AI Impacts on Deskilling and Reskilling Software Engineers

Hanh Le
https://orcid.org/0009-0007-8172-0809
University of the Cumberlands, USA

IGI Global
Scientific Publishing
Publishing Tomorrow's Research Today

Vice President of Editorial Melissa Wagner
Director of Acquisitions Mikaela Felty
Director of Book Development Jocelynn Hessler
Production Manager Mike Brehm
Cover Design Jose Rosado

Published in the United States of America by
IGI Global Scientific Publishing
701 East Chocolate Avenue
Hershey, PA, 17033, USA
Tel: 717-533-8845 | Fax: 717-533-7115
Website: https://www.igi-global.com E-mail: cust@igi-global.com

Library of Congress Cataloging-in-Publication Data

LCCN: 2026017853 (CIP Data Pending)
ISBN13: 9798260010211
Isbn13Softcover: 9798260010228
EISBN13: 9798260010235
British Cataloguing in Publication Data
A Cataloguing in Publication record for this book is available from the British Library.

Table of Contents

Detailed Table of Contents

The growing adoption of generative AI assistants such as GitHub Copilot and ChatGPT is reshaping software engineering practices. While these tools promise faster development and reduced repetitive work, their effects on developer skills, workflow efficiency, and architectural decision-making remain insufficiently examined. This qualitative study explores the interactions between professional software engineers and AI-assisted programming tools, as well as their impact on technical skills, confidence, and system design practices. Data were collected through in-depth interviews with representatives from diverse organizations and observational analysis of AI-assisted coding sessions. Findings reveal a complex interplay of skill augmentation and cognitive offloading, alongside risks of deskilling, shifts in architectural reasoning, and overreliance on AI-generated solutions.

The emergence and incorporation of AI-based coding assistant tools in the software development process mark an unprecedented paradigmatic shift in the profession of software developers with significant implications for the essence and personality of problem-solving, learning, and software developers' profession. The current chapter undertakes an in-depth exploration of the intricate relationship between artificial

This chapter examines how multi-agent artificial intelligence systems are reshaping the skill profile of software engineers by shifting emphasis from traditional coding toward orchestration, evaluation, and human–AI collaboration. Using a real-world multi-agent AI framework as a case study, the chapter analyzes how tasks such as boilerplate coding, documentation generation, query formulation, and initial debugging are increasingly automated. While these capabilities deliver clear productivity gains, they also introduce risks of deskilling if engineers disengage from foundational technical knowledge. The chapter addresses this tension by identifying emerging reskilling pathways, including prompt engineering, agent coordination, system oversight, and ethical validation of AI outputs. Practical deployment experiences are used to highlight common failure modes and best practices for integrating AI-assisted tools into software engineering workflows, offering actionable insights for educators, practitioners, and decision-makers navigating AI-augmented development environments.

As AI is automating traditional programming, the role of humans in software development is moving to higher-level cognitive and evaluative skills. This chapter outlines how systems and architecture design and the coordination of AI-generated code are developing into critical competencies for software developers in an era of AI-aided development. This chapter further describes how oversight, verification and evaluation will become increasingly important as engineers begin to assume the role of "quality gatekeepers," ensuring the accuracy, safety, trustworthiness and sustainability of computer systems. By examining the capabilities that are expected to increase in importance as the automation of computer systems continues to expand, this chapter presents a plan for the reskilling of engineers, development teams and academic programs within a strategic context.

Generative AI is transforming software engineering, expanding from code assistance to producing full implementations, architectures, tests, and infrastructure. As these tools become semi-autonomous collaborators, they reshape engineering workflows, skills, and responsibilities. While AI-driven development boosts productivity, it also carries risks. Overdependence on AI outputs can weaken core engineering skills, reduce system understanding, and blur accountability. This chapter argues that the key challenge is not automation itself, but the absence of deliberate governance over how skills evolve in AI-enabled environments. Drawing on industry practice and research on human–AI collaboration, the chapter introduces a governance-focused framework that distinguishes skills vulnerable to deskilling, emerging high-value skills, and mechanisms to balance automation with human judgment. By reframing deskilling and reskilling as governance issues, it offers guidance for sustaining quality, security, and trust in the era of generative AI.

The integration of generative artificial intelligence into software engineering is reshaping how programming work is carried out, learned, and assessed. AI-assisted tools now automate many tasks that once defined technical expertise, including coding, debugging, and testing. While this shift offers clear efficiency and productivity benefits, it also raises important concerns about deskilling, growing cognitive dependence on automated systems, and the weakening of foundational programming knowledge. At the same time, generative AI opens new pathways for reskilling by moving human effort toward higher-level activities such as oversight, critical reasoning, and system-level design. This chapter examines these parallel processes of deskilling and reskilling in AI-augmented software engineering, focusing on their effects on cognitive engagement, professional identity, and learning pathways.

Let's start with something honest: most software teams didn't sit down and decide to adopt AI coding tools. The tools just showed up—in IDEs, in search results, in what colleagues started pasting into Slack—and adoption happened organically, often before anyone thought much about the implications. That's not a criticism. It's just how useful tools tend to spread. But now that GitHub Copilot, ChatGPT, and half a dozen competitors are embedded in real development workflows, the question of what to actually do about them—how to teach engineers to use them well, how to keep security from quietly eroding, how to prevent the gradual atrophy of skills that no one noticed they were losing—has become genuinely urgent. This chapter tries to address that question with something more than general advice. What follows is a framework built around three interconnected competencies: understanding how AI code generation tools actually work (what we're calling AI literacy), maintaining rigorous security habits when using them, and developing the judgment to critically evaluate what they produce. None of these stands alone. Together, they describe what it means to use AI tools as a skilled professional rather than a passive recipient of output. The framework is grounded in recent empirical research—and there's quite a bit of it now, which is useful. It's designed for educators building curricula and for organizations trying to upskill engineering teams. The core argument is simple even if the details aren't: AI assistance is only as good as the human judgment wrapped around it.

Artificial intelligence is transforming software engineering skills, creating deskilling risks while highlighting urgent reskilling imperatives and evolving workforce pathways. This chapter per the authors examines the adoption of intelligent code generation, automated testing, and AI-assisted development tools, showing how these technologies reshape programming practices, cognitive demands, and professional identities. It explores the tension between productivity gains and the potential loss of foundational competencies, emphasizing adaptive skill frameworks that integrate computational thinking, system-level reasoning, and human–AI collaboration. Organizational and educational responses, including continuous learning, industry–academia partnerships, and competency-based training, are discussed to future-proof the workforce. The chapter synthesizes research and industry trends to outline strategies for resilient, ethically grounded, and innovation-oriented software engineering roles in the age of AI.

Transforming the future of software engineering and have been dubbed augmented engineers since they have been intersecting intelligent automation, artificial intelligence, and the human-centered design. With this dynamism, day-to-day coding, testing, and deploying applications have become more in line with AI-based solutions, and engineers are left to work on more challenging issues and innovative design and ethical decision-making. When the factors of judgment, contextualization and strategic thinking are paramount, augmented engineers with the help of these intelligent systems may achieve a greater productivity, decrease the number of errors and hasten the software delivery process without losing the control over the process to humans. The transformation is also curling the conventional software

aims to support engineering managers in navigating the transition while preserving long-term capability alongside near-term productivity gains.

Preface

The rapid advancement of artificial intelligence (AI), particularly generative AI and large language models, has profoundly reshaped the landscape of software engineering. Tools such as ChatGPT and GitHub Copilot have moved from experimental novelties to everyday development companions, assisting programmers in writing code, generating documentation, debugging systems, designing architectures, and even explaining complex algorithms. As AI systems increasingly participate in core software development tasks, they are redefining what it means to be a software engineer in the twenty-first century.

Much like earlier waves of automation, AI introduces both promise and disruption. On one hand, research has demonstrated that AI-assisted development can increase productivity, reduce routine cognitive load, and accelerate prototyping cycles. Developers can focus more on higher-level problem-solving, system thinking, and creative design. On the other hand, scholars have raised critical concerns about deskilling—the potential erosion of foundational programming competencies due to over-reliance on automated tools. Questions emerge: If AI writes the code, what becomes of the coder? If debugging is automated, how deeply must one understand the underlying logic? How do we balance augmentation with dependency?

This book responds to these pressing questions by examining AI's dual impact on deskilling and reskilling within software engineering. Rather than positioning AI as either a threat or a savior, the contributors adopt a nuanced perspective: AI is a transformative force that simultaneously automates, augments, and redistributes skills. Some technical tasks may become commoditized, while new competencies—such as prompt engineering, AI oversight, verification, ethical reasoning, and system-level orchestration—emerge as critical capabilities.

Across its chapters, this volume explores several key themes:

- **Automation and Task Redistribution:** How AI reshapes coding, testing, documentation, and maintenance practices.

- **Cognitive Offloading and Skill Atrophy:** The risks of reduced deep problem-solving engagement and declining algorithmic fluency.
- **Human–AI Collaboration:** Emerging models of co-development in which engineers supervise, critique, and refine AI-generated artifacts.
- **Professional Identity and Role Evolution:** How software engineers transition from "code writers" to "AI supervisors," "system integrators," and "architects of intelligent systems."
- **Educational and Organizational Implications:** How universities, training programs, and technology firms must redesign curricula and professional development to cultivate adaptive expertise rather than narrow technical proficiency.
- **Ethics, Security, and Responsibility:** The heightened importance of accountability, bias detection, secure code validation, and trustworthy AI deployment.

Contributors to this volume represent diverse disciplinary backgrounds, including software engineering, information systems, computer science education, organizational studies, and human–computer interaction. Drawing on empirical studies, theoretical frameworks, case analyses, and industry observations, the chapters collectively illuminate how AI is reshaping both the technical and socio-cognitive dimensions of programming work.

Importantly, this book does not treat deskilling as inevitable. Instead, it conceptualizes skill transformation as dynamic and context-dependent. While certain low-level coding tasks may be automated, higher-order competencies—critical evaluation, architectural reasoning, secure system design, ethical judgment, and collaborative problem-solving—become even more essential in AI-enhanced environments. The future software engineer must not only know how to code, but also when to trust AI, how to question it, and how to correct it.

This volume is intended for researchers, educators, industry leaders, policy makers, and software professionals who seek to understand how AI is reconfiguring the software development profession. For doctoral students and scholars examining technological change, it provides theoretical grounding in automation, skill formation, and human–AI interaction. For practitioners, it offers insights into workforce adaptation and sustainable professional growth. For educators, it underscores the urgency of redesigning curricula to prepare learners for an era in which programming is no longer solely a human endeavor.

AI is not replacing software engineers. It is transforming them. Whether this transformation leads to diminished expertise or expanded capability depends on how thoughtfully we integrate AI into practice, pedagogy, and policy. By critically examining both the risks of deskilling and the opportunities for reskilling, this book aims to contribute to a more informed, balanced, and forward-looking conversation about the future of software engineering in the age of intelligent automation.

We invite readers to engage deeply with the chapters that follow and reflect on their own roles in shaping a profession at the intersection of human creativity and machine intelligence.

ORGANIZATION OF THE BOOK

AI Impacts on Deskilling and Reskilling Software Engineers brings together interdisciplinary research that explores how artificial intelligence is transforming the practice of software engineering. As generative AI tools increasingly support activities such as coding, debugging, and system design, developers are experiencing substantial shifts in their workflows, skill requirements, and professional roles. While these technologies offer significant gains in productivity and innovation, they also raise critical concerns about deskilling, cognitive dependence, and the shifting boundaries between human expertise and intelligent automation.

Chapter 1 examines how generative AI assistants, including GitHub Copilot and ChatGPT, influence software engineers' skills, workflow efficiency, and decision-making processes. Chapter 2 analyzes the relationship between AI tools and developer confidence, competence, and self-efficacy, emphasizing both productivity benefits and the risks of overreliance on automated systems. Chapter 3 explores the psychological dimensions of deskilling and reskilling, particularly the mental health challenges faced by IT professionals in AI-integrated work environments.

Chapter 4 examines how multi-agent AI systems are shifting the focus of software engineering from traditional coding tasks toward orchestration, coordination, and oversight. Chapter 5 highlights the growing importance of high-level reasoning, system design, and quality assurance as developers increasingly assume the role of evaluators of AI-generated code. Chapter 6 introduces governance strategies for managing skill transformation in AI-augmented development environments. Chapter 7 synthesizes these developments by examining how generative AI reshapes cognitive engagement, learning pathways, and professional identity among software engineers.

Chapter 8 presents a framework for integrating AI literacy, secure coding practices, and critical evaluation skills into software engineering education. Chapter 9 examines the broader transformation of software engineering competencies and the emerging need for reskilling in an AI-driven workforce. Chapter 10 introduces the concept of the "augmented engineer," emphasizing the continued importance of human judgment and creativity in AI-assisted development. Chapter 11 discusses the increasing demand for continuous learning in response to rapid technological change. Finally, Chapter 12 reflects on the long-term implications of AI-driven development, offering practical insights for engineering managers seeking to balance productivity gains with the preservation of foundational technical expertise.

Collectively, these chapters provide a comprehensive examination of how artificial intelligence both challenges and expands the skill boundaries of software engineers. By integrating theoretical perspectives, empirical evidence, and industry insights, the book offers a balanced analysis of deskilling risks, reskilling opportunities, and the evolving relationship between human capability and intelligent automation.

Hanh Le
University of the Cumberlands, USA

Acknowledgement

This book is the culmination of years of inquiry, discipline, reflection, and lived experience. Although my name appears on the cover, this work is the product of a much larger community that has shaped, challenged, and supported me along the way. I am deeply grateful to the colleagues, and collaborators who sharpened my thinking. Your encouragement, intellectual rigor, and generosity of spirit made this work possible.

I am especially thankful for my family. Your patience during long nights of writing, your understanding during seasons of absence, and your unwavering belief in me provided the quiet foundation upon which this work was built. Academic achievements are often measured in publications and credentials, but behind every milestone stands a family that sacrifices, supports, and sustains.

I dedicate this book to my beloved mother and father, who are no longer here to see its completion. Their lives were marked by perseverance, humility, and quiet strength. From them, I learned the value of hard work, the dignity of integrity, and the transformative power of education. Their sacrifices created opportunities they themselves never had, and every accomplishment I achieve rests upon that foundation.

Mom and Dad, though you are no longer physically present, your lessons guide me daily. Your resilience echoes in every challenge I overcome, and your love lives in every page of this work. This book is a tribute to you and to the enduring power of family.

With gratitude, love, and remembrance.

Editorial Advisory Board

Geeta Sandeep Nadella, *University of the Cumberlands, USA*

Hanh Le
University of the Cumberlands, Kentucky, USA

Chapter 1
Impact of Generative AI Assistants on Software Engineers' Skills, Workflow Efficiency, and Decisions

Hanh Le
http://orcid.org/0009-0007-8172-0809
University of the Cumberlands, USA

ABSTRACT

The growing adoption of generative AI assistants such as GitHub Copilot and ChatGPT is reshaping software engineering practices. While these tools promise faster development and reduced repetitive work, their effects on developer skills, workflow efficiency, and architectural decision-making remain insufficiently examined. This qualitative study explores the interactions between professional software engineers and AI-assisted programming tools, as well as their impact on technical skills, confidence, and system design practices. Data were collected through in-depth interviews with representatives from diverse organizations and observational analysis of AI-assisted coding sessions. Findings reveal a complex interplay of skill augmentation and cognitive offloading, alongside risks of deskilling, shifts in architectural reasoning, and overreliance on AI-generated solutions.

DOI: 10.4018/979-8-3373-8450-4.ch001

INTRODUCTION

As AI assistants become a normal part of everyday development, the way developers interact with their tools is changing pretty dramatically. These systems aren't just autocomplete on steroids anymore; they're starting to feel like collaborators that offer ideas, point out patterns, and nudge projects forward. That shift brings a lot of excitement, but it also raises some very real questions about how much we should trust these suggestions and how developers can stay in the driver's seat. After all, an AI can generate code, but it doesn't understand the long-term goals of a product, the quirks of a team's workflow, or the subtle trade-offs that shape good architecture.

This change is especially interesting in education. For beginners, AI can act like a helpful assistant by letting them test ideas, solve problems faster, and see examples of code that works. That said, there are drawbacks. Overreliance on AI—especially early on—may reduce opportunities for students to learn through trial and error, debugging, and independent problem-solving. That's why teachers and mentors still play an important role.

In industry, teams are still figuring out what it means to have AI-generated code living inside real, long-term codebases. Speed is great, but not if it comes at the cost of hidden bugs, security gaps, or architectural drift. As more machine-generated code makes its way into production, teams will need clearer practices for reviewing, documenting, and maintaining it. That might mean new standards for transparency, new tools for code auditing, or even new roles focused on AI-assisted development.

At the end of the day, the rise of generative AI isn't just a technical shift — it's a cultural one. It's reshaping what it means to be a developer, how expertise is built, and how humans and machines share creative work. By studying these changes and talking openly about their impact, the software community can make sure AI becomes a partner that strengthens human skill rather than overshadowing it.

Research Objective / Questions:

The main goal of this study is to understand how generative AI assistants are shaping modern software engineering, especially when it comes to skill development, workflow efficiency, and architectural decision-making. By gathering perspectives from both software engineers and IT managers, the study looks at how these tools are changing day-to-day responsibilities, influencing how teams work, and guiding long-term system design choices.

> *RQ1:* How do software engineers and IT managers perceive the shifts in required skills, technical expertise, and professional roles as they begin working alongside generative AI assistants?

RQ2: How are generative AI tools being used in everyday software development work, and how does feedback from developers affect productivity, code quality, and responsibility?
RQ3: How do software engineers and IT managers think generative AI influence system design, long-term maintainability, and the future of software engineering?

BACKGROUND AND THEORETICAL FRAMEWORKS

This section lays the theoretical groundwork for exploring how generative artificial intelligence (AI) is reshaping software development and IT management. The rapid uptake of large language model (LLM)–driven tools such as GitHub Copilot and ChatGPT is altering how software is designed, built, reviewed, and governed. These systems now influence far more than coding speed—they are beginning to shape architectural thinking, decision-making authority, and accountability structures within development teams. As AI becomes woven into daily workflows, it brings significant consequences for how technical skills are applied, how work is organized, and how professionals adjust to evolving technological environments.

The adoption of generative AI aligns with broader Industry 4.0 transformations, where intelligent automation and human–AI collaboration redefine job roles and organizational processes. Developers are shifting from writing most of the code themselves to checking, shaping, and managing what AI creates. Meanwhile, IT managers are stepping up to handle more of the big-picture responsibilities—like setting AI rules, making sure it's used ethically, and managing risks. To better understand these changes, this chapter draws on three related theories. Deskilling of Jobs Theory focuses on how automation can reduce human skills and autonomy. Job Characteristics Theory explains how the way work is designed affects motivation, engagement, and professional identity. Technology Threat Avoidance Theory focuses on how individuals and organizations respond to risks created by new technologies. Together, these frameworks help explain how software professionals are adapting to generative AI.

Research shows that AI-assisted software development is widely useful but not adopted evenly. A 2024 global survey by Daigle, which included 2,000 software professionals from the United States, India, Brazil, and Germany, showed that people mostly use AI in official work environments. In fact, 17% to 27% of participants said they use AI exclusively at work. That finding pushes back against the common belief that most AI experimentation happens at home in people's free time. Many participants also reported strong benefits, especially better code quality—90% in the United States and 81% in India, with similar results in Brazil and Germany. These findings suggest that AI tools are providing real value across different countries and organizations, while also highlighting the need for proper oversight and skill development.

Using these three theories together, this study explores both the benefits and challenges of using AI in software development and IT management. Deskilling theory raises concerns about whether developers may lose important skills over time. Job Characteristics Theory helps explain how AI changes autonomy, motivation, and responsibility at work. Technology Threat Avoidance Theory sheds light on how developers and managers think about risks such as reliability, security, and ethics. Together, these frameworks provide a useful way to understand how professionals are responding to the technical, cognitive, and organizational changes brought by generative AI.

Deskilling of Jobs Theory

Deskilling of Jobs Theory, which comes from early labor studies and was later expanded by Braverman (1974), argues that new technology can reduce workers' skills and independence by moving control from people to machines and management systems. In the past, this often meant turning complex industrial work into simpler, repetitive tasks. Today, a similar pattern is emerging in software engineering, where generative AI tools automate cognitive and creative tasks that were once core to the profession—things like writing code, debugging, planning architectures, and reasoning about systems.

When we apply deskilling theory to AI-assisted development, a clear concern comes into view: developers may gradually move from being active problem solvers to mainly reviewing what AI systems produce. As these tools produce more code and even suggest design choices, engineers may spend less time thinking through the logic and structure themselves. Over time, this can reduce their technical depth, confidence, and ability to solve complex problems on their own.

The implications go beyond individual skill. If teams rely too heavily on AI, organizations may lose some of their adaptability, creative capacity, and long-term expertise—qualities that are essential for innovation and sustainable system design (Samuels & Pelser, 2025). In this way, deskilling theory provides a useful lens for examining whether AI is ultimately supporting or undermining the human capabilities that software engineering depends on.

Job Characteristics Theory

Job Characteristics Theory (Hackman & Oldham, 1976) offers a helpful counterpoint to Deskilling Theory by focusing on how the structure of work shapes motivation, engagement, and satisfaction. While Deskilling Theory looks at how technology can erode human skills, Job Characteristics Theory highlights five elements that make work feel meaningful: autonomy, feedback, task identity, skill variety, and task significance. As generative AI reshapes software development—and changes how humans and machines share thinking and decision-making—these elements become even more crucial for understanding how work is experienced.

When we apply JCT to generative AI, the message is clear: the impact of automation depends heavily on how these tools are woven into everyday work. If AI reduces a developer's role to simply checking or approving machine-generated output, it can erode autonomy, weaken ownership, and make the work feel less significant. That kind of shift can easily lead to disengagement or the sense that the job has lost its depth. But when AI is used to support—not replace—human judgment, the story changes. Tools that help with complex problem-solving, architectural thinking, creative exploration, or ethical decision-making can actually broaden skill variety and make the work more engaging. In these cases, developers can spend less time on repetitive tasks and more time on the intellectually rich parts of the job.

For IT managers, generative AI introduces new and growing responsibilities. They are becoming more involved in governance, policy making, risk assessment, and ethical oversight. This work often feels more meaningful and gives them more strategic control, placing them in leadership roles for responsible AI use. Instead of focusing on daily operations, their role is shifting toward shaping long-term organizational values and technology direction.

Seen through the lens of JCT, generative AI has the potential to either enrich or diminish software development roles. The deciding factor is how organizations choose to redesign tasks, distribute responsibilities, and frame human–AI collaboration. When used carefully, AI can make work more motivating and rewarding. When used poorly, it can break work into disconnected tasks that feel less meaningful (Khurana et al., 2024). This shows why intentional work design is important, so AI supports—rather than weakens—human motivation and professional development.

Technology Threat Avoidance Theory

Technology Threat Avoidance Theory (TTAT) (Liang & Xue, 2009) offers a helpful way to understand how people and organizations interpret and respond to risks that come with new technologies. Although TTAT was originally created to explain cybersecurity decision-making, its core idea still applies here: people take protective action based on how serious they think a threat is, how vulnerable they feel to it, and how effective they believe their safeguards will be. This logic translates naturally to the world of generative AI in software engineering and IT management.

In AI-supported development environments, both developers and IT managers often see generative AI tools as carrying real risks. These concerns can range from security flaws introduced by AI-generated code to biased or hallucinated outputs, unclear intellectual property ownership, and reduced human oversight in important decisions. When teams view these risks as significant, they tend to adopt stronger protective measures—such as requiring human review, limiting AI use in production systems, or keeping detailed logs to track AI-generated contributions.

IT managers may be under even more pressure because they are accountable to leadership, clients, and regulators. They often create specialized oversight procedures, tighten internal policies, or formalize governance structures to ensure AI is used responsibly. When organizations underestimate or misunderstand the risks of generative AI, they may adopt these tools without proper safeguards, exposing themselves to operational failures, security issues, or ethical dilemmas (Song et al., 2024). These differences in how people judge risk reflect a core idea of Technology Threat Avoidance Theory (TTAT): perceptions of risk strongly shape behavior.

TTAT helps explain why organizations vary so widely in their preparedness, caution, and governance practices. The theory shows that decisions about adopting AI—and the broader culture that forms around its use—are shaped by how individuals and organizations interpret potential threats, vulnerabilities, and the need for protective measures. It also shows the importance of clear communication, proper training, and transparent policies to make sure AI is used effectively and responsibly. In this way, Technology Threat Avoidance Theory helps explain how professionals deal with the uncertainties and risks that generative AI brings into software development.

MAIN FOCUS OF THE CHAPTER

When combined, Deskilling Theory, Job Characteristics Theory, and Technology Threat Avoidance Theory help explain how generative AI is changing software development and IT management. Deskilling Theory highlights the risk that as AI takes on more creative and technical tasks, professionals may lose important skills and autonomy. Job Characteristics Theory shows how changes in tasks, independence, and feedback can affect developers' motivation, engagement, and sense of identity at work. Technology Threat Avoidance Theory helps us understand how developers and IT managers see and respond to risks like ethics, security, control, and reliability. These concerns influence the rules, safeguards, and governance practices that organizations put in place when using AI.

Using these three theoretical perspectives, this chapter offers a critical examination of how generative AI reshapes professional roles, skill trajectories, and organizational accountability within software engineering. Instead of treating AI as purely good or purely harmful, this discussion takes a balanced, evidence-based view that acknowledges both its benefits and its challenges. To build long-term organizational resilience in an increasingly automated world, it emphasizes the importance of preserving human expertise, designing workflows that keep human judgment at the center, and developing sustainable models of collaboration between people and AI systems.

LITERATURE REVIEW

The rapid rise of generative artificial intelligence (AI) in software development and IT management is transforming how digital systems are imagined, built, and maintained. Tools powered by large language models (LLMs)—including GitHub Copilot and ChatGPT—are now embedded across many stages of the software development lifecycle. They help with everything from writing code and producing documentation to exploring architectural options and supporting high-level decision-making. While early industry discussions often focus on gains in productivity, speed, and ease of use, more academic research is taking a more cautious approach. Researchers are starting to question how long-term reliance on AI may affect developers' ability to keep essential skills, maintain ethical standards, and adapt to changing professional roles in AI-driven workplaces.

Programmers and Software Development

For a long time, programmers—also referred to as developers or coders—have been essential to the development, design, and upkeep of software (Fauzi & Andreswari, 2022). Traditionally, their job has involved translating human concepts and requirements into commands that computers can comprehend and execute. These responsibilities span a wide range of tasks, from building system software to keeping it running smoothly. As Robillard (1999) pointed out, writing a program has always required people to organize and structure the knowledge behind it before any code is written. There is no discussion of how the role of the programmer is changing as AI tools become more sophisticated in this earlier literature. The impact of AI on programmers' abilities, daily tasks, and overall job functions is still largely unexplored, despite the fact that the traditional duties are well described.

Programmers have long been a crucial component of software development teams, collaborating with engineers, designers, and quality control personnel to produce solutions that advance organizational objectives. Their abilities have fueled technological progress and innovation. But there are difficulties in the field as well. Michels et al. (2024) found that many programmers experience high stress and burnout, which can reduce productivity and lead to poor work outcomes. What this research does not explore is how AI may be changing this situation. While it shows the pressures programmers face, it does not examine whether AI tools might reduce these stresses—or make them worse—by changing workflows, expectations, or job satisfaction.

Software development itself requires navigating large amounts of information across multiple, often overlapping, knowledge areas (Robillard, 1999). Within this complexity, the Software Development Life Cycle (SDLC) has served as a guiding framework, helping programmers move through each stage of a project. Pothukuchi et al. (2023) described the SDLC as a structured roadmap for completing software engineering tasks. Even so, there is a gap in the research. While the literature explains the software development life cycle in detail, it does not explore how new AI technologies might affect it. Important questions about how AI could change development stages, shift programmer roles, or alter how knowledge is shared and managed within projects remain largely unanswered.

Generative AI in Software Engineering

The growing use of generative artificial intelligence (AI) tools in software engineering is changing the way software is imagined, built, tested, and maintained across its entire lifecycle. Tools like GitHub Copilot, ChatGPT, and TabNine—powered by large language models (LLMs)—now assist developers with a wide range of tasks, from generating boilerplate code and helping with debugging to refactoring, writing tests, and producing documentation. By taking over repetitive, syntax-heavy, and mentally draining work, these systems aim to boost productivity, shorten development timelines, and reduce cognitive load, especially during routine or low-level programming tasks (Barke et al., 2023; Sridhara et al., 2023). For many developers, generative AI has become a natural part of daily work, shaping not just how code is written but also how problems are framed and solutions are evaluated.

Generative AI has moved well beyond simple code completion. Developers now rely on these tools for higher-level tasks such as interpreting requirements, proposing architectural patterns, evaluating design trade-offs, and assisting with quality checks. AI helps teams explore design alternatives, spot edge cases, and consider system-wide impacts earlier and more thoroughly than before. As a result, AI is shifting from a basic productivity tool to an active collaborator, creating a more interactive workflow where developers continually prompt, assess, and refine AI-generated ideas.

Although this collaboration offers clear advantages—faster ideation, more creative design possibilities, and stronger support for complex tasks—it also raises important questions about the future of software engineering expertise. As AI becomes more involved in design and implementation, many worry about its long-term effects on developers' skills, independence, and professional judgment. Accountability also becomes more difficult to define when AI-generated suggestions shape system design or introduce subtle errors that are hard to detect. These concerns underscore the importance of understanding how AI-supported workflows influence skill development, decision-making authority, and responsibility within modern engineering teams.

Overall, the adoption of generative AI is not just a technical upgrade. It represents a major shift in how software engineering knowledge is created, evaluated, and sustained over time.

Skill Development and Deskilling

More research is looking at how generative AI affects software engineers' ability to build and keep their skills over time. Studies based on deskilling theory warn that relying too much on AI-generated code and suggestions can slowly weaken important skills such as algorithmic thinking, breaking problems into smaller parts, debugging, and understanding how programs work (Crowston & Bolici, 2025; Rinta Kahila et al., 2023). When developers accept AI output without questioning the reasoning or trade-offs behind it, learning can shift from active problem-solving to passive checking.

This pattern aligns with the idea of cognitive offloading, which explains how people transfer mental effort to external tools—sometimes reducing long-term learning and deep understanding. In AI-assisted programming, this can show up as accepting AI suggestions without questioning them, giving up more quickly during debugging, or taking a smaller role in design decisions. Research suggests that heavy reliance on AI can make developers less confident in their own problem-solving abilities and less proactive when facing new or challenging tasks (Crowston & Bolici, 2025). These trends raise concerns about weakening professional judgment and adaptive expertise—skills that are essential in complex or high-stakes engineering work.

Kuhail et al. (2023) note that although AI-generated code is usually syntactically correct, it can still include subtle logic flaws, performance issues, or security weaknesses. Finding and fixing these problems requires strong knowledge of algorithms, data structures, and secure coding practices. Without these skills, developers may fail to catch errors, increasing the chance that faulty code reaches production. This risk is especially high for beginners and students who are still developing foundational knowledge and professional identity.

While AI can be a useful learning tool when used carefully, research generally cautions that using generative AI carelessly can result in dependence and skill loss. These results highlight the necessity of well-thought-out tools, transparent organizational guidelines, and instructional strategies that promote introspection, critical thinking, and active participation when working with AI. By prioritizing human oversight, accountability, and continuous learning, educators and organizations can benefit from generative AI while protecting—and potentially strengthening—the core skills essential to effective software engineering.

One of the main benefits of generative AI in software engineering is that it helps developers work more efficiently. AI tools offer quick support with syntax, logic, and context, which can reduce development time, speed up prototyping, and make complex tasks easier to handle (Barke et al., 2023; Sridhara et al., 2023). These improvements often show up as faster task completion, quicker debugging, shorter development cycles, and better responsiveness in agile and continuous integration workflows. At the organizational level, this can lead to faster releases, more reliable delivery schedules, and higher overall productivity.

In addition to saving time, generative AI helps developers spend less effort on repetitive, low-level tasks and more on higher-level thinking. Automating things like boilerplate code, routine syntax, and early documentation allows developers to focus on system design, architecture, and problem solving. Research supports this shift in both educational and professional settings. For example, Avila Chauvet et al. (2023) found that students using AI tools spent more time on analysis and experimentation rather than mechanical coding. Likewise, professionals report paying more attention to long-term system design, architectural trade-offs, and teamwork.

Gains in productivity from generative AI are not always assured.

AI can write code quickly, but the time savings may be outweighed by the effort required to review, edit, and modify the output. Developers often need to carefully review AI-generated code to check for accuracy, security issues, compliance requirements, and coding standards. AI suggestions can sometimes include small errors or miss important context, which may increase the time needed for debugging or refactoring. This shows that productivity is not only about speed, but also about maintaining quality and long-term sustainability.

Research suggests that long-term productivity gains depend on how well AI tools are integrated into development workflows. Organizations that embed AI within structured processes—such as testing, code reviews, human oversight, and clear documentation—are more likely to see consistent benefits. In these settings, AI supports expert judgment rather than replacing it. When combined with strong governance and quality control processes, generative AI can aid in the development of software that is more effective, moral, and sustainable.

Architectural Decision-Making

Software architecture plays a central role in software engineering because it determines a system's quality, scalability, performance, security, and long-term maintainability. The architectural choices made early on shape the system's overall structure and influence how easily it can be updated, expanded, or integrated with other technologies. Traditionally, these decisions have depended on human expertise—engineers drawing on their experience, contextual knowledge, and ability to weigh technical, organizational, and social trade-offs

As generative AI tools increasingly suggest architectural patterns, compare design options, and analyze trade-offs, important questions arise about the appropriate role of AI in system-level decision-making and how much influence it should have over architectural choices. Research shows that generative AI is especially useful during the early stages of architectural design. By quickly producing design alternatives, identifying common patterns, and flagging potential risks based on past projects, AI can support idea generation and reduce mental workload for developers (Sridhara et al., 2023). In modern Industry 4.0 environments—where systems are often distributed, cloud-based, and closely linked to data and physical processes—AI-assisted reasoning helps teams handle complexity and explore more design options in less time (Yen et al., 2023). This allows architects to spend more time evaluating the consequences of different designs rather than creating each option manually.

At the same time, studies warn against relying too heavily on AI-generated recommendations. AI can miss real-world limits that are not well represented in its training data, such as domain-specific needs, legacy systems, regulations, or organizational priorities. Relying too much on common AI-suggested patterns can also lead to similar-looking designs and hidden technical debt. These risks show why human judgment, context awareness, and critical thinking are still essential in architectural decisions.

As a result, software architecture is increasingly viewed as a collaborative effort between humans and AI rather than a fully automated process. For this collaboration to be effective, architects must keep final decision-making authority, carefully review AI input, and think about long-term, ethical, and organizational impacts. Rather than replacing architects, generative AI reshapes their role by shifting their focus toward more strategic, evaluative, and integrative work in a changing software engineering environment.

Ethical and Human Factors

Recent research shows that generative AI raises important ethical and human-centered questions in software engineering. Researchers warn about risks such as bias, privacy concerns, plagiarism, unclear ownership, and over-reliance on systems that are hard to understand. The rapid adoption of AI tools is making these problems more pressing. AI is also changing professional roles. Developers are spending more time reviewing and supervising AI-generated work, while IT managers are taking on greater responsibility for strategy, risk management, and ethical oversight. New concerns regarding authorship, liability, and accountability are brought up by this change. Researchers emphasize the significance of clear organizational policies, robust human oversight, and transparency in addressing these issues. To ensure responsible use, many teams are implementing procedures like audit trails, ethics committees, formal AI guidelines, and human-in-the-loop reviews.

The conversation has moved beyond productivity to include long-term skill development, professional identity, and ethical responsibility as AI tools become integrated into the full software development lifecycle. Finding the ideal balance between efficiency and expertise is one of the main conflicts in the literature. While some research indicates that an excessive dependence on AI may erode fundamental abilities, other studies demonstrate that, when humans are still actively involved, AI can foster creativity and higher order thinking. Governance issues that organizations must deal with include ambiguous ownership, inconsistent results, bias, and privacy risks.

The use of AI in software engineering, skill development and deskilling, workflow efficiency, architectural decision-making, and ethical and human factors are the five interrelated areas that are highlighted in the literature. Together, these perspectives show that generative AI is a sociotechnical force that is reshaping human expertise, software development practices, and collaboration.

Research Gap

Although generative AI is reshaping software engineering at a rapid pace, the current research landscape is still fragmented. Many studies focus on isolated topics—such as productivity, skills, architecture, or ethics—without examining how these issues interact in real development environments. As a result, we still lack a clear picture of how generative AI affects software engineering as a whole.

Most research focuses on the short-term efficiency benefits of generative AI, but far fewer studies look at its long-term impact on technical depth, adaptive expertise, or professional autonomy. While interest in workflow integration and human–AI collaboration is growing, there is still little evidence on how AI shapes architectural decisions, long-term system sustainability, or organizational structures.

Another gap is the lack of managerial perspectives. The perspectives of IT managers, who are responsible for risk, governance, and strategic adoption, are largely absent from the daily experiences of developers, which are more commonly documented. Without these viewpoints, it remains unclear how companies, especially in high-stakes or regulated environments, balance accountability and rapid innovation.

Despite the widespread awareness of ethical issues like bias, privacy, and unclear authorship, little is known about how teams actually handle these risks in practical settings or how human and AI systems share accountability.

When taken as a whole, these gaps demonstrate the need for a deeper understanding of AI's impacts. This study looks at the experiences of IT managers and software engineers to provide a more thorough understanding of how generative AI is altering roles, decision-making, and the future of software engineering.

METHODOLOGY

This study used a qualitative design based on hermeneutic phenomenology to explore how software developers and IT managers experience generative AI in their everyday work. Because hermeneutic phenomenology centers on how people interpret and find meaning in their lived experiences, it is well suited for examining how professionals make sense of changing roles, evolving skill requirements, and new ethical responsibilities in AI-influenced work environments (Peoples, 2021).

As tools like GitHub Copilot and ChatGPT become part of coding, architectural reasoning, and decision-making, practitioners are continually reinterpreting their expertise, authority, and professional identity. This approach makes it possible to move beyond surface-level observations and uncover the deeper cognitive, emotional, and organizational shifts that occur when people work alongside AI. It helps illuminate how professionals negotiate trust, preserve autonomy, and balance their own judgment with machine-generated suggestions.

Choosing this method also fits well with the study's theoretical foundations—Deskilling of Jobs Theory, Job Characteristics Theory, and Technology Threat Avoidance Theory. These frameworks help link individual experiences to the larger sociotechnical forces shaping how AI is changing work, expertise, and organizational practices. By using hermeneutic phenomenology, the study captures the nuanced and evolving ways professionals understand generative AI—revealing not just what is changing, but how those changes are felt and integrated into modern software engineering practice.

Research Design

This study used a qualitative research strategy based on semi-structured, in-depth interviews to explore how software developers and IT managers engage with and adapt to generative AI in real organizational settings. This approach was chosen to capture rich, detailed accounts that reveal how professionals interpret changes in autonomy, accountability, skill development, and governance as AI becomes part of their everyday work. Semi-structured interviews offered enough flexibility to follow individual experiences while still keeping a clear thematic direction, allowing participants to describe not just what has changed, but how those changes feel and how they shape their evolving professional identities.

The aim was not to generate statistically generalizable results, but to identify recurring patterns, points of tension, and strategies of adaptation across different organizational contexts. By emphasizing depth over breadth, the study was able to surface both shared experiences and meaningful differences in how people understand and respond to AI-enabled work. This level of interpretive detail is crucial for examining the complex dynamics of human–AI collaboration, where personal agency, organizational culture, and technological capabilities intersect. Overall, this qualitative approach helped reveal how professionals interpret the growing presence of AI in their work, how they deal with the challenges it introduces, and how they envision their roles changing as software engineering and IT management continue to evolve.

Participant Selection

Participants were recruited using purposive sampling, targeting professionals with direct, hands-on experience using generative AI in software development or IT management. The final group consisted of twelve people, including mid-level and senior developers, IT managers, and technical leads from both public and private sector organizations. This range of roles provided a balanced view of AI use in day-to-day work and in higher-level governance.

All participants had practical experience with tools such as ChatGPT, GitHub Copilot, and other LLM-based systems used for coding, architectural exploration, documentation, and decision support. In order to reach practitioners who are actively using generative AI, participants were recruited through industry referrals, LinkedIn outreach, and professional networks. An informed consent form outlining the study's objectives, methods, confidentiality precautions, and participants' right to withdraw at any time was given to each participant prior to their enrollment. Since participation was voluntary and unpaid, contributions were guaranteed to represent sincere interest and pertinent experience.

Data were gathered through semi-structured, in-depth Zoom interviews lasting 45–75 minutes. The interview guide's primary focus was on participants' real experiences with generative AI and how it is impacting both the technical and managerial aspects of their work. Expectations for future human-AI cooperation were discussed, along with the use of AI in coding and architectural reasoning, changes in roles and autonomy, effects on professional identity and skill development, and ethical and security concerns.

The semi-structured format, which offered a balance between consistency and flexibility, allowed participants to discuss topics that were most relevant to their own circumstances while still enabling cross-interview comparison. Subtle insights regarding perceptions of technological risk, job redesign, deskilling, and accountability were found using this method. All interviews were audio recorded with consent and verbatim transcribed to maintain context and detail for in-depth qualitative analysis.

Data Collection

The study included twelve participants with a wide range of professional backgrounds and experience levels. The majority of participants were seasoned professionals with over ten years of experience, including programmers, system analysts, designers, AI and machine learning engineers, and cybersecurity analysts. One participant was a computer science student with less than a year of experience, while the other two had five to ten years of experience.

Despite the group's mixed gender makeup, most members, particularly the programmers and technical specialists, identified as female. Because they worked for large companies with more than 500 employees, several participants offered insight into the adoption of AI in enterprise-level settings. Others, like entrepreneurs and designers, came from much smaller businesses with one to fifty employees, offering perspectives from more flexible or resource-constrained settings. Two participants who did not fit into a specific organization size were a system analyst and a student.

Analytical Approach

Data were analyzed using a thematic analysis approach that combined inductive exploration with deductive, theory-informed interpretation. The process began with several holistic readings of each transcript to develop a broad understanding of participants' experiences, noting recurring language, emotional cues, and points of emphasis. Initial codes were generated inductively from the data and refined through memo-writing, constant comparison across transcripts, and ongoing reflection on how participants described their interactions with generative AI.

The study's theoretical underpinnings—Deskilling Theory, Job Characteristics Theory, and Technology Threat Avoidance Theory—directed the interpretive phase of the analysis. These perspectives helped explain trends related to changing skills, autonomy, motivation, and perceptions of technological risk by linking personal experiences to broader socioeconomic shifts surrounding the adoption of AI.

Related ideas were grouped into broader themes as the coding process progressed, reflecting how participants understood and adapted to AI in their professional roles. These themes, which highlighted emerging conflicts, coping mechanisms, and novel forms of human–AI collaboration, captured both what participants described occurring in their daily work and the meanings they attached to those experiences.

This process was aided by qualitative analysis software (MAXQDA), which managed codes, arranged transcripts, and allowed for methodical participant comparisons. This made it possible to develop the themes in a way that was transparent, rigorous, and closely aligned with the data and the conceptual framework of the study.

Coding and Theme Development

The study used thematic analysis following Braun and Clarke's (2006) six-phase framework to identify meaningful patterns in the data. This method is often recommended for qualitative research because it offers a clear and structured path from raw data to well-supported findings. Lester et al. (2020) note that thematic analysis is especially useful for researchers who are still gaining confidence in qualitative research methods. Similarly, Aguas (2022) points out that phenomenological analysis is an iterative process, meaning researchers need to repeatedly revisit, reorganize, and refine their codes as their understanding deepens. Guided by these ideas, this study used a data analysis approach that was both well-structured and flexible.

The first phase focused on becoming familiar with the data. This involved carefully listening to interview recordings, reading transcripts multiple times, and reviewing related documents. Listening to the audio recordings was particularly helpful, as it revealed early patterns and provided emotional tone and contextual details that were not always clear in the written transcripts.

In the second phase, initial codes were developed to capture key ideas and recurring points raised by participants. Following the recommendations of Williams and Moser (2019), this step aimed to reflect the full range and richness of participants' experiences without oversimplifying their views.

The third phase involved grouping related codes and refining them into broader themes. As Aguas (2022) explains, this repeated process helps deeper and more meaningful patterns emerge from participants' lived experiences. In the fourth phase, the themes were reviewed and adjusted to ensure they accurately represented the data and contributed clearly to the overall story of the dataset.

The fifth phase focused on clearly defining each theme, making sure they were consistent, connected to the research questions, and easy to understand. In the final phase, all themes were brought together into a coherent narrative that reflected the complexity and depth of participants' perspectives.

Throughout the analysis, MAXQDA software supported the process by helping organize transcripts, manage codes, and compare data across participants (Silver, 2024). Its ability to work with text, audio, and video made it a practical tool for maintaining accuracy and streamlining the overall workflow.

Trustworthiness

A range of strategies was used to enhance the trustworthiness of the study, following well-established qualitative standards for credibility, dependability, and confirmability. Credibility was strengthened by comparing insights from participants across different roles and organizations, helping ensure that the findings reflected broader patterns rather than isolated viewpoints.

Several participants also engaged in member checking by reviewing early interpretations of the data. Their feedback helped verify that the analysis accurately captured their experiences and contributed to refining the themes. This process confirmed that the interpretations aligned with participants' perspectives (Riazi et al., 2023).

To support confirmability and dependability, the researcher engaged in ongoing reflexive practice. A reflective journal was maintained throughout the study to document analytical decisions, track the evolution of codes and themes, and acknowledge any potential biases or assumptions. This continuous self-reflection helped keep interpretations grounded in participant accounts rather than the researcher's expectations. Together, these practices strengthened the study's dependability and created a clear, transparent audit trail.

Ethical Considerations

Ethical approval for the study was obtained from the Institutional Review Board (IRB) at the University of the Cumberlands before data collection began. All participants received an informed consent form that explained the purpose of the study, the procedures involved, and the protections in place. Participation was completely voluntary.

To protect privacy, confidentiality and anonymity were carefully maintained. Pseudonyms were used in all written materials, and any identifying information was removed from transcripts and analysis records. All data were stored securely on encrypted, password-protected devices, with access limited to the researcher.

Participants were reminded that they could withdraw from the study at any time without penalty, ensuring their autonomy throughout the research process. The study followed core ethical principles—including transparency, respect, and participant-centered decision-making—to ensure that all interactions were conducted responsibly and with care.

RESEARCH FINDINGS

RQ1: Developing Skills and Shifting Roles

Participants reported a discernible change from practical coding to more interpretive and supervisory work. Instead of writing every line of code themselves, many now spend more time assessing, refining, and validating AI-generated outputs. AI was often viewed as a helpful learning tool, especially for exploring new ideas. At the same time, participants saw it as a possible risk if it replaced basic problem-solving skills. Because of this shift, many participants began to rethink what professional expertise means. They placed more value on judgment, contextual understanding, and ethical responsibility, rather than focusing only on technical skills.

RQ2: Workflow Efficiency and Feedback Practices

Participants reported that AI tools are now a regular part of their daily work, particularly for routine activities such as coding, testing, debugging, and documentation. These tools were seen as helpful for speeding up tasks and reducing mental workload, especially for repetitive work. However, participants consistently noted that AI feedback alone was not sufficient. To ensure quality and reliability, they emphasized the importance of hybrid feedback loops that combine AI-generated suggestions with peer review and managerial oversight. Participants also raised concerns about unclear accountability when AI-generated outputs result in errors or security issues.

RQ3: Architectural Decision-Making and Future Directions

Participants viewed AI as a helpful tool for exploring architectural options but not for making final decisions. They emphasized that architectural work depends heavily on deep contextual understanding, domain expertise, and long-term thinking—areas where AI was seen as limited. Many participants expressed concerns about technical debt and system maintainability, noting the risk that AI-generated solutions may favor speed over long-term sustainability. Looking to the future, participants expected their roles to evolve toward more cross-functional, ethical, and strategic responsibilities, with AI supporting rather than replacing human judgment.

Overall, the findings show that generative AI is reshaping workflows, skill sets, and architectural thinking in software engineering and IT management. The next section connects these themes to the study's theoretical framework and the broader research literature.

DISCUSSION

This study examined how software engineers and IT managers experience and understand the use of generative AI assistants in their daily work. The findings show that AI is more than just an automation tool—it actively changes how people build skills, organize their work, and make architectural decisions. AI does not affect everyone in the same way. Instead, it creates mixed effects, combining efficiency gains with changes in skills, professional identity, and responsibility.

Skill Development and Changing Roles

For *Research Question 1 (RQ1)*, the study found that working with generative AI shifts developers away from constant hands-on coding toward higher-level tasks such as interpretation, supervision, and decision-making. Job Characteristics Theory (JCT) helps explain this shift by showing how AI changes skill variety, autonomy, and task importance. While AI reduces repetitive work, it increases the need for judgment, contextual understanding, and oversight—skills that help developers stay engaged and find meaning in their work.

Participants also expressed concerns about losing core programming skills, which aligns with Deskilling of Jobs Theory (DJT). These concerns differed by experience level. Senior developers often saw AI as a useful productivity tool, while early-career developers were more likely to rely on it too much. This highlights the importance of intentional training, mentoring, and skill development.

Technology Threat Avoidance Theory (TTAT) helps explain how participants responded to these risks. Many used strategies such as careful code review, limiting AI use, and regularly practicing foundational skills to stay relevant. Rather than rejecting AI, participants adjusted their roles to focus on uniquely human strengths, showing that AI leads to role evolution rather than simple job replacement.

Workflow Efficiency, Feedback, and Accountability

For *Research Question 2 (RQ2)*, generative AI was found to speed up work while also creating new challenges. In line with JCT, participants said AI reduced mental effort and improved efficiency for routine tasks. Fast, automated feedback helped them work faster and feel more productive.

At the same time, participants stressed the importance of hybrid feedback systems. These systems combine AI input with peer review, management oversight, and manual checks. Because AI feedback often lacks context and ethical awareness, human judgment remains essential.

Accountability was a major concern. When AI-generated code caused problems, it was often unclear who was responsible. From a TTAT perspective, this uncertainty is seen as a technological risk, leading participants to call for clearer rules, governance, and responsibility structures. These issues connect everyday development work to larger discussions about responsibility in AI-based systems.

Architectural Decision-Making and the Future

For Research Question 3 (RQ3), participants generally saw AI as a helpful assistant rather than the one making the final calls in architectural work. They emphasized that architecture is a field with big, long-term consequences—one that relies on ethical judgment, strategic thinking, and deep technical expertise. This view aligns well with Job Characteristics Theory, which highlights how important meaningful work and professional autonomy are.

Some concerns tied to Deskilling Theory also came up, especially around technical debt and system maintainability. Participants worried that AI might focus too much on speed and not enough on truly understanding system design. To protect long-term organizational knowledge, they stressed the importance of clear communication, solid documentation, and transparent reasoning behind architectural decisions.

Looking ahead, participants expect their roles to shift toward more governance, systems thinking, and continuous learning. This perspective fits with TTAT, which frames AI as both a challenge and an opportunity to rethink professional value and expertise. Overall, participants believe humans will continue to guide strategic decisions, with AI serving as a supportive partner rather than a replacement.

Overall Meaning

Overall, the findings show that generative AI is reshaping professional norms, skill expectations, and organizational practices. Across all three research questions, participants worked to balance efficiency with responsibility, automation with skill preservation, and innovation with long-term sustainability. Using JCT, DJT, and TTAT together helps explain these dynamics and shows that successful AI integration depends more on how work is designed and managed than on the technology itself.

Implications for Research and Practice

To safeguard essential human skills in increasingly AI-supported environments, organizations must look beyond simply adopting advanced AI tools. Equal attention should be given to investing in continuous training programs, robust governance frameworks, and effective feedback mechanisms that help professionals understand, evaluate, and guide AI use. These supporting structures are critical for ensuring that AI enhances human capabilities rather than diminishing critical thinking, judgment, and technical expertise.

This study emphasizes the need for sustained, long-term research into system sustainability, professional identity, and skill retention as AI becomes more deeply embedded in everyday work practices. Understanding how roles, responsibilities, and expertise evolve over time is essential for managing both the opportunities and risks introduced by generative AI. The findings also highlight the importance of intentional and reflective AI adoption, where clear accountability, transparency in decision-making, and regular evaluation are prioritized. Together, these practices can help organizations responsibly integrate AI while preserving the core human elements that underpin professional work and long-term architectural integrity.

FUTURE RESEARCH DIRECTIONS

This study sheds light on how generative AI assistants are shaping architectural decision-making, improving workflows, and influencing skill development. At the same time, there are a few limitations to keep in mind. Because the research involved only a small group of organizations and participants, the findings can't be easily applied to a wider population. The qualitative approach also depends on people's own accounts of their experiences, which may be influenced by personal context or bias. On top of that, the fast pace of AI innovation makes it challenging to predict long-term effects, since tools and practices are constantly changing.

Looking ahead, future research could strengthen these insights by using long-term studies and combining different research methods. This would help reveal how professional identities and AI-supported skills evolve over time. Broadening the scope to include more industries, job roles, and organizational environments would also offer a fuller picture of how AI is being adopted. There's still much to learn about how AI affects technical debt, long-term system sustainability, and architectural decision-making. Finally, future work should explore training approaches that maintain deep technical expertise while still taking advantage of the efficiency gains AI can provide. As organizations increasingly integrate AI into daily operations, further research on governance and accountability is essential. Continued study in these areas will support responsible and sustainable use of generative AI, helping to protect human expertise and architectural integrity while still encouraging innovation in software engineering.

CONCLUSION

This study explored how generative AI assistants shape software engineers' skills, workflows, and architectural decision-making, drawing on the lived experiences of developers and IT managers. Using a hermeneutic phenomenological approach, the research shows that generative AI tools—especially LLM-based coding and conversational assistants—are not neutral productivity boosters or simple substitutes for human labor. Instead, they act as sociotechnical agents that reshape professional identities, redistribute cognitive work, and influence decision-making across the software development lifecycle.

The findings show that generative AI boosts workflow efficiency by handling repetitive tasks, speeding up coding, and helping teams brainstorm ideas more quickly. At the same time, it is changing the nature of engineering work. Developers now spend less time on routine implementation and more time supervising AI outputs, making judgments, and thinking at a broader system level. This shift introduces new ways of thinking. Developers now spend more time crafting effective prompts, reviewing AI-generated suggestions, and keeping an eye on potential risks. As a result, strong technical expertise remains essential—even as AI takes on more routine tasks. From an architectural perspective, AI can help teams move faster, but it also introduces new risks that need to be carefully managed. It can hide the reasons behind design choices, create hidden connections between systems, and push teams toward short-term solutions. Participants stressed that human oversight is still critical, especially for complex systems. Using AI well requires clear rules, clear responsibility, and intentional human involvement in the workflow.

The findings also show that deskilling is more complex than people often think. While some routine skills may decline, developers are also gaining new skills. These include system-level thinking, ethical decision-making, and AI governance. These changes match Job Characteristics Theory and Technology Threat Avoidance Theory, which help explain shifts in autonomy, task ownership, and how professionals manage risk.

In practice, organizations need to shift away from casual or ad hoc uses of AI and move toward more structured approaches. This includes establishing clear feedback loops, putting architectural safeguards in place, and developing appropriate governance frameworks. Training should blend AI literacy with solid foundations in software architecture, critical thinking, and ethics. Overall, generative AI is reshaping human expertise rather than replacing it. Its long-term value depends on balancing efficiency with ongoing skill development and thoughtful architectural judgment.

REFERENCES

Avila-Chauvet, L., Mejía, D., & Acosta Quiroz, C. (2023). CHATGPT as a support tool for online behavioral task programming. *SSRN*. Obtenido de https://ssrn.com/abstract=4329020

Barke, S., James, M., & Polikarpova, N. (2023). Grounded copilot: How programmers interact with code-generating models. *Proceedings of the ACM on Programming Languages, 7*(OOPSLA1), 85-111. DOI: 10.1145/3586030

Braverman, H. (1974). *Labor and monopoly capital.* Monthly Review Press. DOI: 10.14452/MR-026-03-1974-07_1

Crowston, K., & Bolici, F. (2025). Deskilling and upskilling with AI Systems. *nformation Research an International Electronic Journal, 30*(iConf), 1009-1023. DOI: 10.47989/ir30iConf47143

Daigle, K. (2024). *Survey: The AI wave continues to grow on software development teams*. Obtenido de https://github.blog/author/kdaigle/

Hackman, J. R., & Oldham, G. R. (1976). Motivation through the design of work: Test of a theory. *Organizational Behavior and Human Performance, 16*(2), 250–279. DOI: 10.1016/0030-5073(76)90016-7

Khurana, A., Subramonyam, H., & Chilana, P. K. (2024). Why and when llm-based assistants can go wrong: Investigating the effectiveness of prompt-based interactions for software help-seeking. *arXiv.org*. Obtenido de /arxiv.2402.08030DOI: 10.1145/3640543.3645200

Kuhail, M. A., Mathew, S. S., Khalil, A., Khalil, A., & Shah, S. J. (2023). "Will I be replaced?" Assessing ChatGPT's effect on software development and programmer perceptions of AI tools. *arXiv.org*. Obtenido de DOI: 10.2139/ssrn.4571482

Liang, H., & Xue, Y. (2009). Avoidance of information technology threats: A theoretical perspective. *Management Information Systems Quarterly*, *33*(1), 71–90. DOI: 10.2307/20650279

Michels, L.-M., Petkova, A., Richter, M., Farley, A., Graziotin, D., & Wagner, S. (2024). Overwhelmed software developers: An interpretative phenomenological analysis. *IEEE Software*, *41*(4), 51–59. Advance online publication. DOI: 10.1109/MS.2024.3374821

Peoples, K. (2021). *How to write a phenomenological dissertation: A step-by-step guide* (Vol. 56). SAGE.

Riazi, M., Rezvani, R., & Ghanbar, H. (2023). Trustworthiness in L2 writing research: A review and analysis of qualitative articles in the Journal of Second Language Writing. *Research Methods in Applied Linguistics*, *2*(3), 100065. Advance online publication. DOI: 10.1016/j.rmal.2023.100065

Rinta-Kahila, T., Penttinen, E., Salovaara, A., Soliman, W., & Ruissalo, J. (2023). The vicious circles of skill erosion: A case study of cognitive automation. *Journal of the Association for Information Systems*, *24*(5), 1378–1412. DOI: 10.17705/1jais.00829

Samuels, A., & Pelser, A.-M. (2025). Transitioning from Industry 4.0 to 5.0: Sustainable supply chain management and talent management insights. *SA Journal of Human Resource Management*, *23*(0), a2874. Advance online publication. DOI: 10.4102/sajhrm.v23i0.2874

Song, F., Agarwal, A., & Wen, W. (2024). The Impact of Generative AI on Collaborative Open-Source Software Development: Evidence from GitHub Copilot. SSRN *Electronic Journal*. https://doi.org//arXiv.2410.02091DOI: 10.48550

Sridhara, G. G, R. H., & Mazumdar, S. (2023). CHATGPT: A study on its utility for ubiquitous software engineering tasks. *arXiv.org*. https://doi.org//arXiv.2305.16837DOI: 10.48550

Yen, R., Zhu, J., Suh, S., Xia, H., & Zhao, J. (2023). Coladder: Supporting programmers with hierarchical code generation in multi-level abstraction. *arXiv preprint arXiv:2310.08699*. https://doi.org//arXiv.2310.08699DOI: 10.48550

KEY TERMS AND DEFINITIONS

AI-Supported Development: A development approach where engineers rely on generative AI to enhance coding, troubleshooting, and design activities.

Architectural Decision-Making: The process of choosing system structures, design patterns, and trade-offs that determine long-term performance, scalability, and maintainability.

Code Quality: How readable, secure, stable, and adaptable software code is, reflecting both engineering standards and development practices.

Cognitive Offloading: Reducing mental effort by delegating tasks like syntax recall or idea generation to AI tools.

Deskilling: The gradual decline of core programming or analytical skills due to increased dependence on automated AI outputs.

Developer Productivity: The degree to which engineers efficiently produce reliable, maintainable software, influenced by skills, tools, and team practices.

Generative AI Assistants: AI-driven tools that create code, documentation, and design ideas by learning from large datasets, helping developers with programming, debugging, and system design tasks.

Human–AI Collaboration: A cooperative working model where developers and AI systems jointly contribute to engineering tasks, with humans maintaining final oversight and responsibility.

Sociotechnical Impact: The combined effect of AI technologies, human roles, and organizational processes on how software engineering work is carried out.

Software Engineering Skills: The technical knowledge and problem-solving abilities engineers use to build, test, deploy, and maintain software systems.

Upskilling: The development of new abilities—such as prompt crafting, AI evaluation, and system-level reasoning—enabled by working with AI tools.

Workflow Efficiency: How quickly and effectively development tasks are completed through streamlined processes, automation, and supportive tools.

Chapter 2

Developer Confidence, Competence, and Self-Efficacy in the Age of AI

Deepak Gupta
http://orcid.org/0000-0003-3929-1362
Institute of Technology and Management, Gwalior, India

Ramazonov Xusniddin
Termez University of Economics and Service, Termez, Uzbekistan

Nasiba Jumaniyazova
Mamun University, Khiva, Uzbekistan

Saipnazarov Sherbek
Tashkent State University of Economics, Uzbekistan

Nilufar Rajabova
Urgench State Pedagogical Institute, Uzbekistan

Rustamov Shavkat
Bukhara State University, Uzbekistan

Oymatova Dilorom
Shahrisabz State Pedagogical Institute, Uzbekistan

ABSTRACT

The emergence and incorporation of AI-based coding assistant tools in the software development process mark an unprecedented paradigmatic shift in the profession of software developers with significant implications for the essence and personality of problem-solving, learning, and software developers' profession. The current chapter undertakes an in-depth exploration of the intricate relationship between artificial intelligence assistants and the confidence, competency, and self-efficacy of software developers, relying on an exhaustive examination of the empirical literature on the subject. The current chapter draws on systematic reviews, large-scale surveys, and experimental studies that examined the impact of AI assistants, including GitHub Copilot, ChatGPT, and LLM-based coding assistants, on the productivity and

DOI: 10.4018/979-8-3373-8450-4.ch002

learning of software developers. The Analysis of the findings presents a paradox: the ability of these AI assistants to improve the rate of task completion and cognitive ease in the performance of routine programming tasks contrasts with the risks of deskilling, over-reliance, and the erosion of problem-solving abilities, especially among novice programmers. In the chapter, the psychological facets of human-AI collaboration are investigated, including the role of self-efficacy beliefs as a mediator of tool adoption and use, and the impact of fear of failure. The new models of deskilling and upskilling are synthesized, and guidelines for the maintenance of developer competence in the face of AI assistants are proposed, which has important implications for software engineering education and developer skill building.

1. INTRODUCTION

1.1 The AI Revolution in Software Development

The domain of software engineering has seen a major paradigm shift with the advent of large language models and coding assistants, which are increasingly becoming an integral part of the coding process. GitHub Copilot, ChatGPT, Amazon CodeWhisperer, and Tabnine are some of the prominent coding assistants that started as a proof-of-concept but are now becoming ubiquitous in modern software development environments, changing the way millions of developers code, debug, and think about code, as described in Peng et al. (2023) and Ziegler et al. (2024). Thus, this technological shift does not just imply the increase of productivity but also a paradigmatic shift in the very essence of programming, which raises pertinent issues of the identity of programmers, their skill sets, and competence in the age of AI. These AI assistants are responsible for creating substantial parts of the codebases in the development environment, with one study indicating that developers are accepting 30-40% of the code written by the AI, thereby passing important creative and technical decisions into the hands of the algorithmic systems. The inclusion of these systems has also significantly compressed the development process, thereby making it possible for developers to undertake prototyping and iteration cycles that were hitherto unthinkable, as well as creating new challenges. dependencies on proprietary systems whose internal workings are opaque to most practitioners.

This transformation, however, is not limited to individual productivity measures but has significant implications for collaborative work, code review, and even the epistemology of software craftsmanship, where knowledge is no longer limited to individuals but to the distributed cognition that occurs between individuals and machines. The implications of this are wide-reaching, touching on educational institutions, hiring, and career development as a consequence of the struggles of organizations in defining competency in a world where being able to prompt and validate AI solutions may be just as important as being able to code them. Furthermore, this evolution is taking place in a world where there are growing concerns about technological unemployment, deskilling, and power imbalance resulting from the few conglomerates that have control over the most advanced form of AI, raising important questions about the future implications for the wider software development community.

1.1.1 Historical Context and Technological Advancement

The development of developer tools has always been geared towards abstracting complexity and maximizing the abilities of the human developer. From assembly languages and programming constructs, through integrated development environments and version control systems, every advancement in technology has been the subject of debate over the deskilling of the developer and the degradation of their ability (Rinta-Kahila et al., 2023). Yet, the latest generation of AI assistants differs from all other advancements in developer tooling, as they have the ability to develop new solutions rather than just automating tasks. Unlike other tooling advancements, such as syntax highlighters and auto-completion, which assist the developer in decision-making, the latest generation of LLMs possesses the ability to develop substantial code artifacts without the involvement of critical cognitive abilities.

1.1.2 Scale and Adoption Patterns

Currently, GitHub Copilot has been adopted by over 1.8 million developers across various settings, from individual hobbyists to professional developers in software organizations, by the year 2024 (Liang et al., 2024). The survey indicates that currently, 46% of professional developers frequently use AI coding assistants, with the adoption rate increasing to over 70% among those who are less than 30 years of age. This has happened without a clear empirical understanding of the long-term consequences in terms of the effect on the developers' competence, career, and software quality, thus making it a pressing concern to study the effect of these tools on developers' competence, confidence, and self-efficacy.

1.2 Theoretical Framework: Competence, Confidence, and Self-Efficacy

1.2.1 Defining Core Constructs

In order to understand the impact of AI tools on their developers, it is important to establish a clear and distinct definition of the following core constructs. Competence involves the capacity to execute programming tasks, including knowledge, problem-solving skills, and proficiency. Confidence involves a person's beliefs about their programming skills, which could be congruent or non-congruent with their competence. Self-efficacy involves a person's judgment of their capacity to execute a programming task, and it could be a function of their experience, knowledge, and skills.This construct, which is rooted in Bandura's social cognitive theory, specifically entails individuals' beliefs about their ability to execute specific behaviors necessary for desired outcomes (Margulieux et al., 2024). In programming, self-efficacy includes individuals' beliefs about their capacity to debug complex systems, as well as their ability to design appropriate algorithms.

1.2.2 The Competence-Confidence Paradox

Investigations into human-AI collaboration have shown a paradox wherein AI systems improve performance indicators, but concurrently, they erode the underlying capabilities to facilitate problem-solving independently (Macnamara et al., 2024). In this case, developers might finish a task in a shorter time and with fewer syntax errors when working with AI systems, thus feeling more confident in their coding skills. Yet, the enhanced performance is the outcome of using AI systems rather than developing a more sophisticated understanding of competence, as revealed through the removal of the AI assistance.

1.3 Chapter Objectives and Structure

The objectives of this chapter are fourfold:

1. Synthesize the empirical research on the impact of AI coding assistants on the productivity, learning, and skill maintenance of developers at different levels of experience
2. Examine the psychological process whereby the AI coding assistants impact the self-efficacy, confidence, and metacognitive strategies of the developer
3. Evaluate the different theoretical models of the process of deskilling or upskilling with the aid of AI coding assistants

4. Discuss the implications of the research for the maintenance of the skills of the developer while utilizing the potential of AI coding assistants

The rest of the chapter is divided as follows: Section 2 presents the empirical findings pertaining to the impact of AI assistants in terms of productivity, code quality, and developers' experience. Section 3 presents the psychological factors such as self-efficacy, overreliance, and metacognitive demands. Section 4 presents the mechanisms of skill erosion and the potential for deskilling. Section 5 presents the implications for education and strategies for reskilling. Section 6 presents the frameworks for human-AI collaboration. Section 7 concludes with the future directions.

2. EMPIRICAL EVIDENCE ON AI ASSISTANT IMPACT

2.1 Productivity and Task Completion

2.1.1 Quantitative Performance Metrics

There have been various empirical research results that indicate that there can be considerable benefits in terms of increased productivity for AI coding assistants. For example, a study by Peng et al. (2023) examined the usage of GitHub Copilot, a coding assistant, by 95,000 users and found that users who had access to the AI coding assistant completed tasks 55.8% faster compared to users who did not have access to it. More specifically, a study by Ziegler et al. (2024) conducted a study on a randomized controlled trial with 95 professional developers on GitHub and examined task completion time, acceptance rate, and perceived productivity. The results of this study revealed that compared to a control group, professional developers who used GitHub Copilot were found to complete an HTTP server implementation task 55% faster, with a median completion time of 1h 11min compared to 2h 41min, and 88% reported feeling more productive.

2.1.2 Task Complexity and Differential Benefits

The benefits of productivity in AI assistants also depend upon the complexity of tasks. Imai (2022) found that AI pair programming substitutes human pair programming in implementing tasks. The benefits of productivity in AI pair programming are low in tasks that are more complex, such as architectural decisions and problem-solving. The effectiveness of AI assistants in tasks shows that these assistants perform better in tasks related to generating boilerplate codes, implementing design patterns, and translating natural language specifications into syntactically correct codes. However, in tasks related to the design of creative algorithms, domain-specific optimizations, and integrating complex systems, the benefits of human pair programming cannot be replicated Moradi Dakhel et al. (2023).

Figure 1. Comparison ofTime Comparison: Developers with and without AI Assistance

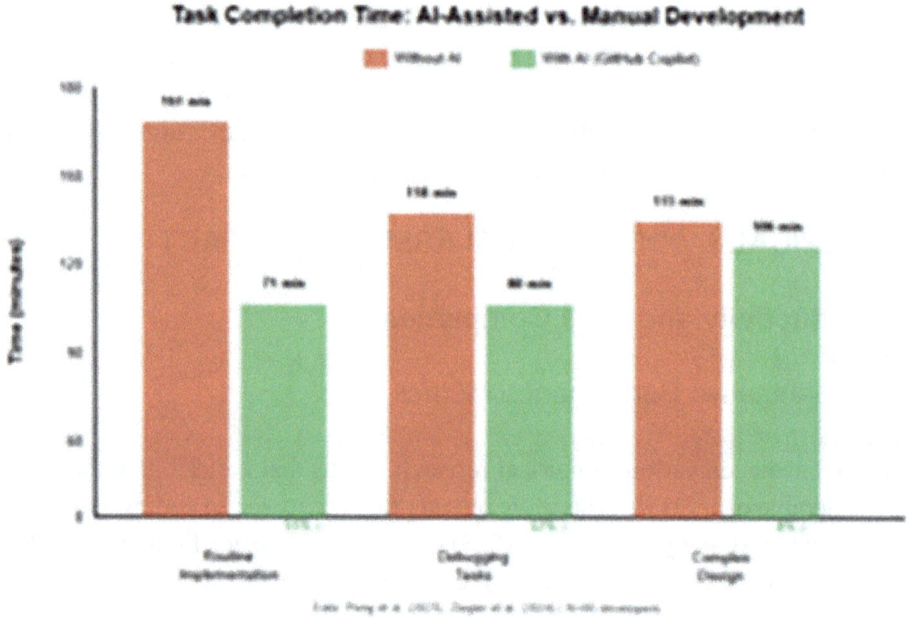

Figure 1 presents the median task completion time for different categories of programming tasks, with and without the assistance of AI coding assistants like GitHub Copilot. The data presented in the graph is synthesized based on the findings of Peng et al. (2023) and Ziegler et al. (2024). It is observed from the graph that the productivity benefits are the highest for routine implementation tasks, with a reduction of 55%, and moderate for debugging activities, with a reduction of 32%. In the case of complex tasks, the time taken with and without the assistance of AI coding assistants differs by only 8%. This indicates that the role of AI assistants is to speed up the solving of well-defined problems rather than to aid creative problem-solving skills.

2.1.3 Code Quality and Security Implications

Although AI assistants help developers speed up the coding process, the quality of the code remains a concern. Perry et al. (2023) conducted controlled experiments in which different security-related coding problems were given to the participants to code with and without the help of AI assistants. The experiments revealed that developers using the help of AI assistants in coding had 40% more security vulnerabilities in their code than developers not using the help of AI assistants. What is more alarming is that developers using the help of AI assistants in coding perceived their code to be more secure than developers not using the help of AI assistants. This is more alarming as this phenomenon leads to "security theater," i.e., developers using the help of AI assistants in coding perceive their code to be correct while in reality, there are security vulnerabilities in their code that cannot be easily identified.

2.2 User Experience and Usability Challenges

2.2.1 Large-Scale Survey Findings

The most extensive research on the usability of AI programming assistants has been performed by Liang et al. (2024), where the authors carried out a survey of 410 developers and examined 48,545 online posts on GitHub and Stack Overflow. The study also showed the existence of systematic usability issues in the following five areas: suggestion quality, output explainability, trust calibration, workflow integration, and mental model alignment. In this study, 38% of the participants experienced "automation surprises," which refer to a situation where AI suggestions differ significantly from the expected automation behavior. In addition, 52% of the participants found it difficult to determine the correctness of the suggestions without extensive testing.

2.2.2 The Problem Landscape

Zhou et al. (2024) provided a taxonomy of the problems faced by developers when working with AI pair programming tools, based on 476 GitHub issues and 378 Stack Overflow questions. They found three types of problems:

1. *Generation problems* (43%): Inaccurate, incomplete, and/or non-functioning code suggestions
2. *Interaction problems* (31%): Interaction problems (31%): Difficulty with controlling and/or guiding the AI, as well as insufficient feedback mechanisms
3. *Conceptual problems* (26%): Misconceptions about the capabilities of the AI, as well as incorrect delegation of tasks

It is interesting to note that most interaction and conceptual issues are the result of the developers' inability to build an accurate mental model of the capabilities and limitations of the AI system, an aspect that affects the use and skill-building process.

2.3 Experience Level and Differential Impact

2.3.1 Novice Developer Outcomes

The impact of AI assistants on learning and development outcomes may be especially strong among novice programmers. In experiments with 69 novice programmers, Kazemitabaar et al. (2023) conducted controlled experiments and showed that the presence of AI code generators significantly increased the number of programming exercises completed by novice programmers (1.8× as many exercises) but also had a negative effect on the conceptual understanding of the novice programmers when the AI support was removed. The novice programmers who heavily used the AI tool had difficulty in articulating the code they had developed, had weak debugging capabilities, and had low ability to generalize the code they had developed.

Figure 2. The Learning Paradox: Task Completion vs. Conceptual Understanding in Novice Programmers

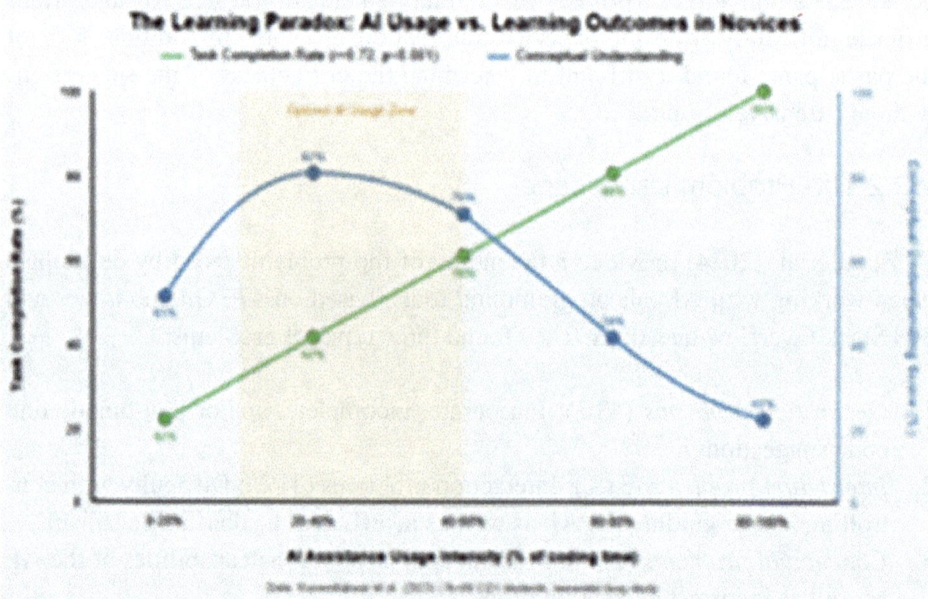

Figure 2 illustrates the relationship between the intensity of the use of AI assistance and the two critical outcomes of novice programmers: task completion rate and scores of conceptual understanding. The graph is based on the experimental study of Kazemitabaar et al. (2023), with 69 CS1 students as participants and the experiment conducted for one semester. The graph shows the trend of task completion, which increases with the intensity of the use of AI assistance in a linear fashion ($r = 0.72$, $p < 0.001$), and the trend of conceptual understanding, which shows the inverted "U" curve, with the highest scores of conceptual understanding occurring with moderate use of AI assistance (20-40% of the time spent coding), and then decreases sharply with heavy use of AI assistance.

2.3.2 Expert Developer Patterns

Expert developers may be better able to harness the productive potential of AI tools, as well as maintain the integrity of their expertise. Barke et al. (2023) carried out ethnographic studies and interviews with experienced programmers working with the Copilot tool and found several advanced interaction patterns, including experts working with the suggestions provided by the tool as starting points for critical evaluation, experts working with the tool in debugging and refactoring the code produced by the tool, and experts disabling the tool's assistance when working with conceptually challenging problems as a means of cognitive engagement. These patterns may be explained by the role of metacognitive awareness and strategic tool use, as products of expertise.

3. PSYCHOLOGICAL DIMENSIONS: SELF-EFFICACY AND CONFIDENCE

3.1 Self-Efficacy Dynamics in AI-Augmented Development

3.1.1 Measurement and Operationalization

To measure programming self-efficacy in an LLM-supported environment, Margulieux et al. (2024) created and validated instruments using traditional self-efficacy scales, extending their application to accommodate tool-supported performance. A longitudinal study of 156 introductory programming students found complex self-efficacy development, with AI users demonstrating higher self-efficacy ratings (M=4.2/5.0) compared to their non-AI using peers (M=3.6/5.0), though this disparity diminished considerably by semester end as non-AI users began to genuinely develop their skills through struggle and perseverance.

3.1.2 Self-Regulation and Fear of Failure

The interplay between self-regulation skills and self-efficacy with the use of AI tools has profound implications for the achievement of desired outcomes. In a study done by Margulieux et al. (2024), it was found that students with high self-regulation skills, i.e., the ability to set goals, monitor their own progress, and adapt strategies, were more likely to use AI tools judiciously as a means of helping their learning, rather than relying on them as a crutch. Students with high fear of failure were more likely to abuse the use of AI tools as a means to cope with the anxiety of attempting to solve problems on their own. The negative coping strategies led to the underdevelopment of skills as the use of AI tools created a dependency that diminished the chances for productive struggle to develop self-efficacy.

3.2 The Confidence-Competence Misalignment

3.2.1 Overconfidence and Dunning-Kruger Effects

Perry et al. (2023) found that there was a worrying trend of confidence inflation for users of AI assistants. In the study, it was found that not only did users of AI assistants write less secure code, but they were also significantly more confident about the security of their code (M=4.1/5.0) compared to a control group (M=3.3/5.0). This finding implies that there might be Dunning-Kruger effects for users of AI assistants, where incompetent users do not understand their own incompetence due to their use of AI assistants.

3.2.2 Calibration and Metacognitive Awareness

Vaithilingam et al. (2022) conducted a study on the calibration of the developers' expectations of the ability of the AI tool. In the study, 21 participants were asked to undertake a survey before and after using the LLM-based code generation tools. The findings indicated that the initial expectations of the participants were extremely unrealistic, as 76% of the participants believed that "the AI would understand my intent perfectly and produce production-quality code." However, after using the AI tools, the participants' expectations were recalibrated, and only 29% believed that "the AI would understand my intent perfectly and produce production-quality code." However, the process of recalibrating the expectations of the participants took extensive direct experience with the tool failures.

3.3 Metacognitive Demands of AI Collaboration

3.3.1 New Cognitive Skill Requirements

According to Tankelevitch et al. (2024), the metacognitive skills that are necessary to collaborate with AI systems effectively are generally not understood. The authors' model proposes that there are five metacognitive skills that are considered critical for the productive use of AI:

1. *Prompt Engineering Competence: The translation of ambiguous problem descriptions into unambiguous specifications for AI systems*
2. *Output Evaluation: The rapid evaluation of the quality of AI-generated solutions in terms of correctness, efficiency, and maintainability*
3. Strategic Delegation: The identification of tasks that are best performed with the assistance of AI and those that require human expertise
4. *Bias Detection: The identification of biases in the data used for the training of AI models*
5. *Integration Planning: The integration of AI-generated system components with the overall system architecture*

Significantly, these metacognitive abilities, too, call for considerable expertise to acquire, thus creating the possibility of competence as a barrier if the novice lacks expertise as well as the "meta-skills" required for the effective use of these AI tools.

Tools like GitHub Copilot, ChatGPT, Amazon CodeWhisperer, and Tabnine have rapidly transformed from the state of prototypes into the "mainstream" development environments, thereby profoundly reshaping the manner in which millions of developers write, debug, and think about code (Peng et al., 2023; Ziegler et al., 2024). This technological change, however, is not merely one of "productivity" but, instead, one of paradigmatic change with regard to the very nature of programming, thereby raising fundamental questions with regard to the very concept of the developer, the required skills, and competence in the age of AI.

Table 1. Metacognitive Skills Required for Effective AI Coding Assistant Use

Metacognitive Skill	Description	Novice Difficulty (1-5)	Expert Proficiency (1-5)	Development Pathway
Prompt Engineering	Translation of problem specifications to precise queries for an AI queries system	4.2	2.1	Practice, and with iterative refinement, explicit instruction
Output Evaluation	Evaluation of correctness, efficiency, and quality of AI suggestions	4.5	1.8	Code review training, testing methodology
Strategic Delegation	Evaluation of whether to apply AI or coding manually	3.8	1.5	Experience with limitations and costs, cost-benefit analysis
Bias Detection	Evaluation of limitations and biases in AI suggestions	4.7	2.3	Training on common AI failure modes, diverse test cases
Integration Planning	Incorporation of AI code with existing systems	4.1	1.9	Architecture expertise, experience with refactoring

Note: Rated on a 5-point scale ranging from 1=Very Easy/High to 5=Very Difficult/Low. Data synthesized from Tankelevitch et al. (2024) and expert interviews conducted by the authors. The development pathways are evidence-based strategies to encourage the development of each skill.

3.3.2 The Expertise Paradox

The expert paradigm in AI-supported development is increasingly yielding a new kind of paradox: the individuals who are best suited to utilize AI tools in a beneficial fashion—those who are experts in the domain of development and have the highest metacognitive abilities—are the same individuals who require the tools the least. Conversely, those individuals who require the tools the most are the ones who do not yet have the foundational knowledge base necessary to utilize the tools in a beneficial fashion.

4. SKILL EROSION AND DESKILLING MECHANISMS

4.1 Theoretical Frameworks for Understanding Deskilling

4.1.1 Automation and Cognitive Offloading

Rinta-Kahila et al. (2023) have established a thorough theoretical framework for understanding skill erosion in cognitive automation scenarios. The authors have identified three interconnected mechanisms through which automation leads to deskilling:

1. **Decreased practice opportunities:** The more human tasks are replaced by AI, the fewer opportunities people have to engage in practice, the only way to gain expertise
2. **Mental model degradation:** The less people engage in problem-solving, the worse developers' internal representations of system behavior, code, and debugging techniques
3. **Metacognitive deskilling:** The more people rely on automated systems, the worse their metacognitive skills, such as self-monitoring, strategy selection, and evaluation of performance, become

The authors' longitudinal case study of robotic process automation implementation identified these mechanisms in action, whereby the skills of knowledge workers showed measurable levels of degradation within 6 to 12 months of automation implementation. The skills took significant retraining to regain, even if they were well-established.

4.1.2 The Deskilling-Upskilling Dialectic

Crowston and Bolici (2025) challenge the simplistic view of deskilling with their demonstration that generative AI systems not only upskill. The authors' analysis of this dialectic reveals three possible outcomes:

1. **Net Deskilling:** The overall level of competence decreases because more skills are lost than gained
2. **Skill Substitution:** The skills that are lost are replaced by new skills, which leaves the overall level of competence unchanged but changes its content
3. **Net Upskilling:** The skills gained outnumber those that are lost, thereby increasing the overall level of competence.

Which of these routes dominates depends critically on the use of AI tools and the educational/organizational support provided for their use. In the absence of such intervention, they propose that the default outcome is net deskilling for routine cognitive tasks.

4.2 Empirical Evidence of Skill Degradation

4.2.1 Experimental Demonstrations

Macnamara et al. (2024) carried out a research in which they sought to investigate the effects of AI on the acceleration of skill degradation through conducting experiments. In the experiment, the research team provided the participants with training on the basics of programming with or without the assistance of AI. Later, the participants who received training with the assistance of AI had to wait for two weeks before being re-assessed without the assistance of AI. Later, the participants who received training with AI assistance were required to wait for a period of two weeks before being re-assessed without AI assistance. The results of the experiment revealed that the participants who initially used AI assistance to acquire the skills demonstrated 34% greater skill degradation compared to the participants who did not use AI assistance. More alarmingly, the experiment revealed that the participants who used AI assistance demonstrated low levels of awareness of their skill degradation and rated their skills significantly higher than they actually were.

4.2.2 The Hidden Nature of Skill Erosion

In a warning call to attention, O'Brien (2025) highlights the silent skill erosion in scientific computing, which may be caused by over-reliance on AI code assistants and lead to a situation where researchers may be unable to detect errors and validate results in a scientific manner. While skill failure can have devastating effects with obvious implications for skill gaps, skill erosion happens in such a slow and ambiguous fashion that people and organizations are not aware of its implications until it is too late, at which point the situation may already be serious. The ambiguous nature of skill erosion, therefore, creates a significant challenge in the sense that while it becomes obvious that there was indeed skill erosion, it may not be easy to solve the situation.

4.3 The Over-Reliance Problem

4.3.1 Automation Complacency

There has been considerable research on "automation complacency" in fields such as aviation and healthcare, which shows that people over-rely on automated systems and consequently under-monitor their results (Gerlich, 2025). Similarly, with regards to software development, Moradi Dakhel et al. (2023) showed that

41% of developers reported that they would accept suggestions made by AI without reviewing them, and this percentage increased with the level of time pressure.

4.3.2 Dependency and Recovery

Another important issue is the reversibility of the effects, or the ability to break the dependency when the developers want to or should go back to the original state. The results are not conclusive, but they suggest that recovery is possible but costly. In the study by Macnamara et al. (2024), it took the participants 2.4 × longer to relearn the skills after the performance degradation caused by AI than it did initially to learn the skills in the first place.

5. EDUCATIONAL IMPLICATIONS AND RESKILLING STRATEGIES

5.1 Computing Education in the Generative AI Era

5.1.1 Pedagogical Challenges and Opportunities

In a comprehensive analysis of the impact of generative AI on computing education, Denny et al. (2024) point out both the challenges and opportunities. The challenges include:

- **Learning bypass**: The possibility of AI being used to bypass learning
- **Assessment validity**: The inability of programming-based assessments to measure student competence in the generative AI era
- **Skill prioritization**: The lack of knowledge of which skills can be bypassed with AI
- **Equity concerns**: The impact of unequal AI adoption on student achievement

At the same time, there are pedagogical opportunities with AI tools, such as personalization of feedback, intelligent tutoring, scaffolding of problem-solving support, and increasing what novices can do on their own.

5.1.2 Curriculum Redesign Principles

Prather et al. (2023) distill the recommendations of a working group of computing education researchers to produce five principles for curriculum design in the AI era:

1. **Explicit AI Literacy**: Educating students on the use of AI coding tools, their limitations, and applications
2. **Metacognitive Scaffolding**: Building the metacognitive skills required for the judicious use of AI
3. **Assessment Innovation**: Going beyond the creation of code to the evaluation of understanding, debugging, and designing
4. **Productive Struggle Preservation**: Ensuring the continuation of appropriately challenging problems for students
5. **Tool-Optional Learning Paths**: Ensuring the continuation of AI-free learning paths for students

5.2 Evidence-Based Teaching Strategies

5.2.1 The Assistance Dilemma

The "assistance dilemma" in the application of educational AI was identified by Kasneci et al. (2023). They suggest that if learning is made easy through AI, it might hinder the development of competence in the long run. The framework they propose suggests that the amount of AI assistance should depend on the competence of the student. More help is required initially, but then it should gradually fade out, which is similar to human tutoring.

5.2.2 Comparative Effectiveness Studies

In a comparative study conducted by Gardella et al. (2024) on the comparative effectiveness of different instructional methods on the learning outcomes of students, the study compared the learning outcomes of students who received traditional teaching methods without the use of AI tools, students who received unrestricted AI tools, and students who received a special type of AI-based teaching referred to as "scaffolded AI." The study revealed that students who received scaffolded AI-based teaching scored significantly higher than students who received unrestricted AI-based teaching and traditional teaching. In the study, the students who received scaffolded AI-based teaching scored the highest on both immediate and delayed tests, i.e., 82.4/100 and 76.1/100, respectively, compared to students who received unrestricted AI-based teaching, who scored 79.2/100 and 61.3/100, respectively, and students who received traditional teaching, who scored

Figure 3. Learning Outcomes Across Instructional Conditions: Immediate Performance vs. Delayed Retention

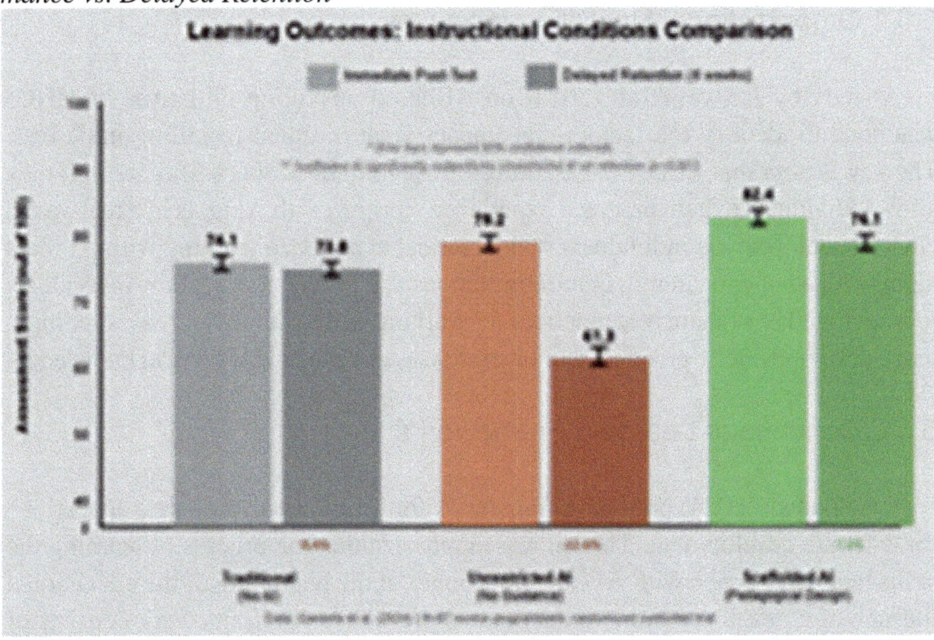

Figure 3 displays the learning outcome results of Gardella et al. (2024), which examined the effectiveness of three instructional conditions: no AI, unrestricted AI, and scaffolded AI. The results, displayed as a bar graph, represent the scores of a 100-point programming competency test administered immediately after instruction and 4 weeks later, or delayed retention. The scaffolded AI had the best results with the highest scores in the immediate test (82.4) and good results in the delayed test (76.1) with only 7.6% decay. The results for the unrestricted AI access had high performance but with a very low retention rate, with only 61.3 being a result of a 22.6% decay. The traditional instruction had moderate performance with high retention, with a low percentage of 0.4% being the decay. The error bars represent the 95% confidence interval. The results show that the inclusion of AI in pedagogy enhances both performance and retention; however, the unrestricted AI access is only an illusion.

5.3 Professional Development and Reskilling

5.3.1 Organizational Upskilling Initiatives

A study by Jaiswal et al. (2022) on AI-based upskilling initiatives in MNCs was done to identify the factors that impact organizational reskilling initiatives. The key factors that make AI-based upskilling initiatives successful are that they allow individuals to gain practical experience working with AI tools in a real-world environment, provide individuals with practical experience working with AI tools along with an understanding of tool limitations and proper usage, allow individuals to work together to share best practices for working with AI tools, and assess competence development by practical demonstration as opposed to theoretical knowledge.

5.3.2 Continuous Learning Frameworks

Sengul et al. (2024) propose a framework for "continuous AI-aware education" for software development. The authors emphasize that the process of learning the skills required to cope with AI cannot be done "at the beginning of the educational journey of a developer but is a continuous process.". The framework consists of competence audit, in which a developer checks his/her skills in the light of new industry requirements; experimentation with new AI technologies under the guidance of a mentor; rotation between AI-based development and manual development to ensure basic skills; and reflection on the impact of AI on the developer's problem-solving skills.

5.4 Assessment and Validation Challenges

5.4.1 Distinguishing Human from AI Contributions

Nikolic et al. (2023) conducted an investigation on engineering education assessments in the ChatGPT age. Their work revealed that "traditional take-home programming assignments have become largely obsolete as an assessment tool." The authors used a benchmarking approach to assess ChatGPT on its capability to accomplish programming assignments for undergraduates, which resulted in a discovery that "ChatGPT can successfully complete 89% of programming assignments at passing quality levels." This is a crisis of validity that requires a fundamental shift in how we assess programming competence, moving from code production to debugging, code explanations, design justifications, and adaptation of existing code to new constraints.

5.4.2 Novel Assessment Approaches

There are emerging strategies for software assessments that focus on the evaluation of skills that AI technologies cannot be used to automate, including the ability to explain someone else's code, debugging of faulty codes, justifying the design of a system, refactoring of codes to comply with newer demands, and the ability to review codes and integrate different components of a system. This is due to the emerging notion that software engineering in the future will involve a greater reading, evaluation, and integration of codes compared to the initial generation of codes.

6. FRAMEWORKS FOR SUSTAINABLE HUMAN-AI COLLABORATION

6.1 Principles for Competence-Preserving AI Use

6.1.1 Strategic Delegation Framework

Tankelevitch et al. (2024) introduced a decision framework to evaluate the delegation of tasks to human AI assistants or performing them manually. The framework takes into account three factors:

1. **Learning value**: The value of the task in terms of learning potential. Novices should manually perform tasks with high learning value
2. **Risk severity**: The severity of the task in terms of reliability and security
3. **Novelty**: The novelty of the task in terms of creativity

This framework asserts that the optimal way to use AI depends on individuals (based on their expertise levels) as well as contexts (based on task requirements), dismissing the idea of a universal tool-use strategy.

6.1.2 Cognitive Engagement

Fakhoury et al. (2024) designed an "active learning" method for the development of code with the aid of AI, in which the user had to engage in test-driven development techniques before being provided with the solutions. The authors' system using an LLM for interactive code generation forced the user to declare test cases first, which actively engages the user cognitively rather than passively accepting the code. The authors' user study showed that the method maintained the effectiveness of the learning (measured by conceptual understanding tests) and still had the benefits of increased productivity, implying that the risk of skill erosion could be mitigated with proper interaction design.

6.2 Designing for Skill Development

6.2.1 Adaptive Assistance Systems

In the domain of AI coding assistants, Kazemitabaar et al. (2024) introduced the concept of "progressive disclosure" of AI coding assistants, which varies depending on the skill levels of users. For a novice user, conceptual hints would be provided by the AI system, and users would be asked to decompose the problem before being given any code solutions. For an intermediate user, implementation-level assistance would be provided by the AI system, while users would be asked to think of overall solution strategies. For an expert user, the AI system would be a productivity accelerator, while it would be "dormant" during the creative process.

6.2.2 Transparency and Explainability

Nguyen et al. (2024) demonstrated that novice programmers misinterpret the code generated by LLMs and accept the solutions they cannot comprehend or change. This, therefore, means that an AI coding assistant not only needs to provide solutions but also an explanation of the logic used in the code, the alternatives considered, and the limitations of the implementation. This would enable the novice programmer to learn by making the reasoning of the AI transparent and teachable, rather than making it seem mysterious or even "magical."

6.3 Organizational and Cultural Factors

6.3.1 Team Dynamics and Knowledge Sharing

In a synthesis of human-AI teaming research, Berretta et al. (2023) identified some of the following best practices in facilitating teamwork between human and AI agents without sacrificing human competence. These best practices include the establishment of "norms regarding when AI use is encouraged or discouraged," the establishment of a mentorship approach in which more senior developers guide junior team members in the use of AI systems judiciously, the implementation of a code review process in which AI-generated code is carefully scrutinized, and the establishment of "AI-free time" in which team members solve problems without the use of AI systems.

6.3.2 Long-Term Competence Planning

There are strategic decisions to be made with regards to competence building in an AI-aided future. Should an organization look to recruit people with strong fundamental skills, built through conventional means, or would they be better off with an AI-first developer who has never known anything else? Should training strategies look to build coding skills, as a means of protection from tool dependency, or would they be better off embracing AI tools for maximum short-term productivity gains? The answer to these questions remains uncertain, but failure to address them means defaulting to maximum automation, which could be a path to regret if skill degradation happens on a large scale.

7. FUTURE TRAJECTORIES AND EMERGING CHALLENGES

7.1 Evolving AI Capabilities

7.1.1 From Code Generation to Software Engineering

The existing code assistants for AI applications are mostly focused on code snippet generation or completion of functions based on context. Yet, emerging coding assistants can already achieve software architecture, test generation, bug localization, and even autonomous debugging. Consequently, with the evolving capabilities of AI, human activities in software development are also bound to change. This has implications for which activities will continue to be human-advantaged, even with the advancement of AI, and which activities will be increasingly "commoditized" by AI advancement.

7.1.2 Multimodal and Context-Aware Systems

Tang et al. (2024) conducted a study on the validation and correction of LLM-generated code by developers using eye tracking and action analysis in the IDE. Their study demonstrated that the validation process is a complex one and includes the integration of different sources of information. AI systems of the future may be multimodal, using vision, dialogue, and context from the entire code base or the entire knowledge base of the company. This may help the developer reason better and decrease the error rates, but the complexity of the human-AI interface and the expertise required may be daunting.

7.2 Research Gaps and Future Directions

7.2.1 Longitudinal Competence Studies

Current studies are based on short-term experiments, which last several weeks or months. Longitudinal studies, which follow the competence of developers over several years of working with AI tools, are urgently needed. For example, do the productivity gains of AI tool usage hold up over time as developers increasingly lose touch with their human coding skills? Do developers who learn to program with AI tools develop different cognitive architectures compared to those who learn to program without AI tool support? Can developers who become tool-dependent successfully maintain their competence when they cannot or should not use AI tools?

7.2.2 Individual Differences and Moderation Effects

Past research has just begun to examine the role of individual differences in moderating the impact of AI tools. Initial findings suggest that personality factors (conscientiousness, openness to experience), cognitive factors (working memory, pattern recognition), and motivational factors (mastery vs. performance goals) all contribute to the adoption of AI tools and competence development. These factors may potentially contribute to the development of recommendations for the use of AI tools based on learning needs.

7.3 Ethical and Societal Implications

7.3.1 Professional Identity and Meaning

Beyond the question of competence, there is the question of professional identity and meaning in the work of software development. If a large part of the work of software development is automated, what does it do to the sense of craft, creativity, and intellectual challenge that many people find attractive in programming? The study of automation psychology indicates that over-automation can lead to decreased job satisfaction, increased burnout, and a feeling of decreased accomplishment, even in the presence of increased objective productivity.

7.3.2 Access, Equity, and Power The Dynamics of Power

The current generation of AI coding assistants represents the dominant Western and English-speaking world of programming and may reflect the biases that exist in the training data. As these coding assistants begin to alter the course and direction that professionals and students take, it becomes obvious that the question of access and equity becomes the most important question of all: will AI coding assistants be able to level the playing field and open the door to more people being able to access programming and coding, or will it continue to exacerbate the problem and only be available to those who can pay for additional educational tools? How will the changes brought about by AI impact the world of software labor and the millions of programmers worldwide?

7.4 Toward Evidence-Based Guidelines

7.4.1 Synthesizing Recommendations

Based on the evidence considered in this chapter, it is possible to outline provisional guidelines for the use of AI coding assistants that take into account both productivity and competence preservation:

For Individual Developers:

- Use AI coding tools strategically for routine coding, but continue to apply manual coding for conceptually difficult problems
- View AI coding suggestions as starting points that need to be critically evaluated, rather than final solutions
- Engage regularly in coding without AI coding assistance to retain basic skills
- Strive to develop a clear understanding of AI coding tool capabilities and limitations through experimentation
- Solicit opinions from experienced programmers regarding proper AI coding tool usage patterns

For Educators:

- Include AI literacy in the curriculum, covering both technical and appropriate contexts of use
- Develop assessment strategies that test AI understanding and problem-solving, not code creation
- Offer AI experiences that balance scaffolding and cognitive load
- Offer students the opportunity to experience productive struggle without AI
- Assess individual student AI use and address the issue if they become dependent on it

For Organizations:

- Develop policies regarding the appropriate use of AI tools in different contexts

- Invest in training programs that build both AI tool and human capabilities
- Implement code review processes that consider AI-generated content
- Assess long-term trends in team competence and adapt AI tool use accordingly
- Encourage diversity in team capabilities rather than relying on universal automation

7.4.2 Adaptive Implementation

Most importantly, these guidelines have to be adaptive to accommodate changes in the evolution of AI techniques and to take into account emerging empirical evidence. What is good practice in terms of using AI tools today may not be good practice in five years' time. The software engineering community has to foster a culture of 'reflective practice' in terms of examining the impact of tools on their own competence.

8. CONCLUSION

8.1 Summary of Key Findings

This chapter provided a discussion on the impact of AI-based coding assistants on the confidence, competence, and self-efficacy of developers based on the latest research studies. Some of the key findings that have been made from the synthesis of the current research studies are as follows:

Performance Paradox: The studies have shown that the use of AI-based coding assistants always improves the performance of developers in the short term but also adds a risk to the development of their competence. The developers are able to show improvement in performance due to the use of AI-based assistants but not necessarily due to better understanding.

Experience-Mediated Effects: The effects of AI assistants differ significantly depending on the level of expertise of the developer. Inexperienced developers are most prone to the loss of expertise and the misuse of AI tools, while skilled developers show a complex pattern of using AI tools that helps maintain their expertise.

Metacognitive Requirements: Collaborating successfully with AI tools requires the developer to have advanced metacognitive capabilities such as engineering, evaluating the output of the AI tools, strategic delegation, detecting biases, and integration planning. However, these capabilities are usually not taught explicitly and are assumed to be present in the developer.

Confidence-Competence Misalignment: AI tools can lead to a situation in which users feel more competent but actually become less competent, resulting in a potentially hazardous overconfidence in the security and correctness of the code.

Deskilling Mechanisms: There are a number of mechanisms by which the adoption of AI tools can lead to deskilling. These mechanisms include the reduction of opportunities for purposeful practice, the degradation of mental models, automation complacency, and metacognitive deskilling. It is the default outcome that skill erosion is the inevitable consequence of AI adoption.

8.2 Practical Implications

The evidence reviewed above implies that the best approach to AI tools' adoption, without the focus on the maintenance of competence, is a risky approach. Therefore, the best approach should be:

- **Trade-offs:** Be aware that productivity may come at the expense of learning and maintenance of competence
- **Experience-based differentiation:** Novice and expert users should be treated differently
- **Metacognitive skills:** Make these skills explicit; don't wait for the developer to be wise about the judicious use of tools
- **Challenge maintenance:** Provide continued exposure to problems that call for genuine cognitive efforts

Trend monitoring: Be aware of the long-term effects of AI tools on competence trends, rather than focusing on short-term productivity

8.3 Limitations and Uncertainties

There are a number of significant limitations that need to be taken into account before drawing a conclusion on the subject matter discussed in this chapter:

Recency of Research: The majority of the research that this chapter is based on was published in 2023-2024, and it would be safe to say that this is an early stage in the adoption cycle of AI tools.

Rapid Technological Evolution: The domain of AI technology is in a continuous state of evolution, and there are possibilities that this research may become irrelevant in the near future. The research done on AI assistants today may not be applicable in the near future, considering the evolution that will take place in the domain of AI technology.

Context Specificity: The empirical research seems to focus on specific contexts (GitHub Copilot, academic settings, Western developers), which may not be representative of other global software development practices.

Measurement Challenges: The ambiguity in the term "competence" in software development is a challenge. There is no consensus on what competencies are significant, what are less significant, what are critical, and what are not critical in the domain of software development.

8.4 Future Research Priorities

To further enhance the understanding of the impact of AI on competence in developers, research investments are needed in the following areas:

Longitudinal Studies: Conducting longitudinal studies on the changes in developer competence, specifically on people who have varying levels of AI tool usage and exposure.

Individual Differences: Thoroughly examining individual differences in personality, cognitive, and motivational factors on AI tool effects on developers.

Cultural Contexts: Conducting research that covers a wide spectrum of geographic, linguistic, and cultural contexts to understand the effects of AI tools on different educational and professional cultures.

Skill Decomposition: Thoroughly examining which skills are more vulnerable to negative AI tool effects and which skills are more resistant to AI tool effects.

Intervention Effectiveness: Thoroughly examining interventions to support the maintenance of developer competence and the effective usage of AI tools.

Tool Design: Conducting research on designing AI tools that can support learning and competence maintenance, unlike AI tools that can efficiently complete tasks.

8.5 Concluding Reflections

What can be said about the implications of AI on software development? It is not an unqualified success or disaster, but rather a complicated change that needs to be carefully managed. We can recognize that there are, indeed, tensions between different goals, such as productivity and learning, or convenience and competence.

Achieving this transition successfully requires a move away from simplistic adoption maximization and towards a more sophisticated understanding of when and how these tools can be beneficial. This is not to say that we should avoid the use of AI tools altogether, as this would mean giving up any hope of achieving the productivity gains and potential of human capabilities; rather, we should be striving to create ecologies of practice where these tools enhance human capabilities without diminishing the cognitive engagement that underpins expertise.

The research discussed in this chapter offers a first indication of the balanced approaches that can be adopted, as well as an indication of just how much remains to be understood. As the capabilities of AI tools continue to evolve and develop at a rapid pace, the software engineering community should be mindful of the trends in competence, flexibility in adapting to the evidence base, and the humility required to recognize the difficulty of predicting the emergent effects of complex systems.

The evidence synthesized within this chapter indicates that the relationship between AI support and developer skill is ultimately dependent on human agency. Organizations that rely on AI as a tool of productivity acceleration without attention to skill maintenance are likely to follow a pattern of deskilling, while organizations that emphasize AI utilization scaffolding and skill maintenance are likely to experience productivity acceleration while improving human capabilities. The distinction is not technology-based but is dependent on human agency.

Among the decisions that are of critical importance are those that affect educational institutions. The computer education that is offered without proper access to AI can lead to a situation where individuals are able to pass through an education program with impressive skills that are actually quite fragile. Such individuals would be able to perform to an impressive standard when AI is an option but would be unable to perform when it is not. It is important to note that other approaches that emphasize AI literacy, cognitive challenge, and metacognitive skills can be quite effective.

With respect to the future, the profession of software engineering will need to contend with basic questions related to the nature of expertise in a highly automated world. If a large percentage of code development is automated, what basic skills define the contributions of human expertise? How will the profession adapt in terms of identity and development if the emphasis shifts from code development to code evaluation, system design, and strategic decisions? What new expertise is being created at the interface of human expertise and artificial intelligence? These are all questions without easy answers but require ongoing dialogue.

The challenge we face ahead is not a technological one; it is a social and organizational one: how to develop norms, practices, and institutions that exploit the transformative potential of AI while preserving the human capabilities that underlie innovation, quality, and professional fulfillment. This means ongoing empirical research to monitor the evolution of competences, refinement of best practices as we gather more evidence, and shared commitment to the sustainability of human development in AI environments.

Ultimately, the question is not whether developers should use AI tools—adoption appears both inevitable and potentially beneficial—but how to integrate these capabilities in ways that enhance rather than undermine human flourishing, learning, and expertise. Answering this question well requires ongoing dialogue among researchers, practitioners, educators, and policymakers, informed by rigorous empirical investigation and guided by commitment to sustainable professional development in an AI-augmented future. The software engineering community stands at a critical juncture where thoughtful choices today will shape competence landscapes for decades to come. The evidence reviewed here provides foundation for making those choices wisely, balancing innovation with preservation of the human expertise that remains irreplaceable.

REFERENCES

Barke, S., James, M. B., & Polikarpova, N. (2023). Grounded Copilot: How programmers interact with code-generating models. Proceedings of the ACM on Programming Languages, 7(OOPSLA1), 85–111. DOI: 10.1145/3586030

Berretta, S., Tausch, A., Ontrup, G., Gilles, B., Peifer, C., & Kluge, A. (2023). Defining human-AI teaming the human-centered way: A scoping review and network analysis. *Frontiers in Artificial Intelligence*, *6*, 1250725. Advance online publication. DOI: 10.3389/frai.2023.1250725 PMID: 37841234

Crowston, K., & Bolici, F. (2025). Deskilling and upskilling with AI systems. Information Research: An International Electronic Journal, 30(iConf), 1009–1023. DOI: 10.47989/ir30iConf47143

Denny, P., Prather, J., Becker, B. A., Finnie-Ansley, J., Hellas, A., Leinonen, J., Luxton-Reilly, A., Reeves, B. N., Santos, E. A., & Sarsa, S. (2024). Computing education in the era of generative AI. *Communications of the ACM*, *67*(2), 56–67. DOI: 10.1145/3624720

Fakhoury, S., Naik, A., Sakkas, G., Chakraborty, S., & Lahiri, S. K. (2024). LLM-based test-driven interactive code generation: User study and empirical evaluation. *IEEE Transactions on Software Engineering*, *50*(9), 2254–2268. DOI: 10.1109/TSE.2024.3428972

Gardella, N., Pettit, R., & Riggs, S. L. (2024). Performance, workload, emotion, and self-efficacy of novice programmers using AI code generation. In *Proceedings of the 2024 Innovation and Technology in Computer Science Education* V. 1 (pp. 290–296). ACM. DOI: 10.1145/3649217.3653615

Gerlich, M. (2025). AI tools in society: Impacts on cognitive offloading and the future of critical thinking. *Societies (Basel, Switzerland)*, *15*(1), 6. Advance online publication. DOI: 10.3390/soc15010006

Imai, S. (2022). Is GitHub Copilot a substitute for human pair-programming? An empirical study. In Proceedings of the ACM/IEEE 44th International Conference on Software Engineering: Companion Proceedings (pp. 319–321). ACM. DOI: 10.1109/ICSE-Companion55297.2022.9793778

Jaiswal, A., Arun, J., & Varma, A. (2022). Rebooting employees: Upskilling for artificial intelligence in multinational corporations. *International Journal of Human Resource Management*, *33*(6), 1179–1208. DOI: 10.1080/09585192.2021.1891114

Kazemitabaar, M., Chow, J., Ma, C. K. T., Ericson, B. J., Weintrop, D., & Grossman, T. (2023). Studying the effect of AI code generators on supporting novice learners in introductory programming. In *Proceedings of the 2023 CHI Conference on Human Factors in Computing Systems* (pp. 1–23). ACM. https://doi.org/DOI: 10.1145/3544548.3580919

Kazemitabaar, M., Ye, R., Wang, X., Henley, A. Z., Denny, P., Craig, M., & Grossman, T. (2024). CodeAid: Evaluating a classroom deployment of an LLM-based programming assistant that balances student and educator needs. In Proceedings of the 2024 CHI Conference on Human Factors in Computing Systems (CHI '24, Article 650, 20 pages). ACM. DOI: 10.1145/3613904.3642773

Kasneci, E., Seßler, K., Küchemann, S., Bannert, M., Dementieva, D., Fischer, F., Gasser, U., Groh, G., Günnemann, S., Hüllermeier, E., Krusche, S., Kutyniok, G., Michaeli, T., Nerdel, C., Pfeffer, J., Poquet, O., Sailer, M., Schmidt, A., Seidel, T., & Kasneci, G. (2023). ChatGPT for good? On opportunities and challenges of large language models for education. *Learning and Individual Differences*, *103*, 102274. Advance online publication. DOI: 10.1016/j.lindif.2023.102274

Liang, J. T., Yang, C., & Myers, B. A. (2024). A large-scale survey on the usability of AI programming assistants: Successes and challenges. In *Proceedings of the 46th IEEE/ACM International Conference on Software Engineering* (pp. 616–628). ACM. DOI: 10.1145/3597503.3608128

Macnamara, B. N., Berber, I., Çavuşoğlu, M. C., Krupinski, E. A., Nallapareddy, N., Nelson, N. E., Smith, P. J., Wilson-Delfosse, A. L., & Ray, S. (2024). Does using artificial intelligence assistance accelerate skill decay and hinder skill development without performers' awareness? *Cognitive Research: Principles and Implications*, *9*(1), 46. Advance online publication. DOI: 10.1186/s41235-024-00572-8 PMID: 38992285

Margulieux, L. E., Prather, J., Reeves, B. N., Becker, B. A., Cetin Uzun, G., Loksa, D., Leinonen, J., & Denny, P. (2024). Self-regulation, self-efficacy, and fear of failure interactions with how novices use LLMs to solve programming problems. In *Proceedings of the 2024 Innovation and Technology in Computer Science Education* V. 1 (pp. 276–282). ACM. DOI: 10.1145/3649217.3653621

Moradi Dakhel, A., Majdinasab, V., Nikanjam, A., Khomh, F., Desmarais, M. C., & Jiang, Z. M. (2023). GitHub Copilot AI pair programmer: Asset or liability? *Journal of Systems and Software*, *203*, 111734. Advance online publication. DOI: 10.1016/j.jss.2023.111734

Nikolic, S., Daniel, S., Haque, R., Belkina, M., Hassan, G. M., Grundy, S., Lyden, S., Neal, P., & Sandison, C. (2023). ChatGPT versus engineering education assessment: A multidisciplinary and multi-institutional benchmarking and analysis of this generative artificial intelligence tool to investigate assessment integrity. *European Journal of Engineering Education*, *48*(4), 559–614. DOI: 10.1080/03043797.2023.2213169

Nguyen, S., Babe, H. M., Zi, Y., Guha, A., Anderson, C. J., & Feldman, M. Q. (2024). How beginning programmers and Code LLMs (mis)read each other. In Proceedings of the 2024 CHI Conference on Human Factors in Computing Systems (CHI '24, Article 650, 20 pages). ACM. DOI: 10.1145/3613904.3642706

O'Brien, G. (2025). Threats to scientific software from over-reliance on AI code assistants. *Nature Computational Science*, *5*(9), 701–703. DOI: 10.1038/s43588-025-00845-2 PMID: 40715786

Peng, S., Kalliamvakou, E., Cihon, P., & Demirer, M. (2023). The impact of AI on developer productivity: Evidence from GitHub Copilot. arXiv. https://doi.org//arXiv .2302.06590DOI: 10.48550

Perry, N., Srivastava, M., Kumar, D., & Boneh, D. (2023). Do users write more insecure code with AI assistants? In *Proceedings of the 2023 ACM SIGSAC Conference on Computer and Communications Security* (pp. 2785–2799). ACM. DOI: 10.1145/3576915.3623157

Prather, J., Denny, P., Leinonen, J., Becker, B. A., Albluwi, I., Craig, M., Keuning, H., Kiesler, N., Kohn, T., Luxton-Reilly, A., MacNeil, S., Petersen, A., Pettit, R., Reeves, B. N., & Savelka, J. (2023). The robots are here: Navigating the generative AI revolution in computing education. In *Proceedings of the 2023 Working Group Reports on Innovation and Technology in Computer Science Education* (pp. 108–159). ACM. DOI: 10.1145/3623762.3633499

Rinta-Kahila, T., Penttinen, E., Salovaara, A., Soliman, W., & Ruissalo, J. (2023). The vicious circles of skill erosion: A case study of cognitive automation. *Journal of the Association for Information Systems*, *24*(5), 1378–1412. DOI: 10.17705/1jais.00829

Sengul, G., Neykova, R., & Destefanis, G. (2024). Software engineering education in the era of conversational AI: Current trends and future directions. *Frontiers in Artificial Intelligence*, *7*, 1436350. Advance online publication. DOI: 10.3389/frai.2024.1436350 PMID: 39268193

Tang, N., Chen, M., Ning, Z., Bansal, A., Huang, Y., & McMillan, C. (2024). Developer behaviors in validating and repairing LLM-generated code using IDE and eye tracking. In *Proceedings of the IEEE Symposium on Visual Languages and Human-Centric Computing* (pp. 40–46). IEEE. DOI: 10.1109/VL/HCC60511.2024.00015

Tankelevitch, L., Kewenig, V., Simkute, A., Scott, A. E., Sarkar, A., Sellen, A., & Rintel, S. (2024). The metacognitive demands and opportunities of generative AI. In Proceedings of the 2024 CHI Conference on Human Factors in Computing Systems (Article 680). ACM. DOI: 10.1145/3613904.3642902

Vaithilingam, P., Zhang, T., & Glassman, E. L. (2022). Expectation vs. experience: Evaluating the usability of code generation tools powered by large language models. In *CHI Conference on Human Factors in Computing Systems Extended Abstracts* (pp. 1–7). ACM. DOI: 10.1145/3491101.3519665

Zhou, X., Liang, P., Zhang, B., Li, Z., Ahmad, A., Shahin, M., & Waseem, M. (2024). Exploring the problems, their causes and solutions of AI pair programming: A study on GitHub and Stack Overflow. *Journal of Systems and Software*, *219*, 112204. Advance online publication. DOI: 10.1016/j.jss.2024.112204

Ziegler, A., Kalliamvakou, E., Li, X. A., Rice, A., Rifkin, D., Simister, S., Sittampalam, G., & Aftandilian, E. (2024). Measuring GitHub Copilot's impact on productivity. *Communications of the ACM*, *67*(3), 54–63. DOI: 10.1145/3633453

KEY TERMS AND DEFINITIONS

AI Coding Assistant: Software tools that rely on large language models to produce, finish, or even suggest code, depending on natural language input or programming context. Some examples of AI Coding Assistants are GitHub Copilot, ChatGPT, Amazon CodeWhispier, and Tabnine.

Automation Complacency: The phenomenon of being overly reliant on automated systems and insufficiently monitoring their responses, which causes a decrease in alertness to errors and critical evaluation of the results provided by automated systems.

Competence-Confidence Misalignment: The disparity between one's skill level and one's perception of their skill level. AI systems can lead to increased confidence and a corresponding decline in competence, causing a dangerous overestimation of one's capabilities.

Developer Self-Efficacy: The extent to which an individual believes he/she is capable of successfully completing programming tasks and coping with programming challenges. Self-efficacy is an important factor that determines an individual's choice of task, effort invested, and how he/she reacts emotionally to programming challenges.

Human-AI Teaming: The manner in which humans and AI systems interact to produce a collaborative outcome that utilizes the best capabilities each partner can offer towards a common objective.

Metacognitive Awareness: The capacity to monitor and manage one's own mental processes, which includes recognizing knowledge deficits, assessing solution quality, choosing strategies, and adapting strategies according to feedback. It is an essential factor when utilizing AI tools effectively.

Skill Erosion: The gradual loss of skills because of insufficient opportunities to utilize them, cognitive offloading to automated systems, or an extended time without practicing certain skills. It is also called "deskilling" when used to describe organizational behavior.

Chapter 3
Deskilling and Reskilling: Mental Health Challenges for IT Professionals in AI-Integrated Workplaces

Akankshya Panda
http://orcid.org/0009-0007-9327-8958
KIIT School of Management, KIIT University, Bhubaneswar, India

Ipseeta Satpathy
http://orcid.org/0000-0002-0155-5548
KIIT School of Management, KIIT University, Bhubaneswar, India

B. C. M. Patnaik
KIIT School of Management, KIIT University, Bhubaneswar, India

Vishal Jain
http://orcid.org/0000-0003-1126-7424
School of Engineering and Technology, Vivekananda Institute of Professional Studies - Technical Campus, New Delhi, India

ABSTRACT

AI is constantly changing the IT industry by continuously transforming work related skills, creating new opportunities and introducing challenges like deskilling, reskilling and job insecurity. This study explores how this AI-driven changes along with deskilling and reskilliling of practical abilities affect employees' mental health focusing on stress, anxiety and fear of job loss. To provide implications for IT Industry this chapter draws on a review from literature and news articles including studies focused specifically on IT employees as well as reviews from other sectors. This

DOI: 10.4018/979-8-3373-8450-4.ch003

broader approach will help organisations to understand and support employees' well-being during AI-driven change. The findings emphasise that organisational support, structured reskilling and mental health programs play a crucial role in helping employees cope with AI-related stress. Overall, the study shows the importance of an employee-centered approach to AI adoption where employee well-being is prioritised alongside technological advancement to create sustainable and resilient AI-driven workplaces.

1. INTRODUCTION

The rapid development and adoption of AI in organisations has transformed the nature of work in the IT sector. These AI systems such as machine learning, robotic process automation, predictive analytics and intelligent decision-support systems have the promise to improve productivity and efficiency but simultaneously they redesign job roles by redefining skill requirements and increasing performance pressure among IT employees. In today's workplaces, getting a job or the idea of stable and long-term job roles is becoming very difficult. IT employees have to continuously update their skills to stay ahead of new technologies because the skills that were essential for one project quickly become outdated as systems change or are replaced, requiring employees to repeatedly learn and adapt. While this constant reskilling has made continuous learning a standard part of professional life, it has also created ongoing job insecurity because employees will be under constant pressure, leading to poor mental well-being.

The global tech industry is going through a difficult period, with constant layoffs creating a lot of uncertainty for IT employees around the world. By around 2025 more than 202,000 IT employees have lost their jobs. Almost 70% of the workforce deductions are based in the U.S. Companies (Economic Times, 2025). These layoffs are generally because of change in technology like automation and AI, as well as by businesses looking to reduce expenses. This demonstrates that learning new skills alone is not sufficient to maintain employment. Now, this circumstance causes employees to worry about losing their skills or becoming obsolete, which causes stress, anxiety, and burnout. As AI continues to change the way companies work the mental health burden of constantly having to learn new skills while worrying about layoffs is becoming an overlooked challenge of IT professionals today. Additionally, according to the New Indian Express, India's IT industry is undergoing rapid changes in 2025 as AI and automation are increasingly taking over routine tasks. Thousands of employees at companies like TCS, Infosys, Wipro, HCLTech and IBM have lost their jobs or need to acquire new skills just to save their positions. This trend is putting a lot of stress and anxiety on employees especially mid-level employees who mostly worry about their careers while considering their families as it is the bread and butter for most of the employees. While the industry still has opportunities in advanced engineering and software development it is clear that helping employees learn new skills and support their mental well-being is more important than ever.

Hidden layoffs and restructuring in the Indian IT sector are creating an environment of uncertainty for IT employees. As companies reduce manpower through hidden actions rather than public announcements many employees are left with fears of job security and about their roles. Even the job of the AI developers is not safe as some organisations lay off the employees who developed this AI (Times of India, 2025). The growing dependency on AI and automation leads to the disappearance of day-to-day tasks by pushing employees into a constant cycle of reskilling to stay relevant. The constant pressure of learning new skills along with limited transparency around workforce changes leads to emotional strain, anxiety and a sense of professional instability leading to poor mental well-being. Thus, in today's work environment navigating deskilling and reskilling is not just a technical challenge but a deeply personal experience that significantly affects the mental well-being of IT professionals (Times of India, 2025).

Recent data from Economic Times India, 2026 also shows that with a significant shift in India's IT sector in the first nine months of 2025 - 2026, the top five IT companies that are TCS, Infosys, Wipro, HCLTech and Tech Mahindra, altogether added just 17 new employees, highlighting a difference of nearly 18,000 hires in the same period the previous year. TCS had the largest reduction, laying off around 25,000 employees, while Infosys, Wipro, HCLTech and Tech Mahindra slightly increased their workforce (Economic Times India, 2026). The Nasscom-Indeed study (2025) shows that employees can remain relevant and contribute effectively through learning new skills as the future of work will be performed by humans and AI working together, not just people using AI occasionally or by AI only. Almost all HR leaders that are around 97% expect this shift by 2027. AI is no longer just a helpful tool. It is becoming a part of everyday jobs, workflows and decisions. In many organisations AI plays a growing role in the workplace. However, AI is not always accurate so human involvement is necessary (The Hindu, 2026). The study also highlights that the most effective human AI teamwork happens in higher-level management. Many routine and repetitive tasks such as writing standard code or running tests are increasingly being handled by AI by highlighting the importance of employees to engage in continuous reskilling to stay relevant and contribute effectively. Nowadays firms are focusing more on employees' skills, which are what they can do for the organisation instead of just their past experiences or educational background. Due to this reason many IT companies, even for technical roles have started hiring across both cross-disciplinary sectors. This situation creates a dual challenge for IT employees as they have to constantly learn new skills while handling stress arising from job insecurity. Employees need to have emotional resilience. Technical skills alone are not enough to adapt to the change of technology. There is a high risk of rise of stress, burnout and anxiety among the employees if the organisation does not provide sufficient support mainly during the time of deskilling and reskilling. Due to the constant AI adoption these challenges affect both low-skilled and highly skilled employees. Hence, deskilling and reskilling are both technical and personal issues that can deeply affect the mental well-being of these employees.

The chapter mainly addresses the psychological and organizational impact of AI integration in today's workplaces by highlighting techno-stress as a key factor through which digital transformation affects employee well-being. Organisations increasingly depend upon AI-driven analytics, automation tools and algorithmic management systems to enhance efficiency and competitiveness (Davenport & Ronanki, 2018). This chapter contributes well to that discussion where employee mental health is a key determinant of AI-enabled transformation. Research consistently shows that technological change reshapes job demands, alters skill requirements and transforms power relations within organisations (Autor, 2015).

1.1 Techno-Stress as a Multidimensional Psychological Response

Technostress was originally described as the stress or difficulty in adapting to new computer technologies (Brod, 1984). Today researchers consider it as a multidimensional stress that arises from the design of digital systems (Tarafdar et al., 2019). The five main sources of techno-stress are techno-overload, techno-invasion, techno-complexity, techno-insecurity and techno-uncertainty which are distinct but interrelated to each other through which technology creates strain. In a workplace where AI is heavily integrated these stressors become more intensified. Techno-overload occurs when AI tools speed up workflow expectations, requiring employees to handle large amounts of information at a greater speed. AI-generated analytics can sometimes increase decision-making pressure instead of reducing it especially when employees are constantly connected to work. Techno-invasion occurs when employees are constantly connected with digital systems. Tools such as remote dashboards, predictive alerts and AI-driven workplaces make it harder for employees to maintain a healthy balance between work and personal life. Constant connectivity has been associated with work-family conflict and emotional exhaustion (Ayyagari et al., 2011). Employees often face difficulties when a change of technologies demands skills for which they have received little or no training leaving them struggling to understand complex systems or interpret unfamiliar outputs on their own. Such situations can reduce self-confidence which is essential in managing mental resilience. Concerns about job insecurity and uncertainty are also common as employees may worry about their skills becoming outdated leading to fear of being replaced. Even the thought of a potential job threat, without any actual loss, can cause considerable stress and anxiety (Sverke et al., 2002). By understanding these challenges including stress, burnout and the pressures of technological change, this chapter highlights the importance of employee well-being while providing awareness of the demands faced in the modern and rapidly evolving work environment.

1.2 Skill Obsolescence and Reskilling Anxiety

Skill obsolescence and anxiety come with reskilling and are increasingly important in the modern workplace. Rapid developments in technology such as automation tools and AI-assisted platforms are leading to changes in the skills that employees need to stay relevant. The World Economic Forum (2023) estimates that nearly half of the workforce skills could shift within just a few years due to technological innovation. In IT sectors, professionals are expected to continuously enhance their knowledge of programming languages, data analytics capabilities and AI literacy to keep up with the changes.

The issue of Skill obsolescence is not just about technical change it also affects professional identity and self-confidence affecting how employees see their value and role within the organisation. When technological change makes previously valuable skills outdated, employees can feel a loss of identity and reduced confidence. This connects closely with research on techno-stress, which shows that learning pressure and cognitive overload are major sources of stress in these digital workplaces (Tarafdar et al., 2019).

Reskilling challenges are important psychological challenges that completely differ from job insecurity. Where Job insecurity is about fear of losing one's job and reskilling anxiety is the fear of falling behind, feeling incapable with new skill demands. Studies show that upskilling opportunities are often unevenly distributed which can increase stress mainly for mid-career employees (OECD, 2019).

1.3 Conceptual Definitions and Operationalisation of Deskilling, Reskilling and Mental Well-Being

Traditionally, deskilling refers to the reduction of task complexity and the loss of previously valued skills due to technological standardisation and automation (Braverman, 1998). In today's AI-integrated workplaces, deskilling occurs when AI systems take over cognitive and decision-making responsibilities that were once performed by employees thereby reducing autonomy, skill utilisation and task variety (Peiró, 2025; Ferdman, 2025). It is important to distinguish deskilling from skill obsolescence. While deskilling refers to the direct reduction or removal from job tasks from an employee's role while skill obsolescence is gradual reduction of the value or requirement of existing skills due to technological change (Battisti, Del Gatto & Parmeter, 2022). In other words, obsolescence does not mean tasks are simplified, instead it reflects a growing mismatch between what employees know and what their jobs now require.

In contrast to deskilling, reskilling means learning entirely new skills to perform for different or transformed job roles while upskilling involves enhancing existing skills to meet changing job demands (McKinsey & Company, 2021). In AI-Driven workplaces reskilling often means developing data literacy, learning to manage AI-based tools and building more advanced analytical, or collaborative capabilities (Bughin, 2024). These new expectations can open opportunities for growth and career development. However, when reskilling becomes continuous without organizational support then it can become a source of stress - contributing to technostress and emotional exhaustion (Morandini et al., 2023).

Mental well-being at any organisation is understood more than simple mental illness that involves positive functioning, resilience and meaningful engagement (Keyes, 2002). In an AI-integrated workplace, it is formed by creating balance between job demands, perceived control and the support provided by the organisation (Demerouti & Bakker, 2022). When this balance is disrupted then it gives rise to burnout, anxiety, emotional exhaustion and lower job satisfaction particularly in a high-pressure technological environment (Maslach & Jackson, 1981). To study these effects researchers depends on validated tools like the Maslach Burnout Inventory (Maslach & Jackson, 1981), job insecurity scales (De Witte, 2005) and techno-stress measures (Tarafdar et al., 2019). Making clear distinctions between these concepts will helps to ensure both empirical accuracy and theoretical clarity.

2. THEORETICAL BACKGROUND:

This study draws ideas from two major existing theories to understand the impact of deskilling and reskilling on IT employees' mental health:1) The Job Demands-Resources theory shows how high job demands such as continuous learning and adapting to new technologies with limited organizational support can lead to stress, anxiety and burnout. Job demands including high work pressure, drain employees' physical and psychological energy leading to increasing risk of poor mental well-being. In contrast, job resources such as independence and social support enable employees to manage these demands and foster personal growth and development (Evangelia Demerouti and Arnold B. Bakker, 2022). According to the JD-R theory, the support from individuals, leaders, organisations and families can reduce stress and enhance performance (Evangelia Demerouti and Arnold B. Bakker, 2022). Maintaining health and motivation during critical periods requires managing demands through job redesign, mental health initiatives and preventive interventions (Evangelia Demerouti and Arnold B. Bakker, 2022). The organisations need to increase skill adaptability and provide sufficient resources/support to reduce burnout particularly during technological changes (Galanakis & Tsitouri, 2022). When employees lack sufficient support or resources then sustained job demands significantly increase burnout, exhaustion and disengagement. Individuals with chronic burnout have diminished capacity to cope with ongoing work pressures, often responding with avoidance, withdrawal and self-undermining behaviors (Bakker et al., 2022). Burnout contributes to resource loss, where reduced energy and motivation heighten vulnerability to future stressors. (Bakker et al., 2022). The perceived technology uncertainty increases technostress, job insecurity and negative outcomes like exhaustion and lower job satisfaction confirming that employees' reactions are not only influenced by implemented technologies but also by predicted changes in the work environment (Liu et al., 2024). In order to build positive ongoing beneficial effects that lower stress and increase engagement, organisations should carefully assess and adjust roles to align technological demands with employee skill development (Liu et al., 2024). Artificial intelligence (AI) presents both opportunities and challenges while offering potential for high quality development while also introducing psychological anxiety, increased workload and role conflicts (Hu et al., 2025). Technology acceptance enabled employees to manage AI anxiety caused by perceived risk in a better way while perceived risks indirectly promoted improvements in human-system compatibility via technology acceptance (Hu et al., 2025).

2) The Skill-Biased Technological Change theory states that AI and automation change job roles & responsibilities by reducing routine work and increasing demand for new skills & also by making reskilling crucial for professional growth. The increasing wage inequality between workers is putting a negative impact on working hours, productivity and wages with stronger effects at higher inequality levels. SBTC increases productivity and wages related problems but reduces working hours by raising inequality while technological upgrades affect all the workers similarly, regardless of their skill level that is increasing working hours in the long run (Christian Hutter & Enzo Weber, 2023). The technical expertise of soft skills such as creativity, critical thinking and problem-solving has become increasingly important. The change in technology highlights the need for continuous learning and manpower training to adapt to this rapid change (Marek Jabłoński, 2025). An analysis done with 38 countries and 30 sectors from the period of 1995 to 2005 shows clear evidence of skill-biased technological change. The productivity of skilled workers increased by approximately 11.5% relative to unskilled workers with this growth largely driven by skill-based technological advancements. AI is changing the types of skills that are in demand at work earlier (Michele Battisti et al., 2022).

Firms that adopt AI early and use it to support rather than replace employees tend to see growth in jobs especially in service sectors. At the same time, basic skills are becoming less relevant by making upskilling more important (Michele Battisti et al., 2022). Across industries advanced technical skills like data and machine learning, along with social and interpersonal skills are increasingly valuable as AI reshapes how work gets done (Jacques Bughin, 2024). Also, using multiple AI tools on integrated platforms can further enhance efficiency, collaboration and the ability of high-skilled employees to focus on higher-value activities while low-skilled workers primarily benefit in routine tasks (Qiang Wu et al., 2025).

Gaps in JD–R and SBTC: Although the Job Demands Resources framework and Skill-Biased Technological Change theory offer important perspectives on technological transformation both are limited when applied separately to AI-driven restructuring. SBTC explains systematic changes in skill appraisal and labor market inequality but pay limited attention to psychological and identity-based consequences. Whereas JD–R highlights individual strain and engagement processes but does not sufficiently explain about the structural and technological factors such as AI that reshape job demands. Therefore, the theoretical gap lies in the absence of a multi-level explanation connecting macro-level skill revaluation to micro-level mental strain. SBTC explains the reason for skills revaluation but not how that revaluation affects employee well-being. JD-R highlights the emergence of strain but not why AI adoption systematically modifies demand structures. Integrating these two frameworks allows for a more detailed understanding of the connection between AI-driven organizational change and restructuring with mental health challenges.

Implications: Together, these above theories can provide an understanding on technical, psychological and organizational challenges faced by employees in AI-integrated workplaces. JD-R and SBTC frameworks show that they both impose technical and psychological demands on employees. When constant learning requirements are combined with job insecurity from layoffs or hidden workforce restructuring, it creates stress, anxiety and burnout even for highly skilled employees. Organisations that provide structured programs, mental health support and clear communication can reduce these negative effects by helping employees remain productive and resilient in AI-driven environments.

3. OBJECTIVES OF THE STUDY:

From the above gaps, it is essential to build a new theory that can provide an understanding on technical, psychological and organizational challenges faced by employees in AI-integrated workplaces. To identify implications for IT employees, the chapter proposes a new model that is AI-Driven Deskilling-Reskilling Strain and Adaptation with the following objectives:

1. To synthesise existing research on common mental health challenges faced by employees due to deskilling and reskilling demands.
2. To analyse the effect of fear of job loss due to AI and technological changes on the mental well-being.
3. To provide an understanding to organisations on how their support helps employees to cope with challenges arises due to AI-driven technology.

Methodological Approach: This chapter adopts a narrative literature review approach to study interdisciplinary research on AI, technological change and employee mental health outcomes. Peer-reviewed journal articles, recent news articles and theoretical contributions were identified through searches in major academic databases including Times of India, The Economic Times, The Hindu, Scopus, Web of Science and Google Scholar. The review of a total of 62 papers or articles was primarily focused on literature published between 2000 and 2025, while major studies are published after 2020 reflecting the contemporary evolution of AI in organizational contexts.

This chapter organises findings around three major factors arising from the literature: reskilling overload, fear of deskilling and job insecurity. This mechanism-based synthesis allows for the integration across economic, organizational and psychological domains by facilitating the development of the AI-Driven Deskilling-Reskilling Strain and Adaptation (AI-DRSA) model.

3.1 Deskilling and Its Impact on Employees' Mental Well-Being

Deskilling has been considered as a major threat in the current workplace scenario due to rapid technological change, particularly with the rise of AI; employees may struggle to keep up with evolving systems which leads to insecurity and negative psychological outcomes. However, when AI acts as a replacement it raises concerns about deskilling, loss of accountability, reduced human interaction and diminished innovation (Jasmine Almer, 2022). These concerns highlight fears that AI could erode human skills and weaken the meaningful role of employees in their work (Jasmine Almer, 2022; Avigail Ferdman, 2025). In the era of automation and AI, deskilling threatens human capacity development as systems replace humans rather than support their activity and reduce opportunities for skill use, learning and meaningful engagement by gradually eroding abilities (Avigail Ferdman, 2025). From a developmental perspective, it is morally essential to design work environments that encourage human engagement and skill cultivation while ensuring technological change strengthens rather than diminishes human capacities (Avigail Ferdman, 2025). In education and workplace, AI automation carries the risk of deskilling students and professionals who completely rely on these tools rather than developing their own critical abilities so making guidance on ethical use, data privacy and responsible tool application of AI is essential to encourage active engagement, critical thinking and problem-solving (Hanh Le, 2026). In the same way that AI automation in education can deskill students who rely excessively on tools, similarly IT employees risk deskilling when AI takes over routine tasks. Providing employees with organizational support through training on critical thinking, problem-solving and responsible AI use can help them maintain and develop their skills, reduce stress and adapt more effectively in AI-driven workplaces.

Collaboration with technologies or AI can sometimes lead to deskilling in practical, cognitive and emotional areas especially when managerial priorities focus more on productivity and control over employee perspectives. Including a diverse range of employee views on AI implementation can reduce bias and help to preserve valued skills (Firuza Huseynova, 2024). While AI can increase human capabilities, drive innovation, create new career opportunities and improve decision-making and productivity it also carries potential risks such as deskilling, job displacement, reduced autonomy and privacy concerns. Tasks that are routine, repetitive, or heavily decision-based are most susceptible to automation, whereas roles that rely on creativity, emotional intelligence, complex problem-solving, and human interaction are far less likely to be replaced (Akhmad Farhan, 2023). AI is constantly transforming the knowledge economy as shown by many industries. Routine day-to-day tasks are increasingly being automated, shifting job demands and creating advantages for highly skilled employees while exposing others to the risks of skill erosion and job displacement. The combination of technical skills with strong interpersonal & leadership skills makes continuous learning effective. Early measures such as specialised courses, professional development programs and employee support policies can help mitigate these negative effects while soft skills like critical thinking, empathy, communication and collaboration are becoming ever more important. (Brent Orrell, 2025). AI should be considered as a partner rather than a replacement for the skills that are uniquely human. Proper planning and employee-centered policies are important to make sure that new tools create opportunities while safeguarding human expertise and well-being (Orrell, 2025). Hence, deskilling remains a growing challenge in digitally transformed work as automation and standardised technologies reduce task variety and autonomy by eroding previously held skills over time. Over time, this erosion of previously acquired abilities has been linked to lower job satisfaction, decreased proficiency and diminished career prospects, particularly when work becomes overly repetitive. (José M Peiró, 2025).

3.2 Psychological Implications of Continuous Reskilling Demands

Upskilling and reskilling allow individuals to develop new abilities or enhance existing ones to meet the evolving demands of their roles (McKinsey & Company, 2021). In today's rapidly changing workforce with continuous technological developments, reskilling has become more than just acquiring new skills, that is it acts as a trigger for psychological and societal transformation (Chaker and Damak, 2024). However, the constant need to learn and adapt in AI-driven workplaces can be stressful and challenging. While acquiring new skills is essential for staying relevant, it can also trigger anxiety, fatigue and uncertainty if employees are not adequately supported (Morandini et al., 2023). As technology, automation and new work practices redesign jobs, workplace mental health has become an urgent concern (Anya Johnson; et al., 2020). Digital tools can provide flexibility and opportunities but may also increase work pressure, disrupt work-life balance and lead to stress, isolation and burnout by highlighting the importance of prioritising mental health and nurturing balanced & meaningful work environments (Anya Johnson et al., 2020). This technological change can both displace and enhance employees' skills. While only a small part of employees face skills displacement because of these technological shifts, those affected often gain access to more training, task variety and complex skill development, particularly in higher-skilled roles. Yet, despite these benefits employees frequently experience high job insecurity and uncertainty about the future (Seamus McGuinness et al., 2023). Many also encounter barriers such as mental health challenges, fear, low confidence, time constraints and limited technological literacy which prevent them from fully engaging in learning programs and simultaneously contributing to stress, anxiety and insecurity (Rosalind Marie Evans, 2022). Thus, reskilling is increasingly necessary to keep pace with digital and organizational change but it often imposes significant demands on employees particularly when new learning occurs alongside existing job responsibilities (José M Peiró, 2025). Programs that focus solely on technological needs and place responsibility primarily on individuals are less effective and can undermine well-being (José M Peiró, 2025). Consequently, while AI improves efficiency, it can also generate technostress, skill insecurity and job polarisation. Digital skill gaps and cognitive overload further exacerbate anxiety and burnout, especially in rapidly changing workplaces (Bhanu Ranjan et al., 2026).

3.3 Fear of Job Loss and Job Insecurity Due to AI and Technological Change

Although AI tools are increasingly common in the IT Sector yet greater exposure to AI does not necessarily reduce fear of job loss. In fact, higher exposure is moderately associated with increased anxiety about job security while a better understanding of AI's impact is linked to greater readiness to adapt to workplace changes (Hobot, 2024). Technological development, job stress and job insecurity greatly contribute to organizational cynicism among recently separated employees whereas higher job involvement appears to act as a shield against such negative attitudes suggesting that engagement in meaningful work can protect employees from feelings of distrust or doubt towards their organisation. Employees' perceptions of technology, job security and their roles strongly shape how they view and respond to their organisations (Kanika Sharma et al., 2025). In Kenya, banks are heavily using AI for tasks such as cybersecurity, fraud detection and understanding customer needs and about 83% of employees reported anxiety about job loss due to task integration and reduced staffing. However, many employees also recognise that learning new skills and adapting to AI can help them remain relevant and protect their job (Angela E. Nwaomah, 2025). So, just as employees in Kenyan banks report anxiety over job loss due to AI-driven task integration in the same way IT employees face similar challenges when automation and AI reduce routine work. Trust in AI is influenced by factors such as confidence in institutions, openness to change and general attitudes toward technology. Notably, greater fear of job loss reduces trust in AI while confidence in one's ability to adapt increases trust (Asvestopoulou, Evdokia, 2024). AI and automation are already replacing certain jobs while improving others with technologies such as chatbots and medical imaging analysis and evidence suggests that AI will also create new roles, especially those requiring specialised skills (Gabriel Kenechukwu Ojiyi et al., 2023). These developments link technological change to human impacts and provide a clear image for exploring strategies to maintain employee well-being. By highlighting that AI can both replace certain roles and create new opportunities requiring specialised skills, it directly connects workplace change to the pressures of deskilling and the need for continuous reskilling. These pressures then contribute to stress, anxiety, burnout and fear of job loss making the investigation of mental health challenges in IT employees highly relevant. The introduction of AI often triggers employee anxiety about being replaced, increasing job insecurity and intentions to leave which can further heighten feelings of uncertainty regarding one's future in the organisation (Cheng, 2024).

Over time, employees have experienced fewer hours along with rising employment and earnings reflecting a shift from declining sectors to growing ones particularly from manual and manufacturing roles to more skilled service positions (Dr. A. Shaji George, 2024). . With adequate training, education and governmental support employees can transition into these new opportunities rather than face prolonged unemployment (Dr. A. Shaji George, 2024). Overall, these findings indicate that AI has the potential to foster more meaningful, higher-value work, provided that individuals and organisations receive the necessary support to adapt their skills effectively (Dr. A. Shaji George, 2024). So, AI adoption can increase anxiety and fear of job loss, particularly among routine workers, it also creates opportunities for skill development and higher-value work. Adequate organizational support, training and employee adaptability are key to mitigating job insecurity and enhancing trust, engagement and mental well-being.

3.4 Impact of AI-Related Job Insecurity on the Mental Well-Being of IT Employees

Mental health plays an important role in controlling the negative effects of technological disruption by offering practical guidance for organisations to design strategies that support employees' mental needs (Sheela Narang Wadhwa et al., 2025). AI adoption has been shown to increase job insecurity, particularly among routine and low-skilled workers leading to stress, anxiety and lower job satisfaction. Psychological resilience can buffer these effects by helping employees manage uncertainty and adapt to changing job roles (Putri & Werdini, 2025). In Ghanaian hospitals adopting AI studies reveal that employees with higher AI awareness are more likely to engage in informal learning at work such as sharing knowledge or experimenting with new tools. This informal learning in turn creates a better well-being among these employees. Furthermore, informal learning influences the relationship between AI awareness and well-being with employees who have a strong learning mindset benefiting even more as it strengthens the connection between AI awareness and informal learning (Francisca Arboh et al., 2025). For IT employees facing deskilling and reskilling pressures in AI-integrated workplaces, developing a strong learning orientation and proactively acquiring new skills may help reduce stress, anxiety and fear of job loss. The findings provide evidence that encouraging continuous learning and skill development can serve as a protective factor for mental health, which directly aligns with the focus on supporting employee well-being during technological change.

AI-based HRM systems also give rise to four key shadow experiences: erosion of interpersonal autonomy, surveillance-induced precarity, algorithmic bias dilemmas and personalised discontent. These experiences negatively impact employee well-being across psychological, physical and social dimensions manifesting as psychological isolation, physical overload and social left out (Jianwen Zheng et al., 2025). Additionally, longitudinal studies show that increased exposure to AI since 2015 is associated with lower life and job satisfaction with creating greater concerns about job security and personal economic conditions though it does not appear to significantly affect mental health outcomes such as anxiety or depression (Giuntella Osea et al., 2023). Employees' AI awareness has also been linked to higher emotional exhaustion. This relationship is influenced by increased job insecurity and increased work interference with family responsibilities both of which independently and sequentially contribute to emotional strain. These findings highlight job insecurity and work–family conflict as key mechanisms through which AI awareness translates into employee emotional exhaustion (Jiansong Zheng and Tao Zhang, 2025). Overall, the literature indicates that fear of job loss arising from AI and technological change is a significant factor affecting employees' psychological, social and emotional well-being.

3.5 Organizational Support in Managing AI-Driven Technology-Related Stress

The COVID-19 pandemic quickened the adoption of AI across various sectors but mainly in the IT sector the organisation was forced to rethink job design, skill development and change acceptance to remain stable and sustainable. As AI rebuilds work structures, employees' satisfaction and commitment increasingly depend on the organisations, that is whether they provide the right knowledge, skills and adequate support to help them adapt to change (Menon and Suresh, 2020). In addition to promoting positive attitudes about the adoption of AI, clear direction, appropriate training and ongoing assistance can reduce the stress related to deskilling and reskilling (Morandini et al., 2023). Training employees with critical thinking, problem-solving and teamwork skills not only prepares them for technological change but also protects their mental well-being by allowing reskilling to be seen as an opportunity for career development rather than a source of stress. As AI and automation continue to transform work, reskilling and upskilling have become essential for keeping the workforce relevant. Organisations that take a human - centered approach prioritising psychological safety, inclusivity and mental health enable employees to adapt confidently by building a resilient and capable workforce (Hajam & John, 2024). So, effective reskilling training can improve both employment opportunities and mental health. These initiatives helped to reduce depression among injured employees by showing that learning can support them during difficult times (Humlum & Plato, 2025). Strategically, Chief Human Resources Officers are inspired to view skill development as a long-term investment rather than a short-term training effort as it helps organisations to ensure sustained competitive advantage in constantly changing business environments (Asiedu & Tenakwah, 2025). Structured and flexible reskilling initiatives such as short courses and adaptable learning can increase employee confidence and skills while addressing the challenges of AI. DEI considerations that include diversity, equity and inclusion consider age, gender and disability; promote psychological safety by reducing feelings of exclusion and strengthening employees' endurance. Thus, structured reskilling strategies can reduce skill gaps by supporting employees' mental well-being and helping them to adapt more effectively in AI-driven workplaces (Gruenewald & Mueller, 2025). Moreover, combining job redesign with reskilling programs improves organizational agility even during sudden disruptions like the COVID-19 pandemic. Integrating HR practices such as job design and employee skilling positively influences both employee behaviour and long-term organizational outcomes (Amani Fathi Jamal et al., 2025). Universities also play an important role in upskilling and reskilling but approaches vary considering the need for stronger collaboration with local partners to address regional workforce and economic needs (Abigail Taylor et al., 2021). Therefore, upskilling and reskilling are essential for organisations seeking adaptability in rapidly evolving technological and market environments. A supportive organizational culture, strong leadership and alignment between training initiatives and business objectives significantly enhance the effectiveness of these programs (Mahedi Hasan et al., 2024). Learning is further supported with social interaction, teamwork and enterprise social networks emerging as effective mechanisms for skill development. Personal factors such as trust, confidence, inclusion and job satisfaction also play a key role in the success of learning initiatives (Ramona Diana Leon, 2023). Transparency, clear communication and organizational support for reskilling help reduce employee fears and build trust in AI systems (Asvestopoulou, Evdokia, 2024). Promoting mental health and resilience enables employees to manage AI adoption effectively while maintaining productivity and engagement (Sheela Narang Wadhwa et al., 2025). Finally, fostering agility, personal growth, streamlined efficiency and resource empowerment helps employees to handle overall well-being challenges related to AI guiding them toward self-reflection, inner strength and resourcefulness (Jianwen Zheng et al., 2025).

3.6 Leadership Support and Change Management in AI Integration

Leadership plays an important role in forming employee responses towards AI-driven transformation. Organizational support is important but leadership behaviour directly impacts on perceptions of fairness, trust and psychological safety during these technological changes (Rhoades & Eisenberger, 2002). Transformational leadership includes clear vision communication, encouragement of innovative thinking and individual consideration has been related with lower employee anxiety and greater adaptability during change processes (Bakker et al., 2022). An AI integrated workplace often introduces uncertainty, role ambiguity and fears of job displacement. To reduce resistance and cynicism through structured transition planning, effective change management programs play a crucial role in clear communication and inclusive decision making (Sharma et al., 2025). In AI contexts ethical leadership is very critical where concerns about algorithmic bias, surveillance and autonomy arises (Zheng et al., 2025). Also, open discussion by leaders on AI implementation strategies by clarifying long term careers and investing in developmental opportunities can decrease job insecurity by increasing trust on AI tools (Asvestopoulou, 2024). Furthermore, leadership also influences whether employees perceive AI as a threat or as a collaborative tool. When leaders show AI adoption is to improve human abilities rather than replacing them then employees are more likely to engage in proactive learning behaviours and actively moderate psychological impact (Hu et al., 2025). Thus, leadership support acts as a critical mitigating factor in the relationship between AI adoption and employee mental well-being.

3.7 Methodological Gaps in Current AI and Mental Health Research

Although research on AI and employee well-being is constantly growing there are several methodological limitations still remaining. Most of the existing literature relies heavily on cross-sectional survey designs which give very little information regarding the relationship between AI exposure and mental health outcomes by making it difficult to establish (Giuntella, König & Stella, 2023). Longitudinal studies are needed to understand how psychological effects change over time as employees adapt to technological change. Second, many studies primarily depend on self-reported measures of job insecurity, technostress and emotional exhaustion by raising concerns about common method bias (Morandini et al., 2023). Incorporating multiple data sources such as organizational records, behavioural metrics and physiological indicators would offer a more comprehensive and reliable picture of how AI integration affects employees.

In addition, research has been largely concentrated in Western economies, with limited empirical focus on recent markets such as India despite significant technological restructuring in these settings (Peiró, 2025). Differences in cultural values, institutional arrangements and labour market conditions may influence how AI-driven change affects employees' well-being. Finally, in many studies the literature often isolates either technological variables or psychological outcomes without integrating multi-level frameworks that include organizational culture, leadership practices and macroeconomic conditions (Demerouti & Bakker, 2022). To understand the complex nature of AI integration future researchers would benefit from interdisciplinary models that combine organizational behaviour, labour economics and digital sociology.

3.8 Policy Implications for Workforce Transition in the AI Era

In this modern era the reason behind the constant change of workplace is AI. It not only affects one sector instead it affects almost all the industries. Because of this evolving situation the government's intervention becomes crucial. Thus, to help employees to adapt to these changes the government is investing more in reskilling programs, supporting digital skills and making sure employees have strong social support if they lose their jobs (George, 2024). To ensure equitable access to learning opportunities the public and private sector should work together. These sectors together then can support a large number of training programs that are aligned with

If some employee does not have the right skills then AI can create a significant gap in between high paid and low paid employees. The increase of this inequality unfairly affects certain workforce functions arising due to AI adoption which is explained with the help of Skill-Biased Technological Change Theory (Hutter & Weber, 2023). Generally mid-career and endangered employees feel left behind. These feelings of employees can be reduced if policies are made with appropriate strategies. Apart from this, National AI strategies should consider both the mental health of employees and economic growth. Effective labour regulations by companies are important for the use of algorithmic transparency, employee data protection and workplace surveillance (Zheng et al., 2025). Fear of losing a job and lower stress associated with constant technological change can be reduced if enough support from organisations such as unemployment support and transition assistance programs are given (George, 2024). Therefore, when human development is included in AI Policies technology can improve employees lives instead of damaging their mental well-being.

4. DEVELOPMENT OF AI-DRSA MODEL

Bridging Gap between SBTC and JD–R: To fill the gap comes from the Job Demands Resources theory and Skill-Biased Technological Change theory this chapter builds a new conceptual framework to explain the impact of AI-related technological change on the mental well-being of employees to provide implications for IT sector that AI adoption must be done in a structured way that is without hampering the well-being of employees. The process of restructuring of job roles and automation of daily tasks are increased because of AI adoption. The primary work-related stressors like fear of deskilling, skill obsolescence, continuous reskilling demands and job insecurity are generated from continuous technological changes. JD-R Theory explains that these changes can raise the demand of jobs requiring the need of sustained psychological effort. Thus, technostress, reskilling anxiety, work-family conflict and emotional exhaustion are activated because of job demands. As the time passes by these stressors will lead to burnout, reduced job satisfaction, dissatisfaction and increased turnover intention ultimately affecting the overall well-being of employees. However, organizational and individual measures serve as critical factors of reducing the effects. Transformational leadership, structured reskilling programs, transparent communication, psychological safety and individual resilience can reduce the negative psychological effects of AI-driven change. In the presence of JD-R theory adequate resources reduce strain and foster engagement even under high technological demands.

The AI-DRSA model fills the gap arises from the above two theories that is introduced to explain:

1. AI adoption gives rise to organisation level skill revaluation.
2. Organisations respond through restructuring and performance reevaluation
3. Job demand is intensified by structural technological change which include learning pressure and performance growth.
4. When organizational resources like autonomy and support do not increase it ultimately leads to poor mental well-being.

Thus, SBTC identifies why skills are revalued while JD-R explains how that revaluation converts into employee strain.

Considering all the above details this chapter proposes the AI-Driven Deskilling-Reskilling Strain and Adaptation (AI-DRSA) Model to explain how AI-driven technological transformation influences employees' mental well-being. The model conceptualises deskilling and continuous reskilling demands as central job stressors emerging from AI integration which activate psychological strain while being moderated by organizational and individual resources.

AI-DRSA Model: The AI-Driven Deskilling-Reskilling Strain and Adaptation (AI-DRSA) model has five constructs to ensure precision. First, AI adoption explains the way organisations change and redesign their work functions when AI tools are integrated into workflows, decision-making and performance management systems. This includes automating tasks, monitoring performance, reducing roles, redefining skills and reallocating staff. Importantly, AI-driven transformation involves a broader idea on reshaping of work structures and expectations.

Second, deskilling is understood as a complex construct. At the task level, it happens when routine parts of work are automated. At the role level, deskilling occurs when responsibilities are redesigned while reducing professional authority.

One's professional value or uniqueness is weakening even if actual skills remain unharmed at the identity level. Due to this weakening employees may keep their jobs but feel less irreplaceable.

Third, job insecurity is another construct where employees believe that their skills or role could be easily replaced by AI tools or more technologically advanced employees. This insecurity acts as a psychological connection between organizational restructuring and stress that affects anxiety, engagement and commitment. Job insecurity can give rise to unnecessary stress even when no one is actually displaced unlike actual layoffs.

Fourth, reskilling anxiety refers to the ongoing pressure that employees feel to constantly update their skills in response to technological change mainly when they lack time, institutional support or psychological resources. This is different from reskilling opportunities which are structured, supported learning programs with dedicated time and organizational investment. The strain comes not from learning itself but from having to meet demands that exceed available resources.

Finally, all this gives rise to poor mental well-being resulting from an imbalance between ongoing demands and available resources which leads to stress, anxiety, burnout and reduced engagement. Mental well-being in relation to burnout explains the earlier stages of stress which can eventually cause more serious outcomes. Within the AI-DRSA model mental well-being is the collective effect of increased demands comes with insufficient organizational support.

AI Adoption → Deskilling / Reskilling / Job Insecurity → Reskilling Anxiety → Poor Mental Well-Being

Boundary Conditions: The introduced model does not speculate that AI adoption automatically leads to negative outcomes. The psychological consequences of AI adoption depend upon multiple variables that are Individual and Organizational level variables. Individual-level facilitators include age, skill accuracy and period of time employees spend in the specific organisation. Employees with highly advanced technical skills may experience AI as an opportunity rather than a threat. In contrast to this employees with proficient and automated skills may have higher susceptibility towards the change. While AI adaptability, leadership transparency, structured reskilling programs and preservation of autonomy are organisation-level facilitators. The restructuring of the organisation can reduce uncertainty while protecting training duration and reducing mental overload through transparent communication. Other factors like national resilience of the labour market, government rules and regulations also influence outcomes. Thus, understanding these boundary conditions helps to prevent certain assumptions and highlights the importance of careful governance planning.

Contradictory Evidence: Although this chapter explains that mental health issues arise from deskilling and reskilling, another piece of evidence suggests that AI can improve engagement and productivity under supportive work conditions. AI tools may reduce repetitive workload, increase decision-making accuracy and create new high-skill roles.

Some studies also highlight that structured reskilling programs can increase employee confidence and career adaptability. Additionally, algorithm tools can standardise performance metrics while potentially reducing role ambiguity. The findings suggest that AI adoption is not inherently strain-inducing; rather it appears when demand growth is not accompanied by resource coordination. Therefore, the AI-DRSA model explains psychological consequences as governance-dependent rather than technologically inevitable.

5. CONTRIBUTIONS:

Although the chapter mainly considers psychological and structural implications of AI-driven transformation in IT workplaces, its wider academic value comes from how it brings several ideas together. Some of these contributions are not always directly stated but are built within the way the chapter is organised and developed. One key strength of the chapter is the integration of technological change with employee mental well-being. Instead of treating AI as only an economic and technical issue the chapter also places AI adoption within organizational and human experiences. It shows how technology affects people, not just systems or profits. This allows the chapter to reduce gaps between technology studies, organizational behaviour, labour economics and occupational psychology.

AI is not only about innovation but also about its consequences for workers and organisations which helps to provide a balanced understanding of digital transformation. A major strength of the chapter is the integration of two important theoretical perspectives which are JD-R theory and SBTC theory. This combined approach supports the analysis as it explains how a large number of technological changes within the economy can directly impact individual experiences at work including stress, motivation and mental health. Thus, the chapter explains not only what is changing in the workplace but also how and why these changes influence employees on a personal level. Its understanding of deskilling and reskilling shows ongoing discussion about automation, job displacement and the growing need for technical skill development. In this way, the manuscript contributes meaningfully to a rapidly evolving academic discussion while remaining closely aligned with current real-world developments.

Finally, the chapter develops a clear conceptual framework that integrates JD–R and SBTC theories to explain how AI adoption, deskilling and reskilling shape employees' mental health. This framework provides a strong foundation for future research particularly within technology-driven industries.

6. IMPLICATIONS

The result of constant technological change is continuous deskilling and reskilling, which affects employees' performance and consequently leads to poor mental well-being and the organisation's growth. When AI is implemented properly then it has the potential to increase productivity, innovation and operational efficiency and if not then it can increase stress, job insecurity and burnout. Organisations that focus more in structured reskilling programs by providing mental health support and communicating openly to employees can help them remain motivated, resilient and engaged. This in turn improves long-term organizational performance with reduced employee turnover.

When all the literature is combined then it becomes clear that mental health challenges are not just individual issues. These are influenced by Organizational culture, practices and the constant change of technology. Managing these changes has become both a personal and professional challenge. Employees constantly have to adapt to new technologies while simultaneously coping with stress and managing job insecurity. Employees feel isolated when they feel their organisations are not supportive or transparent. This shows that addressing technology adoption is just as important as supporting employees' mental and emotional well-being during this phase.

7. LIMITATIONS AND FUTURE RESEARCH DIRECTIONS

This chapter adopts a conceptual approach that requires empirical verification. By using a longitudinal plan the future researchers can verify the AI-DRSA model to illustrate evolving psychological reactions to the change of technology. There is a need for sectoral differentiation as the pattern of AI adoption differs across industries. Moreover, future studies should explore interaction effects among different factors, mainly the combined influence of leadership transparency and skill specificity. Quantitative testing using structural equation modelling or multilevel analysis could strengthen the model. Finally, qualitative research may illuminate identity-based deskilling processes that remain underexplored in existing literature.

8. CONCLUSION

The growing adoption of AI has driven organisations to implement it in all sectors, but major layoffs due to technological change are occurring in the IT sector by creating both multiple opportunities and complex challenges which is why the study focuses on the IT sector. These implementations of AI can help employees to work efficiently by reducing repetitive or unnecessary tasks and creating career opportunities. However, these opportunities also come with mental stress, uncertainty and anxiety especially for employees who have to reskill constantly while simultaneously worrying about deskilling. If both the technical and emotional nature of work are considered then these problems can be solved by applying an employee-centred approach. This study emphasises mental health challenges arising from deskilling and reskilling not only in the IT sector but also across other sectors. By studying multiple sectors the findings provide insights and implications for both the IT Industry and its employees.

One of the major concerns of the IT Sector is deskilling and reskilling where layoffs are more frequent compared to other industries. Thus, understanding these issues can help employees adjust better to uncertainty and help organisations to design strategies that promote an adaptable workplace rather than a technologically dominated workplace.

This chapter introduced a new framework, the AI-Driven Deskilling-Reskilling Strain and Adaptation model to explain the impact of AI adoption in generating psychological strain through an interconnected process of reskilling overload, fear of deskilling and job insecurity. By integrating Skill-Biased Technological Change theory with the Job Demands-Resources theory the model covers the gap between macro-level labour market dynamics and micro-level employee experiences. In doing so, it highlights how structural skill revaluation gives rise to job demands and how insufficient resource collaboration can produce anxiety, emotional exhaustion and disengagement.

However, the model also highlights that AI-driven strain is not technologically predetermined. Instead it is influenced by governance choices, leadership transparency, training investment and autonomy preservation. Organisations that proactively align learning expectations with a supportive work environment may reduce psychological risk and improve adaptive capacity. In contrast, increasing demand without adequate resources can improve innovation, quiet disengagement and weakened trust. Thus, this chapter encourages leaders and policymakers to treat psychological sustainability as an integral part of an organisation mainly during the change of technology.

9. REFERENCES

Almer, J. (2022). Deskilling as an effect of AI: A group of students' attitudes towards AI and their worries about deskilling.

Arboh, F., Zhu, X., Atingabili, S., Yeboah, E., & Drokow, E. K. (2025). From fear to empowerment: The impact of employees AI awareness on workplace well-being–a new insight from the JD–R model. *Journal of Health Organization and Management*. Advance online publication. DOI: 10.1108/JHOM-06-2024-0229 PMID: 39875341

Asiedu, E., & Tenakwah, E. S. (2025). Future-proofing your workforce: Upskilling and reskilling as HR's top priorities. *Strategic HR Review*, *24*(4), 169–173. Advance online publication. DOI: 10.1108/SHR-01-2025-0008

Asvestopoulou, E. (2024). AI revolution: Trust and the perceived threat to job security (Master's thesis). http://hdl.handle.net/10071/33859

Autor, D. H. (2015). Why are there still so many jobs? The history and future of workplace automation. *The Journal of Economic Perspectives*, *29*(3), 3–30. DOI: 10.1257/jep.29.3.3

Ayyagari, R., Grover, V., & Purvis, R. (2011). Technostress: Technological antecedents and implications. *Management Information Systems Quarterly*, *35*(4), 831–858. DOI: 10.2307/41409963

Battisti, M., Del Gatto, M., & Parmeter, C. (2022). Skill Biased Technical Change and Labor Market. Available at *SSRN* 3977544. DOI: 10.1016/j.jedc.2022.104428

Braverman, H. (1998). Labor and monopoly capital: The degradation of work in the twentieth century. nyu Press.

Brod, C. (1984). Technostress. Addison-Wesley. https://cir.nii.ac.jp/crid/1970023484968949634

Bughin, J. R. (2024). Corporate Ai Play and Skill-Biased Ai Change. Available at *SSRN* 4852540. DOI: 10.2139/ssrn.4852540

Chaker, B., & Damak, C. (2024). Navigating tomorrow: Strategies for effective workforce reskilling. In *Reskilling the Workforce for Technological Advancement* (pp. 62–81). IGI Global Scientific Publishing., DOI: 10.4018/979-8-3693-0612-3.ch004

Cheng, Z., & Jin, X. (2024). The Impact of Job Anxiety Caused by Artificial Intelligence Substitution on Organizational Members' Turnover Intention: The Mediating Role of Job Insecurity and the Moderating Effect of Job Uncertainty. : , 38(3), 67-103.https://www.dbpia.co.kr/Journal/articleDetail?nodeId=NODE12011895

Davenport, T. H., & Ronanki, R. (2018). Artificial intelligence for the real world. *Harvard Business Review*, *96*(1), 108–116.

De Witte, H. (2005). Job insecurity: Review of the international literature on definitions, prevalence, antecedents and consequences. *SA Journal of Industrial Psychology*, *31*(4), 1–6. https://hdl.handle.net/10520/EJC89073. DOI: 10.4102/sajip.v31i4.200

Demerouti, E., & Bakker, A. B. (2022). Job demands-resources theory in times of crises: New propositions. *Organizational Psychology Review*, *13*(3), 209–236. DOI: 10.1177/20413866221135022

Evans, R. M. (2022). Perceived benefits of upskilling and reskilling by persons who are among the employed, underemployed, and unemployed.https://digitalcommons.acu.edu/etd/482

Farhan, A. (2023). The impact of artificial intelligence on human workers. *Journal of Communication Education*, *17*(2), 93–104. DOI: 10.58217/joce-ip.v17i2.350

Ferdman, A. (2025). AI deskilling is a structural problem. *AI & Society*, •••, 1–13. DOI: 10.1007/s00146-025-02686-z

Galanakis, M. D., & Tsitouri, E. (2022). Positive psychology in the working environment. Job demands-resources theory, work engagement and burnout: A systematic literature review. *Frontiers in Psychology*, *13*, 1022102. DOI: 10.3389/fpsyg.2022.1022102 PMID: 36204770

George, A. S. (2024). Artificial intelligence and the future of work: Job shifting not job loss. *Partners Universal Innovative Research Publication*, *2*(2), 17–37. DOI: 10.5281/zenodo.10936490

Giuntella, O., König, J., & Stella, L. (2023). Artificial intelligence and workers' well-being (No. 16485). IZA Discussion Papers. https://hdl.handle.net/10419/282612

Gruenewald, H., & Mueller, M. (2025). Challenges and Opportunities in Reskilling and Upskilling. In *Reskilling and Upskilling in a Globalized Economy. Future of Business and Finance*. Springer., DOI: 10.1007/978-3-658-48384-5_7

Hajam, A. A., & John, A. S. (2024). Reskilling and Upskilling Strategies in the Era of Automation: A Human-Centered Approach to Workforce Development. *International Journal of Multidisciplinary Research Transactions*, *6*(10). Advance online publication. DOI: 10.5281/zenodo.13912971

Hasan, M., Haque, M. A., Nishat, S. S., & Hossain, M. M. (2024). Upskilling and reskilling in a rapidly changing job market: Strategies for organizations to maintain workforce agility and adaptability. *European Journal of Business and Management Research*, *9*(6), 118–126. DOI: 10.24018/ejbmr.2024.9.6.2502

Hobot, Z. (2024). *Navigating the Artificial Intelligence Revolution: Trust*. Fear, and Job Security in the Modern Workplace.

Hu, Y., Xu, Y., & Wu, B. (2025). A dual-pathway model of teacher-AI collaboration based on the job demands-resources theory. *Education and Information Technologies*, *30*(11), 15125–15146. DOI: 10.1007/s10639-025-13421-y

Humlum, A., & Plato, P. (2025). *Reskilling and Resilience (No. w34095)*. National Bureau of Economic Research., DOI: 10.3386/w34095

Huseynova, F. (2024). Addressing Deskilling as a Result of Human-AI Augmentation in the Workplace.

Hutter, C., & Weber, E. (2023). Labour market effects of wage inequality and skill-biased technical change. *Applied Economics*, *55*(27), 3063–3084. DOI: 10.1080/00036846.2022.2108751

Jabłoński, M. (2025). Changes of Employees' Skill Requirements Caused by Technological Progress. In Moussa, M., & McMurray, A. (Eds.), *The Palgrave Handbook of Breakthrough Technologies in Contemporary Organisations*., DOI: 10.1007/978-981-96-2516-1_17

Jamal, A. F., El Nemar, S., & Sakka, G. (2025). The relationship between job redesigning, reskilling and upskilling on organizational agility. *EuroMed Journal of Business*, *20*(2), 474–492. DOI: 10.1108/EMJB-10-2023-0279

Johnson, A., Dey, S., Nguyen, H., Groth, M., Joyce, S., Tan, L., Glozier, N., & Harvey, S. B. (2020). A review and agenda for examining how technology-driven changes at work will impact workplace mental health and employee well-being. *Australian Journal of Management*, *45*(3), 402–424. DOI: 10.1177/0312896220922292

Keyes, C. L. M. (2002). The mental health continuum: From languishing to flourishing in life. *Journal of Health and Social Behavior*, *43*(2), 207–222. DOI: 10.2307/3090197 PMID: 12096700

Le, H. (2026). Design and Development Effective Learning AI Education: Navigating Deskilling in the Age of Intelligent Automation. In The Intersection of AI and Student Development in Learning (pp. 307-338). IGI Global Scientific Publishing. DOI: DOI: 10.4018/979-8-3373-2927-7.ch010

Leon, R. D. (2023). Employees' reskilling and upskilling for industry 5.0: Selecting the best professional development programmes. *Technology in Society*, *75*, 102393. DOI: 10.1016/j.techsoc.2023.102393

Liu, N.-C., Wang, Y.-C., & Lin, Y.-T. (2024). Employees' Adaptation to Technology Uncertainty in the Digital Era: An Exploration Through the Lens of Job Demands–Resources Theory. *IEEE Transactions on Engineering Management*, *71*, 7286–7297. DOI: 10.1109/TEM.2023.3264293

Maslach, C., & Jackson, S. E. (1981). The measurement of experienced burnout. *Journal of Organizational Behavior*, *2*(2), 99–113. DOI: 10.1002/job.4030020205

McGuinness, S., Pouliakas, K., & Redmond, P. (2023). Skills-displacing technological change and its impact on jobs: Challenging technological alarmism? *Economics of Innovation and New Technology*, *32*(3), 370–392. DOI: 10.1080/10438599.2021.1919517

McKinsey & Company. (2021). How Companies are Reskilling to Address Skill Gaps. https://www.mckinsey.com/business-functions/organization/our-insights/how-companies-are-reskilling-to-address-skill-g

Menon, S., & Suresh, M. A. (2020). Organizational agility assessment for higher education institution. *Journal of Research on the Lepidoptera*, *51*(1), 561–573. DOI: 10.36872/LEPI/V51I1/301050

Morandini, S., Fraboni, F., De Angelis, M., Puzzo, G., Giusino, D., & Pietrantoni, L. (2023). The impact of artificial intelligence on workers' skills: Upskilling and reskilling in organisations. *Informing Science*, *26*, 39–68. DOI: 10.28945/5078

Nwaomah, A. E. (2025). Utilization of Artificial Intelligence (AI) and Fear of Job Loss in the Banking Industry: Perspectives of Bank Employees. Pan-African Journal of Education and Social Sciences, 6(1), 88-103.https://www.ajol.info/index.php/pajes/article/view/296667

OECD. (2019). OECD skills outlook 2019: Thriving in a digital world. OECD Publishing. https://www.oecd.org/en/publications/2019/05/oecd-skills-outlook-2019_c8896fe0.html

Ojiyi, G., Oji, I., Aikabeli, B. O., Oji, I. N., & Ayegbusi, W. E. (2023). Job Security in the Artificial Intelligence and Automation Era. no. December.https://repositorio.iscte-iul.pt/handle/10071/33859

Orrell, B. (2025). De-Skilling the Knowledge Economy.https://cosm.aei.org/wp-content/uploads/2025/06/De-Skilling-the-Knowledge-Economy-1.pdf

Peiró, J. M. (2025). Applied Psychology and Careers in the 21st Century. Challenges and Opportunities. *Australian Journal of Career Development, 34*(2), 114–123. DOI: 10.1177/10384162251350691

Putri, K. M. H., & Werdini, Y. E. (2025). Artificial Intelligence Adoption, Job Insecurity, and Psychological Resilience: Challenges for Employee Adaptation in Future Work Environments. *International Journal of Issue Science, 1*(5). Advance online publication. DOI: 10.71364/ijiss.v1i5.12

Ranjan, B., Sivanesan, I., & Bernie, S. B. (2026). Artificial intelligence and anxiety: The human price of adapting to a smarter workplace. Inspire Intelligence, 1(1), 52-67.https://inspirequill.org/index.php/inspireAI/article/view/12

Rhoades, L., & Eisenberger, R. (2002). Perceived organizational support: A review of the literature. *The Journal of Applied Psychology, 87*(4), 698–714. https://psycnet.apa.org/buy/2002-15406-008. DOI: 10.1037/0021-9010.87.4.698 PMID: 12184574

Sharma, K., Davidson, B. G. J., George, J. P., & Muttungal, P. V. (2025, October). Breeding distrust during artificial intelligence (AI) era: how technological advancements, job insecurity and job stress fuel organizational cynicism? In Evidence-based HRM: a Global Forum for Empirical Scholarship (Vol. 13, No. 4, pp. 763-779). Emerald Publishing Limited. DOI: 10.1108/EBHRM-05-2024-0159

Sverke, M., Hellgren, J., & Näswall, K. (2002). No security: A meta-analysis and review of job insecurity and its consequences. *Journal of Occupational Health Psychology, 7*(3), 242–264. https://psycnet.apa.org/buy/2002-01632-005. DOI: 10.1037/1076-8998.7.3.242 PMID: 12148956

Tarafdar, M., Cooper, C. L., & Stich, J. (2019). The technostress trifecta. *Information Systems Journal, 43*(3), 683–712. DOI: 10.1111/isj.12169

Taylor, A., Green, A., & Hassan, S. (2021). Priorities for up-skilling and re-skilling: what role can and should universities play?.

The Economic Times. 2025;https://economictimes.indiatimes.com/news/new-updates/reskilling-wont-help-200000-tech-jobs-gone-30000-more-lay-offs-likley-in-next-two-months-says-report/articleshow/124989112.cms?from=mdr

The Hindu. 2026; https://www.thehindu.com/business/human-ai-will-define-the-future-of-work-by-2027-nasscom-indeed/article70505399.ece

The times of India, 2025; https://timesofindia.indiatimes.com/education/careers/news/silent-layoffs-on-the-rise-in-indian-tech-sector-subtle-signs-employees-should-watch-out-for/articleshow/124498098.cms

Wadhwa, S. N., Bhardwaj, G., Srivastava, A. P., & Malik, R. (2025). AI-driven job insecurity and work performance: Unveiling the mediating role of psychological well-being. *International Journal of Information Technology : an Official Journal of Bharati Vidyapeeth's Institute of Computer Applications and Management, 17*(7), 1–12. DOI: 10.1007/s41870-025-02602-0

World Economic Forum. (2023). The Future of Jobs Report 2023. https://www.weforum.org/publications/the-future-of-jobs-report-2023/

Wu, Q., He, P., & Zhou, P. (2025). Skill-biased Productivity Effects of AI Adoption: Evidence from a Financial Shared Service Center Reform. DOI: 10.2139/ssrn.5759446

Zheng, J., Zhang, J. Z., Kamal, M. M., Liang, X., & Alzeiby, E. A. (2025). Unpacking human-AI interaction: Exploring unintended consequences on employee Well-being in entrepreneurial firms through an in-depth analysis. *Journal of Business Research, 196*, 115406. DOI: 10.1016/j.jbusres.2025.115406

Zheng, J., & Zhang, T. (2025). Association between AI awareness and emotional exhaustion: The serial mediation of job insecurity and work interference with family. *Behavioral Sciences (Basel, Switzerland), 15*(4), 401. DOI: 10.3390/bs15040401 PMID: 40282023

Chapter 4
From Coding to Orchestration:
How Multi-Agent AI Systems Are Reskilling Software Engineers – Deskilling Risks and Reskilling Pathways in AI-Augmented Development

Arpan Shaileshbhai Korat
http://orcid.org/0009-0001-0227-4967
Barclays Services Corporation, USA

ABSTRACT

This chapter examines how multi-agent artificial intelligence systems are reshaping the skill profile of software engineers by shifting emphasis from traditional coding toward orchestration, evaluation, and human–AI collaboration. Using a real-world multi-agent AI framework as a case study, the chapter analyzes how tasks such as boilerplate coding, documentation generation, query formulation, and initial debugging are increasingly automated. While these capabilities deliver clear productivity gains, they also introduce risks of deskilling if engineers disengage from foundational technical knowledge. The chapter addresses this tension by identifying emerging reskilling pathways, including prompt engineering, agent coordination, system oversight, and ethical validation of AI outputs. Practical deployment experiences are used to highlight common failure modes and best practices for integrating AI-assisted tools into software engineering workflows, offering actionable insights for educators, practitioners, and decision-makers navigating AI-augmented development environments.

DOI: 10.4018/979-8-3373-8450-4.ch004

1. INTRODUCTION

1.1 Background and Context of Large Language Models

The past few years have witnessed a transformative evolution in Artificial Intelligence (AI), largely driven by the advances in transformer-based Large Language Models (LLMs). LLMs have demonstrated superior ability in natural language understanding, reasoning, and the generation of text. LLM models such as GPT-4, LaMDA, and LLaMA have significantly advanced natural language processing. These models have enabled the development of AI tools that can perform tasks once considered exclusive to human expertise, including technical writing, multilingual translation, and software development support.

1.2 Background and Context of Large Language

Modern AI applications, despite their ability to perform many functions, are largely based on monolithic architecture, which requires that one large model serve many functions. Despite great success in controlled environments, this type of architecture has demonstrated its limitations in real-world scenarios utilizing diverse, specialized, and contextually relevant forms of reason. In real-world scenarios, tasks often require a combination of capabilities for example, summarizing technical documents, translating specialized language, and generating domain- specific code. Complex queries from users are often broken down into multiple smaller sub-queries that require unique types of skill sets to accomplish. Only one LLM has a limited ability to excel at all three aspects of this complex task, regardless of size.

1.3 Motivation for Multi-agent AI Tool Development

The growing complexity of AI-augmented software development has exposed the limitations of single-model approaches, motivating increased interest in collaborative intelligence and multi-agent systems. As software engineers transition from writing isolated code to orchestrating AI-driven workflows, AI tools must support specialization, coordination, and adaptive decision-making rather than monolithic automation. Multi-agent frameworks, inspired by human teamwork and distributed problem-solving, enable autonomous or semi-autonomous agents often powered by heterogeneous, task-specialized large language models to collaborate effectively on complex tasks that exceed the capabilities of any single model.

When we consider AI being integrated into software development training and education, some issues are raised regarding development of new skills without degrading basic skills. Some literature has systematically reviewed AI-based programming educator tools that will positively impact people, engagement, and task completion speed in a programming class. The use of these tools must be carefully shaded to prevent dependency, critical thinking and debugging skills of developers. Separate studies presented the use of AI-assisted coding by comparing the approach of cognitive AI support for completing routine tasks faster to the approaches without assistance. The AI assisted workflows are proven to increase the productivity of the developers and speed of software development. But, the limitation of AI assisted approaches put developer's creativity and algorithmic reasoning at risk. Developers will not think critically about the machine-generated code as mentioned in Alanazi, 2025. Therefore, there is a need for new learning paradigms focused on the development of high-order capabilities (e.g., verification knowledge, architectural constructs, and the architecture of a prompt), rather than simply on demonstrating fluent execution of the process while assisting with the transition to the new way of thinking about the integration of human-AI collaboration into software development in the industry.

1.4 Concrete Deskilling Mechanisms in AI-Augmented Software Engineering

Emerging evidence suggests there are specific mechanisms by which deskilling may happen, as mentioned in previous subsection 1.3. Automation limits developers' efficiency and creativity of the algorithm development as well as the reasoning of edge cases, potentially eroding deep conceptual understanding over time. In addition, reduced access to debugging and tracking errors (especially as developers accept AI-generated code with minimal changes) can erode their diagnostic expertise, which is a critical component of a developer's professional competency. An over-reliance on and automated bias towards AI may cause low-level validation loops, where developers only check for surface correctness, without fully understanding how the implementation works. Lastly, as designers prompt for specifications as opposed to doing low-level designs, it could create abstraction drift which would move their expertise further away from developing algorithms toward paths of orchestration and evaluative review. Although AI adoption in development do not always indicate an overall loss of skills, they do indicate a change in the way that cognitive labour will have to be organized through intentional strategies for reskilling in verification literacy, architectural reasoning and system-level oversight.

1.5 Problem Statement and Objectives

The core problem addressed in this chapter is: How can collaborative multi-agent AI frameworks, built on diverse LLMs, be designed to mitigate deskilling risks while enabling meaningful reskilling pathways for software engineers in AI-augmented development environments? This chapter presents a comprehensive discussion of a collaborative multi-agent architecture for integrated AI tool development using heterogeneous LLMs, with a specific focus on software engineering contexts. The proposed framework leverages multi-agent systems, reinforcement learning, and distributed AI principles to support adaptive task routing and continuous learning, as illustrated in *Figure 1* (a high-level architecture depicting the User Interface, Orchestration Layer, and Agent Layer). By introducing a centralized orchestration layer that manages specialized agents through shared memory and feedback-driven optimization, the chapter extends prior research by connecting architectural design choices to emerging shifts in developer roles and competencies.

The primary objectives of this chapter are threefold:

(i) To examine the theoretical and practical foundations of collaborative intelligence as they relate to AI-augmented software engineering;
(ii) To describe the design and implementation of a multi-agent LLM-based framework that supports integrated tool development and developer-in-the-loop workflows; and
(iii) To analyze the advantages, limitations, and future research directions of such frameworks, particularly in relation to deskilling risks and reskilling opportunities.

2. FOUNDATIONS OF COLLABORATIVE INTELLIGENCE

Increasing requirements for the ability of AI systems to adapt and apply context-relevant reasoning or knowledge from other fields threaten the effectiveness of monolithic models. This need has given rise to the concept of collaboration between multiple intelligent agents in the same system. This is termed "Collaborative Intelligence". Collaborative intelligence emphasizes the value of a diversity of agents working together to solve complex problems as opposed to relying solely on one generalized model. This section outlines the conceptual foundation of collaborative intelligence.

2.1 Concept of Collaborative Intelligence

In general, collaborative intelligence as applied to AI is based on systems that incorporate multiple agents that perform specialized functions, such as reasoning, perception, planning, and communication. To work together effectively, the agents share information, negotiate decisions, and generate solutions cumulatively. To be effective, the performance of individual agents is important; however, this is only part of the equation. Collaborative intelligence systems must also be well-coordinated and have a strong degree of orchestration among all the agents. Contemporary collaborative intelligence systems increasingly employ adaptive learning mechanisms to allow for the continuous improvement of the coordination strategies of the agents as time progresses. Techniques such as reinforcement learning, the use of a shared memory structure, and optimizing via feedback allow the agents to dynamically align their actions to the evolving requirements of the tasks and users. The collaborative intelligence paradigm is particularly applicable to AI technologies that must provide multi-dimensional answers to complex questions and thereby employ a wide range of expertise.

2.2 Historical Evolution of Multi-Agent Systems

Collaborative Intelligence (CI) in the field of Artificial Intelligence (AI) originated in the last few decades of the 20th century from early research in Multi-Agent Systems (MAS) as mentioned in Wooldridge & Jennings, 1995. The initial work in MAS was focused on creating autonomous agents that could autonomously operate in shared environments using decision-making techniques and processes similar to those used by humans, and ultimately to replicate the ability of humans to reach agreement through Distributed Problem-Solving (DPS) using game theory. Subsequently, early research efforts in MAS looked at coordination protocols, communication languages, and negotiation strategies that provided agents with capabilities to cooperate and/or compete with each other more effectively.

2.3 Human-Inspired Collaboration Models in AI

Collaborative efforts between humans provide an excellent example of how we can design multi-Agent systems (AI). Humans break down complex jobs into smaller parts, assigning them to those who have the skills to complete them. This process occurs by assigning communication roles, coordinating the work, supervising the work, managing the work via the use of project managers, establishing common goals, and fostering collaboration to accomplish shared objectives. Collaborative teamwork relies not only on each individual's ability but on many factors, such as how disputes are resolved, how feedback is shared, and how roles are adjusted and changed to meet the needs of all members of the team. AI developers have turned to using many of the organizational models found in human teams as the basis for developing collaborative systems. Role specialization, hierarchical coordination, and joint situational awareness are now part of the design of most multi-agent AI systems as mentioned in Isaacs, 1999.

2.4 From Ensemble Learning to Agent-Based Collaboration

Agent-based collaborative learning represents the next iteration of ensemble learning referred by Dietterich, 2000. Whereas ensemble learning typically uses pre-defined procedures, such as bagging, boosting, or stacking, to aggregate multiple models' outputs into a single prediction, agent-based collaboration knows no bounds when it comes to how models interact and communicate with one another. Collaboration via agent-based learning will be a critical element of the next generation of AI tools that leverage the advantages of integrating multiple LLMs with distinct advantages and will be able to form a collective output that is better contextualised and more coherent than any individual output produced by using a single agent or using an ensemble of agents.

2.5 Automation Bias, Trust Calibration, and Human Oversight

When software developers work with AI tools and technical assistants like Copilot, building trust and cognitive bias are important factors in how they will use the tools as part of their job, thereby impacting their overall performance as well as how they oversee the tool's usage. Trust levels among participants in controlled studies assessing the evolution of programmers' trust when using Copilot tend to increase as they gain experience with the product as reported by Shah et al., 2025. However, the majority of participants were adamant that they could not solely rely on Copilot for verifying or debugging source code before it was deployed because they didn't possess core debugging and verification skills necessary to appropriately evaluate the AI tool's suggestions. In addition, researchers have discovered that there are many types of cognitive bias that can emerge when developers utilize automated outputs in LLM-assisted software development. These biases can result in a significant increase in precarious actions taken by the developer or misjudgments made by the developer without having appropriately reflected on critical reasoning. The noted/cited research surrounding this potential emergence of cognitive bias is tied to more formal studies of human-automation interaction, and supports the need for calibrated trust, whereby an appropriate balance must be achieved between AI reliance and active human management, which can eliminate or reduce automation bias, assure quality, and protect professional accountability in software engineering processes.

2.6 Collaborative Multi-Agent AI as a Reskilling Enabler for Software Engineers

When applied to software engineering, collaborative intelligence shifts the focus of the engineer from performing low-level coding to a higher-level role involving the orchestration, evaluation, and management of systems. Collaborative AI systems distribute tasks between specialized agents, allowing for increased productivity while preserving the critical human judgment that is needed in the software development process. Furthermore, the use of collaborative intelligence in AI systems will continue to grow as new AI applications are developed in various domains.

3. LARGE LANGUAGE MODELS AS SPECIALIZED AGENTS

This section provides that foundation, setting the stage for multi-agent orchestration in integrated AI tools.

3.1 Overview of Transformer-Based LLMs

Transformer-based architectures introduced by Vaswani et al. (2017) revolutionized natural language processing by employing self-attention mechanisms to capture long-range dependencies in text. Transformers were originally designed to overcome the parallel-processing limitations of earlier types of neural networks (CNNs) by utilizing a self-attention mechanism that allows them to determine how words/concepts relate to one another over long distances within the source text. By utilizing this architecture, the model's context can be processed more efficiently, enabling it to produce coherent and relevant responses based on the context of the source text.

Over time, transformer-based architecture has greatly increased in terms of size (number of parameters), amount of training data, and amount of computational power as shown in *Figure 2* (A timeline graph depicting key milestones in LLM development - from early RNNs to GPT-3/4, LaMDA, and LlaMA, with annotations highlighting transformer breakthroughs). Transformer-based models such as GPT-3/4, LaMDA, and LLaMA were developed from very large (millions of documents) and diverse training datasets that enabled these models to determine linguistic patterns, factual relationships, and implicit reasoning methods within the domain and across languages and cultures. As a consequence, these models are now able to generate fluency and versatility far beyond any other systems in the field of NLP.

3.2 Strengths and Task-Specific Limitations of LLMs

The most important advantage of LLMs is their ability to generalize to different tasks with little or no specialized instructions, such as summarizing large documents and translating from one language to another. In addition, LLMs can create code through their understanding of natural languages. Because of this flexibility,

LLMs will be attractive foundational components for developing AI tools for many different types of workflows.

However, due to this generality, LLMs also have significant limitations. LLMs might generate outputs that are linguistically reasonable, but technically inaccurate, in specialized fields and/or in situations where mistakes would have catastrophic impacts. In addition, LLMs struggle to maintain long-term consistency, to perform precise logical reasoning, and to operate under strict constraints. Finally, LLMs' performance will likely drop dramatically for any tasks that require advanced specialized knowledge that is not adequately covered by the LLM's training data.

3.3 Fine-Tuning and Specialization of Language Models

The purpose of fine-tuning is to further develop and refine large pre-existing language model capabilities to make them better suited as an agent in a specific area. Fine-tuning involves re-training the language model on datasets and/or examples that are specifically related to that area of specialization (i.e., training a language model for technical summarization, multi-lingual translations, or code generation), thereby greatly increasing its ability to perform the tasks required in that area. Fine-tuning also allows the language model to learn conventions, terminology, and evaluation criteria that are specific to that area and cannot necessarily be learned through general training methods. As a result of fine-tuning, the outputs generated by the fine-tuned model will be more accurate, relevant, and reliable for that particular use case.

In multi-agent AIs, fine-tuned models and more general-purpose language models exist together. The combination of the two types of models within the multi-agent AI system creates a balance between depth and breadth, with the specialized agents performing specialized tasks and providing depth of knowledge about the topic, while the general agents provide context, clarification, and fallback reasoning when necessary.

3.4 Role of LLMs as Autonomous and Semi-Autonomous Agents

LLMs can act as either completely third-party automated (self-sufficient) or semi-automated (dependent on a monitoring layer) components of a multi-user or multi-component software app when integrated into this environment.

- Complete self-sufficient LLMs work autonomously on a specific assignment from start to finish without the need for any outside input after initial task assignment.

- Semi-automated LLMs follow a performance review process guided by the presence of a monitoring layer or feedback as performance reviews..

Some examples of how these types of agents work in practice include how they would interpret end-user intent, generate intermediate outputs based on that interpretation, and validate other agents' performance and results based on defined rules of performance.

The framework in which these types of agents are designed and operate is still bounded by specific tasks assigned to them based on safety constraints, operating constraints, or successful results from previous evaluations. Viewing these types of agents through an agent-based lens helps to re-frame how LLMs are perceived from a passive tool to an active participant in any problem-solving process and helps to create a new set of expectations for participants involved in agent-based solutions.

3.5 Challenges in Coordinating Heterogeneous LLMs

A major limitation of employing multiple specialized LLMs is the various coordination challenges from having heterogeneous models. Because agents may have trained on different data sets, have different output styles, have been trained to generate responses with different levels of confidence, and have been designed to use various formats to generate their responses, it is likely that inconsistencies will result when agent outputs are combined. Therefore, if not carefully orchestrated, these systems may produce separated or contradictory outputs.

There are also concerns regarding latency and computational expense associated with multi-agent interaction, as it usually requires both sequential processing and the exchange of information between agents. Developing effective and efficient ways to communicate while maintaining context fidelity necessitates building robust shared memory mechanisms and designing intelligent routing processes.

Furthermore, an additional challenge associated with generating output is interpretability. Understanding the process behind producing output becomes more complicated, since the output was generated based on the interaction between multiple agents. This complicates the debugging process for developers and technology evaluators, as well as building user trust, especially within the context of a professional or regulated environment.

Recent efforts in reinforcement learning for coordination by Foerster et al., 2018 have laid the ground- work, yet the challenge remains to create an integrated system where specialized agents can interact fluidly and adaptively. Developing solutions that allow for consistent, robust, and flexible system designs, including defining clear agent roles within the agent architecture, developing adaptive policies for orchestrating the agents' individual contributions, and developing mechanisms for ongoing monitoring and refinement of each agent by other agents, will address many of these challenges. The successful implementation of this approach will establish a strong foundation for creating coordinated LLM-based agents capable of creating integrated, flexible, and human-aligned artificial intelligence tools.

3.6 Empirical Studies on LLM/AI Assistants in Developer Workflows

In a recent study by (Koripalli, 2025), the adoption of GitHub Copilot in software teams showed that while Copilot helped improve productivity in routine tasks. However, there were concerns among developers about how using Copilot might affect their skill development or confidence levels. Separate large surveys of programmers (481 respondents in total) in Sergeyuk et al., 2025, showed that developers use AI assistants to help them with tasks they prefer - natural language documentation, refactoring, and documenting their work rather than the core logic behind the design of their code. The results from a long-term case study within an organization by Kumar et al., 2025 concluded that integrated AI tools into their workflow showed statistically significant reductions in the number of days required to complete pull request cycles, an increase in throughput from coding being shipped, and some concerns from management about how to develop proper change management processes. All of these findings provide a basis for discussing how AI will impact day-to-day engineering practices while highlighting issues regarding deskilling developers and the resulting shift of expertise among developers.

4. DESIGN RATIONALE OF A MULTI-AGENT AI FRAMEWORK FOR RESKILLING SOFTWARE ENGINEERS

As artificial intelligence systems move beyond research environments into everyday software development and business workflows, the complexity of the decisions they must support has increased substantially. Real-world development challenges rarely present themselves as well-defined problems with a single objective; instead, they involve layered goals, evolving constraints, and the need to balance technical, organizational, and user-centric considerations. In such settings, software engineers are no longer responsible only for writing code but must increasingly design, supervise, and refine AI-driven decision processes. Real-world problems rarely arrive as neatly defined inputs with a single objective; instead, they involve layered goals, evolving constraints, and diverse forms of reasoning. Therefore, the design and structure of the model for AI systems will transition from a typical monolithic architecture to a multi-agent or modular architecture that distributes decision-making responsibilities, has the ability to dynamically change as requirements or objectives change, has a dynamic way of building/partitioning the logical tasks across agents, and uses agent-to-agent peer communications in decision-making. *Figure 3* differentiates centralized collective intelligence with collaborative intelligence with autonomous agents. The collaborative model highlights key advantages such as adaptability, richer contextual reasoning, and improved responsiveness to complex problem structures. The development of multi-agent AI systems is motivated both by the need for technical diversity across tasks and by practical experience gained from deploying such systems within organizational environments.

4.1 Problem Decomposition in Complex AI Tasks

To effectively manage advanced artificial intelligence tasks, complex tasks must be divided into groups or sub-tasks that have interdependencies but are different enough at the scope level and at the level of expertise required to effectively perform the task. For instance, within one end-user request, there may be an element of intent detection, retrieval of associated information, creating an appropriately structured set of outputs, followed by verification that the outputs adhere to a specific domain's criteria. Given the level of complexity in each end-user request, it is unreasonable to expect that the entire group of sub-tasks can be accomplished in a single work unit of labor.

By decomposing AI tasks into sub-tasks, it allows for greater clarity of the purpose of the task, prevents errors from rolling from one step to another, and enables the ability to carry out sub-tasks concurrently. sub-tasks allow for improved accountability and performance measurement, variables that are equally important in the continuous improvement of artificial intelligence performance.

4.2 Need for Dynamic Task Routing

Once we break a problem apart into smaller pieces, we need to decide which agent(s) will best perform each piece. Static routing strategies assign all pieces to agents based on predetermined rules. These strategies become obsolete when there are frequent changes in task characteristics and system performance, as is frequently the case in dynamic systems. Dynamic task routing makes it possible for the system to use context, previous experience, and current status in order to identify which agents will perform best, depending on circumstances. The resulting framework allows for both increased accuracy and efficiency. This flexibility is crucial in AI tool-chains serving diverse user populations and use cases. By implementing dynamic routing features into an AI workflow system, the system will also be able to accommodate any failures or inconsistencies as they arise. For example, if an agent produces an output that is of low-confidence or if the agent becomes unavailable for some reason, then other agents can take over those tasks without any impact on the overall workflow. Thus, this type of flexibility is necessary for creating resilient AI systems that can operate in dynamic environments.

4.3 Orchestration vs. Centralized Control

At first glance, orchestration may appear similar to centralized control, as both involve a coordinating component. However, the distinction lies in how authority and intelligence are distributed. A centralized control system makes all decisions via top-down authority and considers all sub-components to be simply passive executors of their respective tasks. In contrast to centralized control, orchestration focuses on collaboration as opposed to command. Within multi-agent AI, orchestration provides communication between agents, management of dependencies between agents, integration of outputs from different agents, and allows agents to maintain autonomy regarding their job functions. Through this balance between coordination and individualization of agents, agents can provide a specific type of service without limiting themselves by means of a strict hierarchy of command.

4.4 Design Principles of the Proposed Framework

The proposed multi-agent system is built according to several fundamental principles:

(1) Modularity: Modularity enables each agent to be developed, deployed, and updated independently, reducing overall system complexity and allowing the framework to evolve without extensive reengineering.
(2) Specialization: Each agent can concentrate on those tasks that relate to its specific competencies (be they developed by fine-tuning existing agents, constructing new agent architectures, or developing training data sets that are tailored to exploit individual pairs of agents). While specialization increases both agent performance and reliability.
(3) Shared Context/Communication: In order to produce coherent agent outputs, agents must be able to share contexts and communicate with other agents. The presence of an associated memory/contextual layer allows agents to leverage the outputs of other agents instead of being required to operate independently from one another.
(4) Adaptability: The adaptive quality of this framework will result from the continual refinement of routing algorithms and coordination strategies through the introduction of mechanisms that incorporate feedback collected from both users

and system performance metric data. Through this process, the framework will continue to evolve in relation to real-world usage.

Together, these principles ensure that the framework can adjust to real-world usage patterns while supporting software engineers in higher-level roles centered on orchestration, evaluation, and system oversight.

4.5 Comparison with Traditional Single-Model Architectures

The traditional single model architecture is simpler than multi-agent systems and less complicated to deploy, however it only works for narrowly defined tasks. As the task complexity increases, the traditional model will be limited to competition between multiple objectives such as accuracy, interpretability, and response time. Multi-agent systems alleviate some of these limitations by distributing tasks to multiple specialized agents. Although this strategy results in more complexity in the design and operating phases of a multi-agent architecture, it also results in increased flexibility and robustness. Errors can be avoided in a multi-agent architecture by isolating the problem to individual agents, making incremental updates easier, and allowing for more efficient analysis of how to optimize system performance. From a practical standpoint, multi-agent computer architectures mirror how many businesses organize their workforces to respond effectively to complex work environments. By promoting the ideals of cooperation and orchestration amongst agents, multi-agent systems create a more sustainable pathway for developing highly advanced artificial intelligence (AI) systems that can grow with the changing technological and user needs.

5. PROPOSED COLLABORATIVE MULTI-AGENT AI FRAMEWORK FOR SOFTWARE ENGINEER RESKILLING

This multi-agent collaborative framework was developed to help with complex, real-world AI workflows. The framework separates out the workload across specialized components but keeps them working together in an organized and consistent way through structured coordination of multiple agents. Instead of having one model do all of the work from input, interpretation, reasoning, and generation of outputs end-to-end, this framework has a layered approach where each agent contributes to the end product gradually over time. The layered approach supports both practical experience from implementation of similar types of solutions, as well as utilizing established principles from collaborative problem solving and distributed systems.

The core principle of the framework is to promote modularity, adaptability, and transparency. Each layer has its own unique responsibility, and by separating them, the overall solution can continue to grow, adapt, and support different user requirements. Beyond architectural modularity, this separation also reflects a shift in professional practice: engineers increasingly operate as designers of coordinated workflows and evaluators of AI-generated outputs rather than solely as direct implementers of low-level logic.

5.1 High-Level Architectural Overview

The architecture of the proposed framework (Figure-1) consists of three primary layers: the user interface layer, the central orchestration layer, and the agent layer.

5.2 User Interface Layer

The user-interface layer mediates interactions between users and the underlying AI system. In addition to gathering user input, it shapes how users articulate goals and interpret outputs. Because the interface allows participants to provide input in natural language, it lowers technical barriers and enables sophisticated requests without requiring deep implementation expertise.

The user-interface layer also provides visibility through clarification prompts, confidence indicators, and summaries of system responses. In professional and decision-critical environments, such transparency mechanisms play a crucial role in building trust in AI-generated outputs and supporting informed human oversight.

5.3 Central Orchestration Layer

The collaborative framework relies heavily on the central orchestration layer. This layer transforms unstructured user input into structured task requests, coordinates agent activities, and produces coherent final outputs. Its role is facilitative rather than executory.

Within this orchestration-based model of shared responsibility, the orchestration layer mirrors the evolving role of software engineers in AI-augmented environments. It enables agents to operate independently while synchronizing efforts through shared objectives and contextual awareness. By separating execution from coordination, the framework allows engineers to focus on workflow design, evaluation of outcomes, and refinement of system behavior. This shift from direct coding to orchestration and oversight represents a key reskilling pathway.

5.3.1 Query Understanding and Intent Recognition

Understanding user intent is a foundational responsibility within the orchestration-driven framework. The orchestration layer analyzes user input to determine goals, constraints, and expected output forms. Natural language understanding techniques transform informal requests into structured task representations that guide coordinated agent activity.

Accurate intent recognition is critical, as misinterpretations propagate downstream and affect task allocation and outcomes. By focusing on semantic understanding rather than keyword matching, the system better handles complex or multi-part queries. This mirrors the evolving responsibility of engineers, who increasingly translate high-level objectives into structured workflows.

5.3.2 Task Decomposition and Agent Selection

Once intent is established, the orchestration layer decomposes the request into logically coherent subtasks. Each subtask is assigned to specialized agents based on functional expertise, historical performance, and system context. This reflects a shift from execution-centric development toward coordination-centric system design.

Routing decisions are dynamic rather than static and are refined through feedback, task complexity, and system conditions. This adaptive selection reduces dependence on any single component and supports flexible system behavior. For engineers, value creation increasingly emerges from designing effective task flows and evaluating agent performance.

5.3.3 Reinforcement Learning–Based Optimization

To support continuous improvement, the orchestration layer incorporates reinforcement learning mechanisms that optimize coordination strategies over time. User feedback such as satisfaction ratings, corrections, or follow-up interactions serves as reward signals for refining routing and aggregation decisions. The framework evaluates performance holistically at the system level rather than optimizing agents in isolation.

From a reskilling perspective, this learning-driven orchestration model reinforces the role of engineers as supervisors and evaluators responsible for guiding adaptive behavior and ensuring that collaborative AI systems evolve in transparent and human-aligned ways.

5.4 Agent Layer and Functional Specialization

The agent layer forms the execution backbone of the collaborative framework and consists of multiple large language model–based agents, each designed to perform a narrowly defined function. Constraining scope improves precision and reliability while reducing cognitive and computational burden on any single model. Although agents operate independently, their outputs are coordinated through the orchestration layer to achieve unified objectives.

This design reflects a broader shift in engineering practice in which developers delegate well-defined operational tasks to specialized AI components while focusing on higher-level concerns such as workflow design, system integration, validation, and quality assurance.

5.4.1 Summarization Agent

The Summarization Agent condenses complex documents into concise representations that preserve core ideas and logical structure. It supports knowledge-intensive workflows by reducing manual review time and enabling engineers to focus on interpretation and decision-making.

5.4.2 Translation Agent

The Translation Agent converts content across languages while preserving semantic meaning and domain-specific terminology. In multilingual development environments, it supports coordination and documentation activities, allowing engineers to validate and integrate outputs rather than perform manual translation.

5.4.3 Code Generation Agent

The Code Generation Agent translates natural language specifications into executable or semi-executable code, assists with prototyping, and supports debugging. Rather than replacing developers, it handles routine implementation tasks, enabling engineers to focus on architectural reasoning, system integration, validation, and security considerations.

5.4.4 Domain-Specific Analysis Agent

The Domain-Specific Analysis Agent performs in-depth analysis within specialized knowledge domains using domain-adapted reasoning strategies. It enables integration of expert-level insights while positioning engineers as evaluators and contextualizers of those outputs.

5.4.5 Conversational Support Agent

The Conversational Support Agent maintains continuity throughout interactions, providing clarifications and guided prompts. It emphasizes the importance of interpretability and user-centered design in AI-augmented development environments.

5.5 Inter-Agent Communication and Shared Memory

Agent cooperation relies on structured communication and shared contextual memory. A shared memory mechanism maintains intermediate data, contextual information, and feedback between agents.

Through shared memory and asynchronous coordination, agents build on each other's outputs while maintaining flexibility. This enables coherent, contextually appropriate responses while preserving modular independence of individual components. The resulting architecture supports adaptable, transparent, and collaborative AI workflows aligned with evolving engineering roles.

6. LEARNING, ADAPTATION, AND CONTINUOUS IMPROVEMENT

A significant trait of strong multi-agent artificial intelligence (AI) systems is their capability to learn from their experiences and subsequently adapt to them over time. In today's deployed environment, where the continual evolvement of user needs due to transitions in the workload and the way users interact with multi-agent systems occur, having a static infrastructure (even one that was created using a high degree of consideration) will become less and less advantageous in terms of being able to address the ever-changing nature of the dynamics in the user's work situation. As such, adaptation and learning are the cornerstones of the proposed multi-agent collaborative framework.

6.1 Reinforcement Learning in Agent Orchestration

Reinforcement learning is a key enabling technology for adaptive orchestration in a multi-agent environment. Rather than use hard-coded routing decisions, the adaptive orchestration system learns from the results of each routing decision, and over time, develops knowledge of which coordination methods have been associated with the best outcome.

The orchestration layer serves as the decision-maker for the adaptive orchestration system. The orchestration layer selects agents and workflows based on the expected utility of the agent and workflow to achieve an overall goal. Each agent and workflow selected by the orchestration layer is assessed against historical performance data, including the quality of completion of tasks and user satisfaction. Thus, over a period of time, the adaptive orchestration system develops a preference for the routing methods that consistently yield positive results, while at the same time decreasing the reliance on those methods that have not delivered positive results.

Reinforcement learning is a system-level enhancement to the adaptive orchestration system, rather than being applied to individual agents. This approach allows the optimization of routing decisions to be based on the overall coherence of the adaptive orchestration system, rather than on the performance of individual agents.

6.2 Reward Modeling Using User Feedback

User input offers acceptable and beneficial feedback for a system to improve its performance, unlike automated metrics that relate only to quantitative information and do not account for qualitative details such as relevance, clarity, and trustworthiness. It is hard to measure qualitative feedback quantitatively.

To achieve this, the framework employs models of reward based on user input. In other words, the user feedback provides cues for the framework regarding how to make future decisions on orchestration. User input can be either explicit in the form of ratings and corrections or it can be implicit, as demonstrated by follow-up queries and interactions. By utilizing user experience as the foundation for learning, the framework continues to meet user expectations and human needs.

When interpreting user input, the framework recognizes that dissatisfaction may occur because of a lack of clarity in the task being performed, rather than a failure of the agent. This perspective enables the framework to avoid overfitting the user input to specific user occurrences, allowing for longer-term, more stable learning.

6.3 Meta-Learning Across Agents

While individual agents may improve through fine-tuning and task-specific updates, additional benefits emerge when learning is shared across the system. Meta-learning technologies allow for the identification of rules that apply across multiple tasks or areas of a domain.

Agents create a "shared memory" that includes performance data (successes and failures); therefore, agents can learn from each other. For example, agents learn from the most successful methods of structuring prompts and by studying agent errors and how they occurred to make improvements across the entire system. Collective learning through these means helps agents reduce redundancies, enabling greater efficiencies and speedier experimentation.

Meta-learning helps speed up the rate of adaptation for new agents as well as agents that have been changed. By applying the experience gained by all agents that previously existed and have now merged or changed, the overall performance of all agents will remain stable.

6.4 Adaptability to New Tasks and Domains

Using a collaborative multi-agent framework provides many benefits because it can easily incorporate new tasks or domains without having to completely redesign the framework. In the event that there are new requirements to be met, any new agents that will perform tasks will be added to the current framework, or existing agents that already perform similar functions will be used to perform these new functions, based on the orchestration and learning capabilities of the framework.

The ability of collaborative multi-agent frameworks to adapt to new tasks and domains is further supported by the framework's separation of concerns. By separating out the components of task understanding, coordination, and execution, the use of different types of coordinated action on multiple agents allows for changes to happen independently of each other. As a result, it is possible to update existing components of the framework independently of the other components, which is less risky and makes deployment faster in fast-changing environments.

Collaborative multi-agent frameworks are designed to assist researchers in performing research tasks; to provide tools and support for the development of software applications; and to assist in making decisions based on knowledge of the past.

6.5 Long-Term System Evolution

Learning and adapting to changing conditions provide a foundation for the collective development of the system over time. Knowledge of User Behavioural Patterns (UBPs), Task Complexity (TCs), and Agent Performance (APs) all support the strategic development of architecture and coordination Management Policies (CMPs) within the system. In addition to Allowing For Long-Term Evolution, learning and adapting through the use of longitudinal evaluations raises challenges with respect to Maintainability, Interpretability and Governance.

Beyond system-level adaptation, long-term evolution of multi-agent orchestration frameworks has parallel implications for human expertise and workforce structures. As reinforcement-driven routing, automated coordination, and adaptive task allocation increase operational efficiency, they may simultaneously reduce the frequency with which engineers engage in low-level implementation, debugging, and algorithmic construction. Over time, diminished exposure to such activities can reshape competency profiles, particularly among early-career engineers who traditionally acquire expertise through sustained hands-on practice. This shift suggests that system evolution must be understood as co-evolution between human and machine capabilities. Consequently, educational programs and professional development pathways must transition from syntax-centric training toward architectural reasoning, evaluation literacy, oversight competence, and ethical accountability. In this framing, orchestration does not merely enhance performance; it redefines the locus of human expertise within adaptive AI ecosystems, positioning engineers as supervisors, validators, and governance actors in continuously learning systems.

7. SYSTEM IMPLEMENTATION AND TECHNICAL ARCHITECTURE

To be effective, the Multi-Agent Collaborative Framework must be implemented with careful consideration of the following elements:

- Implementation Details: Implementation details will differ based on the capabilities of the technologies that will be used as the basis of the Framework. Implementation details will vary based on factors such as operational constraints, technical limitations, safety, and security requirements. The objective of this section is to address the most important implementation details of the proposed Framework.
- System Environment: The system environment will be determined by the types of hardware and software used in an organization's operating environment. Implementation considerations take into account the organization's operating environment to design the Framework for an implementation that best fits the organization's existing resources.

7.1 Technology Stack Overview

Figure 8 represents architecture diagram detailing the full technical stack: the user interface connects to the API gateway; the gateway communicates with agent micro-services, the shared memory module, the message broker, and the database; monitoring tools are shown on the side.

The front end is built using React.js, allowing a user interface with an adaptable and interactive experience regardless of the device used to access the system. The front end is also the primary interface that users will use to interact with the system by submitting queries and receiving synthesized results. The backend of the system includes an API Gateway built using FastAPI (using the Python programming language). The API Gateway on the backend accepts incoming requests, parses the incoming requests into query components, and identifies the Type of Query component to Route to the correct Agent for Processing. FastAPI was chosen because it was able to provide fast performance and support Asynchronous/in-parallel operations. The Asynchronous feature is especially useful in coordinating multiple agents at the same time. All of the Agents on the system are Containerized Components (Docker) and are deployed as Microservices. All of the Microservices expose RESTful APIs that allow Users to Send Requests for Sub-Tasks and Provide Structured Responses Based on the Processing Results. The Message Broker used in the system is RabbitMQ, which enables Asynchronous communication between the orchestration layer of the system and the agent services. All Persistent Data stored in the system (such as Logs and Feedback from Users) is stored in a PostgreSQL database.

7.2 Microservices-Based Agent Deployment

In a micro-services architecture, agents are deployed as independent services (i.e., containers). The use of containers provides an environment that is consistent across different infrastructures, which greatly eases the deployment of containers. Each agent operates independently from the other agents and can be developed, tested, and scaled without affecting the overall system.

The ability to isolate agents and decouple them from the orchestration logic increases system fault isolation and resilience. If one of the agents becomes unavailable or experiences degraded performance, the orchestration logic can redirect tasks to other agents/fallback methodologies. This design allows the system to continue operating as long as there are agents available and is conducive to the easy integration of upgraded/new agents.

7.3 Orchestration Algorithms and Decision Pipelines

The orchestration layer allows for the overall management of task flow and agent executions by employing a structured decision pipeline that processes user queries and produces actionable sub-tasks and combines agent responses into a single, coherent output.

7.3.1 Query Understanding and Intent Recognition

User queries are first processed by a natural language understanding (NLU) module that transforms raw input into a structured representation. *Figure 6* represents flowchart of query decomposition, where an input query "Summarize and translate this paper" splits into two branches with corresponding agent selection. This representation includes the user's intent, entities (objects), and any required subsections of action. Accurate intent recognition at this stage is critical, as it determines subsequent task decomposition and routing decisions.

7.3.2 Task Routing and Agent Selection

The routing mechanism using a decision tree that has been augmented by means of reinforcement learning enables the determination of the optimal individual or group of individuals to complete a task after it has been broken down into various sub-tasks. Routing decisions are made based on both historical performance information, as well as the current contextual environment of the system and the complexity associated with the task. Consequently, the process by which agents to complete the sub-tasks are selected continues to become increasingly efficient with the passage of time.

7.3.3 Result Aggregation and Post-Processing

The outputs from agent execution return at the orchestration layer. Here, the outputs are merged using a weighted aggregation function. The responses given by the different agents have gone through Natural Language Processing post-production to ensure they flow naturally together and fit within the context. This step is critical to ensuring the final result is presented as a single cohesive response to the user rather than as a set of unrelated agent responses.

7.4 Agent Module Specifications

The framework consists of several agents that serve distinct functional roles, allowing for accurate, dependable execution of tasks for those distinct areas. *Figure 5* shows different agents of the proposed framework represented as boxes (Summarization, Translation, Code Generation, Domain Analysis, and Conversational), all connected to the orchestration layer via a shared memory module. The agents are explained in detail in Section 5.

7.5 Security, Privacy, and Robustness Considerations

The system's architectural foundation supports security and robustness. All inter-service data exchanged between systems are subjected to transport layer security (TLS) encryption, which protects the data from interception while it is in route. The agent APIs are protected with an authorization mechanism based on OAuth 2.0. Only those components authorized through authentication can issue requests to an agent's API.

To ensure high reliability for the system, redundancy and failover methodologies are being used at the orchestration and on the agents. Whenever an agent becomes unresponsive or fails for whatever reason, any tasks assigned to that agent will automatically be transferred to backup services. The personal information associated with a user will be anonymized, and any confidential user logs generated will be securely stored in order to safeguard user privacy. As well, the robustness of the system has been validated by way of performing stress tests and creating simulated failure scenarios to assess how well it will continue to function in adverse conditions.

7.6 Scalability and Performance Optimization

Containerized deployment and asynchronous communication provide a method for implementing a scalable deployment model. As workloads increase, agents can be replicated on demand to accommodate the added workload; message queues decouple execution timing from the time of request intake. Additionally, using Redis caching allows for the prevention of repeated computation of commonly accessed contextual data.

Tools for monitoring system performance provide visibility into what is happening with the system at any given time, allowing for immediate action to optimize performance and plan for future capacity. The combination of these approaches helps keep the framework responsive and efficient across different sizes of deployments and workloads.

7.7 Experimental Settings

To evaluate performance, scalability, and robustness, controlled experiments were conducted under standardized conditions.

Hardware Environment

- NVIDIA A100 GPU (40GB VRAM)
- 64GB RAM

- 16-core CPU
- Ubuntu 22.04

Software Environment

- Python 3.10
- FastAPI backend
- Docker containerization
- Redis 7.x
- RabbitMQ 3.x
- PostgreSQL 14

8. COMPARATIVE ANALYSIS AND DISCUSSION

In order to evaluate the effectiveness of the proposed collaborative multi-agent framework, the results were evaluated against those of a standard monolithic AI system. Analyses of how both types of systems perform will consider the quantitative performance measure and the qualitative measures of end user interaction (experience), adaption to change and circumstance, and an overview of system transparency.

8.1 Performance Comparison with Monolithic AI Systems

The experimental evaluation designed a composite research assistant task that required the user to summarize, translate and generate code all within one query. In the real world, many knowledge-work activities require simultaneous use of different types of reasoning as well as output generation.

In every task evaluated, the multi-agent collaborative framework significantly outperformed the single-agent baseline. The multi-agent platform generated higher ROUGE scores the scores were greater for the agent that produced summaries and therefore provided a higher level of coverage and coherence as compared to the single-agent collaborator. The translation agent had higher BLEU scores than the baseline, reflecting greater fluency and contextual accuracy. The code generation agent performed better than the baseline, as evidenced by higher unit test pass rates; therefore, it was more closely aligned with functional requirements. *Figure 12* shows bar charts comparing ROUGE, BLEU, and code generation success rates between our collaborative framework and a baseline single-model system.

User satisfaction measures supported these conclusions. Participants rated the multi-agent system higher than the single-agent collaborative system because participants reported that the multi-agent system provided a more comprehensive response to a specific task in one interaction than the single-agent collaborative system. Thus, the data indicate that distributing collaborative tasks among specialized agents results in an increase in both the technical performance of the agents as well as the perceived usefulness of the agents. *Figure 13* shows screenshots of the system's outputs for summarization, translation, and code generation, with callouts highlighting key features

8.2 Critical Evaluation and Socio-Technical Trade-offs

Although improvements in ROUGE, BLEU, and unit test pass rates indicate measurable task-level gains, these metrics alone do not fully capture long-term robustness, cross-agent error propagation, or lifecycle maintenance complexity. Unlike a purely conceptual architecture, the proposed multi-agent framework was validated through controlled deployment experiments that simulated production-like conditions, including concurrent workloads, agent-level failures, and routing instability. Observability mechanisms such as structured logging, latency tracing, and agent-specific diagnostics were used to evaluate coordination overhead and failure recovery behavior. Results indicated that while the multi-agent architecture introduces additional orchestration complexity, modular fault isolation reduced cascading failures compared to a monolithic baseline under stress scenarios. Nevertheless, the distributed nature of responsibility across agents increases challenges related to debugging, traceability, version control, and governance. Furthermore, improved automated metrics and user satisfaction do not eliminate the need for human accountability in AI-generated engineering decisions, particularly in security-sensitive or compliance-critical contexts. Engineers remain responsible for validating outputs, auditing reasoning chains, and ensuring alignment with organizational and ethical standards. Therefore, a comprehensive evaluation of collaborative multi-agent systems must integrate quantitative performance metrics, controlled deployment evidence, longitudinal reliability assessment, maintenance cost analysis, and structured human oversight evaluation to accurately assess the trade-off between specialization benefits and governance complexity.

8.3 Advantages of Collaborative Multi-Agent Design

- Heterogeneous Expertise: By integrating specialized agents, the system leverages domain-specific knowledge that no single model could fully capture.
- Dynamic Adaptability: Real-time query decomposition and routing enable the system to adjust to diverse and complex tasks dynamically.
- Collaborative Learning: The reinforcement learning loop and shared memory foster continuous improvement and cross-agent knowledge transfer.

- User-Centric Design: The system's design prioritizes user satisfaction, ensuring that the final output is coherent, context-rich, and actionable.

8.4 Interpretability and Transparency Challenges

- Inter-Agent Synchronization: Managing communication and ensuring consistency among agents can introduce overhead and complexity.
- Latency Issues: The dynamic routing and aggregation processes can increase response times compared to simpler, single-model systems.
- Data Dependency: The quality of each agent's output depends on the availability and diversity of training data, which may vary by domain.
- Interpretability: While output quality is enhanced, understanding the detailed decision pathways within the orchestration layer remains challenging.
- Failure Modes: The multi-agent pipelines have the potential to produce conflicting outputs when the agents use different solutions to optimize their respective objectives and thus require human intervention/oversight for resolution of any issues that would cause a negation of the trade offs they had originally intended to make.
- Hallucination: LLM generated code may contain hallucinated APIs, deprecated library calls and/or insecure characteristics such as improper input validation and unsafe deserialization that could be passed downstream if they are not properly vetted/assessed. Also, if context is improperly aligned between retrieval-augmented and/or tool-using systems, agents may end up reasoning from inappropriate either by virtue of being outdated or irrelevant data sets, resulting in outputs that are logically consistent, but operationally or functionally unsound. Additionally, there is the potential for cascading failure to occur if you have a flaw created by an agent operating early in the pipeline and none of the subsequent agents catch that flaw and, instead, all further amplify it.

8.5 Implications for Industry

- Healthcare: Integrated systems can support diagnostics, personalized treatment planning, and medical research.
- Education: Collaborative AI tools can assist in literature reviews, automated tutoring, and research synthesis.
- Software Development: Enhanced code generation and documentation can streamline development workflows.
- Robotics: Multi-agent integration can improve autenuous decision-making in complex, dynamic environmints.

9. FUTURE RESEARCH DIRECTIONS AND CONCLUSION

This section outlines key research opportunities and concludes with a summary of the chapter's contributions. Future research will explore following:

9.1 Hierarchical and Distributed Orchestration

- Hierarchical Clustering: Implementing a multi-level orchestration system that groups agents into clusters for faster, more efficient processing.
- Edge Computing: Investigating lightweight agent deployment on edge devices to reduce latency and improve real-time performance.

9.2 Advanced Learning and Adaptation

- Meta-Learning Strategies: Integrating advanced meta- learning approaches to enhance agents' ability to learn from feedback more rapidly.
- Cross-Domain Knowledge Transfer: Enabling agents to share insights across domains, thereby expanding their collective intelligence and problem-solving capabilities.

9.3 Enhancing Interpretability

- Visualization Tools: Developing dashboards to visualize inter-agent communication and decision pathways, help in users understand the collaborative process.
- Explainable AI Modules: Incorporating methods to generate human-understandable explanations for routing decisions and agent outputs.

9.4 Ethical and Responsible AI Considerations

As collaborative AI systems become increasingly independent and intricate, questions about ethics and management are raised. To ensure they are used in a morally sound way, we must consider issues such as Data Privacy, Bias Mitigation, Accountability, and Oversight by Humans when designing these systems. To build an ethical orchestration mechanism, we need to include principles of ethical design in the learning processes for these systems. Therefore, it will be necessary to monitor the behaviors of agents for unintended bias, provide users with some level of control over where their decisions are made, and create clear audit trails to track the actions of the agents. Building Trust in Users through Responsible AI requires that all members of our society benefit from the Use of Collaborative Intelligence.

The translation of orchestration-driven AI frameworks from experimentation to real-world operation presents a number of issues including management of costs (API usage, infrastructure scaling), reliable performance under changing-functionality, and managing errors among multiple agents working together. Enterprises must also deal with governance issues such as data privacy and ownership of intellectual property, security flaws in created software, audit-ability of automated decision-making, particularly around regulated industries. In agentic systems where task decomposition, tool invocation, and output synthesis occur across many components, there are additional challenges regarding accountability and the assignment and traceability of responsibilities. Initiatives focused on interoperability such as the Model Context Protocol (MCP) and structured tool calling standards have been started in an attempt to standardize the means of communicating specifications between models, memory stores and outside tools ultimately leading to better re-produce ability and efficiency with respect to the governance of these types of systems. However, establishing a standard (or multiple standards) will not eliminate the ethical and regulatory challenges that need to be addressed through the establishment of robust oversight systems, logging architecture and Human-in-the-loop validations of effective, safe, accountable and economically viable deployment of multi-agent AI systems within the software engineering discipline.

9.5 Conclusion

This chapter describes a novel framework to develop a collaborative multi-agent system using various LLMs to solve complex problems by breaking down queries into smaller components for each agent. Each agent performs a specific task and returns the results to an orchestration layer for aggregation and combination before returning to the user. The framework illustrates an important shift in the role of software engineers from direct coding toward orchestration, supervision, and evaluation of AI-driven systems. Experimental evaluation using research assistance tasks demonstrated that the multi-agent framework significantly improves the quality of generated summaries, translations, and code outputs, while also achieving higher levels of user satisfaction. These findings highlight the effectiveness of specialization and orchestration in handling multifaceted AI workflows. At the same time, the framework illustrates an important shift in the role of software engineers - from direct coding toward orchestration, supervision, and evaluation of AI-driven systems. In addition, empirical evaluations of research assistance tasks have shown that the collaborative approach has significantly improved the quality of generated summaries, translations, and code and provided users with higher levels of satisfaction.

REFERENCES

Alanazi, M., Soh, B., Samra, H., & Li, A. (2025). The Influence of Artificial Intelligence Tools on Learning Outcomes in Computer Programming: A Systematic Review and Meta-Analysis. *Computers, 14*(5), 185. DOI: 10.3390/computers14050185

Foerster, J. N., Assael, Y. M., de Freitas, N., & Whiteson, S. (2018). Counterfactual multi-agent policy gradients. In *Proceedings of the Thirty-Second AAAI Conference on Artificial Intelligence* (pp. 2974– 2982).

Isaacs, W. (1999). Dialogue: The art of thinking together. Crown Business. Dietterich, T. G. (2000). Ensemble methods in machine learning. In Kittler, J., & Roli, F. (Eds.), *Multiple Classifier Systems* (pp. 1–15). Springer.

Koripalli, M. (2025). Copilot Impact Studies: Measuring Productivity, Trust, and Skill Evolution in Enterprise Developer Teams. *International Journal of Computational and Experimental Science and Engineering, 11*(4). Advance online publication. DOI: 10.22399/ijcesen.4217

Kumar, A., Khare, V., Sharma, D., Kumar, S., Saini, V., Yadav, A., Jain, S., Rana, A., Verma, P., Meena, V., & Edubilli, A. (2025). Intuition to evidence: Measuring AI's true impact on developer productivity (arXiv:2509.19708). arXiv. https://arxiv .org/abs/2509.19708

Sergeyuk, A., Golubev, Y., Bryksin, T., & Ahmed, I. (2025). Using AI-based coding assistants in practice: State of affairs, perceptions, and ways forward. *Information and Software Technology, 178*, 107610. DOI: 10.1016/j.infsof.2024.107610

Shah, A., Rexin, T., Tomson, E., Porter, L., Griswold, W. G., & Soosai Raj, A. G. (2025). Evolution of programmers' trust in generative AI programming assistants (arXiv:2509.13253). arXiv. https://arxiv.org/abs/2509.13253 DOI: 10.1145/3769994.3770029

Vaswani, A., Shazeer, N., Parmar, N., Uszkoreit, J., Jones, L., Gomez, A. N., Kaiser, Ł., & Polosukhin, I. (2017). Attention is all you need. In Advances in Neural Information Processing Systems, 30 (pp. 5998– 6008). https://papers.nips.cc/paper/2017/file/3f5ee243547dee91fbd053c1c4a8 45aa-Paper.pdf

Wooldridge, M., & Jennings, N. R. (1995). Intelligent agents: Theory and practice. *The Knowledge Engineering Review, 10*(2), 115–152. DOI: 10.1017/S0269888900008122

Chapter 5
Beyond Coding: High-Level Reasoning, System Design, and Quality Gatekeeping in an AI-Driven Development Landscape

Neha Yadav
http://orcid.org/0000-0002-7793-2063
JSS University, Noida, India

Mayank Singh
http://orcid.org/0000-0002-8393-3652
JSS University, Noida, India

Vipin Tyagi
http://orcid.org/0000-0003-4994-3686
Jaypee University of Engineering and Technology, Guna, India

ABSTRACT

As AI is automating traditional programming, the role of humans in software development is moving to higher-level cognitive and evaluative skills. This chapter outlines how systems and architecture design and the coordination of AI-generated code are developing into critical competencies for software developers in an era of AI-aided development. This chapter further describes how oversight, verification and evaluation will become increasingly important as engineers begin to assume the role of "quality gatekeepers," ensuring the accuracy, safety, trustworthiness and sustainability of computer systems. By examining the capabilities that are ex-

DOI: 10.4018/979-8-3373-8450-4.ch005

pected to increase in importance as the automation of computer systems continues to expand, this chapter presents a plan for the reskilling of engineers, development teams and academic programs within a strategic context.

INTRODUCTION

Artificial Intelligence (AI) or, more specifically, Generative AI is transforming the practice of software engineering. Tools like GitHub Copilot and Code Whisperer from Amazon, in addition to the ability to integrate Large Language Models (LLMs) into existing development workflows, provide developers with greater abilities to implement entire functions, modules and complex multi-file scenarios than ever before (Karim et al., 2025). This chapter examines three interconnected shifts in software engineering driven by AI: a move from manual code production to logical reasoning about system capabilities and trade-offs as routine implementation tasks become automated; a transition from localized coding to the design of centralized architectural blueprints, requiring engineers to ensure AI-generated components align with organizational, regulatory and contextual constraints; and a shift from writing code to quality control, as the probabilistic nature of AI-generated outputs increases the need for rigorous verification, validation and oversight to ensure correctness, security, compliance and trustworthiness. These changes show the urgent need to re-train the upcoming generation of software engineers. Instead of being replaced by an AI model, software engineers are being repositioned from an implementation-focused role to one that involves overseeing and evaluating the work of the AI model and to becoming systems-oriented thinkers.

Coding automation is no longer a theoretical concept. It is now proven that engineers using AI complete work faster, with higher satisfaction and lower cognitive load and AI-generated code is increasingly deployed in production. This raises concerns about long-term quality, maintainability and risk propagation, particularly in distributed and microservices architectures.

Many critics believe that depending too much on AI tools leads to deskilling, or an engineer slowly losing the knowledge and ability to produce or understand foundational code. This notion is supported by research conducted in various other fields. In industries that have overstudied the use of automation without sufficient supervision, automation has been found to eliminate many of the situational awareness skills needed by professionals to successfully oversee their systems (Bainbridge, 1983). Deskilling is avoidable and can be mitigated through intentional reskilling. Reskilling is required to cultivate architectural literacy, quality assurance and failure-mode analysis, reasoning about constraints, ethical and security awareness, socio-technical awareness and use of generative AI tools. With appropriate educational and organizational scaffolding, AI will rise to elevate the profession rather than diminish it (Becker et al., 2023). This framework will have three interrelated domains, High-Level Reasoning (problem framing, abstraction, trade-off analysis and Specification Engineering); System and Architecture Design (interface design, dataflows, failure modes, observability and distributed systems thinking); Oversight, Verification and Evaluation (positioning engineers as quality gatekeepers who validate the artifacts produced by AI, assure correctness and manage governance processes). The chapter utilizes Research, Industry Reports and Case Studies, creating a useful roadmap for educational institutions, engineering teams and individual practitioners to follow. In addition, the sections following this introduction will outline how these human competencies will become increasingly important, rather than decreasing, in the rapidly changing development landscape driven by AI.

The Automation Landscape

The tremendous advancement of Generative AI has produced significant automating technologies for Software Development (McIntosh et al., 2025). An example is Large Language Models (LLMs) (e.g. GPT-4, Codex, StarCoder, etc.), which provide a wealth of information about how to generate code in various programming languages successfully. Using such tools, developers can generate simple code snippets to complex, integrated modules. These tools enable developers to refactor their code, write documentation, draft design specifications and much more. However, the performance of these tools varies significantly across the Software Engineering field.

The Spectrum of AI Automation in Software Engineering

The automation of Software Engineering will not be evident through a binary state of replacing human work entirely. It will reside along an automation continuum with generative AI tools performing micro-automation at the low end (i.e. generating boilerplate code, converting between one programming construct to the other, or generating test case inputs) and macro-automation at the opposite end (i.e. AI generating an entire application, system component from a natural language description).

Figure 1. The Automation Spectrum in Software Engineering.

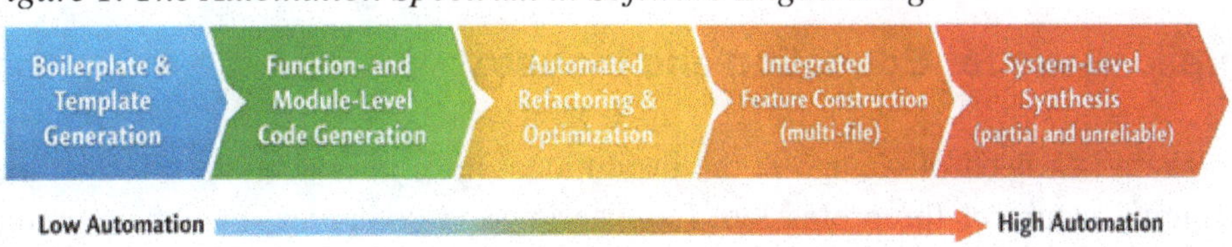

In Figure 1, levels 1-3 represent assistive and semi-automated coding, while levels 4-5 correspond to end-to-end system generation with human oversight. As shown in Figure 1, Automation reliability deteriorates significantly beyond Level 3, with Levels 4 & 5 requiring a high degree of human intervention.

Examples of tasks AI can automate reliably include boilerplate pattern generation, language translation, unit test creation, SQL queries, data models and common syntax or logic fixes (Karim et al., 2025). It remains difficult to automate high-level engineering tasks that require judgment and awareness of the situation. Examples include the systems' architecture, design decisions, rationale for the tradeoffs made between security versus scalability, latency versus cost and detail in resolving ambiguity surrounding requirements; understanding how to interpret ethical versus regulatory constraints (e.g. GDPR); combining multiple services into distributed systems; anticipate failure modes, resiliency post-facto; identify long-term maintainability; perform risk, threat, compliance analyses. These tasks rely on an understanding of an organization's objectives (goals) and the organizational, economic, social context in which it operates, an area in which AI presently falls short (Amershi et al., 2019).

Automation Boundary for Engineering Roles

The growing trend toward automation means that engineering jobs will likely shift away from writing code and toward thinking critically about the way a system works as a whole. The majority of the work involved in creating a system will still take place in the mind of a human engineer. Human engineers are responsible for ensuring that systems are designed correctly; they are also the ones primarily responsible for performing quality assurance on the system. Humans will develop new skills to coordinate the use of generative tools. Although AI is capable of doing many tasks very well e.g., pattern replication, syntactic fluency, producing known structures and accelerating repetitive tasks, there are a number of areas in which AI does not perform as well as a human, such as the ability to think critically, identify risk, make ethical judgments and coordinate social and technical constraints among various stakeholders (Brown et al., 2020). The engineers who will be most successful in the future will be the ones who can combine a solid technical foundation with an ability to effectively oversee the entire development process.

Implications for Education and Industry

There is a need of change at the institutional level in education to reflect the changing nature of the profession. Engineering and computer science programs should de-emphasize the use of implementation-only type assignments and instead emphasize problem framing, systems thinking, architecture, testing and governance. Implementation of a product in isolation is becoming less and less valuable, so institutions will be able to deliver the most value to their students by emphasizing the areas of focus mentioned above and allowing for a more in-depth exploration of the way systems work. Teams in Industry should begin to evolve from using output metrics, such as lines of code, to using outcome metrics, such as quality, resilience, safety and maintainability. While developing these outcome metrics, teams must ensure that software engineers have strong review skills and critical reasoning, as well as not rely too heavily on AI.

HIGH-LEVEL REASONING

As Generative AI is automating the majority of lower level coding tasks, the value proposition for software engineers has shifted from implementation to the elements of human cognition that are currently not able to be automated. High-level reasoning is the primary differentiator for engineers as well as the manner in which engineers approach creating software solutions in an ever evolving AI based environment. This section examines the nature of high level reasoning, the reasons why it is unique to humans and how it serves as the basis of how engineers create and execute directions on the implementation of AI based systems.

Importance of High-Level Reasoning in Automated Coding

As routine implementation work is being increasingly automated, the non-routine work performed by humans is beginning to focus on resolving non-routine issues and therefore require a greater understanding of conceptual clarity, complexity of decisions, the ability to interpret contexts, the requirement to assess and manage risk and to ultimately apply both moral and regulatory judgments and the mindset of long-term thinking. People performing routine jobs that were previously performed by another person may be assigned supervisory tasks, since they will now be responsible for managing unforeseen interference and unusual incidents that necessitate a higher level of analytical judgement (Buschmann et al., 2007). Although a faster code production using AI can increase an individual's efficiency in developing a software application, there is potential for error in the outcome because the AI cannot identify logical flaws resulting from a lack of well-developed critical thinking.

Components of High-Level Reasoning in Software Engineering

High-level reasoning is not a singular skill, but rather encompasses multiple interconnected capabilities that are integrated into the daily workflow of building Generative AI Systems. These capabilities, when established, help determine whether the outputs produced by the generative AI system will be a coherent and reliable system or a series of hastily produced fragments of code. In order to be able to properly solve an issue that is being addressed by leveraging AI, an engineer is still required to define the true nature of the issue, identify constraints to the solution, variables required to determine the relative success of the solution and the user or business objectives that determine the behaviour of AI-based solution. Examples are decisions made to determine whether to maximize latency or throughput, prioritize privacy over personalization, or give up redundancy for cost savings (Ford et al., 2017). To make such decisions, a high level of situational awareness and an ability to make sense of things will be necessary; however, these characteristics are not capabilities of AI. Software engineers working in a real-world environment will face competing constraints such as scalability vs. cost, performance vs. reliability, speed vs. quality; privacy vs. personalization and innovation vs. compliance.

Reasons High-Level Reasoning is Unique to Human

There are many reasons why high-level reasoning continues to be a distinctly human capability that is not available to AI (Li et al., 2019). Human beings typically have an intention when forming goals and creating plans and priorities, whereas an AI system's output is based completely on the programmed algorithm and it does not have the same degree of intention or purposefulness. Humans have contextual knowledge of the socio-technical world around them, which includes organizational politics, legal requirements of business and cultural expectations; therefore, humans can exercise their own individual values while evaluating whether an action is ethical or unacceptable, regardless of statistically-derived predictions. AI systems do not have experience as humans do and there are many verifiable cues that are used by humans to form judgments that are typically unavailable to AI systems (Benraouane, 2024). In conclusion, technology intersects with economic, psychological and law concepts, where humans can utilize their understanding of the integration of these disciplines to better understand what we want to achieve (the system). These disciplines will provide information about the things to avoid (outcome of the technology). It is important to note that the technology and the disciplines need to be considered together when developing the integrated solution.

Integration of High-Level Reasoning into AI-Augmented Workflows

High-Level reasoning will not be eliminated through the use of AI; it will be given an increased priority because the rate and quantity of implementation will increase. Engineers, using AI, will integrate high-level reasoning throughout the workflow; during the development, set the problem, establish a specification of requirements, identify constraints and create an architectural model and use AI-assisted coding to improve their prompts, break the work down into logical components and choose an appropriate tool or model (Karekezi et al., 2025). Following the creation of the code by AI, engineers will check for the correctness of the code, assess the overall compatibility of the code with the existing architecture, find any missed risks and reconcile conflicting assumptions between the services that were provided by the AI (Ford et al., 2017). Finally, high-level reasoning will help engineer AI-generated artifacts to maintain their functionality and be maintainable and as a result of the increasing volume of AI-generated artifacts, engineers will be able to achieve their objectives more quickly and efficiently than ever.

SYSTEM AND ARCHITECTURE DESIGN

As AI continues to automate the activity of constructing functions, classes, modules and in many cases even functional software application skeletons, software engineering will begin shifting from "how to build an application" (implementation) to "what to build" (design, architecture) and "how to get those component pieces to work together" (Buschmann et al., 2007). As system design had been considered the activity of an experienced senior engineer, AI is putting new emphasis on the design of systems as it - even though it will produce code - cannot yet intelligently identify the context of business, stakeholder needs, sociotechnical boundaries, compliance obligations and long-term architecture trade-offs. Once businesses began automating assembly lines, the role of the employee subsequently is transitioned to supervising the machinery, planning assembly procedures and validating quality control (Kim et al., 2014). As software is progressively being built by machines, engineers too will need to transition to cognitive activities which build abstractions of the system and architecturally mitigate the short-term vs long-term of engineering decision- making. In AI-driven development, system design ensures coherence among AI-generated components, supports long-term modularity, scalability and maintainability and embeds reliability, security and governance into the system foundation. Therefore, system design becomes the guiding "north star" for directing AI-Driven coding toward sustainable, interpretable and ethically aligned technical results.

The Human Role

As programming becomes easier and less expensive due to increasing levels of automation, organizations will continue to distinguish engineers from one another based on their conceptual abilities rather than their level of programming fluency. Engineers are now expected to provide clarity on the conceptual level of product design as well as developing the architecture of the products. An engineer must effectively frame problems by converting unclear specifications into clear design intent; develop abstraction models with the necessary interaction boundaries that must be observed; and decompose all appropriate code components into discrete modules. As the engineer becomes an integral member of the technical architecture development team, their role shifts from being a component developer to being an architect who is responsible for integrating and coordinating the use of AI generated software with the other aspects of the entire architecture. The Human-in-the-Loop architecture workflow for AI-Augmented development is shown in Figure 2.

Figure 2. Human-in-the-Loop Architecture Workflow for AI-Augmented Development.

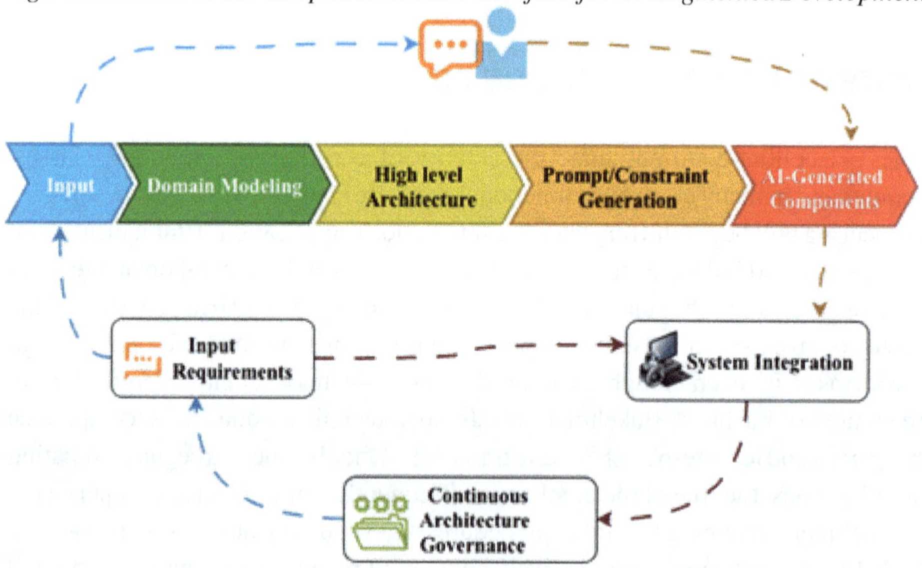

Core Architectural Competencies Elevated by AI Automation

AI-generated outputs shift greater responsibility onto architects, as output quality depends on the clarity of human-defined architectural intent. Architects must ensure AI-generated components align within a coherent system vision, a role increasingly formalized as Intent or Specification Engineering, which bridges design and AI generation through explicitly defined goals. Because AI lacks domain understanding, Domain-Driven Design is essential to align generated code with business intent by defining entities, bounded contexts and dependencies. Ultimately, selecting appropriate architectural patterns remains a human responsibility, as it depends on organizational maturity, team capabilities, regulatory constraints and runtime readiness beyond AI's contextual awareness.

It is important for engineers to find when using a monolithic design vs microservices is best, whether applying either event-driven or reactive approaches to their desired domain is appropriate and when an orchestration model should supplement a choreography model or vice-versa to address the growing complexity and accountability of systems under development. The ultimate architectural challenge lies in governance rather than algorithm; if governance is not deployed the speed at which development occurs accelerates entropy, thereby eroding the long-term integrity of the system.

Designing Systems for AI Collaboration

AI development tools should be viewed as partners or co-creators versus replacing humans. Therefore, architects must design architectures that support human-AI collaboration. Architectural characteristics that support human, AI collaboration need to be clear, modular and enforceable constraints that enable automated code creation and integration safely and uniformly into existing systems. An architectural decision should always be documented, constraints expressed as structures and represented in machine-readable format wherever feasible; this will reduce ambiguity and enhance the ability of AI tools to consistently follow the design rules instead of generating code "that looks good" but does not meet standards. Finally, given the possibility of verbosity or tight coupling when AI tools create code, the use of modular boundaries provides a safety buffer to limit the size of change and facilitate review.

The assistance of engineers for Hybrid systems does not diminish the need for clear interfaces, contracts with clear separation of concerns, rules of dependency injection and the design of failure isolation zones to contain inconsistencies and regressions in the generated code rather than allowing for systemic failures at scale. Hybrid systems also provide a declarative set of constraints that may be easily restated, enforced, tested. Therefore, early embedding of guardrails prevents the rise of insecure patterns. Therefore, it is critical for the architect to define the threat models, implement least-privileges rules, establish data handling constraints and identify where encryption is expected, then publicize audit log requirements that view security and compliance as first class constraints of the architecture instead of a patchwork downstream effectively.

Architecture Prompts and Template-Driven System Design

As generative AI becomes embedded in development, architectural artifacts are evolving from static documents into dynamic, reusable controls that encode design intent directly into generative workflows. Through Architecture-as-Prompt, artifacts such as Infrastructure as Code, event-driven rules and Domain-Driven Design definitions guide AI behavior, reduce design drift and improve alignment across AI-generated components.

Ensuring Scalability, Robustness and Maintainability in AI-Generated Codebases

Generative AI has an incredible ability to create code quickly and therefore is a large source of structural risk if it is not constrained by disciplined architecture. Therefore, architectural oversight is the primary method by which System Teams can maintain Scalability, Robustness and Maintainability. If no guidance is provided to the generative AI about how to generate code and how to evolve it, it will produce code using very simplistic models, such as synchronous blocking calls, excessive database queries, or excessive use of in-memory caches, which will degrade Scalability as loads increase. Architectural governance and review mechanisms facilitate the discovery of these patterns prior to widespread adoption in the code base. Designing for operational resilience should never be assumed; rather, engineers should specify operational resiliency requirements as part of their architecture, such as reducing the likelihood of failure through fault-tolerant messaging, retry logic, circuit breakers, handling backpressure and conducting chaos resilience testing. Architectural governance must implement a consistent approach to enforce maintainability through the use of refactoring cycles, linters and static analysis and architecture fitness functions, which are used to maintain the system's coherence throughout growth. Table 1 shows the human system design skills that gain value in the AI driven development.

Table 1. Human System Design Skills That Gain Value in AI-Driven Development

Skill	Why it Gains Value	AI Limitations
Domain modeling	Anchors AI code in business semantics	Lacks full context
Architecture pattern selection	Ensures long-term scalability	Cannot reliably choose global patterns
Intent engineering	Guides generative models	Misinterprets ambiguous instructions

continued on following page

Table 1. Continued

Skill	Why it Gains Value	AI Limitations
Governance design	Controls AI-generated complexity	Does not enforce policies
Trade-off reasoning	Balances cost, performance, risks	Cannot weigh contextual constraints

Framework of an AI-Integrated Architecture Review Process

The combination of AI and human intelligence provides a structured workflow for implementation and conduct their architecture reviews. The architecture review workflow starts with alignment of intent, identifying the goals of the system and establishing constraints, creating a preliminary model of the system; followed by the development of an overall architecture outline, which is initially created by humans, then validated against data produced by AI. A team can then use AI to explore various architectural options before humans perform a trade-off analysis on the identified options. After examining this scenario briefly, it very likely will be repeated often because the business demands for many clients in this industry are causing an increase in the number of systems that can use this technology to develop applications. Following example shows how to define this kind of platform and develop an AI-generated system.

ORCHESTRATION OF AI-GENERATED CODE

As AI systems assume responsibility for generating increasingly large portions of application logic, a new category of engineering work emerges-code orchestration. Unlike traditional programming, orchestration involves coordinating, integrating, constraining and supervising AI-generated components so that they function as a coherent whole. While AI excels at producing syntactically correct and semantically plausible code fragments, it lacks the capacity to ensure alignment with global system structure, domain rules, cross-cutting concerns and long-term maintainability. Human engineers thus become the conductors of AI-generated codebases, ensuring that thousands of automatically generated elements operate in harmony (Leveson, 2012).

AI-assisted software development relies on an integrated orchestration workflow in which engineers define high-level intent and architectural constraints, then iteratively validate, test and refine AI-generated components to ensure coherence, correctness and well-defined module boundaries before integration.

Prompt Engineering for Code Orchestration

Prompt engineering for orchestration systems entails much more than just requesting short snippets of code. Multi-component systems require prompts that represent all architectural patterns, boundaries of modules and interfaces, contracts on the type of data exchanged across modules, cross-cutting rules (e.g., error handling, security, etc.) and the desired levels of performance of all components that are generated by AI (P. L. Li et al., 2019). The teams utilize both structured prompts, which can be thought of as standard templates for encoding architectural intent and constraint prompts which allow teams to explicitly instruct the model on what functionality to include and exclude. Multi-level prompting is critical for large scale implementations. High-level prompts establish global expectations and guidance at component level provide local guidance; together they can serve as a coordination mechanism for a complex generation pipeline.

Patterns of Orchestration

As orchestration type(s) may vary in patterns based on team maturity and system complexity, Teams may use one of the following orchestration patterns to coordinate the work of AI: Top-down Orchestration - The Architect provides the overall Structure, then utilizes AI to complete the details of the Implementation. This pattern is also referred to as "Classical Model Driven Engineering." Bottom-up Orchestration - The AI provides the team with candidate solutions first whereby the team "Reverse Engineers" the patterns in candidate solutions, prior to determining the solutions to retain, modify, improve, etc.). Middle-out orchestration combines the strengths of Top-down and Bottom-up since humans define key abstractions and constraints and the AI builds upon the key abstractions and constraints. Teams utilize a multi-agent orchestration strategy to focus on many specialized agents for different tasks (such as architecture generation, test creation, documentation, refactoring and performance optimization) while the engineer oversees the coordination of outputs and resolves conflicts among agents in the ecosystem. Figure 3 shows a circular workflow of collaborative pipeline.

Figure 3. Human-AI Collaborative Orchestration Pipeline.

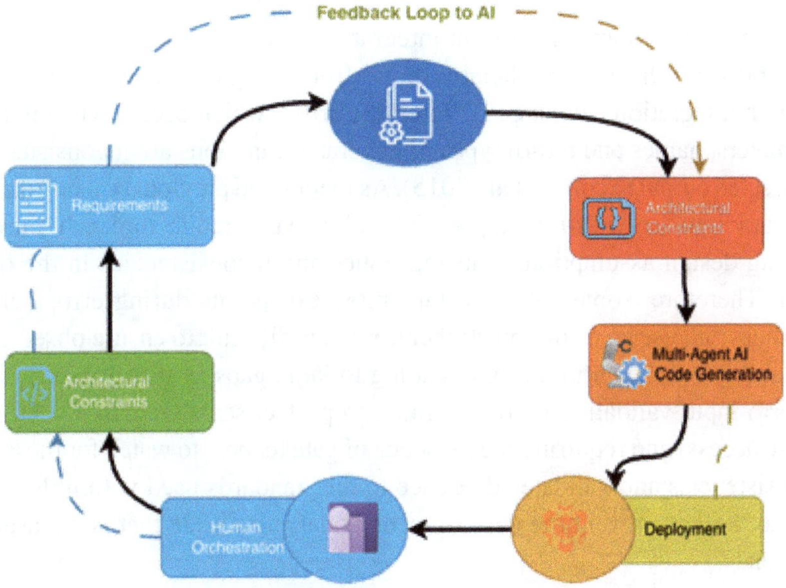

Managing the Complexity Explosion in AI-Generated Codebases

As well as providing large amounts of code at high speed, generative AI also increases the potential for structural risks such as hidden coupling, semantic drift, duplicate logic, unused branches and inconsistent naming. Therefore, orchestration will require mechanisms for managing these increased levels of complexity. These include: automatic deduplication and pattern detection tools to search for duplicate code and patterns, as well as semantic code search and mapping tools that enable engineers to conduct behaviour-based queries instead of searching through file names and structural integrity checks to validate that generated code contains the correct interfaces, dependencies and adherence to architectural fitness functions. Continuous refactoring pipelines, which are usually AI-assisted, are beneficial for helping to keep code bases clean; however, they still necessitate human oversight to validate that the intent of the refactored code is preserved, that regression testing is performed and that the refactored code is achieved using long-term goals in mind.

Integration Challenges Unique to AI-Generated Components

AI-generated components present integration challenges because their outputs are probabilistic rather than predictably drawn from a single, coherent design model. A common integration challenge is "interface drift", which occurs when the order of parameters, names and return types of generated functions are inconsistent with their expected output (Sculley et al., 2015). As mentioned previously, using different design paradigms-such as merging MVC with Clean Architecture may introduce conflicting design assumptions, causing issues and inconsistencies in the overall solution. Therefore, some modules will throw exceptions during error handling while others will use an error object; therefore, it is difficult to ensure observability and reliability for the entire design, leading to large gaps in security (e.g., failure to perform input validation on data, failure to protect sensitive data, or failure to authorize access) and requiring the presence of gatekeepers to watch for these types of inconsistencies and validate adherence to the standards used within the overall system, as well as prevent the development of defective code that is released into production.

AI-Assisted Integration Testing and Verification

AI has the potential to improve the efficiency of verifying applications by automatically generating Unit Tests, Integration Tests, Mocks, Stubs and Test Data. However, humans still determine what tests are useful, how to organize test suites and how to verify new behaviors (i.e., behaviors that only occur when components interact). While AI-generated tests enable faster test coverage, they can also contain anti-patterns; e.g., they may be created with too high a level of abstraction, exclude edge cases, fail to simulate concurrency, or misinterpret the nature of external dependencies. Accordingly, proper orchestration of AI-generated tests and human judgment is critical for achieving appropriate balance between the speed of AI and the accuracy of human-created tests and for scaling coverage with the use of AI while relying on the engineers for accurate and thorough test coverage and realistic risk-based prioritization of testing.

Governance Models for AI-Generated Code

Governance prevents increased autonomy from creating inconsistencies and introducing risks into systems. Architectural governance provides a framework for approved coding patterns, coding standards, documentation formats, dependencies on other systems, data-sharing policies so that AI-generated codes will always adhere to the organization's standards. Ethical governance protects patient privacy through regulatory compliance and responsible handling of algorithmic fairness and auditability; both of these are essential for any system dealing with personal, sensitive information or substantial decisions; these requirements enable accountability and build trust in these kinds of systems. Finally, operational governance standardizes practices, monitoring techniques, error-reporting methods that implement and rely on these systems (Shneiderman, 2020). Without these governance structures in place at the organizational level, AI-generated solutions have a high probability of diverging from organization-level standards, making them much more challenging to support and believe in as credible.

VERIFICATION, OVERSIGHT AND QUALITY GATEKEEPING

As the Generative AI models continue to automate many aspects of software development, implementation, resulting in significant changes in how we approach development. However, AI-generated code has a fundamentally different risk profile (Sculley et al., 2015), introducing exposure to hidden logic errors from nondeterministic behavior, hallucinated APIs or libraries, latent security vulnerabilities, fragile edge-case handling and subtle misalignment between stated intent and actual behavior. Because of this, Oversight, Verification and Quality Gatekeeping of Generative AI code has become critical and the strategically important activity has shifted from writing code to ensuring AI-generated code is "safe," "correct" and "trustworthy." Thus, Engineers are developing a dual role where they not only validate the technical specifications of a product (correctness, performance, reliability) but also manage the risk associated with having products that comply with Safety, Compliance, Ethics and Readiness for Use (Vaswani, A. et al., 2017) This balance of Quality Gatekeeping is now considered one of the pillars of professional engineering practice.

The Evolution of Verification in the Age of Generative AI

Validation in traditional Software Engineering had primarily focused on Syntax and requirement matching, as AI Technology has matured, there is a need to develop a more comprehensive validation strategy. Validation should occur at many levels during the Development Life Cycle including, semantic validation to ensure the output will maintain the original intent, Architectural validation to ensure the output is consistent with the systems design, Behavioural validation to identify unexpected, emergent behaviours, data validation to verify the data used for training and AI generated data is clean, free from bias where applicable and compliance validation to verify that the product meets or exceeds all statutory and industry requirements.

Engineers as "Quality Gatekeepers"

The workflow for engineering using AI has a designated gatekeeping function, which is an individual tasked with ensuring the safe and accountable operation of AI-generated engineering products, such as software. While Quality gatekeeping can sometimes slow down the delivery process, its core goal is to keep unsafe errors from accumulating within the software development process, thus producing systemic risk. A quality gatekeeper is an engineering professional who governs the outputs of generative AI, evaluates the correctness of the outputs and their reliability and ethical consequences, enforces architectural and policy controls, maintains traceable audit trails for their decisions and produces the necessary documentation before releasing or deploying the outputs. The Quality Gatekeeper's function is to assure AI-based Development Pipelines produce products and other output that are functional, accountable and Safe and not just syntactically correct. Examples of primary responsibilities of a Quality Gatekeeper are reviewing AI-generated code, running behavioural testing to find latent defects, verifying the outputs conform to the system architecture, confirming compliance with security, privacy and regulatory compliance, documenting decisions to allow for traceability and evaluating the reliability and mode of operation of the AI agents that produced the output (Cheng et al., 2024).

Verification Techniques for AI-Generated Codebases

AI-generated code can look 'correct' on the surface, but underneath it may contain many errors that can be hard to find or detect. Consequently, this necessitates a multi-layered approach to verifying that AI-generated code is correct: one must combine static inspections (analysis of the code without executing it) with runtime and behavioral evaluations (Bird et al., 2015). The disadvantages of static analysis tools lead to situations where AI-generated code could pass a superficial static analysis only for hidden structural or semantic issues to become evident when running it. In addition, Dynamic testing must incorporate more rigorous testing to determine how an AI-generated code's logic will operate on edge-case inputs and with other concurrent running instances.

Property-Based testing is essential for AI-Generated codes because generative models will fail in unexpected ways and for unpredictable reasons. Instead of testing with a limited set of inputs as with standard testing, Property-Based testing approach will validate generic properties over a broad spectrum of applicable input ranges. As such, property-based testing provides validation that counteracts assumptions made when writing logic that depend solely on a few examples. This is important because of the speed with which code could potentially be developed and redeveloped. In areas of Safety Critical domains (e.g. healthcare, autonomous transportation, defence systems and financial auditing) formal methods and verification based on mathematical reasoning are regaining importance. Characteristics of AI, the way it produces results, makes the value of independent guarantees (unlike the results produced by a person or model) very important, especially when a failure means that a significant and serious problem will occur in the real world.

Oversight in Multi-Agent AI Development Pipelines

Therefore, more and more organisations now utilise many different kinds of specialised AI agents to generate code and create tests, documentation, refactor code, performance tune output, etc. Although this was an excellent boost in productivity, it also significantly increases the risk of conflicts caused by coordination failure among agents before code can be merged into a single version of code. An example is inconsistent assumptions made by agents; incompatible outputs produced by agents; version drift caused by confusion among agents; and conflicting interpretations of requirements by different agents. A critical success factor for humans in this regard is providing the oversight necessary to ensure that agents are aligned with one another, have a means of communicating, provide a single merged output and maintain consistent interfaces across multiple versions of the output. Therefore, it is essential that the human monitors the role and limitations of each agent, prevents agents from producing outputs that contradict one another, enforces consistency through the use of meta-prompts or shared constraints for each agent's output and maintains a human oversight of approval for each critical step of the process. The objective is to ensure that multiple agents do not act as separate agents who produce potentially incompatible artefacts, but rather act together as a cohesive unit.

Security and Privacy Verification in AI-Generated Systems

AI code generation can result in subtle security vulnerabilities caused by a lack of sanitization, insecure default settings, etc. Security verification and privacy verification for each piece of AI-generated code require a sustained architectural approach because of the potential profusion of these security vulnerabilities across numerous generated modules. Threat modelling and the assessment of trust boundaries, configuration weaknesses and access-control paths, as well as the identification of attack surfaces prior to the large-scale generation of code are critical components of security verification and privacy verification in AI-generated code. Threat models also provide the foundation of the constraints on what code should be developed and what code should not be developed with AI assistance. Security testing methodologies, including fuzz testing, penetration testing and dependency vulnerability scanning continue to be vital. These methodologies are the primary means of identifying security vulnerabilities that may not be identifiable through just reviewing a given code base, especially when the AI-generative design processes embed common coding patterns in the generated output, allowing the replication of minor coding errors across multiple generated modules. In the case of regulated industries, compliance checks of privacy law requirements are also necessary, particularly in the context of frameworks, such as GDPR, HIPAA, PCI DSS and India's DPDP Act. In conclusion, in order to avoid the negative effects of using AI to create potentially insecure or non-compliant software, it is essential to ensure that there is full coordination among multiple agents as they produce the software. Whether the implementation is automatically produced or not, Gatekeepers are responsible for making sure that all data handling, logging, storage, retention and access procedures comply with legal requirements and the organization's policies.

Ethical and Interpretability Oversight

Verification of AI-augmented systems involves not only checking for technical correctness but also ensuring that the system is fair, transparent, free from bias and explainable, particularly in areas such as safety, financial, health and rights decisions, where the consequences of the decisions made by AI systems are significant. Because AI systems can produce hallucinated results and because both completeness and accuracy in the development and use of AI systems are generally not established through clear and accessible provenance, ethical oversight for AI systems has transitioned from being viewed as an abstract notion to a practical necessity for engineers working with such technologies. Engineers must be able to determine whether or not their AI-augmented systems can be interpreted and to provide a complete audit trail from which to make the necessary evaluations about AI's reasoning process.

Human-AI Feedback Loops

As AI systems generate and revise code, engineers will need to continually evaluate the quality of the changes. Working in most cases from a system that proposes changes, generates options and proposes solutions, there will be a continual feedback loop from engineers and AI systems that results in the continued evolution of a verification process. As new systems develop, the limitations on engineers' ability to complete their work will continue to change and architects and management will continue to provide oversight to ensure that AI systems are safe to use, maintain correct operation and operate consistently throughout the entire life of the system. Figure 4 shows the human AI verification loop stages.

Figure 4. Human AI Verification Loop.

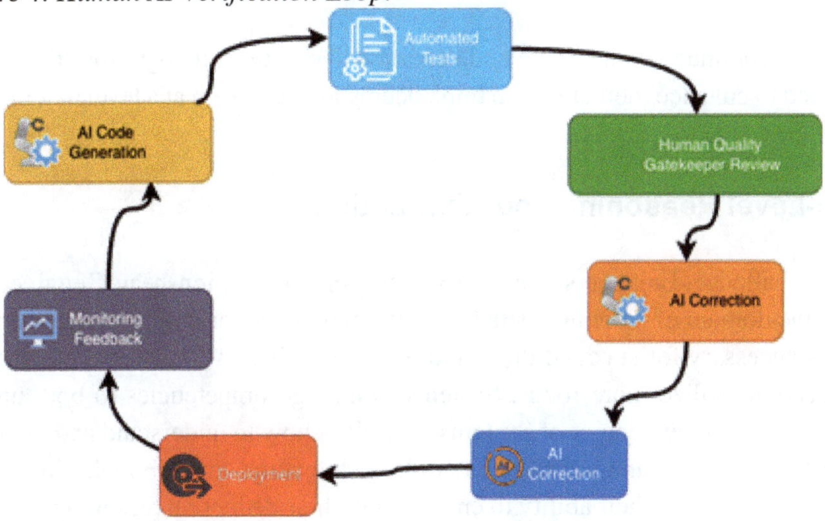

RESKILLING PATHWAYS AND COMPETENCY FRAMEWORKS FOR THE AI-AUGMENTED ENGINEER

With the evolution of AI-driven automation in software engineering (i.e., AI is freely implemented in all software engineering processes), what practitioners, educators and companies are asking now is not just what jobs will be replaced by AI but what types of human-centered skills will determine how successful a person will be working with software that has been developed with automation capabilities. The following framework demonstrates a clearly defined progression to update the existing skill sets of the Future Workforce to accommodate the evolving AI, human workflow and is composed of following components: Skills for Cognitive and Conceptual Development; Technical Knowledge & Architectural Knowledge; Skills for AI Orchestration and Prompt Engineering; Skills relating to the Quality, Verification, Safety of Computational Intelligence; and Professional, Ethical, Cross-Disciplinary Skills. Taken together, all of these areas create a multi-dimensional competency model to support Software Engineers transitioning into roles within the higher-level design, oversight, integration and evaluation of AI development ecosystems (Karekezi et al., 2025).

Cognitive and Conceptual Skill Development

As AI continues to automate code creation and pattern recognition, Engineers will need to enhance their ability to think deeply and to reason at a level that models are still not able to achieve.

High-Level Reasoning and Abstraction

The challenges Engineers face when working on "abstraction-heavy" engineering tasks (the domain of incoming data to be interpreted and, or modified) and competencies necessary for successfully working within this new landscape will require Engineers to utilize more robust Systems Thinking competencies to both understand the Interdependencies of Systems, as well as how to understand and interpret emergent behaviour and interactions at the architectural level. Equally important to Engineers will be their ability to engage both their deductive reasoning and also their ability to engage in Abductive Reasoning as they expand their knowledge of how to troubleshoot AI-generated output and identify subtle integration errors. In order to do this, engineers also need to compensate for the lack of contextual sensitivity that may exist in code generated by artificial intelligence (AI) as well as to ensure that the designs created by AI-generated code are aligned with business and regulatory and organizational objectives.

Problem Framing and Domain Modeling

When implementation of a code-based solution is easier than implementation of the solution through other means, the process by which engineers define the appropriate problem to address becomes more important. Engineers must be able to take very vague requirements provided by users and develop these vague requirements into well-structured domain models and to identify implicit constraints and non-functional requirements, model potential failure modes and risk scenarios and develop algorithmic or architectural patterns to achieve system-level goals. Engineering advantage in this case has moved from problem-solving at the level of the generated code to framing the problem at the level of the system. In other words, the explicit definition of the problem will determine whether the use of automation will create value or simply provide further acceleration of the misalignment.

Technical and Architectural Upskilling

As AI systems will generate code components but will not be able to ensure that the final product will be coherent at a system level, engineers will need to build their understanding of how to design the architecture that provides a resilient, maintainable and governable framework for code generated by AI systems to ensure the code will not degrade into a condition that is inconsistent with the architecture. The future success of engineering will depend on the development of modular, resilient, explainable systems that can incorporate code generated by AI systems without collapsing into a state of inconsistency. AI will generate modules much faster than human architects can create, but human architects still need to define boundaries, contracts, failure modes and observability assumptions to preserve performance, safety and maintainability. AI-intensive systems will introduce new challenges that traditional software does not have to deal with in regard to drift management and safe model updates; therefore, organizations need to reskill their workers to add capabilities such as MLOps pipelines and automation workflows (that include A, B testing), AI reliability engineering, Model Versioning and Dependency Management tooling, explainability (explanation of how a model makes decisions), introspection interfaces (documenting how models are performing) and Data Engineering capabilities to ensure engineers will have the tools and knowledge they need to continue bridging the world of traditional software engineering with the newly created AI lifecycle governance to maintain stability and accountability of the systems as models evolve.

AI Orchestration and Prompt Engineering Competencies

As organizations begin to embed LLMs into workflows, engineers must learn how to organize or orchestrate the generative tools they use so that they can produce outputs that are consistent, constrained and verifiable rather than random bursts of potentially plausible code. Completing this task requires an applicable skill set including understanding structured prompting, breaking down tasks into solvable units, using role-based prompts, iterating through refinements during the process, utilizing prompt correction and developing scaffolding techniques that apply ethically and securely to improve the reliability of reasoning without compromising safety or confidentiality. The newest LLM ecosystems support an increasing number of multi-agent workflows in which multiple specialized agents are working together to complete various functions related to architecture generation, testing, documentation, refactoring and optimization. As such, engineers will need to learn how to create agent hierarchies, assign roles, define goals and constraints, connect agents to system APIs and software development toolchains, evaluate agent actions and performance and avoid potential failure modes such as feedback loops, hallucination cascades and unsafe action chains. Effective orchestration relies upon how well humans manage agents and systemizes their operations while creating rules for policy and safety.

AI systems may be able to create syntactically correct code but they can also produce code that is semantically inconsistent with enterprise constraints, this means that the engineer must develop orchestration techniques for safe integration, for example, code reviews developing patterns used by AI code generation, integration testing that stresses non-functional requirements, refactoring strategies and techniques to reduce duplication in code developed by AI, security validation processes to identify subtle vulnerabilities in automated coding practices. In the enterprise environment, the question will not be based upon whether an AI can generate code but rather upon whether the engineer can consistently integrate an AI generated piece of code into a system that will still be secure, dependable and in alignment with the enterprise.

Quality, Verification and Safety Skills

As artificial intelligence moves engineering away from traditional methods of review, validation and oversight, the focus on quality shifts from being a downstream check point to a primary discipline within engineering. The role of an engineer is shifting to become a "trust guarantor" for AI-generated artifacts as they are responsible for ensuring that these types of artifacts function correctly, safely and consistently in the context of real-world constraints. In addition to the typical responsibilities of gatekeeping, engineers in an AI-mediated development ecosystem are tasked with blending technical diligence with risk understanding. This includes, but is not limited to, carefully evaluating code and artifacts to identify any discrepancies, conducting audits of model performance to uncover patterns of failure, assessing potential bias and fairness wherever AI is used to impact people's lives or influence decisions, completing traceability analysis to ensure that the responsible parties are held accountable if failures occur and doing robustness testing of AI artifacts through adversial inputs (adversarial incidence) to verify if they break. In essence, engineers are now responsible for assuring that automation produces both executable codes but also accountable and responsible systems. The aspect of testing should adapt to include more than a deterministic assumption of AI-generated components because AI-produced components can vary between executions and may even include hidden failure-prone logic.

Therefore, modern testing engineering practices are expanding to include AI differential testing, evaluation of model drift to recognize when degradation occurs, evaluation of non-deterministic behavior to understand how stable and repeatable a product can perform over time and evaluation of component or system performance through scenario simulation in realistic environments. Engineers need to establish strong human validation loops when using AI-based test generation in order to ensure that their tests address meaningful risk rather than just superficial behaviour. Human-in-the-loop (HITL) guidelines dictate how engineers should build oversight pipelines to ensure accountability, safety, compliance, transparency and operational integrity throughout the entire development life cycle. These guidelines should define what needs to be reviewed by people, what sign-offs need to occur, what audit trails need to be maintained and how exceptions should be escalated. Since many risks are either legal, regulatory, or reputational, as well as technical, engineers have to work closely with their legal, compliance and risk management teams to establish that the compliance obligations are enforced in practice and not just documented.

Professional, Ethical and Cross-Disciplinary Fluencies

As software systems continue to embed AI capability and influence human results, engineering expertise must evolve from a focus on simply providing technical solutions to understanding the ethical implications of technology on human beings, creating human-centric designed products and collaborating with multiple disciplines during the engineering process. Engineers will need to acquire knowledge regarding ethics, law, data governance and privacy. Additionally, they will also need to know how to create truly fair, unbiased algorithms and provide transparent communications regarding the risks associated with AI on humans, such as system limitations and how to conduct a safe deployment of AI technology. Therefore, because legal obligations and ethical responsibilities are core systems defining requirements, responsible AI cannot simply be an option; it has to be a fundamental part of creating technically correct software systems.

Reskilling increasingly requires engineers to design AI-based systems that effectively support users, combining UX principles, cognitive ergonomics and interaction design with an understanding of trust, error and misalignment in human–AI collaboration. Success depends on integrating social and psychological insight with technical expertise, collaborating across domains such as business, policy, cybersecurity and data science and translating technical constraints into organizational and strategic decisions.

A Unified Reskilling Framework

This competency framework provides an integrated capability model for the future of engineering. The competency pyramid consists of five blended layers that build upon and reinforce each other. The first layer is the foundational level, which consists of cognitive skills and strategies for reasoning, abstracting and systems thinking; the second layer contains the architectural knowledge of advanced overall system design and development; the third layer is considered the AI orchestration layer, encompassing the ability to design and coordinate many different agents or AI systems to solve complex problems; the fourth layer is the verification and safety layer, which involves establishing safety and quality gatekeeping processes, developing utilisation guidelines for the AI and creating an appropriate governance framework for the safe implementation of the AI system. Finally, the fifth level is the professional fluency level, which includes core values of ethical conduct and collaboration across all domains of expertise. The pyramid illustrates the continuum of engineering advantage resulting from increasing automation of systems and the resulting transition of engineers' roles from system implementers to systems thinkers and subsequently, overseers and, or governors.

Structured Learning Pathways

The implementation of this framework will require organizations to create phased reskilling pathways that will be built on a foundation from basic skills to the point at which individual employee has the skill set necessary to oversee others at the leadership level. In the first phase (0-3 months), engineers will develop foundational skills, such as an ability to use systems thinking principles, an understanding of the fundamentals of prompt engineering, be able to refresh their existing architectural knowledge and skills and understand the ethical use of AI. In phase two (3-9 months), Engineers will begin to increase their technical skills and their ability to orchestrate AI solutions by learning to create ML Ops pipelines, creating AI, Human Workflow Designs, Training inconsistently in regards to (but not limited to) creating multi-agent orchestrations and to Build Secure Designs (threat modelling). The third phase (9-18 months) will include Developing Leadership and Gatekeeping Skills through creating Audits of AI Models, creating Explainable AI, creating Safe & Reliable AI and Developing additional Domain-Specialization in areas such as Health-care, Finance and Manufacturing.

Implications for Academia, Industry and Policy

Enabling this reskilling shift requires coordinated action across education, industry and public policy. Academia should integrate AI coding assistants into curricula, move beyond measuring code volume toward evaluating reasoning and design skills and strengthen training in AI ethics and governance through interdisciplinary programs. Industry should establish new roles such as AI code reviewer and AI safety engineer, alongside structured reskilling initiatives and internal governance frameworks. Policymakers should prioritize national reskilling efforts, standards for AI safety and reliability and funding for interdisciplinary research to align technological progress with economic and societal resilience.

CASE STUDIES IN AI-AUGMENTED ENGINEERING PRACTICE

Following case studies provide evidence of the shift in how AI-assisted development changes engineering workflows, redistributes cognitive load and increases strategic value of higher-order reasoning, verification, & orchestration. This section takes examples from industry, open-source ecosystems & enterprise engineering environments to show opportunities and challenges that arise from scaling AI tool integration. The selected cases are drawn from the following five representative domains: large-scale enterprise modernization; AI-assisted rapid prototyping in start-ups; open source adoption of AI-enabled contribution tools; safety-critical deployments with strict oversight; experimental multi-agent development workflows.

Case Study 1: Enterprise Legacy Modernization at Scale

A background examination of how Legacy COBOL, Java Systems and the resulting constraints caused delays and mistakes in Modernization Projects. A Fortune 500 Financial Services Company collected Legacy COBOL, Java Systems over approximately two decades, resulting in modernisation projects that were slow, cumbersome, error-prone and expensive to implement. The Corporation initiated an LLM-based Modernization Assistant to provide automated code parsing for Legacy COBOL, Java Systems, suggest equivalent Modern Patterns such as Transitioning from Java to Kotlin or COBOL to Java services and to facilitate the initial production of Microservices.

Pre-AI adoption, senior engineers worked predominantly as implementers of brittle legacy systems and reverse-engineering existing systems, requiring extensive effort to translate undocumented behavior into maintainable code. Based on the estimates provided, post-AI implementation, the AI produced approximately 40-60% of the modernization code base, while engineers focused on architectural validation, refactoring and semantic validation. System designers began to lead the "deconstruction" of traditional monolithic systems into micro-services and domain experts began to work more closely with engineers to validate that business logic transformations maintained their original intent and correct behavior.

It was observed that the company has seen approximately a 35% reduction in Time to Migration (TTM), as engineers now spend significantly less time writing boilerplate code and significantly more time interpreting business logic and ensuring that the system is functioning correctly. A new workflow has evolved, in which quality gatekeeping has become a core element of the process; engineers are now reviewing AI outputs for their correctness against security directives internal to the company and to ensure that service boundaries and interfaces have been constructed to achieve the intended architectural model rather than simply compiling successfully.

Although productivity gains have been achieved with the implementation of AI, the AI has not been able to effectively replicate and utilize undocumented legacy abstractions, resulting in engineers having to develop additional semantic test suites to demonstrate equivalence between old and new modules. Additionally, to mitigate operational and compliance risk, governance teams have also created a requirement that all AI-generated outputs have associated traceability logs be submitted to ensure that modernization decisions and transformation history can be audited and revisited over time. Figure 5 gives an overview of pipeline for AI assisted legacy code parsing.

Figure 5. A pipeline showing AI-assisted legacy-code parsing, modernization suggestions, human review and integration testing.

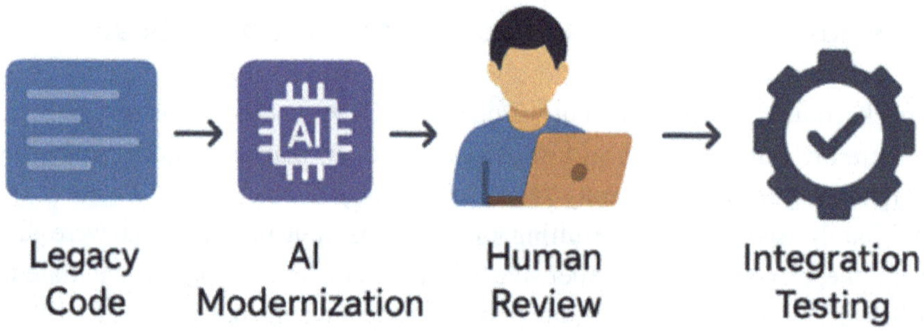

Case Study 2: Rapid Prototyping in Early-Stage Startups

A health-tech startup developing a telemedicine platform used Large Language Models (LLMs) to accelerate early prototyping. The small team leveraged LLMs for UI scaffolding, database schemas, API stubs, business logic, integration tests and early documentation. As AI adoption increased, the senior engineer shifted toward platform design and governance, making decisions on security models, data governance, architectural boundaries and AI trade-offs. Junior developers became AI orchestrators, iteratively generating, integrating, testing and refactoring AI-produced modules while ensuring quality and standards compliance. The UX designer co-created interface mock-ups with AI, which were later refined by engineers for feasibility, accessibility and maintainability.

The outcomes of this was that prototyping time was reduced from approximately 12 weeks to 4 weeks, demonstrating how LLMs compress time-to-first-system. However, hallucinated SQL relationships revealed the need for human verification even at early stages.

The team observed AI-induced race conditions in asynchronous workflows and a tendency for developers to over-trust AI outputs. These risks were mitigated through added review checkpoints and a "verify by default" development approach.

Case Study 3: Safety-Critical Industry with Stringent AI Oversight

AI in Safety-Critical industries such as aerospace and automotive (including Automated Driver Assistance Systems (ADAS)), health care and industrial automation, have stringent and low tolerances for failure to meet specific regulatory obligations, which requires AI adoption to include layered verification and compliance mechanisms to ensure they meet established regulations. An example of this is an embedded firmware code generation project for a medical device that implemented AI to assist with generating the code for the sensor interface, generating the scaffolding for error handling, generating unit test and assisting in generating regulatory documentation. AI did not replace engineers but changed their roles: engineers are increasingly becoming an auditor of a model, become verification specialist and become custodians of documentation. While AI can generate firmware modules, engineers remain responsible for verifying the real-time safety of a model, the timing constraints, memory safety and the requirements of the medical device software.

As a result, the organization reduced the Time to Prototype by 40%, which shows that AI does accelerate Engineering Work under High Constraint when it serves as a Scaffold Generator and not as a Dictator, but required 20% additional Testing, documentation review and compliance validation over the increasing time to produce. However, overall time from prototype to production improved due to the reduced organisation time because automation was used to reduce the implementation work and the engineers spent their time performing the higher risk validation. An organization spent a greater percentage of its engineering time on hazard analysis and failure mode modeling, AI still struggles to perform these tasks reliably due to the need of contextual judgment and safety reasoning that encompasses a wide range of factors.

The case supports the belief that AI-Generated Code cannot be used directly in safety critical environments without rigorous human oversight structuring in the verifying pipeline and human expertise in training for regulatory literacy and ethical reasoning because compliance and accountability, correctness alone is not sufficient (Leveson, 2012). AI-assisted compliance documentation can help increase the speed of compliance audits and traceability, but human oversight will still be necessary to ensure accuracy, consistency and regulatory alignment.

CONCLUSION AND FUTURE DIRECTIONS

As AI reshapes software engineering, the role will shift from mostly writing code to higher-level responsibilities such as architecture, evaluation and oversight. Future development tools will likely use multiple coordinated agents to build features, generate tests, optimize performance and produce documentation, while IDEs will embed AI collaborators for refactoring, debugging explanations and risk assessment. This will make orchestration and traceability essential, with clear links between AI-generated code, its rationale and its constraints.

AI will increasingly generate design patterns, architectures, pipelines and threat models, requiring engineers to evaluate outputs against technical constraints, organizational needs and long-term maintainability. As AI enters production workflows, demand will rise for governance, compliance and audit expertise, particularly in regulated sectors. Education must therefore emphasize abstraction, systems thinking, responsible AI and interdisciplinary collaboration.

Key challenges include skill erosion from over-reliance on AI, increased security and reliability risks from flawed generated code and widening workforce inequality due to uneven access to tools and reskilling. Ethical questions around accountability, verification, fairness and societal impact will require strong governance and human judgment.

Engineers operating within this type of environment will not be replaced but will be elevated in importance due to the fact that their value will reside not in the creation of software but in providing a means for safely, coherently and meaningfully developing and aligning AI-generated systems with human needs.

REFERENCES

Amershi, S., Begel, A., Bird, C., DeLine, R., Gall, H., Kamar, E., Nagappan, N., Nushi, B., & Zimmermann, T. (2019). Software engineering for machine learning: A case study. *Proceedings of the 41st International Conference on Software Engineering: Software Engineering in Practice (ICSE-SEIP)*, 291–300. DOI: 10.1109/ICSE-SEIP.2019.00042

Bainbridge, L. (1983). Ironies of automation. *Automatica, 19*(6), 775–779. DOI: 10.1016/0005-1098(83)90046-8

Becker, B. A., Denny, P., Finnie-Ansley, J., Luxton-Reilly, A., Prather, J., & Santos, E. A. (2023). Programming is hard—or at least it used to be. *Proceedings of the 54th ACM Technical Symposium on Computer Science Education*, 500–506. DOI: 10.1145/3545945.3569759

Benraouane, S. A. (2024). AI management system certification according to the ISO/IEC 42001 standard. In *Productivity Press eBooks*. DOI: 10.4324/9781003463979

Bird, C., Menzies, T., & Zimmermann, T. (Eds.). (2015). *The art and science of analyzing software data*. Elsevier.

Brown, T. B., Mann, B., Ryder, N., Subbiah, M., Kaplan, J., Dhariwal, P., Neelakantan, A., Shyam, P., Sastry, G., Askell, A., Agarwal, S., Herbert-Voss, A., Krueger, G., Henighan, T., Child, R., Ramesh, A., Ziegler, D. M., Wu, J., Winter, C., & Amodei, D. (2020). Language models are few-shot learners. *Advances in Neural Information Processing Systems*, *33*, 1877–1901. DOI: 10.48550/arXiv.2005.14165

Buschmann, F., Henney, K., & Schmidt, D. C. (2007). *Pattern-oriented software architecture: A pattern language for distributed computing* (Vol. 4). John Wiley & Sons.

Cheng, R., Wang, R., Zimmermann, T., & Ford, D. (2024). "It would work for me too": How online communities shape software developers' trust in AI-powered code generation tools. *ACM Transactions on Interactive Intelligent Systems*, *14*(2), 1–39. DOI: 10.1145/3651990

Ford, D., Zimmermann, T., Bird, C., & Nagappan, N. (2017). Characterizing software engineering work with personas based on knowledge worker actions. *Proceedings of the 2017 ACM/IEEE International Symposium on Empirical Software Engineering and Measurement (ESEM)*, 394–403. DOI: 10.1109/ESEM.2017.54

Karekezi, P., Moore, G., & Luo, J. (2025). Human-centered AI design: Developers' perspectives. *Journal of Engineering Design*, •••, 1–16. DOI: 10.1080/09544828.2025.2518907

Karim, M. M., Khan, S., Van, D. H., Liu, X., Wang, C., & Qu, Q. (2025). Transforming data annotation with AI agents: A review of architectures, reasoning, applications, and impact. *Future Internet*, *17*(8), 353. Advance online publication. DOI: 10.3390/fi17080353

Kim, M., Zimmermann, T., & Nagappan, N. (2014). An empirical study of refactoring challenges and benefits at Microsoft. *IEEE Transactions on Software Engineering*, *40*(7), 633–649. DOI: 10.1109/TSE.2014.2318734

Leveson, N. G. (2012). *Engineering a safer world: Systems thinking applied to safety*. MIT Press., DOI: 10.7551/mitpress/8179.001.0001

Li, P. L., Ko, A. J., & Begel, A. (2019). What distinguishes great software engineers? *Empirical Software Engineering*, *25*(1), 322–352. DOI: 10.1007/s10664-019-09773-y

McIntosh, T. R., Susnjak, T., Liu, T., Watters, P., Xu, D., Liu, D., & Halgamuge, M. N. (2025). From Google Gemini to OpenAI Q* (Q-Star): A survey on reshaping the generative artificial intelligence (AI) research landscape. *Technologies*, *13*(2), 51. Advance online publication. DOI: 10.3390/technologies13020051

Sculley, D., Holt, G., Golovin, D., Davydov, E., Phillips, T., Ebner, D., Chaudhary, V., Young, M., Crespo, J., & Dennison, D. (2015). Hidden technical debt in machine learning systems. *Advances in Neural Information Processing Systems*, *28*, 2503–2511.

Shneiderman, B. (2020). Human-centered artificial intelligence: Reliable, safe & trustworthy. *International Journal of Human-Computer Interaction*, *36*(6), 495–504. DOI: 10.1080/10447318.2020.1741118

Vaswani, A., Shazeer, N., Parmar, N., Uszkoreit, J., Jones, L., Gomez, A. N., & Polosukhin, I. (2017). Attention is all you need. *Advances in Neural Information Processing Systems*, *30*, 6000–6010.

KEY TERMS AND DEFINITIONS

AI-Assisted Software Development: Use of AI to support coding tasks e.g. generation, debugging and testing, shifting developers toward design-focused roles.

Cognitive Load Redistribution: Transfer of routine coding to AI

Emergent Code Orchestration: Coordinating AI-generated components into cohesive software systems

Explainable AI: Making AI outputs interpretable

Human-AI Collaboration: Joint development by humans and AI

Prompt Engineering: Designing structured inputs to guide generative AI outputs effectively

Socio-Technical Systems: Integration of technical infrastructure with human and organizational factors

Static Code Analysis: Code inspection to detect defects and vulnerabilities

System-Level Thinking: Viewing software as interconnected systems emphasizing architecture, scalability and maintainability.

Technical Debt: Future maintenance costs

Chapter 6
From Copilot to Colleague:
Governing Skill Transformation in AI-Augmented Software Engineering

Jasdeep Singh Bhalla
http://orcid.org/0009-0002-0462-055X
GoDaddy, USA

ABSTRACT

Generative AI is transforming software engineering, expanding from code assistance to producing full implementations, architectures, tests, and infrastructure. As these tools become semi-autonomous collaborators, they reshape engineering workflows, skills, and responsibilities. While AI-driven development boosts productivity, it also carries risks. Overdependence on AI outputs can weaken core engineering skills, reduce system understanding, and blur accountability. This chapter argues that the key challenge is not automation itself, but the absence of deliberate governance over how skills evolve in AI-enabled environments. Drawing on industry practice and research on human–AI collaboration, the chapter introduces a governance-focused framework that distinguishes skills vulnerable to deskilling, emerging high-value skills, and mechanisms to balance automation with human judgment. By reframing deskilling and reskilling as governance issues, it offers guidance for sustaining quality, security, and trust in the era of generative AI.

DOI: 10.4018/979-8-3373-8450-4.ch006

INTRODUCTION: FROM CODE AUTHOR TO AI COLLABORATOR

Software engineering is transforming as significant as the introduction of high-level programming languages or the rise of open-source ecosystems. For much of its history, the profession has been defined by the ability of human engineers to translate intent into executable logic through direct engagement with code. Writing, debugging, refactoring, and reasoning about software artifacts were not merely tasks but formative practices through which engineers developed intuition, judgment, and professional identity. Generative artificial intelligence fundamentally disrupts this model by inserting an increasingly capable non-human agent directly into the act of software creation.

Early generations of developer tooling focused on assisting engineers at the margins: syntax highlighting, autocomplete, static analysis, and automated testing frameworks reduced friction while preserving the engineer's central role as author and decision-maker. Contemporary generative AI systems operate at a different level of abstraction. They generate entire functions, infrastructure definitions, architectural suggestions, test cases, and even remediation strategies for production failures. In doing so, they shift the locus of authorship away from the human engineer toward a shared space in which intent, validation, and oversight become as important as manual implementation.

This shift marks a transition from viewing AI as a "copilot"—a passive assistant responding to explicit commands—to treating it as a quasi-"colleague" capable of initiating solutions, proposing designs, and influencing technical direction. The metaphor is not merely rhetorical. As AI systems gain autonomy and context awareness, engineers increasingly interact with them through dialogue, constraint specification, and post hoc evaluation rather than line-by-line construction. The engineer's role evolves from primary producer of code to curator, reviewer, and governor of machine-generated artifacts.

While this evolution promises substantial productivity gains, it also introduces profound questions about skill, responsibility, and trust. Software systems today underpin critical infrastructure, financial systems, healthcare platforms, and national security capabilities (Fitts, 1951). In such contexts, the erosion of foundational engineering skills or the dilution of accountability can have consequences far beyond reduced efficiency. The central concern is therefore not whether generative AI can write code—this capability is already established—but how its integration reshapes what it means to be a competent and responsible software engineer.

A growing body of discourse frames this transformation in binary terms: either generative AI will deskill engineers by automating core tasks, or it will reskill them by freeing cognitive capacity for higher-order problem solving. This chapter argues that such framing is incomplete. Deskilling and reskilling are not inevitable outcomes dictated solely by technology (Autor, 2015; Raisch & Krakowski, 2021); they are mediated by organizational choices, governance structures, tooling constraints, and cultural norms. In other words, skill transformation in AI-augmented software engineering is a governance problem.

Without deliberate governance, AI-assisted development risks amplifying existing weaknesses in software practice. Engineers may accept plausible-looking outputs without deep understanding, security vulnerabilities may be introduced through unvetted code generation, and accountability for failures may become diffuse as responsibility is shared between humans and machines. Conversely, when governed intentionally, generative AI can serve as a catalyst for elevating the profession—shifting emphasis toward system-level reasoning, architectural stewardship, risk assessment, and ethical judgment.

This chapter introduces a governance-centered perspective on AI-augmented software engineering that treats skill transformation as a socio-technical process rather than a purely technical one. From this perspective, the key question becomes: how can organizations design workflows, controls, and incentives that preserve and enhance human expertise while leveraging the strengths of automated generation? Answering this question requires moving beyond tool-centric discussions toward an integrated understanding of skills, roles, and institutional mechanisms.

The transition from code author to AI collaborator also has implications for professional identity. Traditional markers of expertise—such as the ability to write complex algorithms from memory or manually debug low-level failures—may diminish in visibility or perceived value. At the same time, new forms of expertise emerge, including the ability to reason about system behavior across layers, to interrogate and validate AI-generated outputs, and to design guardrails that constrain automated systems within acceptable risk boundaries. These competencies are less tangible than raw coding speed, yet they are central to maintaining trust in AI-mediated development.

Importantly, this transformation does not affect all engineers equally. Junior engineers face altered learning trajectories in which exposure to foundational practices may be reduced. Senior engineers encounter new supervisory burdens as they are asked to validate outputs generated at unprecedented speed and scale. Engineering managers must reconcile productivity metrics with long-term capability development, while educators grapple with how to prepare students for a profession in which code generation is no longer the primary differentiator.

The remainder of this chapter explores these challenges through the lens of skill transformation governance. It begins by examining how automation reshapes traditional engineering skills and identifies areas most vulnerable to deskilling. It then analyzes cognitive offloading and overreliance as mechanisms through which skill atrophy can occur. Building on this analysis, the chapter identifies emergent high-value skills required in AI-augmented environments and proposes governance mechanisms that balance automation with human judgment. Finally, it considers the implications of these changes for education, workforce development, and the future design of software engineering roles.

By reframing generative AI not as a replacement for engineers but as a collaborator requiring oversight and governance, this chapter sets the foundation for a more resilient and trustworthy model of AI-augmented software development. The goal is not to resist automation, but to shape it deliberately—ensuring that the evolution from copilot to colleague strengthens, rather than undermines, the long-term integrity of the software engineering profession.

EVOLUTION OF AUTOMATION IN SOFTWARE ENGINEERING

Automation has been a defining force in the evolution of software engineering since the discipline's earliest days. From the introduction of assemblers that abstracted away raw machine code to the development of high-level programming languages that emphasized human-readable logic, each wave of automation has sought to reduce cognitive burden while increasing reliability and productivity. Historically, these shifts altered *how* engineers worked, but not *who* held primary agency over software creation. Generative AI represents a departure from this pattern.

Early automation in software engineering focused on mechanizing repetitive or error-prone tasks (Parasuraman et al., 2000) while preserving human control over core design and reasoning. Compilers automated instruction translation, linkers resolved dependencies, and build systems coordinated increasingly complex toolchains. Later innovations, such as version control systems, automated testing frameworks, and continuous integration pipelines, further abstracted operational complexity, enabling teams to scale without sacrificing quality. In each case, automation reinforced human intent rather than substituting for it.

The rise of integrated development environments (IDEs) and static analysis tools marked a gradual shift toward more proactive assistance. Features such as autocomplete, refactoring suggestions, and linting provided real-time feedback, subtly shaping developer behavior. Yet these tools remained fundamentally reactive. They operated within boundaries explicitly defined by human-authored code and required engineers to retain a deep understanding of underlying logic to resolve issues or make architectural decisions.

Generative AI introduces a qualitatively different form of automation (Autor, 2015; Raisch & Krakowski, 2021). Instead of operating solely on existing artifacts, AI systems can synthesize new ones from high-level descriptions, examples, or partial context. Code generation models trained on vast corpora of software repositories are capable of producing solutions that appear idiomatic, contextually appropriate, and complete. This capability collapses the traditional separation between design, implementation, and documentation, allowing large portions of the development lifecycle to be traversed in a single interaction

Figure 1. Evolution of Automation in Software Engineering

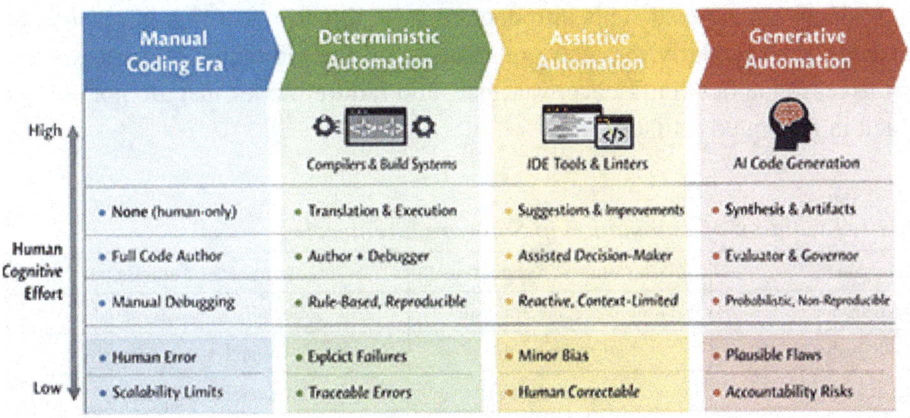

Figure 1 illustrates the progression from deterministic automation toward generative AI–driven development, highlighting the corresponding shift in the software engineer's role. It emphasizes how responsibility moves from direct code authorship toward validation, governance, and system-level reasoning as automation becomes more autonomous.

This shift is not merely an incremental improvement in tooling efficiency; it reconfigures the locus of expertise. When an engineer prompts an AI system to "implement a secure API endpoint" or "generate infrastructure-as-code for a scalable deployment," the system draws upon patterns learned across countless projects, many of which the human engineer has never encountered. The resulting artifact may encode best practices—or outdated assumptions, insecure defaults, or contextually inappropriate trade-offs. The engineer's task becomes one of evaluation rather than construction.

Historically, the pace of automation allowed skill adaptation to occur organically. Engineers learned new abstractions as older ones faded, often over decades. The acceleration of generative AI adoption compresses this transition into years or even months. Organizations can deploy AI-assisted tooling at scale with minimal friction, immediately altering workflows across entire engineering teams. This rapid adoption magnifies both benefits and risks, as skill erosion can occur faster than compensatory reskilling mechanisms are established.

Another distinguishing characteristic of generative AI is its probabilistic nature. Traditional automation systems behave deterministically (Parasuraman et al., 2000): given the same inputs, they produce the same outputs. Generative models, by contrast, operate under uncertainty, producing outputs that are statistically likely rather than logically guaranteed. This introduces a new dimension of risk into software engineering, particularly in safety- or security-critical domains. Engineers must learn to reason about confidence, variance, and failure modes that are not always explicit in generated artifacts.

Table 1. Evolution of Automation in Software Engineering

Dimension	Deterministic Automation	Generative AI Automation
Core behavior	Rule-based, deterministic	Probabilistic, pattern-based
Output predictability	Fully reproducible	Variable across runs
Role of an engineer	Author and debugger	Evaluator and governor
Failure visibility	Explicit errors	Plausible but flawed outputs
Governance focus	Input/output validation	Process, oversight, and accountability

Table 1 contrasts traditional deterministic automation with generative AI–driven automation across key dimensions such as predictability, failure visibility, and the engineer's role. It highlights why legacy validation-focused governance models are insufficient for probabilistic, AI-mediated development workflows.

The evolution of automation also intersects with organizational incentives. Metrics such as velocity, throughput, and cost efficiency strongly favor tools that accelerate delivery. In the absence of countervailing controls, teams may prioritize short-term productivity gains over long-term capability development. This dynamic can create feedback loops in which reliance on AI-generated outputs increases as human proficiency declines, further entrenching automation dependence.

It is important to note that generative AI does not emerge in isolation. Its impact is amplified by complementary trends such as cloud-native architectures, microservices, and infrastructure-as-code, which already abstract away physical resources and operational complexity. In these environments, AI-generated artifacts can be deployed rapidly and at scale, making errors or vulnerabilities equally scalable. The combination of high abstraction and high automation raises the stakes for effective governance.

Understanding the evolution of automation in software engineering is essential for contextualizing current debates about deskilling and reskilling. Previous waves of automation enhanced human capability without displacing core competencies. Generative AI challenges this equilibrium by automating elements of reasoning and synthesis that were once considered uniquely human. Whether this results in diminished expertise or elevated professional practice depends not on the technology itself, but on how it is integrated, constrained, and governed within engineering organizations.

The following sections build on this historical perspective to examine where skill erosion is most likely to occur in AI-augmented development and how deliberate governance can redirect automation toward sustainable skill transformation rather than unintended deskilling.

DESKILLING RISKS IN AI-AUGMENTED DEVELOPMENT

As generative AI becomes embedded in everyday software engineering workflows, concerns about deskilling move from speculative to practical. Deskilling in this context does not imply the wholesale disappearance of engineering expertise, but rather a gradual erosion of specific competencies that were historically reinforced through direct practice. Understanding which skills are most vulnerable—and why—is essential for designing governance mechanisms that prevent unintended degradation of professional capability.

One of the most immediately affected areas is low-level coding fluency. Traditionally, engineers developed proficiency through repeated exposure to syntax, control flow, data structures, and language-specific idioms. This fluency enabled rapid comprehension of unfamiliar codebases and precise reasoning about program behavior. When AI systems generate large portions of code automatically, engineers may interact primarily with finished artifacts rather than constructing them incrementally. Over time, this can weaken the mental link between intent and implementation, particularly for engineers early in their careers.

Manual debugging is another skill at heightened risk (Endsley, 2017). Debugging has long served as a crucible for engineering judgment, requiring hypothesis formation, systematic experimentation, and deep understanding of runtime behavior. AI-assisted tools increasingly propose fixes, suggest likely root causes, or regenerate entire functions in response to failures. While these capabilities can accelerate resolution, they may also bypass the diagnostic process that builds intuition. Engineers who routinely accept suggested fixes without reconstructing the underlying failure mode risk losing the ability to diagnose novel or emergent issues.

Configuration-heavy development, especially in cloud-native environments, presents a subtler deskilling risk. Infrastructure-as-code, security policies, and deployment configurations encode critical assumptions about isolation boundaries, permissions, and failure domains. Generative AI can synthesize these artifacts rapidly, but often without full awareness of organizational context or threat models. When engineers treat generated configurations as opaque outputs rather than objects of scrutiny, they may lose familiarity with the mechanics that govern system behavior under stress or attack.

Deskilling risks are amplified by the plausibility of AI-generated outputs (Shneiderman, 2020). Unlike traditional automation failures, which often manifest as explicit errors, generative systems tend to produce artifacts that appear correct at a glance. This plausibility bias can discourage deeper inspection, particularly under time pressure. Engineers may conflate syntactic correctness with semantic or security correctness, leading to overconfidence in generated solutions.

Another contributing factor is the compression of feedback loops. Historically, mistakes in code or configuration produced visible consequences that reinforced learning. AI-mediated workflows can obscure these loops by presenting polished solutions that work in common cases but fail under edge conditions. When failures do occur, they may be attributed to system complexity rather than gaps in understanding, further reducing incentives for skill development.

Table 2. Deskilling Risks and Corresponding Governance Controls

Skill at Risk	Deskilling Mechanism	Governance Control
Coding fluency	Direct code generation	Mandatory explanation of generated changes
Debugging intuition	AI-proposed fixes	Root-cause analysis requirements
Configuration reasoning	Generated infrastructure	Policy-as-code validation
Security awareness	Plausible insecure defaults	Threat modeling reviews

Table 2 maps specific engineering skills vulnerable to deskilling against the mechanisms through which erosion occurs and the governance controls that mitigate these risks. It illustrates how intentional workflow and policy interventions can preserve foundational expertise in AI-augmented environments.

The distribution of deskilling risk is uneven across experience levels. Junior engineers are particularly vulnerable because AI tools can substitute for foundational learning experiences. Tasks that once required grappling with errors, reading documentation, and experimenting with alternatives can now be resolved through a single prompt. While this accelerates onboarding, it may also create shallow competence that collapses when AI assistance is unavailable or insufficient.

Senior engineers face a different form of deskilling. As AI systems take on implementation tasks, senior practitioners may spend less time engaging directly with code and more time coordinating, reviewing, or approving outputs. While these activities are valuable, reduced hands-on exposure can erode familiarity with evolving language features, libraries, and runtime behaviors. Over time, this can weaken the ability to detect subtle flaws or challenge incorrect assumptions embedded in generated artifacts.

Empirical and survey-based analyses of LLM-assisted development report that the plausibility of generated outputs, combined with limited visibility into model reasoning, increases the risk of uncritical adoption and skill erosion across multiple phases of the SDLC (Bhalla & Jodhka, 2025).

Organizational dynamics can further entrench deskilling. Productivity metrics that reward output volume or delivery speed may implicitly discourage deep inspection or manual exploration. Teams that celebrate rapid AI-assisted delivery without parallel investment in validation and learning risk normalizing superficial engagement with code. In such environments, engineers who insist on thorough review may be perceived as bottlenecks rather than stewards of quality.

Importantly, deskilling is not an inevitable outcome of AI adoption. It emerges when automation displaces practice without replacing it with alternative forms of skill reinforcement. Recognizing deskilling as a risk created by specific workflow choices allows organizations to intervene intentionally. The next section examines cognitive offloading and overreliance as mechanisms through which deskilling occurs, providing a foundation for identifying effective reskilling and governance strategies.

COGNITIVE OFFLOADING, OVERRELIANCE, AND SKILL ATROPHY

The deskilling risks outlined in the previous section do not arise solely from the presence of generative AI, but from deeper cognitive and organizational mechanisms that shape how humans interact with automated systems. Among the most significant of these mechanisms are cognitive offloading and overreliance—phenomena well-documented in human–computer interaction research and increasingly relevant in AI-augmented software engineering. Understanding these mechanisms is essential for explaining why skill atrophy can occur even when productivity appears to improve.

Cognitive offloading refers to the practice of delegating cognitive tasks (Simon, 1956; Wickens et al., 2013) —such as memory, calculation, or reasoning—to external tools. In software engineering, offloading has long been normalized. Engineers rely on documentation, search engines, libraries, and frameworks to reduce mental load. Historically, however, offloaded tasks were discrete and bounded. An engineer might look up an API signature or reuse a known pattern, but still had to integrate these elements through active reasoning.

Generative AI expands cognitive offloading from retrieval to synthesis. Instead of recalling information or assembling components, engineers can now delegate entire chains of reasoning to an AI system. For example, prompting an AI to "design a fault-tolerant service" implicitly outsources architectural decision-making, trade-off analysis, and even risk prioritization. While this can accelerate solution generation, it also reduces opportunities for engineers to exercise and reinforce the cognitive skills involved in system design.

Overreliance emerges when offloaded tasks are not periodically reclaimed or validated (Parasuraman et al., 2000; Endsley, 2017). In AI-mediated workflows, overreliance is often reinforced by positive early experiences. When AI-generated outputs work correctly in common scenarios, trust accumulates rapidly (Hancock et al., 2011). This trust, however, may not be calibrated to the system's actual capabilities or limitations. Engineers may begin to assume correctness by default, intervening only when failures become visible.

This dynamic is particularly problematic because generative AI systems lack an explicit understanding of context, intent, or consequence (Bender et al., 2021). They operate by predicting plausible outputs based on learned patterns, not by reasoning about system behavior in a causal or normative sense. When engineers treat AI outputs as authoritative rather than provisional, they risk importing hidden assumptions, outdated practices, or insecure patterns into production systems.

Skill atrophy occurs when offloaded cognitive functions are not exercised over time. In software engineering, this can manifest as diminished ability to reason about concurrency, memory management, security boundaries, or failure modes. These skills are rarely lost suddenly; instead, they erode gradually as engineers encounter fewer situations that demand active engagement. AI-assisted tooling can inadvertently accelerate this process by smoothing over difficulties that would otherwise prompt learning.

Organizational structures can exacerbate cognitive offloading and overreliance. Teams operating under tight delivery timelines may implicitly reward acceptance of AI-generated solutions that "work well enough," discouraging deeper examination. Code review processes may shift focus from understanding logic to checking surface-level compliance, further reducing opportunities for skill reinforcement. Over time, these practices can normalize shallow interaction with complex systems.

Figure 2. Cognitive Offloading Spectrum in AI-Augmented Engineering

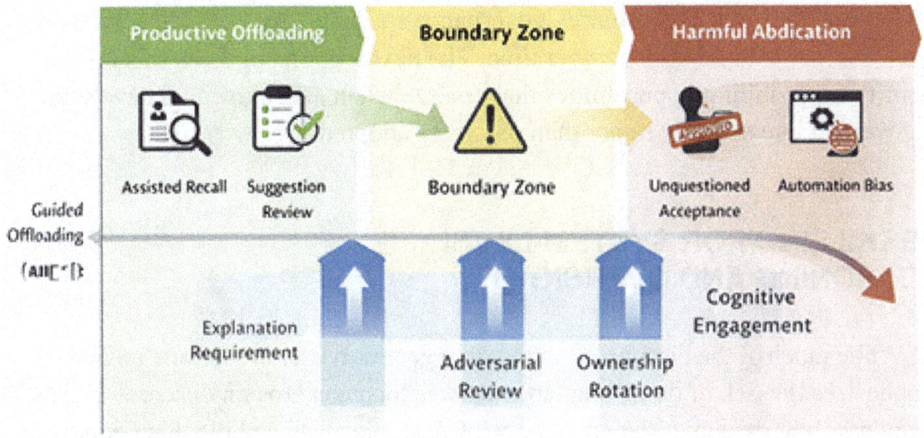

Figure 2 depicts cognitive offloading as a continuum ranging from productive assistance to harmful overreliance and automation bias. It highlights governance interventions that help engineers remain actively engaged in reasoning and decision-making rather than passively accepting AI-generated outputs.

Another factor contributing to skill atrophy is the opacity of AI systems themselves. Unlike traditional tools, generative models do not provide transparent reasoning traces. Engineers evaluating an AI-generated artifact often see only the final output, not the intermediate steps that led to it. This lack of visibility makes it difficult to reconstruct or critique the underlying logic, reinforcing passive consumption rather than active reasoning.

The effects of cognitive offloading are not uniformly negative. When managed deliberately, offloading can free cognitive resources for higher-order tasks such as strategic planning, cross-system integration, and risk assessment. The challenge lies in distinguishing productive offloading from abdication of responsibility. Without explicit norms and controls, teams may drift toward the latter, mistaking reduced effort for increased effectiveness.

Crucially, cognitive offloading and overreliance are reversible dynamics. Skills can be preserved and even enhanced if organizations design workflows that require periodic re-engagement with foundational reasoning. Practices such as mandatory explanation of AI-generated changes, adversarial review of generated code, and rotation of responsibilities can counteract atrophy by reintroducing deliberate cognitive effort.

By situating deskilling within the broader context of cognitive offloading and overreliance, this section highlights why technical solutions alone are insufficient. Addressing skill atrophy requires governance mechanisms that shape how engineers interact with AI systems over time. The next section builds on this insight by identifying reskilling opportunities that emerge when AI-augmented development is governed intentionally rather than passively adopted.

RESKILLING FOR SYSTEM-LEVEL REASONING AND OVERSIGHT

While much of the discourse surrounding generative AI in software engineering emphasizes the risk of deskilling, an exclusive focus on erosion obscures a critical countervailing dynamic: the emergence of new, high-value skills that become essential in AI-augmented environments. Reskilling in this context does not simply involve learning new tools or prompt syntaxes. Rather, it reflects a reorientation of professional expertise away from localized implementation tasks toward system-level reasoning, validation, and governance.

One of the most significant reskilling domains is system-level reasoning. As AI systems assume responsibility for generating localized code artifacts, the engineer's comparative advantage shifts toward understanding how components interact across layers, services, and organizational boundaries. This includes reasoning about data flows, failure propagation, security boundaries, and performance trade-offs at a scale that exceeds any single code unit. Engineers must develop the ability to assess whether AI-generated components align with architectural intent and long-term system evolution.

Closely related is the skill of validation and verification of AI-generated outputs. In traditional development workflows, correctness emerged through construction: engineers built artifacts incrementally and tested them as they went. In AI-mediated workflows, engineers are often presented with complete solutions that must be evaluated post hoc. This requires a different cognitive stance—one oriented toward skepticism, adversarial thinking, and risk identification. Engineers must ask not only whether the code works, but under what conditions it might fail, be exploited, or produce unintended consequences.

Security oversight becomes a particularly critical reskilling area. Generative AI systems may reproduce insecure patterns present in their training data or fail to account for organization-specific threat models. Engineers must therefore cultivate the ability to recognize subtle security implications in generated artifacts, including overly permissive access controls, insecure defaults, and insufficient isolation. Secure-by-design thinking—once embedded implicitly through hands-on configuration—must now be articulated explicitly and enforced through review and policy mechanisms.

Another emergent competency is intent specification. Interacting effectively with generative AI requires engineers to translate high-level goals, constraints, and non-functional requirements into prompts or structured inputs that guide generation. This process resembles requirements engineering more than traditional coding. Engineers must learn to express intent precisely, anticipate ambiguities, and iteratively refine instructions based on observed outputs. Mastery of intent specification determines not only output quality but also the efficiency and reliability of AI-assisted workflows.

Reskilling also encompasses the ability to reason about uncertainty. Unlike deterministic systems, generative AI produces outputs with implicit confidence distributions that are rarely exposed directly. Engineers must develop heuristics and practices for assessing confidence indirectly—through testing, redundancy, and comparative evaluation. This includes understanding when AI outputs are likely to be brittle, when additional validation is required, and when human judgment must override automated suggestions.

Table 3. Emerging Skills in AI-Augmented Software Engineering

Skill Category	Description	Organizational Value
System-level reasoning	Cross-layer understanding of behavior	Resilience and scalability
AI output validation	Adversarial evaluation of outputs	Risk reduction
Intent specification	Translating goals into constraints	Output quality and efficiency
Governance design	Creating guardrails and policies	Trust and accountability

Table 3 summarizes the high-value skills that gain prominence as generative AI assumes greater responsibility for implementation tasks. It emphasizes the organizational importance of system-level reasoning, validation, and governance-oriented competencies in sustaining long-term software quality and trust.

These emergent skills demand a shift in educational and professional development priorities. Traditional curricula emphasize algorithmic problem-solving and language-specific proficiency. While these remain important, AI-augmented engineering places increasing value on abstraction, systems thinking, and ethical judgment. Engineers who can navigate ambiguity, integrate diverse signals, and design robust oversight mechanisms will be disproportionately valuable.

Importantly, reskilling is not an automatic consequence of AI adoption. Without intentional design, organizations may fail to recognize or reward these new competencies. Performance metrics focused narrowly on output volume or delivery speed may undervalue validation work, architectural reasoning, and risk mitigation. To enable reskilling, organizations must align incentives, career paths, and evaluation criteria with the skills that sustain long-term system integrity.

Reskilling for oversight also reshapes collaboration within engineering teams. As AI systems take on more generative tasks, human collaboration shifts toward review, discussion, and decision-making. Engineers must communicate assumptions, justify trade-offs, and collectively reason about system behavior. These social dimensions of engineering—often underemphasized in technical training—become central to effective practice.

Ultimately, reskilling in AI-augmented software engineering represents an elevation rather than a diminution of the profession. By moving engineers closer to questions of intent, risk, and accountability, generative AI creates an opportunity to redefine expertise around stewardship of complex socio-technical systems. The next section examines how governance mechanisms can institutionalize these skills, ensuring that reskilling is reinforced rather than left to chance.

GOVERNING AI-GENERATED CODE: SECURITY, ETHICS, AND ACCOUNTABILITY

As generative AI becomes an active participant in software development, governance emerges as the central mechanism through which organizations can reconcile automation with responsibility. Governance in this context extends beyond compliance checklists (NIST, 2023; EU High-Level Expert Group on AI, 2020) or ethical principles; it encompasses the concrete processes, controls, and accountability structures that determine how AI-generated artifacts are created, evaluated, and deployed. Without such mechanisms, the risks associated with deskilling and overreliance are amplified, particularly in security- and safety-critical systems.

Security provides a clear lens through which to examine the governance challenge. Software vulnerabilities are rarely the result of isolated coding errors; they emerge from mismatches between assumptions, configurations, and operational realities. Generative AI systems, trained on heterogeneous data sources, may produce code that reflects generic best practices but fails to account for organization-specific threat models, regulatory requirements, or architectural constraints. When such artifacts are integrated without rigorous review, they can introduce latent vulnerabilities that scale with deployment.

Governing AI-generated code, therefore, requires shifting security from a downstream concern to an explicit design constraint. Secure-by-design principles must be encoded not only in human practices but also in the interfaces through which AI systems are used. This includes constraining prompts, templates, and generation contexts to reflect approved patterns, as well as enforcing automated checks that validate generated artifacts against security policies. In this model, governance is enacted through both social and technical controls.

Human-in-the-loop review is often cited as a safeguard against automation risk, but its effectiveness depends on how it is implemented. Superficial review processes that focus on stylistic conformity or basic functionality provide little protection against deeper flaws. Effective governance requires that human reviewers are empowered—and expected—to interrogate AI-generated outputs critically. This includes assessing threat boundaries, questioning implicit assumptions, and challenging outputs that appear plausible but lack justification.

Figure 3. Skill Transformation Governance Framework

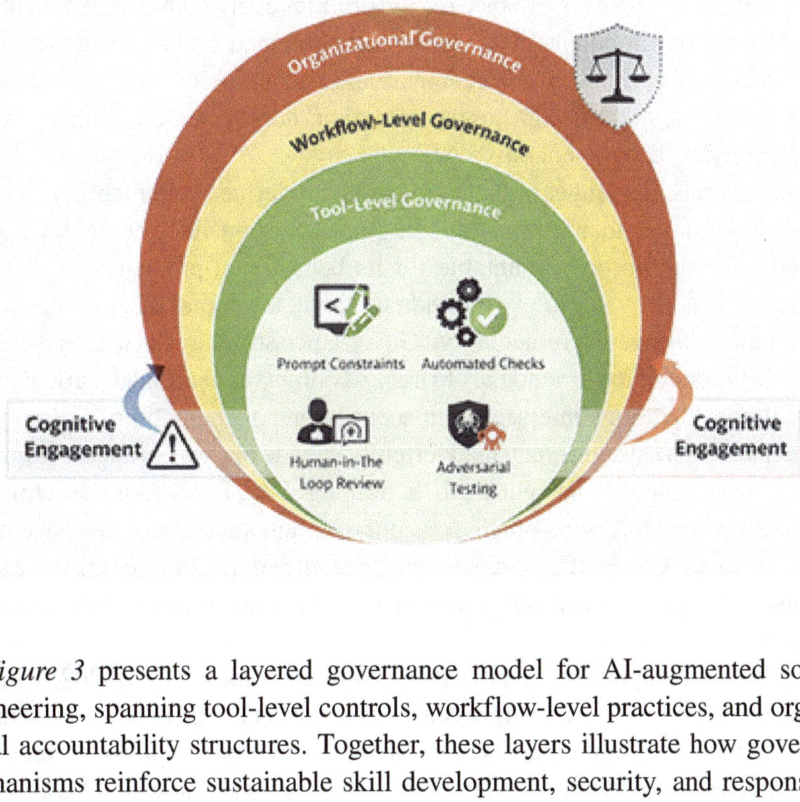

Figure 3 presents a layered governance model for AI-augmented software engineering, spanning tool-level controls, workflow-level practices, and organizational accountability structures. Together, these layers illustrate how governance mechanisms reinforce sustainable skill development, security, and responsibility in human–AI collaboration.

Accountability becomes particularly complex when humans and AI systems jointly produce software artifacts (Rahwan et al., 2020; Zuboff, 1988). Traditional accountability models assume a clear chain of authorship and decision-making. In AI-augmented workflows, responsibility is distributed across tool designers, model trainers, prompt authors, reviewers, and deployment owners. Without explicit delineation of roles, failures may be attributed to the technology itself, obscuring human agency and undermining incentives for careful oversight.

Table 4. Governance Mechanisms Across the Software Lifecycle

SDLC Phase	AI Involvement	Governance Focus	Human Responsibility
Design	AI proposes architectures	Constraint & threat modeling	Assumption validation
Implementation	Code generation	Secure-by-design checks	Code review & testing
Deployment	Config generation	Policy-as-code enforcement	Risk approval
Operations	AI remediation suggestions	Observability & rollback	Incident ownership

Table 4 illustrates how governance responsibilities evolve across different phases of the software development lifecycle in AI-augmented environments. It shows how human oversight, policy enforcement, and accountability mechanisms must be integrated throughout design, implementation, deployment, and operations to ensure responsible use of generative AI.

To address this challenge, organizations must redefine accountability in terms of stewardship rather than authorship. Engineers responsible for deploying AI-generated code should be accountable for its behavior in production, regardless of its origin. This does not imply individual blame, but rather clear ownership of validation, monitoring, and remediation. Governance structures that assign explicit responsibility counteract the tendency to treat AI outputs as external or authoritative.

Ethical considerations intersect with security and accountability in important ways. Generative AI systems may inadvertently encode biases, unsafe assumptions, or exclusionary practices present in their training data. In software systems that mediate access to services, resources, or opportunities, such biases can have material consequences. Governing AI-generated code, therefore, requires ethical review mechanisms that go beyond abstract principles and are integrated into development workflows.

Policy-as-code represents a powerful governance tool (NIST, 2023) in AI-augmented environments. By expressing organizational rules—such as security controls, compliance requirements, and architectural constraints—in executable form, teams can automatically evaluate AI-generated artifacts at scale. This approach reduces reliance on individual vigilance and creates consistent enforcement across teams. Importantly, policy-as-code shifts governance from reactive enforcement to proactive design, shaping outputs before they reach production.

Another critical governance mechanism is observability. AI-generated systems must be instrumented in ways that allow engineers to detect anomalous behavior, performance degradation, or security incidents. Observability supports accountability by making system behavior visible and traceable, enabling timely intervention when automated decisions produce unintended outcomes. In the absence of such visibility, trust in AI-mediated systems erodes quickly.

Governance also entails managing the evolution of AI usage over time. As models improve and capabilities expand, previously acceptable practices may become risky or obsolete. Organizations must therefore treat AI governance as a living process, subject to periodic review and adaptation. Static policies are insufficient in the face of rapidly changing tooling and threat landscapes.

Ultimately, governing AI-generated code is not about constraining innovation but about enabling it responsibly. By embedding security, ethics, and accountability into the fabric of AI-augmented development, organizations can harness the benefits of automation while preserving trust, reliability, and professional integrity. The following section explores how these governance demands give rise to new roles and team structures in AI-driven engineering organizations.

EMERGING ROLES IN AI-DRIVEN ENGINEERING TEAMS

As generative AI becomes embedded in software development workflows, its influence extends beyond individual tasks to reshape team structures and professional roles. Traditional engineering roles, organized primarily around implementation and ownership of specific components, are increasingly supplemented by responsibilities centered on oversight, validation, and governance. These emerging roles reflect the need to manage AI as a persistent collaborator rather than a transient tool.

One prominent role is that of the AI system steward. Unlike conventional tool owners, AI stewards are responsible for curating how generative systems are used within an organization. This includes defining approved use cases, maintaining prompt templates and guardrails, monitoring output quality, and coordinating updates as models evolve. The steward role bridges technical understanding with organizational policy, ensuring that AI capabilities align with architectural standards and risk tolerance.

Another emerging role is the automation auditor. Automation auditors focus on evaluating AI-generated artifacts for correctness, security, and compliance. Their work resembles that of traditional quality assurance, but with a stronger emphasis on adversarial review and systemic risk identification. Rather than validating individual features, auditors assess patterns across generated outputs, looking for recurring weaknesses or unsafe assumptions that may reflect biases in training data or prompt design.

Security-focused organizations are also seeing the rise of AI security reviewers. These practitioners specialize in threat modeling and vulnerability analysis for AI-generated code and configurations. They work closely with development teams to identify potential attack surfaces introduced through automation and to refine guardrails that constrain generation within secure boundaries. This role reinforces the idea that security oversight must evolve alongside automation capabilities.

Prompt and intent engineers represent another adaptation, though the title itself remains fluid. These engineers specialize in translating high-level requirements, constraints, and non-functional goals into structured inputs that guide generative systems. Their expertise lies not in writing code directly, but in shaping the conditions under which code is generated. Effective intent engineering reduces ambiguity, improves output consistency, and minimizes downstream validation effort.

Engineering managers and technical leads also experience role evolution. As AI accelerates implementation, leadership attention shifts toward prioritization, risk management, and capability development. Managers must balance short-term productivity gains against long-term skill health, ensuring that teams retain the ability to operate independently of automation when necessary. This requires new metrics that capture quality, resilience, and learning—not just delivery speed.

These emerging roles challenge traditional career ladders that equate seniority with direct code output. Expertise in governance, validation, and system stewardship may not produce visible artifacts, yet it is critical for organizational resilience. Recognizing and rewarding such contributions requires deliberate changes to performance evaluation and promotion criteria.

Team collaboration patterns also evolve in AI-driven environments. Code reviews become forums for reasoning and debate rather than mechanical checks. Design discussions shift toward defining constraints and success criteria for automated generation. Cross-functional collaboration increases as legal, security, and compliance considerations intersect more directly with day-to-day development.

Importantly, these roles are not necessarily distinct positions in all organizations. In many cases, they represent responsibilities distributed across existing roles. What matters is not the creation of new titles but the explicit acknowledgment that AI-augmented development demands sustained attention to governance, oversight, and skill cultivation.

By articulating and legitimizing these emerging roles, organizations can better align their structures with the realities of AI-driven engineering. Doing so supports reskilling by creating pathways for engineers to develop and apply new competencies, reinforcing the chapter's central argument that skill transformation must be governed intentionally rather than left to chance.

IMPLICATIONS FOR EDUCATION AND WORKFORCE DEVELOPMENT

The shift toward AI-augmented software engineering has profound implications for education and workforce development (Dwivedi et al., 2021). Traditional models of training, which emphasize mastery through repeated manual implementation, are increasingly misaligned with professional practice (Faraj et al., 2018; Raisch & Krakowski, 2021) in environments where generative AI mediates much of the development lifecycle. Addressing deskilling and enabling reskilling, therefore, requires rethinking how engineers are prepared, evaluated, and supported throughout their careers.

In formal education, computer science curricula have historically prioritized algorithmic problem-solving, language proficiency, and individual coding assignments. These foundations remain important, but they are no longer sufficient. As generative AI systems assume responsibility for producing large portions of code, educational programs must place greater emphasis on system-level reasoning, architectural design, and critical evaluation of automated outputs. Students should be trained not only to write code, but to interrogate, validate, and govern code produced by others—including machines.

One implication is a renewed focus on conceptual understanding over rote implementation. Courses can leverage AI-assisted tooling as a pedagogical aid while simultaneously requiring students to explain, critique, and modify generated solutions. Assignments that ask students to identify weaknesses, security risks, or inefficiencies in AI-generated code reinforce active engagement and discourage passive acceptance. In this way, AI becomes a catalyst for deeper learning rather than a shortcut that bypasses it.

Ethics and security education must also evolve. While many programs include standalone courses on ethics or secure coding, AI-augmented development demands that these considerations be integrated throughout the curriculum. Students should encounter ethical trade-offs, bias considerations, and security constraints as routine aspects of software design rather than exceptional topics. Embedding these concerns into project-based learning mirrors the realities of professional practice and reinforces the governance perspective advanced in this chapter.

Workforce development within organizations faces similar challenges. On-the-job training programs often assume that experience accumulates naturally through exposure to tasks. In AI-mediated environments, this assumption no longer holds. Organizations must design deliberate learning pathways that ensure engineers continue to develop foundational reasoning skills alongside new oversight competencies. This may include structured rotations, mentorship programs, and deliberate constraints on AI usage in certain contexts to preserve hands-on experience.

Performance evaluation systems play a critical role in shaping workforce behavior. Metrics that reward speed and output volume risk discouraging the validation, reflection, and learning necessary for sustainable skill development. Organizations should expand evaluation criteria to recognize activities such as thorough review of AI-generated artifacts, identification of systemic risks, and contributions to governance frameworks. Making these activities visible and valued reinforces reskilling incentives.

Continuous learning becomes especially important as AI capabilities evolve rapidly. Static training programs cannot keep pace with changing tools and practices. Instead, organizations should cultivate cultures of ongoing education, supported by internal communities of practice, shared documentation, and regular review of AI usage policies. Encouraging engineers to reflect on failures and near-misses involving automation can transform incidents into learning opportunities rather than sources of blame.

The implications for workforce diversity and inclusion are also significant. AI-assisted tooling has the potential to lower barriers to entry by reducing reliance on prior exposure or informal knowledge networks. However, without careful governance, it may also reinforce existing inequities if certain groups are disproportionately channeled into oversight roles that are undervalued or invisible. Educational institutions and employers must therefore attend to how reskilling pathways are structured and rewarded.

Ultimately, preparing engineers for AI-augmented practice requires aligning education and workforce development with the realities of governed automation. By emphasizing critical reasoning, ethical judgment, and system stewardship, educators and organizations can ensure that the next generation of engineers is equipped not merely to use AI tools but to shape and govern them responsibly. The following section synthesizes these themes to outline a vision for the future of the augmented software engineer.

DESIGNING THE FUTURE OF THE AUGMENTED SOFTWARE ENGINEER

The preceding sections have examined the risks, opportunities, and governance mechanisms associated with AI-augmented software engineering. Taken together, they point toward a reframing of the profession—one in which the defining attributes of expertise shift from individual code production to stewardship of complex socio-technical systems. Designing the future of the augmented software engineer therefore, requires intentional choices about roles, incentives, and institutional norms.

At the core of this future is a redefinition of expertise. Traditional measures of engineering skill—such as the ability to rapidly implement features or recall language-specific details—are increasingly complemented by competencies in judgment, validation, and risk management. Augmented engineers distinguish themselves by their capacity to reason across abstraction layers, to anticipate failure modes, and to impose structure and constraints on automated systems. This form of expertise is less visible but more consequential in environments where errors can propagate at scale.

Professional identity must evolve accordingly. Engineers are no longer solely authors of code, but collaborators with generative systems that influence design and implementation choices. This collaboration requires a mindset oriented toward critical engagement rather than deference. Augmented engineers must be comfortable challenging AI-generated outputs, articulating reasons for rejection, and taking responsibility for final decisions. Such practices reinforce human agency even as automation accelerates production.

Designing effective workflows is central to supporting this identity shift. Workflows should be structured to create moments of deliberate reflection and review, counteracting the tendency toward passive acceptance of automated outputs. For example, requiring engineers to document assumptions underlying AI-generated changes, or to present alternative solutions generated through different prompts, encourages comparative reasoning and deeper understanding. These practices embed reskilling into daily work rather than relegating it to formal training sessions.

Institutional incentives play a decisive role in shaping the future of the profession. Organizations that reward only speed and volume risk undermining the very skills needed to manage AI responsibly. By contrast, incentives that recognize validation work, architectural foresight, and governance contributions signal that these activities are integral to engineering excellence. Career progression pathways should reflect this broader conception of value, enabling engineers to advance through stewardship and leadership as well as implementation.

The future augmented engineer also operates within a broader ecosystem of stakeholders, including product managers, security teams, legal advisors, and users affected by automated decisions. Effective collaboration across these boundaries requires communication skills and ethical sensitivity that have not always been emphasized in technical roles. As AI systems mediate increasingly consequential decisions, engineers must be prepared to engage in dialogue about trade-offs, risks, and societal impact.

Technology itself will continue to evolve, presenting new challenges and opportunities. As generative models become more capable, the boundary between human and machine contributions may blur further. Designing for resilience in this context means assuming that AI systems will fail in unpredictable ways and preparing organizational responses accordingly. Augmented engineers must therefore cultivate humility about automation and vigilance in oversight.

Ultimately, the future of the augmented software engineer is not predetermined by technological progress. It is shaped by choices about governance, education, and professional norms. By foregrounding stewardship, accountability, and system-level reasoning, organizations can ensure that automation elevates rather than diminishes the profession. The final section synthesizes these insights and reinforces the chapter's central argument for deliberate governance of skill transformation.

CONCLUSION

Generative artificial intelligence has introduced a structural inflection point in the evolution of software engineering. Unlike prior waves of automation—such as compilers, build systems, and static analysis tools—that operated through deterministic, rule-based transformations, generative systems introduce probabilistic synthesis into the core of software development. This distinction is not merely technical; it fundamentally reshapes how engineers reason about correctness, accountability, and professional competence. Where traditional automation could be governed primarily through input–output validation, generative AI requires governance of process itself, including how intent is specified, how outputs are evaluated, and how responsibility is assigned in human–machine collaboration.

This chapter has argued that the central challenge posed by AI-augmented software engineering is not automation per se, but the absence of deliberate governance over how automation reshapes skills, roles, and institutional practices. Through analysis of historical automation trends, contemporary AI-assisted workflows, and established research on human–automation interaction, the chapter demonstrates how ungoverned adoption of generative AI can accelerate deskilling through mechanisms such as cognitive offloading, overreliance, and automation bias. These mechanisms do not eliminate expertise abruptly; rather, they erode it gradually by displacing opportunities for active reasoning, diagnosis, and judgment.

At the same time, the chapter has shown that deskilling is neither inevitable nor irreversible. When governed intentionally, AI-augmented development environments give rise to new, high-value competencies centered on system-level reasoning, validation, security oversight, and stewardship of complex socio-technical systems. As generative systems assume responsibility for localized implementation tasks, the comparative advantage of human engineers shifts toward evaluating assumptions, reasoning across abstraction layers, managing uncertainty, and constraining automation within acceptable risk boundaries. These emergent skills represent an elevation of the profession, not a diminution, provided they are recognized, reinforced, and rewarded.

A central contribution of this chapter is the articulation of governance as the connective tissue between automation and responsibility. Governance mechanisms—including human-in-the-loop review, policy-as-code enforcement, secure-by-design constraints, observability practices, and explicit accountability models—shape how AI systems are integrated into engineering workflows and how skills are exercised over time. The proposed three-layer governance perspective highlights the need for complementary controls at the tool, workflow, and organizational levels. Weakness in any one layer increases reliance on the others, underscoring the importance of balanced and intentional design.

The chapter has also emphasized that skill transformation in AI-augmented software engineering is a collective and institutional phenomenon. Emerging roles such as AI system stewards, automation auditors, and security-focused reviewers reflect the redistribution of responsibility that accompanies generative automation. Educational institutions, engineering organizations, and policymakers all play a role in determining whether AI becomes a catalyst for learning and professional growth or a driver of fragility and dependence. Traditional apprenticeship models, which assume skill acquisition through incremental implementation, must be rethought in environments where generation is increasingly automated and reasoning risks being obscured.

Ultimately, the transition from copilot to colleague marks a redefinition of what it means to be a software engineer. Expertise in AI-augmented environments is no longer measured solely by the ability to produce code, but by the capacity to govern its creation, deployment, and impact. By framing deskilling and reskilling as a governance problem rather than a purely technical or educational one, this chapter provides a foundation for sustaining long-term engineering quality, security, and trust in the age of generative AI.

The future of software engineering will be shaped as much by institutional choices as by technological capability. Organizations that foreground governance, accountability, and deliberate skill development can ensure that generative AI strengthens the profession's foundations instead of eroding them. In doing so, they affirm a vision of the augmented software engineer not as a passive consumer of automation, but as a steward of systems, a guardian of trust, and an active participant in shaping the ethical and technical trajectory of modern software development.

REFERENCES

Autor, D. H. (2015). Why are there still so many jobs? The history and future of workplace automation. *The Journal of Economic Perspectives*, *29*(3), 3–30. DOI: 10.1257/jep.29.3.3

Bender, E. M., Gebru, T., McMillan-Major, A., & Shmitchell, S. (2021). On the dangers of stochastic parrots: Can language models be too big? *Proceedings of the 2021 ACM Conference on Fairness, Accountability, and Transparency*, 610–623. DOI: 10.1145/3442188.3445922

Bhalla, J. S., & Jodhka, M. K. (2025). Leveraging large language models in the software development lifecycle: Opportunities and challenges. *International Journal of Advanced Computer Science and Applications*, *16*(11). Advance online publication. DOI: 10.14569/IJACSA.2025.0161105

Dwivedi, Y. K., Hughes, D. L., Ismagilova, E., Aarts, G., Coombs, C., Crick, T., Duan, Y., Dwivedi, R., Edwards, J., Eirug, A., Galanos, V., Ilavarasan, P. V., Janssen, M., Jones, P., Kar, A. K., Kizgin, H., Kronemann, B., Lal, B., Lucini, B., & Williams, M. D. (2021). Artificial intelligence (AI): Multidisciplinary perspectives on emerging challenges, opportunities, and agenda for research, practice and policy. *International Journal of Information Management*, *57*, 101994. DOI: 10.1016/j.ijinfomgt.2019.08.002

Endsley, M. R. (2017). From here to autonomy: Lessons learned from human–automation research. *Human Factors*, *59*(1), 5–27. DOI: 10.1177/0018720816681350 PMID: 28146676

EU High-Level Expert Group on AI. (2020). *Ethics guidelines for trustworthy AI*. European Commission.

Faraj, S., Pachidi, S., & Sayegh, K. (2018). Applied extensively 2020–2024). Working and organizing in the age of the learning algorithm. *Information and Organization*, *28*(1), 62–70. DOI: 10.1016/j.infoandorg.2018.02.005

Fitts, P. M. (1951). *Human engineering for an effective air-navigation and traffic-control system*. National Research Council.

Hancock, P. A., Billings, D. R., Schaefer, K. E., Chen, J. Y. C., de Visser, E. J., & Parasuraman, R. (2011). A meta-analysis of factors affecting trust in human–robot interaction. *Human Factors*, *53*(5), 517–527. DOI: 10.1177/0018720811417254 PMID: 22046724

NIST. (2023). *AI Risk Management Framework (AI RMF 1.0)*. National Institute of Standards and Technology. https://www.nist.gov/itl/ai-risk-management-framework

Parasuraman, R., Sheridan, T. B., & Wickens, C. D. (2000). A model for types and levels of human interaction with automation. *IEEE Transactions on Systems, Man, and Cybernetics. Part A, Systems and Humans, 30*(3), 286–297. DOI: 10.1109/3468.844354 PMID: 11760769

Rahwan, I., Cebrian, M., Obradovich, N., Bongard, J., Bonnefon, J.-F., Breazeal, C., Crandall, J. W., Christakis, N. A., Couzin, I. D., Jackson, M. O., Jennings, N. R., Kamar, E., Kloumann, I. M., Larochelle, H., Lazer, D., McElreath, R., Mislove, A., Parkes, D. C., Pentland, A. S., & Wellman, M. (2020). Machine behaviour. *Nature, 568*(7753), 477–486. DOI: 10.1038/s41586-019-1138-y PMID: 31019318

Raisch, S., & Krakowski, S. (2021). Artificial intelligence and management: The automation–augmentation paradox. *Academy of Management Review, 46*(1), 192–210. DOI: 10.5465/amr.2018.0072

Shneiderman, B. (2020). Human-centered artificial intelligence: Reliable, safe & trustworthy. *International Journal of Human-Computer Interaction, 36*(6), 495–504. DOI: 10.1080/10447318.2020.1741118

Simon, H. A. (1956). Rational choice and the structure of the environment. *Psychological Review, 63*(2), 129–138. DOI: 10.1037/h0042769 PMID: 13310708

Wickens, C. D., Hollands, J. G., Banbury, S., & Parasuraman, R. (2013). *Engineering psychology and human performance* (4th ed.). Pearson.

Zuboff, S. (1988). *In the age of the smart machine: The future of work and power*. Basic Books.

KEY TERMS AND DEFINITIONS

AI-Augmented Software Engineering: A mode of software development in which human engineers collaborate with generative AI systems that actively contribute to design, implementation, and validation.

Cognitive Offloading: The delegation of cognitive tasks such as memory, reasoning, or synthesis to external tools, which can increase productivity but may contribute to skill atrophy if unmanaged.

Deskilling: The gradual erosion of professional competencies caused by reduced opportunities to practice foundational skills due to automation.

Governance: The organizational, technical, and social mechanisms that shape how AI systems are constrained, evaluated, and held accountable in practice.

Human-in-the-Loop Review: A governance practice in which human judgment is deliberately integrated into automated workflows to validate, challenge, and contextualize machine-generated outputs.

Policy-as-Code: The expression of organizational rules and constraints in executable form to enable automated validation and enforcement at scale.

System Stewardship: A professional orientation emphasizing oversight, accountability, and long-term system integrity over direct code production.

Chapter 7
Rethinking Software Engineering Skills in the Age of AI

Rampelli Manojkumar
http://orcid.org/0000-0002-8141-0321
BVRIT HYDERABAD College of Engineering for Women, India

Morri Prashanth
BVRIT HYDERABAD College of Engineering for Women, India

Aditya Sai Srinivas T.
Ravindra College of Engineering for Women, India

Bandreddi Venkata Seshukumari
VNR Vignana Jyothi Institute of Engineering and Technology, India

Chamakura Krishna Reddy
http://orcid.org/0009-0000-7811-5981
BVRIT HYDERABAD College of Engineering for Women, India

Arunima Dutta
National Institute of Technology, Meghalaya, India

ABSTRACT

The integration of generative artificial intelligence into software engineering is reshaping how programming work is carried out, learned, and assessed. AI-assisted tools now automate many tasks that once defined technical expertise, including coding, debugging, and testing. While this shift offers clear efficiency and productivity benefits, it also raises important concerns about deskilling, growing cognitive dependence on automated systems, and the weakening of foundational programming knowledge. At the same time, generative AI opens new pathways for reskilling by moving human effort toward higher-level activities such as oversight, critical reasoning, and system-level design. This chapter examines these parallel processes of deskilling and reskilling in AI-augmented software engineering, focusing on their effects on cognitive engagement, professional identity, and learning pathways.

DOI: 10.4018/979-8-3373-8450-4.ch007

INTRODUCTION

Software engineering is defined by a close connection between human thought and technical tools. Writing code, debugging logic, designing systems, and checking system behaviour are not just tasks; they are ways developers form internal models of systems and develop professional judgment. Over the decades, as tools evolved from structured programming to integrated development environments, automation mainly sped up execution while keeping the human developer at the center of decision-making. The rise of generative artificial intelligence (AI) represents a significant change. Modern AI systems are involved in tasks like code creation, explanation, and decision support, changing how software work is done and how we understand expertise (Ozkaya, 2023; Sauvola et al., 2024).

AI-augmented software engineering refers to environments where machine learning systems act as active collaborators instead of being mere tools. Large language models and generative assistants can suggest implementations, restructure code, create tests, and explain behaviour in plain language. These abilities push automation into areas traditionally tied to human reasoning. Such tools are embedding themselves throughout the software lifecycle (Pangavhane et al., 2024; Pham et al., 2022; Ramos et al., 2025; Schieferdecker, 2025; Fui-Hoon Nah et al., 2023). Practically speaking, this means developers now often start their work by reviewing machine-generated suggestions instead of building solutions entirely from scratch. This shift is viewed as a new form of collaborative programming, where AI serves as a continuously responsive partner (Spinellis, 2024; Treude & Gerosa, 2025; Ahmad et al., 2023).

This change is not just technical; it also alters the nature of cognitive labor. Developers now work within hybrid human–AI systems, where reasoning is partially handed off to algorithmic agents. Studies on program generation indicate that while AI outputs can speed up iteration, they may also introduce subtle issues related to correctness, security, or maintainability which require human oversight (Idrisov & Schlippe, 2024). This leads to a redistribution of effort: developers spend less time on routine tasks and more on validation, interpretation, and integration. This change raises important questions about what expertise means when machine systems are directly involved in coding.

In educational settings, these tensions become especially clear. Students use generative AI tools to help with programming tasks and lower entry barriers. The literature shows improvements in confidence, perceived accessibility, and quick feedback cycles when conversational AI is used in education (Yan et al., 2024; Yilmaz & Yilmaz, 2023). However, educators find it challenging to assess understanding. A student may produce a working solution but struggle to explain its logic or constraints. Moreover, the generative AI challenges traditional views which link effort, learning, and assessment, calling for teaching methods (Becker et al., 2023; Daun & Brings, 2023; Petrovska et al., 2024; Yabaku et al., 2024).

These changes relate to broader discussions of deskilling, which is how automation affects practiced expertise by taking over cognitively demanding tasks. In fields which require knowledge, deskilling is often gradual, changing what professionals regularly practice. When important programming tasks shift to AI, developers may engage less in foundational reasoning, which could weaken their understanding over time (Le, 2025; Ferdman, 2025). Further, the dependence on automated help can impact engagement, confidence, and willingness to put in cognitive effort (Valový & Buchalcevova, 2023). Figure 1 illustrates how AI-assisted workflows simultaneously introduce deskilling pressures and reskilling opportunities. However, looking at AI solely through the lens of deskilling overlooks the parallel trend of reskilling. As routine tasks become automated, new skills arise around oversight, reasoning, and system-level judgment. Software engineers act as intermediaries between AI-generated outputs and real-world outcomes, ensuring security, fairness, and sustainability (Zhu, 2023; Sharma, 2024; Cruz et al., 2025). There is a rising demand for skill sets that blend technical knowledge with analytical thinking and governance awareness (Goel et al., 2024; Bodea et al., 2024; Ersanlı et al., 2025; Pradhan & Saxena, 2023).

Figure 1. Human–AI collaboration workflow.

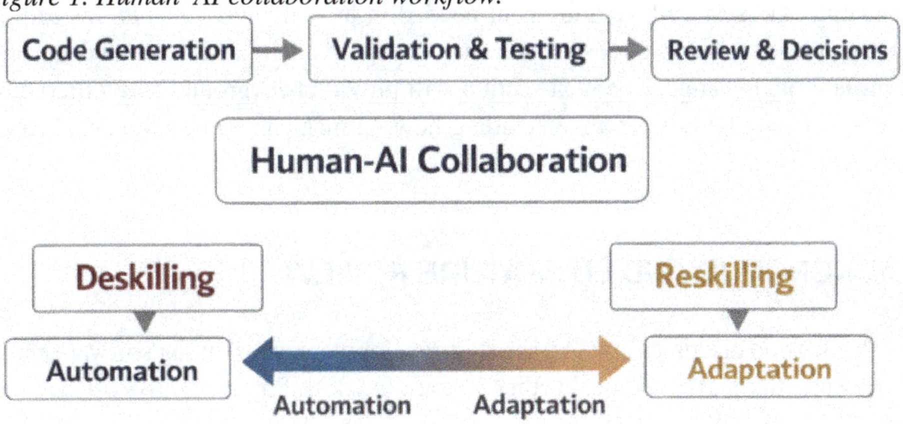

The trust, transparency, and mental models influence how people rely on AI (Weis & Wiese, 2022; Kahr et al., 2024; Klingbeil et al., 2024; Wanner et al., 2022). Too much reliance can increase automation bias and lower opportunities for critical evaluation (Chattopadhyay et al., 2022). Studies in algorithm-based areas indicate that sustained dependence may affect how agency and authority are perceived (Mieczkowski, 2022; Sun & Xu, 2025; Schaetz et al., 2025).

These changes go beyond individual thinking and into how organizations operate. Companies which use AI must weigh efficiency gains against long-term skill development, making sure automated access to information does not undermine tacit knowledge (Uren & Edwards, 2023; Felemban et al., 2024; Gausen et al., 2024; Mitra et al., 2024). Early-career professionals face identity issues as expectations shift towards AI-driven workflows, impacting their sense of professional value and career paths (Bjerg, 2024; Hicks et al., 2024; Tan, 2024; Mulgund et al., 2025; Xu & He, 2024).

In summary, AI-augmented software engineering signifies a major change in professional practice, not just an upgrade in tools. Expertise is shared between humans and machines, raising important questions about learning, accountability, and authority. Approaches which focus on design thinking and human-centered integration highlight the need to keep reflective judgment in AI-driven workflows (Krolikowski et al., 2022; Sarma, 2025). Comprehensive views reveal that integration issues go beyond simple correctness, encompassing larger architectural and lifecycle challenges (Gemlau et al., 2022; Sergeyuk et al., 2026).

This chapter explores AI-augmented software engineering through the linked concepts of deskilling and reskilling. Deskilling shows how automation reshapes expertise and cognitive involvement. Reskilling establishes the new skills of oversight, reasoning, and system-level judgment needed in hybrid environments. Instead of viewing these forces as opposing, the chapter regards them as interrelated aspects of professional change. The next section will provide background and a literature review, forming a basis for understanding how AI influences cognition, expertise, and organizational practice.

BACKGROUND AND LITERATURE REVIEW

This section discusses how AI-assisted development is reshaping software engineering practice and expertise. Further, it examines deskilling, cognitive offloading, and organizational adaptation in AI-augmented workflows.

AI-Assisted Software Development

The generative systems mark a shift from automating execution to participating in reasoning. Early scholarship treats AI-assisted development as the next frontier of software tooling, in which machine learning models function as co-creators rather than simple assistants (Ozkaya, 2023). This view is reinforced by studies documenting the role of large language models across the development lifecycle, including implementation, refactoring, testing, and documentation (Pangavhane et al., 2024; Pham et al., 2022). Moreover, alongside productivity gains, new quality challenges emerge, making careful validation of automated outputs essential (Ramos et al., 2025; Schieferdecker, 2025).

Human–AI collaboration characterizes these tools as partners within iterative workflows. Pair-programming metaphors describe AI as an always-available collaborator capable of proposing candidate solutions while relying on human judgment for contextual appropriateness (Spinellis, 2024). The collaboration ranges from suggestion-based assistance to co-creation and partial autonomy, each imposing distinct cognitive demands on developers (Treude & Gerosa, 2025). Although AI accelerates routine work, outputs may contain hidden assumptions or vulnerabilities, reinforcing the need for human oversight (Idrisov & Schlippe, 2024). Moreover, the integrated environments blur the boundary between authoring and evaluation, reshaping what developers perceive as core expertise (Sergeyuk et al., 2026).

These findings converge on a central insight: AI augmentation does not remove human agency but redistributes cognitive responsibility. Developers remain accountable for correctness, maintainability, and ethical implications even when code originates from machine synthesis (Fui-Hoon Nah et al., 2023; Ahmad et al., 2023). The future of the profession will depend on engineers' ability to integrate AI functions into system-level reasoning rather than treating them merely as productivity enhancers (Sauvola et al., 2024; Zhu, 2023).

Deskilling and the Transformation of Technical Work

The concept of deskilling originates in labor process theory, where automation reshapes work by transferring knowledge and decision-making from humans to machines. Contemporary scholarship revisits this structure in the context of digital and cognitive technologies. Deskilling rarely occurs as an abrupt loss; instead, it unfolds gradually through changes in what workers practice on a regular basis (Cavestro, 2024). Generative AI intensifies this process by externalizing conceptual tasks which were once central to programming expertise.

The sustained reliance on automated synthesis can weaken procedural understanding, particularly among early-career practitioners (Le, 2025). Structural critiques highlight that such effects are embedded in organizational adoption patterns rather than individual shortcomings (Ferdman, 2025). Studies of human–automation skill distribution introduce the notion of unequal deskilling, whereby experienced professionals leverage automation strategically while novices are more vulnerable due to underdeveloped mental models (Mbelekani & Bengler, 2023).

Workplace research links deskilling to managerial systems which prioritize efficiency over reflective engagement. Algorithmic management environments can promote superficial interaction with automated tools, reducing autonomy and increasing pressure to conform to system-driven metrics (Kinowska & Sienkiewicz, 2023). The automated assistance affects confidence and engagement, sometimes lowering tolerance for cognitive effort when solutions are readily available (Valový & Buchalcevova, 2023). The opaque systems limit learning opportunities by concealing underlying reasoning processes (Grimmelikhuijsen, 2023). Complementary educational studies document correlations between heavy AI reliance and erosion of analytical skills when learners accept generated outputs without critique (Miranda et al., 2025).

Deskilling scholarship also recognizes adaptive responses. The structured exposure to AI tools can promote deeper understanding when learners are encouraged to critique rather than accept outputs (Aspra & Chong, 2025). These findings underscore that deskilling is setting-dependent: whether automation undermines or reinforces expertise depends on how workflows are designed and governed.

Cognitive Offloading and Human–AI Collaboration

Alongside deskilling debates, recent works on cognitive offloading offers insight into how humans delegate mental effort to external systems. Studies show that individuals are more likely to offload when tools are perceived as reliable and aligned with internal mental models (Weis & Wiese, 2022). Under conditions of cognitive load, people readily transfer attentionally demanding tasks to algorithmic agents in exchange for efficiency gains (Wahn et al., 2023). Generative AI extends this phenomenon by mediating reasoning rather than simple calculation.

Trust calibration emerges as a critical factor in this relationship. Moreover, users often over-rely on automated advice, even when accuracy is imperfect, particularly in complex domains (Kahr et al., 2024; Klingbeil et al., 2024). Transparency and explainability moderate this effect only when explanations meaningfully support understanding rather than merely simulating it (Wanner et al., 2022). Moreover, automation bias and anchoring as mechanisms through which AI suggestions shape decision-making and narrow evaluative diversity (Chattopadhyay et al., 2022).

Theoretical perspectives extend these findings into broader models of distributed cognition. Externalized cognition structures conceptualize human–machine teams as integrated cognitive systems in which reasoning emerges from interaction rather than isolated human deliberation (Diaz Alfaro et al., 2024). Within such systems, authority becomes hybrid. Moreover, the expertise and ownership are negotiated across human and algorithmic actors (Mieczkowski, 2022; Sun & Xu, 2025). Organizational analyses further warn that algorithmic mediation can influence how knowledge is accessed and interpreted, increasing the risk of dependence and erosion of tacit understanding (Gausen et al., 2024; Schaetz et al., 2025).

Educational and Organizational Perspectives

The influence of generative AI extends into educational settings and organizational structures. Educational research documents both opportunities and challenges associated with AI-assisted programming. The conversational AI can scaffold learning, enhance engagement, and provide personalized feedback (Yan et al., 2024). At the same time the unrestricted reliance may obscure conceptual gaps, necessitating assessment models which prioritize reasoning over output (Becker et al., 2023; Daun & Brings, 2023; Petrovska et al., 2024; Yabaku et al., 2024). Therefore, AI use can boost confidence without consistently strengthening deep problem-solving skills (Yilmaz & Yilmaz, 2023).

Workforce and organizational research treats AI adoption as a capability-building challenge. Models of AI-driven reskilling emphasize hybrid competencies which combine technical literacy, critical reasoning, and governance awareness (Goel et al., 2024; Bodea et al., 2024; Ersanlı et al., 2025; Pradhan & Saxena, 2023). The effective integration depends on cultural alignment and knowledge management practices, not merely technological infrastructure (Uren & Edwards, 2023; Felemban et al., 2024). Moreover, the overreliance on AI-mediated access can weaken institutional memory if human expertise is not simultaneously cultivated (Gausen et al., 2024; Mitra et al., 2024).

Early-career perspectives reveal identity tensions as professional expectations shift. Guides for emerging professionals mention the need to reinterpret expertise in AI-mediated environments (Bjerg, 2024). Both anxiety and opportunity as practitioners negotiate new roles (Hicks et al., 2024). The AI systems can shape career trajectories by influencing perceptions of competence and value (Tan, 2024; Xu & He, 2024). Concerns about role attractiveness, particularly in domains such as software testing, illustrate how automation narratives can affect talent pipelines (Mulgund et al., 2025).

Governance and sustainability considerations further broaden the discussion. Responsible AI architectures position software engineering as central to ensuring fairness, accountability, and environmental stewardship (Zhu, 2023; Cruz et al., 2025; Sharma, 2024). Design thinking approaches advocate human-centered integration strategies which preserve reflective judgment within automated workflows (Krolikowski et al., 2022; Sarma, 2025). AI components must be evaluated within broader architectural contexts to maintain reliability and adaptability (Gemlau et al., 2022; Sergeyuk et al., 2026).

This literature portrays AI-augmented software engineering as a multifaceted transformation spanning cognition, skill formation, education, and organizational practice. The next section builds on this foundation by examining how AI-assisted workflows reshape practiced expertise, professional identity, and everyday development behaviour.

DESKILLING DYNAMICS IN AI-ASSISTED PROGRAMMING

This section discusses how automation of core programming tasks can lead to deskilling and cognitive dependence. It also highlights how context, trust, and organizational practices determine whether AI weakens or strengthens expertise.

Automation of Core Programming Tasks

One of the most visible drivers of deskilling is the automation of programming tasks which once functioned as foundational learning experiences. Generative AI systems can produce boilerplate code, implement common algorithms, translate between programming languages, and propose solutions to syntactic or runtime errors. While these accelerate routine development work and reduce friction, they also alter how often developers directly engage with underlying programming mechanisms.

Skills tend to deteriorate through disuse rather than outright loss (Cavestro, 2024). As developers depend on automated generation for tasks such as loop construction, exception handling, or design pattern implementation, opportunities for repeated cognitive rehearsal diminish. The early-career practitioners are particularly susceptible to this transition. When learners progress through tasks without independently constructing solutions, procedural competence may develop without deep conceptual understanding (Le, 2025). Further, the deskilling is not merely an individual learning issue but a systemic outcome of how AI tools are embedded within development workflows and productivity-oriented cultures (Ferdman, 2025).

A concrete example illustrates this process. A developer may rely on an AI assistant to generate database access logic. Although the resulting code executes correctly, implicit assumptions about concurrency or error handling remain unclear. Because the implementation appears to function as intended, further investigation may be postponed. Over time, repeated acceptance of such outputs can normalize superficial engagement, shifting expertise from construction toward orchestration. Experienced developers are often able to compensate by critically interrogating outputs, whereas novices may lack the mental models required for effective evaluation (Mbelekani & Bengler, 2023).

Cognitive Offloading and Skill Atrophy

Deskilling is closely connected to cognitive offloading, or the delegation of mental effort to external systems. Generative AI extends this practice into areas which traditionally supported deep learning. Moreover, the automated assistance can lower perceived effort while simultaneously reducing engagement with problem-solving processes (Valový & Buchalcevova, 2023). As a result, developers may become less willing to tolerate ambiguity or engage in extended debugging when automated suggestions are readily available.

Recent works on system transparency identifies how opaque AI systems exacerbate this tendency. When developers cannot meaningfully examine the reasoning behind generated outputs, opportunities for reflective learning decline (Grimmelikhuijsen, 2023). Educational studies similarly report correlations between heavy reliance on AI and reduced analytical reasoning when learners accept generated solutions without critique (Miranda et al., 2025).

Related findings from other algorithmically mediated domains reinforce this pattern. The prolonged reliance on algorithmic support can narrow evaluative engagement and weaken critical judgment (Schaetz et al., 2025). In programming settings, comparable changes emerge when developers treat AI-generated code as authoritative defaults rather than provisional hypotheses requiring verification. Deskilling thus appears less as a visible decline and more as a gradual erosion of practice intensity.

Uneven Distribution of Deskilling

Deskilling does not affect all practitioners in the same way. There are asymmetries in how skills are redistributed (Mbelekani & Bengler, 2023). Senior developers with well-established mental models often use AI strategically, accelerating routine tasks while preserving conceptual oversight. Early-career developers, by contrast, may experience disproportionate dependence because foundational reasoning skills are still developing. This imbalance has long-term implications for professional pipelines. When early learning stages are heavily mediated by automation, organizations risk weakening the development of system-level expertise.

Organizational setting further shapes these changes. Algorithmic management environments which prioritize speed of output over understanding of process can unintentionally encourage shallow engagement with AI tools (Kinowska & Sienkiewicz, 2023). When performance metrics reward rapid delivery, developers may default to automated solutions without adequate evaluation. Over time, such practices embed deskilling into workplace culture rather than leaving it as an individual choice.

Transparency, Trust, and Learning Opportunities

Trust calibration plays a central role in determining whether AI augmentation strengthens or undermines expertise. Developers must continually decide when to rely on automated outputs and when to question them. Users frequently overestimate system reliability, particularly in cognitively demanding settings (Kahr et al., 2024; Klingbeil et al., 2024). Without meaningful transparency, explanations risk creating the appearance of understanding rather than genuine insight (Wanner et al., 2022).

In educational settings, this illusion of understanding can conceal learning gaps. Students may arrive at correct solutions with AI assistance while lacking the reasoning needed to reproduce or adapt those solutions independently (Miranda et al., 2025). Conversely, structured exposure to AI tools can foster productive engagement when learners are encouraged to critique and refine generated outputs. Deliberate friction such as requiring explanation or modification can transform automation into a catalyst for deeper learning (Aspra & Chong, 2025).

Psychological and Identity Dimensions

Deskilling is not only a cognitive phenomenon; it also intersects with professional identity. Programming is traditionally associated with mastery, creativity, and autonomy in problem solving. When AI systems assume visible portions of this work, developers may experience uncertainty about their role and value. Studies of developer identity highlight tensions between perceiving AI as an empowering collaborator and viewing it as a threat to expertise (Hicks et al., 2024). Emotional responses such as reduced confidence or anxiety about skill relevance can reinforce reliance patterns, creating feedback loops in which diminished self-efficacy leads to greater dependence (Valový & Buchalcevova, 2023).

These psychological changes are particularly salient in early-career development. New practitioners working within AI-mediated environments must reconcile expectations of independence with the realities of collaborative automation.

Deskilling as a Context-Dependent Transformation

Despite these concerns, deskilling is not an inevitable consequence of AI adoption. The outcomes depend on workflow design and institutional context. When automation is paired with reflective practices such as code review, explanation, and structured critique, it can reinforce rather than replace expertise. Productive failure architectures illustrate how learners exposed to imperfect AI outputs can develop stronger reasoning skills by diagnosing limitations (Aspra & Chong, 2025). Organizational cultures which prioritize understanding alongside efficiency can similarly mitigate skill erosion.

From this perspective, deskilling is best understood as a context-dependent transformation rather than a deterministic decline. Automation redistributes cognitive effort, and whether that redistribution weakens or strengthens expertise depends on how humans engage with the technology. Recognizing this contingency is essential for designing educational and professional environments which preserve depth while benefiting from increased efficiency.

The next section examines these mediating processes more closely by exploring cognitive dependence and the redistribution of expertise within human–AI systems.

COGNITIVE DEPENDENCE AND THE REDISTRIBUTION OF EXPERTISE

In this section, cognitive offloading is examined as a normalized practice in AI-assisted software development to highlight its effects on reasoning, trust, and authority.

Cognitive Offloading as a Normalized Practice

Cognitive offloading is the delegation of mental effort to external artefacts and a feature of technical work. Software developers routinely use compilers, debuggers, and documentation to manage complexity. Generative AI extends this offloading into domains traditionally associated with conceptual reasoning, including problem decomposition and solution construction. Offloading preferences are shaped by perceptions of system reliability and alignment with users' mental models (Weis & Wiese, 2022). When AI outputs appear competent and contextually appropriate, developers naturally shift from constructing solutions to evaluating machine-generated alternatives.

In general, the individuals are willing to offload cognitively demanding tasks under conditions of time pressure or uncertainty (Wahn et al., 2023). In programming settings, this tendency becomes visible when developers rely on AI to suggest architectural patterns or resolve unfamiliar syntax. The immediate benefit is reduced cognitive effort and faster progress. However, repeated offloading can change engagement patterns. Reasoning becomes episodic, activated primarily when AI outputs fail rather than continuous. Although this change does not eliminate understanding, it reduces opportunities for sustained mental rehearsal and may weaken internal representations over time. This redistribution of cognitive effort is illustrated in Figure 2.

Figure 2. Cognitive offloading in AI-assisted software engineering.

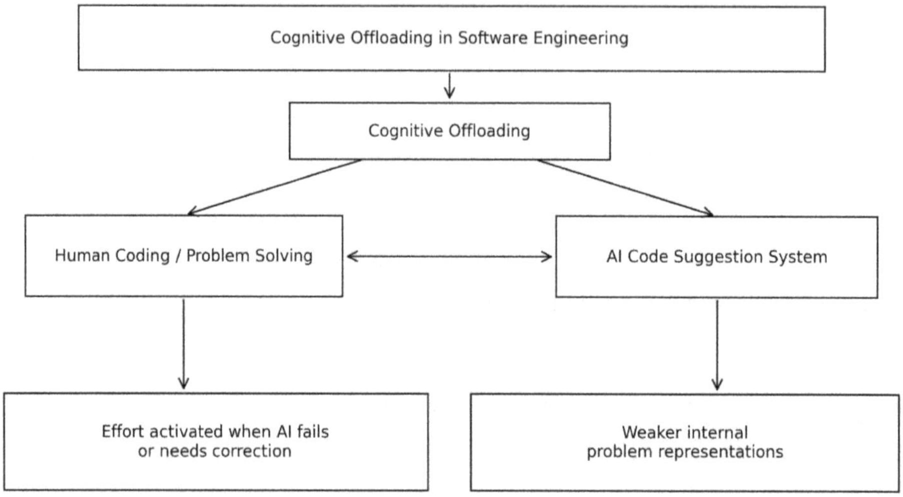

Theoretical models of externalized cognition conceptualize these environments as hybrid systems in which reasoning is distributed across human and machine components (Diaz Alfaro et al., 2024). From this perspective, cognitive dependence is not inherently problematic; it reflects an adaptive strategy for managing complexity. The challenge lies in maintaining balance. When external systems dominate core reasoning processes, human oversight risks becoming reactive rather than proactive.

Mental Models and AI-Mediated Reasoning

The consequences of offloading depend on how well users understand the merits and limitations of external systems (Weis & Wiese, 2022). Developers with strong conceptual foundations can treat AI as an amplifier, using it to explore alternatives while preserving independent reasoning. Those with weaker foundations may substitute AI outputs for understanding, producing fragile expertise which only becomes visible in edge cases.

Studies of AI-mediated communication frame this redistribution as a negotiation of agency and ownership (Mieczkowski, 2022). Knowledge becomes co-produced: developers access and interpret AI-generated content rather than authoring it entirely themselves. Further, the algorithmic systems subtly influence norms of what is considered "correct" or "optimal," shaping decision-making even when human oversight is retained (Sun & Xu, 2025). Over time, developers may internalize patterns favoured by the model, reducing the diversity of problem-solving approaches.

Cognitive Biases Amplified by Automation

Human reasoning is subject to well-documented cognitive biases, and AI-mediated environments can intensify these tendencies. Automation bias is the inclination to favour machine recommendations over personal judgment and becomes particularly pronounced when AI systems present confident outputs.

Anchoring effects occur when an AI-generated solution serves as the initial reference point. Developers may hesitate to deviate from this structure even when alternatives would be more appropriate. Confirmation bias further reinforces acceptance: outputs which align with expectations are readily trusted, while discrepancies are rationalized. Users often over-rely on AI advice even when accuracy is imperfect, particularly under high cognitive load (Kahr et al., 2024; Klingbeil et al., 2024).

Transparency can mitigate, but not eliminate these effects. Explanations which meaningfully reveal reasoning support calibrated trust, whereas superficial explanations risk creating an illusion of understanding (Wanner et al., 2022). Without deliberate reflection, cognitive biases can narrow evaluative engagement and limit the range of solutions considered.

Parallel findings from algorithm-mediated domains illustrate how sustained reliance shapes perceptions of authority and agency. The algorithmic mediation influences what users regard as credible or relevant (Schaetz et al., 2025). In software engineering, similar interactions emerge when developers treat AI-generated code as a default baseline rather than as a hypothesis requiring scrutiny.

Trust, Authority, and Reliance Calibration

Trust is central to cognitive dependence. Developers must continually calibrate when to rely on AI outputs and when to intervene. Perceived accuracy, prior experience, and explanation quality shape reliance patterns (Kahr et al., 2024). Moreover, trust does not scale linearly with reliability. Even imperfect systems can elicit overreliance when tasks are complex or time-sensitive (Klingbeil et al., 2024).

Authority negotiation further complicates this relationship. Moreover, the authority in AI-mediated systems is distributed rather than singular (Sun & Xu, 2025). Developers may implicitly defer to algorithmic recommendations while retaining nominal responsibility for outcomes. This diffusion of authority can obscure accountability, particularly when reasoning pathways are opaque (Grimmelikhuijsen, 2023).

The algorithmic management structures may reinforce default reliance by embedding AI recommendations into performance metrics or workflow norms (Kinowska & Sienkiewicz, 2023). In such environments, questioning automated outputs may be perceived as inefficiency, subtly discouraging critical evaluation.

Learning, Recursive Dependence, and Expertise Development

Cognitive dependence has significant implications for learning. AI-mediated pedagogy can accelerate access to information while reducing opportunities for productive struggle, a key driver of deep understanding (Turvey & Pachler, 2025). When learners rely on AI to resolve uncertainty, they may internalize navigation strategies rather than conceptual reasoning.

Recursive learning frameworks describe how AI systems transform individual interactions into organizational knowledge, creating feedback loops that shape collective practice (Mitsugi et al., 2025). While this process can enhance knowledge sharing, it also risks reinforcing dependence if individual mastery is deprioritized. The algorithmic mediation may erode tacit knowledge when explicit access replaces experiential learning (Gausen et al., 2024).

These transitions extend into professional development. Early-career practitioners operating within AI-assisted workflows must balance efficiency with foundational learning. Without structured opportunities for independent reasoning, cognitive habits may skew toward reliance, shaping long-term expertise formation.

From Individual Dependence to Structural Redistribution

The readiness depends on aligning technological integration with human capability development (Uren & Edwards, 2023; Felemban et al., 2024). AI primarily as an efficiency mechanism risk cultivating dependence without resilience. By contrast, environments that mention reflective oversight and knowledge retention can leverage cognitive redistribution as a strength (Mitra et al., 2024).

The following section turns to reskilling, examining how developers, educators, and organizations can cultivate oversight, reasoning, and system-level competencies that sustain expertise in AI-mediated environments.

RESKILLING FOR OVERSIGHT, REASONING, AND SYSTEM-LEVEL DESIGN

One of the most important themes in workforce studies is that AI-driven transformation is not only about changing tasks but also about the cognitive stance that needs to be adopted to accomplish these tasks effectively. Reskilling models in the AI era focus on hybrid skills that integrate technical literacy with analytical judgment and governance awareness (Goel et al., 2024; Bodea et al., 2024). International assessments of reskilling projects mentions the key to successful transformation is to develop reflective and systems-level thinking along with technical skills (Ersanlı et al., 2025; Pradhan & Saxena, 2023). In software engineering, this means that there are three interconnected areas: oversight capability, reasoning beyond automation, and system-level design.

Oversight as a Core Professional Competency

In AI-assisted software engineering, oversight is not a marginal task; rather, it is a critical task which ensures that the automatically generated code is consistent with technical, ethical, and organizational requirements. Oversight involves scrutinizing AI-generated code, pinpointing subtle errors, and contextualizing suggestions within the larger system objectives. Governance-focused analyses highlight oversight as a nexus between automated code generation and accountability, with a focus on the fact that accountability is human even when it is informed by AI (Sharma, 2024; Zhu, 2023).

AI-generated code can contain inefficiencies, hidden errors, or security risks that need to be carefully assessed (Idrisov & Schlippe, 2024). Oversight within this structure requires more than superficial examination. Programmers need to be aware of the limitations of the model, the structures in which automated code generation is not reliable, and the design of verification strategies for probabilistic outputs. This is in line with trust calibration studies, which suggest that successful human–AI collaboration requires the ability to modulate trust rather than defaulting to acceptance or rejection (Kahr et al., 2024; Klingbeil et al., 2024).

Oversight also involves cognitive and emotional aspects. Overseeing AI systems can introduce stress when professionals are held responsible for opaque processes (van Voorst, 2024). In software development, related stress comes from having to defend AI-influenced decisions without complete visibility into generation processes. Reskilling must therefore cover approaches to dealing with uncertainty, reasoning documentation, and preserving professional confidence in hybrid processes.

In terms of specific skills, oversight involves interpreting AI explanations and identifying gaps, designing validation and testing processes for generated code, recognizing when to override automated suggestions, and maintaining audit trails that record human judgment. These skills shift software developers' roles from tool operators to guardians of system integrity.

Reasoning Beyond Automation

Generative AI systems are highly adept at pattern synthesis and probabilistic reasoning but lack structure awareness, ethical judgment, and long-term foresight. Reskilling must therefore provide reasoning approaches that complement, rather than duplicate, automated reasoning. Analytical reasoning, trade-off analysis, and decision-making under uncertainty are important as software developers incorporate AI system outputs into larger socio-technical systems.

It is important to strengthen critical thinking and systems reasoning skills rather than focusing primarily on tool mastery (Pradhan & Saxena, 2023; Goel et al., 2024). In software engineering, this entails reasoning across abstraction levels, considering the long-term implications of design decisions, and aligning them with organizational constraints. Responsible AI structures further position software engineers as translators of ethical values into system behaviour (Zhu, 2023). Issues of fairness, privacy, and sustainability cannot be delegated to generative models and instead require reflective human judgment (Cruz et al., 2025).

Studies on cognitive bias further underline the importance of deliberate reasoning. Developers must learn to treat AI-generated outputs as hypotheses rather than definitive conclusions, resisting automation and anchoring biases (Chattopadhyay et al., 2022). Moreover, the meaningful explanations can support this approach by enabling developers to examine reasoning pathways rather than accepting outputs at face value (Wanner et al., 2022; Grimmelikhuijsen, 2023).

System-Level Thinking as Durable Expertise

The system-level coordination remains resistant to full automation (Gemlau et al., 2022). Developers must anticipate timing interactions, resource limitations, and long-term effects that extend beyond local correctness. The firms adopting AI may underestimate the importance of architectural expertise by prioritizing tool deployment over integration strategy (Bodea et al., 2024). This imbalance can result in fragile systems that are optimized for short-term efficiency but difficult to maintain or govern.

Human-centered design practices offer an alternative perspective. Design thinking methodologies provide empathy, feedback, and contextual awareness, encouraging developers to see systems as socio-technical networks rather than purely technical constructs (Krolikowski et al., 2022). Contemporary software practices integrate these ideas with AI-assisted collaboration, treating generative tools as exploratory partners while reserving framing and synthesis for human judgment (Sarma, 2025).

AI Literacy as Foundational Infrastructure

Educational research identifies AI literacy as a prerequisite for effective participation in AI-mediated work, enabling professionals to move from passive use to active collaboration (Asrifan et al., 2025).

Organizational frameworks describe AI literacy as a dynamic capability that supports sensing, seizing, and reconfiguring opportunities within digital ecosystems

(Malik, 2023). In software engineering, this literacy underpins trust calibration, oversight, and ethical reasoning. Without it, developers risk treating AI outputs as black-box authority, reinforcing dependence rather than agency.

AI literacy is not static. As AI models evolve, developers must continuously update their understanding. Lifelong learning becomes a core component of professional resilience, aligning with broader reskilling initiatives that view adaptation as an ongoing process rather than a one-time intervention (Ersanlı et al., 2025).

Organizational Conditions for Sustainable Reskilling

Reskilling does not occur in isolation; it is shaped by organizational incentives and cultural values. The effective AI adoption requires strategic alignment between technology deployment and human capability development (Uren & Edwards, 2023; Felemban et al., 2024). Organizations that reward speed alone may inadvertently suppress reflective engagement, accelerating deskilling interactions. In contrast, environments that value explanation, review, and learning create conditions in which AI augmentation sustains expertise.

It is important to preserve tacit knowledge alongside automated access (Gausen et al., 2024; Mitra et al., 2024). Structured mentorship, documentation practices, and collaborative review processes help ensure that expertise remains distributed across people as well as systems. Early-career development initiatives must explicitly address identity formation in AI-mediated structures, guiding practitioners toward balanced reliance (Bjerg, 2024; Hicks et al., 2024; Tan, 2024).

The next section examines how these reskilling priorities are enacted in educational and early-career environments, where foundational habits of reasoning and professional identity are established.

EDUCATIONAL TRANSFORMATION AND EARLY-CAREER DEVELOPMENT

In this section, programming education is reconsidered in light of generative AI. It explores how assessment design, identity formation, and lifelong learning must evolve to prevent shallow competence and cultivate reflective, resilient professionals.

Reframing Learning Objectives in AI-Augmented Education

The traditional education in programming is based on the premise that conceptual understanding is achieved through extensive engagement with syntax, debugging, and iterative problem-solving activities. The presence of generative AI in education disrupts this paradigm by allowing students to quickly generate functional code, often without engaging in the prolonged struggle that was previously conducive to learning. Conversational AI can enhance engagement and confidence, especially for beginners who require immediate feedback (Yan et al., 2024; Yilmaz & Yilmaz, 2023). Mpreover, the correctness of the output is no longer an indicator of conceptual understanding (Becker et al., 2023).

Educational scholarship contends that curricula need to move from product assessment to reasoning assessment. Instead of asking if a program is effective, teachers ask students to justify why it is effective, analyze and evaluate AI-suggested solutions, and justify design choices (Daun & Brings, 2023; Petrovska et al., 2024). Investigative studies on AI integration within programming classes indicate that when students are asked to interrogate AI output i.e., altering, annotating, or justifying, the use of automation becomes a reflection tool rather than a crutch (Yabaku et al., 2024). Productive failure theories support this method: controlled exposure to suboptimal AI suggestions promotes diagnostic thinking and enhances conceptual understanding (Aspra & Chong, 2025).

This paradigm supports learning outcomes in line with reskilling requirements. Students need to learn not only how to code but also how to evaluate, trust, and ethically apply AI-mediated solutions.

Assessment, Integrity, and Reflective Practice

The presence of generative AI makes traditional assessment paradigms problematic. Tasks intended to assess autonomous implementation can be achieved through automated synthesis, making it difficult to distinguish between aid and authorship. Educational scholarship asserts that the objective should not be to ban AI use but to develop assessments that assess reasoning processes (Becker et al., 2023).

Process-based assessment methods include oral defense, annotated code analysis, and reflective journaling where students describe AI tool usage and rationale behind design choices (Daun & Brings, 2023). These methods focus on metacognition rather than product creation. Studies on student engagement demonstrate that reflective activities enable students to distinguish between AI as a learning aid and AI as a replacement for comprehension (Yan et al., 2024).

Learning Trajectories and the Risk of Shallow Competence

Asymmetry is introduced in the learning pathways by generative AI. Students who have a solid foundation in a subject can use AI to investigate alternatives and enhance their knowledge, whereas students who lack foundations in a subject can move ahead without grasping the essential concepts. AI can either illuminate or cloud learning based on the learning structure (Yabaku et al., 2024). Learners can show procedural fluency but lack reasoning skills.

This disparity sparks equity issues. Educational institutions may widen the gap in metacognitive abilities: students skilled at reflection have an advantage, and others rely on AI-generated results. Studies showing the degradation of analytical abilities in AI-using students illustrate the need for systematic access to independent problem-solving (Miranda et al., 2025). Good pedagogy integrates AI-assisted inquiry with tasks involving construction from first principles.

Early-Career Identity and Professional Development

The move from education to professional life is a defining moment for identity. Early-career developers are confronted with AI not as a supplement but as a system integral to modern practice. To succeed in this context, one must reframe what it means to be competent: importantly, it is in evaluation and integration, not mere execution (Bjerg, 2024).

Recent works illustrates the ambivalence of developers towards AI tools. While anxiety can be mitigated and time saved by automation, it can also erode confidence if machine-generated results seem better (Hicks et al., 2024). Open discussion of the role of AI can help early-career professionals accurately assess their own contributions, avoiding overdependence and maintaining a sense of professional control (Tan, 2024).

Skill signalling becomes even more nuanced in AI-mediated environments. Recruitment and assessment strategies need to separate tool orchestration from conceptual knowledge. The ambiguity regarding authorship and autonomy can impact legitimacy perceptions (Xu & He, 2024). Such trade-offs also exist in software engineering, where reasoning ability and effective tool use are necessary.

Role attractiveness is also impacted by automation discourse. Areas of high automation, such as software testing, may have difficulty attracting new entrants despite their continued strategic relevance (Mulgund et al., 2025). A shift in these roles to intellectually demanding oversight roles is necessary for maintaining professional talent streams. Figure 3 illustrates how perceived prestige and growth narratives can shape career attractiveness and identity in AI-mediated software roles.

Figure 3. Perceived career value shift in software roles.

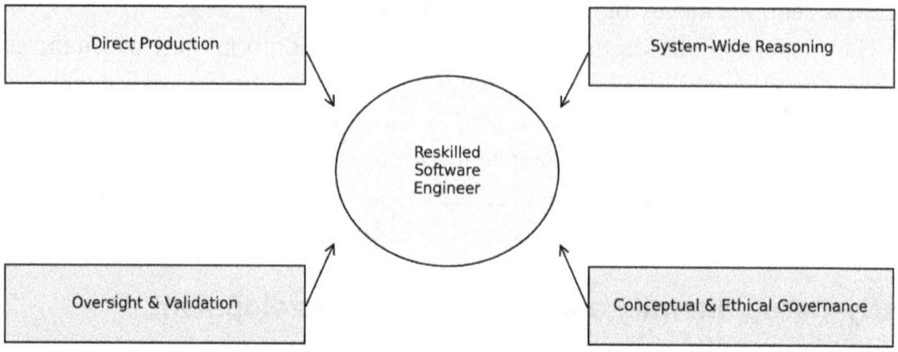

Educational Resilience and Lifelong Learning

Adaptation for AI-mediated practice is not limited to the educational setting. Lifelong learning paradigms view adaptability as a central professional skill (Goel et al., 2024; Ersanlı et al., 2025). Educational institutions thus have a dual role: developing basic reasoning skills and modeling thoughtful engagement with dynamic tools. Moreover, the new entrants are aware of model limitations, bias, and ethics (Asrifan et al., 2025).

ORGANIZATIONAL CAPABILITY AND SUSTAINABLE AI ADOPTION

The organizational readiness for AI adoption is examined through the lenses of capability alignment, knowledge retention, governance, and workforce transformation as discussed follows.

Organizational Readiness and Capability Alignment

The literature on organizational readiness characterizes AI adoption as a phased process that requires alignment between technological infrastructure and human capabilities (Uren & Edwards, 2023). Initial efforts typically focus on experimenting with tools and integrating them into existing workflows. However, meaningful transformation requires sustained investment in oversight, coordination, and learning. Organizations that fail to develop these capabilities risk superficial adoption to achieve short-term productivity improvements while gradually undermining internal expertise.

Moreover, the cultural readiness is as critical as technical preparedness (Felemban et al., 2024). Teams need a shared understanding of AI's purpose, limitations, and accountability boundaries. Without this shared perspective, misunderstandings arise, and reliance on AI becomes inconsistent or poorly calibrated.

Dynamic capability models further position AI literacy as an organizational asset that enables firms to identify opportunities, create value, and adapt processes over time (Malik, 2023). In software-intensive organizations, this literacy must be distributed across developers, managers, and leadership. Shared understanding supports more informed decision-making and helps organizations maintain balanced trust in AI systems.

Knowledge Retention and Institutional Memory

Generative AI mainly alters how organizations access and manage knowledge. Automated documentation and retrieval tools can improve efficiency, but they also introduce new risks of dependency. When institutional memory is embedded primarily in AI-mediated systems, tacit knowledge can gradually erode (Gausen et al., 2024). Employees may retrieve information quickly without deeply understanding it, reducing the organization's ability to respond creatively to unfamiliar or complex situations.

AI adoption must be accompanied by continued investment in human expertise to preserve adaptability (Mitra et al., 2024). Practices such as peer review, collaborative debugging, and mentorship play a vital role in maintaining experiential knowledge that automation cannot fully replicate. Organizational learning thus becomes a balancing act: leveraging AI for efficiency while safeguarding human judgment and insight.

Governance, Accountability, and Responsible Integration

As AI systems mainly shape decisions, governance models must clearly define responsibility and accountability. Recent literature identifies developers as stewards who remain accountable for outcomes influenced by AI, even when underlying reasoning processes are opaque (Sharma, 2024). Responsible AI scholarship extends this responsibility to ethical and environmental considerations, emphasizing fairness, transparency, and sustainability (Zhu, 2023; Cruz et al., 2025).

Effective governance requires explicit guidance on when AI-generated recommendations must be validated by humans, how decisions are documented, and how accountability is shared. In the absence of such structures, responsibility gaps emerge, undermining trust in automated systems. Design thinking approaches argue for embedding human-centered values into development practices, ensuring that automation supports rather than replaces reflective judgment (Krolikowski et al., 2022; Sarma, 2025).

The AI components must be evaluated within the structure of broader software architectures. Many integration failures stem not from isolated errors but from unexpected interactions across subsystems (Gemlau et al., 2022). Human oversight is therefore essential for maintaining system coherence and resilience. The effective human–AI collaboration depends on interfaces that enable inspection, interpretation, and critical evaluation of AI outputs (Sergeyuk et al., 2026).

Workforce Dynamics and Professional Sustainability

The organizational adoption of AI also reshapes workforce expectations and professional roles. Developers are assessed not only on their technical output but on their ability to orchestrate AI tools while exercising independent judgment. For early-career professionals, these shifting expectations can be perceived as threats to traditional notions of expertise, affecting motivation and professional identity (Hicks et al., 2024). Structured mentorship and transparent evaluation criteria help address these concerns by reinforcing the idea that AI augments rather than replaces human contribution (Bjerg, 2024).

Role distribution within organizations also evolves as automation advances. Oversight-oriented functions such as testing, validation, and architectural design become more prominent as routine coding tasks are automated. Organizations must actively communicate the intellectual and strategic value of these roles to sustain engagement and maintain talent pipelines (Mulgund et al., 2025). Continuous professional development initiatives which integrate AI literacy with reflective practice are essential for supporting long-term workforce resilience.

The next section synthesizes these organizational changes with earlier discussions of deskilling and reskilling, bringing them together into a unified model for sustainable human–AI collaboration.

INTEGRATING DESKILLING AND RESKILLING: TOWARD SUSTAINABLE HUMAN–AI COLLABORATION

AI-augmented development signals a fundamental shift in the cognitive ecology of software engineering. Automation increasingly takes on forms of routine reasoning, while simultaneously elevating the importance of oversight, interpretation, and system-level thinking. This redistribution does not inherently diminish expertise;

instead, it reshapes what developers repeatedly practice and, over time, internalize. The skills erode primarily when automated workflows remove opportunities for deliberate engagement (Cavestro, 2024; Ferdman, 2025). Yet those same workflows can strengthen higher-order reasoning when they are paired with reflective practices such as explanation, critique, and verification (Aspra & Chong, 2025).

Cognitive dependence provides the mechanism that links these divergent outcomes. Reliance on AI becomes problematic only when trust is poorly calibrated or transparency is lacking. Across studies of human–AI interaction, a consistent finding is that calibrated reliance neither blind acceptance nor reflexive rejection and supports effective collaboration (Kahr et al., 2024; Klingbeil et al., 2024; Wanner et al., 2022). In software engineering, this calibration takes the form of an epistemic stance in which AI-generated outputs are treated as hypotheses to be examined rather than authoritative answers to be followed. When developers adopt this stance, automation functions as a catalyst for learning rather than a substitute for understanding.

A sustainable model therefore depends on the reciprocal reinforcement of deskilling awareness and reskilling practice. Recognizing the risk of skill erosion encourages the deliberate design of workflows that preserve cognitive engagement. Reskilling initiatives such as training in oversight, structured reasoning, and system-level design provide the scaffolding needed to maintain professional autonomy. Educational and organizational structures play a critical mediating role in this process, shaping whether developers ultimately experience AI as an empowering collaborator or a constraining force (Uren & Edwards, 2023; Goel et al., 2024).

PRACTICAL IMPLICATIONS AND IMPLEMENTATION FRAMEWORK

Although conceptual synthesis helps clarify the dynamics of deskilling and reskilling, sustainable integration ultimately depends on action. Educators, organizations, and developers need practical guidance on how to embed reflective uses of AI into everyday practice. The framework that follows translates theoretical insights into concrete strategies aligned with research on AI adoption, governance, and learning.

Implications for Software Education

Software education must be redesigned so that AI supports reasoning rather than replacing it. This requires a shift in how learning environments are structured and how progress is evaluated. Main strategies include process-centered assessment that prioritizes explanation, critique, and justification over simple artifact correctness (Becker et al., 2023; Daun & Brings, 2023). Structured AI critique exercises can require students to identify and analyse the limitations of AI-generated code, encouraging deeper engagement with underlying concepts (Aspra & Chong, 2025). Integrating AI literacy into curricula helps learners understand model functions, bias, and ethical implications (Asrifan et al., 2025), while reflective documentation practices prompt students to articulate how AI tools influenced their decisions (Yan et al., 2024). Together, these approaches position AI as a pedagogical scaffold that strengthens metacognitive awareness rather than a shortcut to results.

Implications for Organizations

Organizations adopting generative AI must balance productivity gains with long-term capability development. Effective practices include human-in-the-loop verification processes that establish formal checkpoints for reviewing AI outputs (Sharma, 2024). Knowledge retention mechanisms such as peer review and mentorship help preserve tacit expertise that might otherwise erode through automation (Gausen et al., 2024; Mitra et al., 2024). Transparent governance models are essential for clarifying accountability in AI-mediated decisions (Zhu, 2023), and continuous reskilling programs should integrate training in oversight and system-level reasoning (Ersanlı et al., 2025; Bodea et al., 2024). These measures ensure that automation complements, rather than displaces, human judgment.

Implications for Developers

Individual practitioners also play a decisive role in shaping patterns of reliance on AI. Effective habits include documenting decision rationales to maintain transparency and accountability, as well as actively updating AI literacy through continuous learning (Goel et al., 2024). Such practices help sustain professional autonomy and critical engagement in automated environments.

Integrated Implementation Model

An effective implementation model connects education, early-career development, organizational practice, and continuous learning into a coherent progression:

Education → Early Career → Organizational Practice → Continuous Learning

At each stage, reflective engagement is reinforced, allowing expertise to evolve alongside technological change. The coordinated action across these levels leads to more resilient and sustainable AI adoption (Uren & Edwards, 2023; Felemban et al., 2024; Sergeyuk et al., 2026).

CONCLUSIONS: REFRAMING SOFTWARE EXPERTISE IN THE AI ERA

Generative AI represents a structural point of inflection in software engineering. Automation has expanded beyond execution into domains of conceptual reasoning, reshaping how expertise is practiced, assessed, and transmitted. This transformation is best understood through the intertwined processes of deskilling and reskilling. Deskilling draws attention to how reduced engagement with foundational activities can weaken practiced expertise, while cognitive dependence explains the mechanisms through which reliance patterns take shape. Reskilling, in turn, illustrates the adaptive competencies such as oversight, analytical reasoning, and system-level thinking which are required to sustain professional judgment in AI-mediated environments. The integrated capability profile of a reskilled software engineer is summarized in Figure 4.

Figure 4. Capability model of the reskilled software engineer.

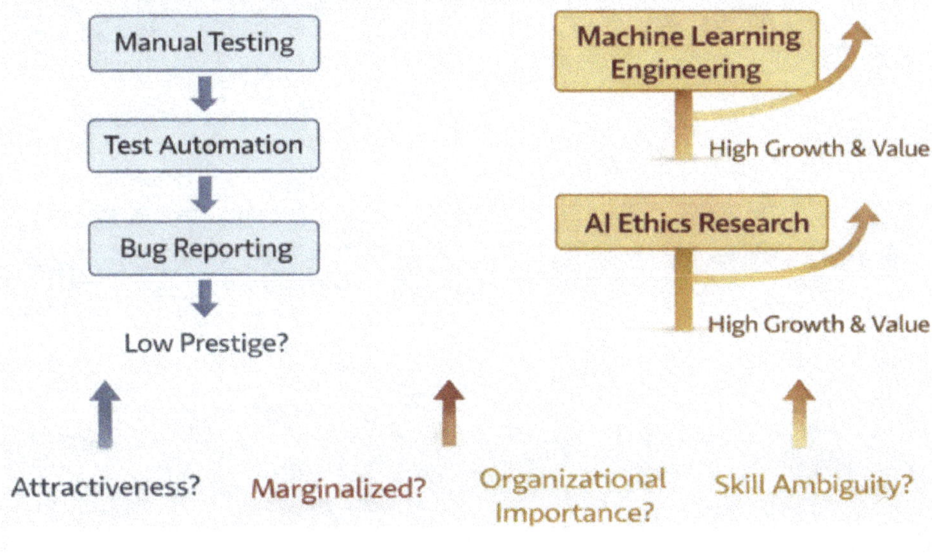

Moreover, these changes are not deterministic. Whether AI ultimately augments or undermines expertise depends on how tools are embedded within educational settings, organizational cultures, and individual practice. The calibrated trust, transparency, and reflective engagement are central to productive partnership (Kahr et al., 2024; Klingbeil et al., 2024). When AI is approached as a collaborator rather than an unquestioned authority, it can broaden the developer's cognitive horizon without displacing human agency.

The future of software engineering, therefore, is neither one of wholesale replacement nor of uncritical augmentation. Instead, it reflects a process of professional reinvention in which expertise becomes distributed across human and machine actors while remaining anchored in human judgment. Achieving sustainable integration requires the deliberate design of workflows, curricula, and governance structures that preserve opportunities for reasoning while leveraging the strengths of automation. By framing AI as a catalyst for reflective practice, the profession can navigate this transition in ways that enhance both productivity and autonomy.

Ultimately, AI-augmented software engineering invites a reconsideration of what it means to be an expert developer. Mastery no longer resides solely in manual implementation, but in the capacity to interpret, evaluate, and integrate automated intelligence within complex socio-technical systems. Preserving that capacity represents both the central challenge and the defining opportunity of the AI era.

ACKNOWLEDGEMENT

The authors used ChatGPT (OpenAI) to assist with language refinement, grammar correction, and improvement of readability during the preparation of this chapter.

REFERENCES

Ahmad, A., Waseem, M., Liang, P., Fahmideh, M., Aktar, M. S., & Mikkonen, T. (2023, June). Towards human-bot collaborative software architecting with chatgpt. In *Proceedings of the 27th international conference on evaluation and assessment in software engineering* (pp. 279-285). DOI: 10.1145/3593434.3593468

Aspra, N. O., & Chong, C. H. (2025, May). Developing an AI-Driven NC Programming Assistant: A Productive Failure Approach in CNC Education. In *2025 Systems and Information Engineering Design Symposium (SIEDS)* (pp. 438-443). IEEE. DOI: 10.1109/SIEDS65500.2025.11021219

Asrifan, A., Said, U. M. R., Jakob, J. C., & Wanci, R. (2025). AI literacy: foundations, importance, and broader implications. In *Transforming vocational education and training using AI* (pp. 17–48). IGI Global Scientific Publishing.

Becker, B. A., Craig, M., Denny, P., Keuning, H., Kiesler, N., Leinonen, J., ... & Quille, K. (2023). Generative ai in introductory programming. Computer Science Curricula, 438-439.

Bjerg, J. (2024). *The Early-Career Professional's Guide to Generative AI*. Apress. DOI: 10.1007/979-8-8688-0456-4

Bodea, C. N., Paparic, M., Mogos, R. I., & Dascalu, M. I. (2024). Artificial intelligence adoption in the workplace and its impact on the upskilling and reskilling strategies. *Amfiteatru Economic, 26*(65), 126–144. DOI: 10.24818/EA/2024/65/126

Cavestro, W. (2024). Automation, new technology and work content. In *The Transformation of Work?* (pp. 219–234). Routledge. DOI: 10.4324/9781003502913-11

Chattopadhyay, S., Nelson, N., Au, A., Morales, N., Sanchez, C., Pandita, R., & Sarma, A. (2022). Cognitive biases in software development. *Communications of the ACM, 65*(4), 115–122. DOI: 10.1145/3517217

Cruz, L., Fernandes, J. P., Kirkeby, M. H., Martínez-Fernández, S., Sallou, J., Anwar, H., Barba Roque, E., Bogner, J., Castaño, J., Castor, F., Chasmawala, A., Cunha, S., Feitosa, D., González, A., Jedlitschka, A., Lago, P., Muccini, H., Oprescu, A., Rani, P., & Yamshchikov, I. P. (2025). Greening ai-enabled systems with software engineering: A research agenda for environmentally sustainable ai practices. *Software Engineering Notes*, *50*(3), 14–23. DOI: 10.1145/3743095.3743099

Daun, M., & Brings, J. (2023, June). How ChatGPT will change software engineering education. In *Proceedings of the 2023 Conference on Innovation and Technology in Computer Science Education* V. 1 (pp. 110-116). DOI: 10.1145/3587102.3588815

Diaz Alfaro, G., Fiore, S. M., & Oden, K. (2024, September). Externalized and Extended Cognition: Cognitive Offloading for Human-Machine Teaming. [). Sage CA: Los Angeles, CA: SAGE Publications.]. *Proceedings of the Human Factors and Ergonomics Society Annual Meeting*, *68*(1), 290–293. DOI: 10.1177/10711813241275506

Ersanlı, C. Y., Çelik, F., Barjesteh, H., Duran, V., & Manoochehrzadeh, M. (2025). A review of global reskilling and upskilling initiatives in the age of AI. *AI and Ethics*, *5*(6), 1–10. DOI: 10.1007/s43681-025-00767-9

Felemban, H., Sohail, M., & Ruikar, K. (2024). Exploring the readiness of organisations to adopt artificial intelligence. *Buildings (Basel, Switzerland)*, *14*(8), 2460. DOI: 10.3390/buildings14082460

Ferdman, A. (2025). AI deskilling is a structural problem. *AI & Society*, •••, 1–13.

Fui-Hoon Nah, F., Zheng, R., Cai, J., Siau, K., & Chen, L. (2023). Generative AI and ChatGPT: Applications, challenges, and AI-human collaboration. Journal of information technology case and application research, 25(3), 277-304.

Gausen, A., Mitra, B., & Lindley, S. (2024, June). A framework for exploring the consequences of AI-mediated enterprise knowledge access and identifying risks to workers. In *Proceedings of the 2024 ACM conference on fairness, accountability, and transparency* (pp. 207-220). DOI: 10.1145/3630106.3658900

Gemlau, K. B., Hasseln, H. V., & Ernst, R. (2022, October). Industry-track: System-level logical execution time for automotive software development. In *2022 International Conference on Embedded Software (EMSOFT)* (pp. 21-23). IEEE. DOI: 10.1109/EMSOFT55006.2022.00017

Goel, A., Dede, C., Garn, M., & Ou, C. (2024). AI-ALOE: AI for reskilling, upskilling, and workforce development. *AI Magazine*, *45*(1), 77–82. DOI: 10.1002/aaai.12157

Grimmelikhuijsen, S. (2023). Explaining why the computer says no: Algorithmic transparency affects the perceived trustworthiness of automated decision-making. *Public Administration Review*, *83*(2), 241–262. DOI: 10.1111/puar.13483

Hicks, C. M., Lee, C. S., & Foster-Marks, K. (2024). The new developer: AI skill threat, identity change & developer thriving in the transition to AI-assisted software development.

Idrisov, B., & Schlippe, T. (2024). Program code generation with generative AIs. *Algorithms*, *17*(2), 62. DOI: 10.3390/a17020062

Kahr, P. K., Rooks, G., Willemsen, M. C., & Snijders, C. C. (2024). Understanding trust and reliance development in ai advice: Assessing model accuracy, model explanations, and experiences from previous interactions. *ACM Transactions on Interactive Intelligent Systems*, *14*(4), 1–30. DOI: 10.1145/3686164

Kinowska, H., & Sienkiewicz, Ł. J. (2023). Influence of algorithmic management practices on workplace well-being–evidence from European organisations. *Information Technology & People*, *36*(8), 21–42. DOI: 10.1108/ITP-02-2022-0079

Klingbeil, A., Grützner, C., & Schreck, P. (2024). Trust and reliance on AI—An experimental study on the extent and costs of overreliance on AI. *Computers in Human Behavior*, *160*, 108352. DOI: 10.1016/j.chb.2024.108352

Krolikowski, K. A., Bi, M., Baggott, C. M., Khorzad, R., Holl, J. L., & Kruser, J. M. (2022). Design thinking to improve healthcare delivery in the intensive care unit: Promise, pitfalls, and lessons learned. *Journal of Critical Care*, *69*, 153999. DOI: 10.1016/j.jcrc.2022.153999 PMID: 35104692

Le, H. (2025). The Deskilling of Software Development and the Impact of AI Chatbots on Programmers' Skills and Roles. In *Generative AI in Software Engineering* (pp. 397–426). IGI Global Scientific Publishing. DOI: 10.4018/979-8-3373-0370-3.ch013

Le, H. (2025). The Deskilling of Software Development and the Impact of AI Chatbots on Programmers' Skills and Roles. In *Generative AI in Software Engineering* (pp. 397–426). IGI Global Scientific Publishing. DOI: 10.4018/979-8-3373-0370-3.ch013

Malik, S. A. (2023). Unlocking Organizational Potential: Harnessing AI literacy for Dynamic Capabilities through sensing, seizing and reconfiguring initiatives in IT firms.

Mbelekani, N. Y., & Bengler, K. (2023, November). Unequally Yoked [Skilled]: Transformative Views on Human-Automation Skilfulness. In *2023 International Conference on Electrical, Computer and Energy Technologies (ICECET)* (pp. 1-8). IEEE. DOI: 10.1109/ICECET58911.2023.10389238

Mieczkowski, H. N. (2022). *AI-Mediated communication: Examining agency, ownership, expertise, and roles of AI systems*. Stanford University.

Miranda, J. P. P., Cruz, M. A. D., Fernandez, A. B., Balahadia, F. F., Aviles, J. S., Caro, C. A., ... & Gaña, E. P. (2025). Erosion of Critical Academic Skills Due to AI Dependency Among Tertiary Students.

Mitra, A., Seetharaman, A., & Maddulety, K. (2024, December). Adoption of Artificial Intelligence Enabling Value Creation in Business. In 2024 4th International Conference on Robotics, Automation and Artificial Intelligence (RAAI) (pp. 213-220). IEEE. DOI: 10.1109/RAAI64504.2024.10949520

Mitsugi, N., Ijuin, K., Oshiyama, C., Hara, E., & Nishimura, T. (2025). An AI-mediated framework for recursive learning: Transforming individual experiences into organizational knowledge and autonomous engagement in elderly care. *Frontiers in Digital Health*, *7*, 1529072. DOI: 10.3389/fdgth.2025.1529072 PMID: 40678716

Mulgund, P., Singh, R., Gillenson, M., Li, Y., & Oliver, C. (2025, May). "Not My First Choice": Why Software Testing Struggles to Attract Early-Career Professionals. In Proceedings of the 2025 Computers and People Research Conference (pp. 1-8).

Ozkaya, I. (2023). The next frontier in software development: AI-augmented software development processes. *IEEE Software*, *40*(4), 4–9. DOI: 10.1109/MS.2023.3278056

Pangavhane, S., Raktate, G., Pariane, P., Shelar, K., Wakchaure, R., & Kale, J. N. (2024, December). AI-augmented software development: Boosting efficiency and quality. In *2024 International Conference on Decision Aid Sciences and Applications (DASA)* (pp. 1-5). IEEE. DOI: 10.1109/DASA63652.2024.10836523

Petrovska, O., Clift, L., Moller, F., & Pearsall, R. (2024, January). Incorporating generative AI into software development education. In *Proceedings of the 8th Conference on Computing Education Practice* (pp. 37-40). DOI: 10.1145/3633053.3633057

Pham, P., Nguyen, V., & Nguyen, T. (2022, October). A review of ai-augmented end-to-end test automation tools. In *Proceedings of the 37th IEEE/ACM International Conference on Automated Software Engineering* (pp. 1-4). DOI: 10.1145/3551349.3563240

Pradhan, I. P., & Saxena, P. (2023). Reskilling workforce for the Artificial Intelligence age: Challenges and the way forward. In The adoption and effect of artificial intelligence on human resources management, Part B (pp. 181-197). Emerald Publishing Limited.

Ramos, T., Dean, A., & McGregor, D. (2025). AI-Augmented Software Engineering: Revolutionizing or Challenging Software Quality and Testing? *Journal of Software (Malden, MA)*, *37*(2), e2741. DOI: 10.1002/smr.2741

Sarma, A. D. N. (2025). FusionFlow: A Software Development Approach in the Era of Design Thinking and AI. In Innovative Design Thinking Approaches in Software Engineering (pp. 53-84). IGI Global Scientific Publishing. DOI: 10.4018/979-8-3693-9531-8.ch003

Sauvola, J., Tarkoma, S., Klemettinen, M., Riekki, J., & Doermann, D. (2024). Future of software development with generative AI. *Automated Software Engineering*, *31*(1), 26. DOI: 10.1007/s10515-024-00426-z

Schaetz, N., Gagrčin, E., Toth, R., & Emmer, M. (2025). Algorithm dependency in platformized news use. new media & society, 27(3), 1360-1377.

Schieferdecker, I. K. (2025, August). Navigating the growing field of research on AI for software testing–the taxonomy for AI-augmented software testing and an ontology-driven literature survey. In International Conference on Formal Methods for Industrial Critical Systems (pp. 3-20). Cham: Springer Nature Switzerland.

Sergeyuk, A., Zakharov, I., Koshchenko, E., & Izadi, M. (2026). Human-AI experience in integrated development environments: A systematic literature review. *Empirical Software Engineering*, *31*(3), 55. DOI: 10.1007/s10664-025-10793-0

Sharma, R. (2024). Governance and Oversight of AI Systems. In *AI and the Boardroom: Insights into Governance, Strategy, and the Responsible Adoption of AI* (pp. 353–370). Apress. DOI: 10.1007/979-8-8688-0796-1_28

Spinellis, D. (2024). Pair programming with generative AI. *IEEE Software*, *41*(3), 16–18. DOI: 10.1109/MS.2024.3363848

Sun, Y., & Xu, C. (2025). Hybrid cognitive authority and algorithmic subjectivity: Rethinking knowledge management in AI-driven communication. *Journal of Knowledge Management*, •••, 1–26. DOI: 10.1108/JKM-02-2025-0252

Tan, L. (2024). Designing an AI Career Mentor for Early Career Researchers. *CERN ideaSquare Journal of Experimental Innovation*, *8*(3), 42–51.

Treude, C., & Gerosa, M. A. (2025, April). How developers interact with AI: A taxonomy of human-AI collaboration in software engineering. In 2025 IEEE/ACM Second International Conference on AI Foundation Models and Software Engineering (Forge) (pp. 236-240). IEEE. DOI: 10.1109/Forge66646.2025.00033

Turvey, K., & Pachler, N. (2025). A topological exploration of convergence/divergence of human-mediated and algorithmically mediated pedagogy. *British Journal of Educational Technology*, bjet.70007. DOI: 10.1111/bjet.70007

Uren, V., & Edwards, J. S. (2023). Technology readiness and the organizational journey towards AI adoption: An empirical study. *International Journal of Information Management, 68*, 102588. DOI: 10.1016/j.ijinfomgt.2022.102588

Valový, M., & Buchalcevova, A. (2023, October). The psychological effects of AI-assisted programming on students and professionals. In *2023 IEEE International Conference on Software Maintenance and Evolution (ICSME)* (pp. 385-390). IEEE. DOI: 10.1109/ICSME58846.2023.00050

van Voorst, R. (2024). Challenges and limitations of human oversight in ethical artificial intelligence implementation in health care: Balancing digital literacy and professional strain. *Mayo Clinic Proceedings. Digital Health*, *2*(4), 559–563. DOI: 10.1016/j.mcpdig.2024.08.004 PMID: 40206522

Wahn, B., Schmitz, L., Gerster, F. N., & Weiss, M. (2023). Offloading under cognitive load: Humans are willing to offload parts of an attentionally demanding task to an algorithm. *PLoS One*, *18*(5), e0286102. DOI: 10.1371/journal.pone.0286102 PMID: 37205658

Wanner, J., Herm, L. V., Heinrich, K., & Janiesch, C. (2022). The effect of transparency and trust on intelligent system acceptance: Evidence from a user-based study. *Electronic Markets*, *32*(4), 2079–2102. DOI: 10.1007/s12525-022-00593-5

Weis, P. P., & Wiese, E. (2022). Know your cognitive environment! Mental models as crucial determinant of offloading preferences. *Human Factors*, *64*(3), 499–513. DOI: 10.1177/0018720820956861 PMID: 32955351

Xu, J., & He, C. (2024, December). Understanding AI Tools Adoption in Academic Work: Case from Chinese Early-Career Researchers. In International Conference on Asian Digital Libraries (pp. 181-193). Singapore: Springer Nature Singapore.

Yabaku, M., Pombo, N., & Ouhbi, S. (2024, September). Exploring the potential use of generative ai in software engineering education. In 2024 IEEE 18th International Conference on Application of Information and Communication Technologies (AICT) (pp. 1-7). IEEE. DOI: 10.1109/AICT61888.2024.10740416

Yan, W., Nakajima, T., & Sawada, R. (2024). Benefits and challenges of collaboration between students and conversational generative artificial intelligence in programming learning: An empirical case study. *Education Sciences*, *14*(4), 433. DOI: 10.3390/educsci14040433

Yilmaz, R., & Yilmaz, F. G. K. (2023). The effect of generative artificial intelligence (AI)-based tool use on students' computational thinking skills, programming self-efficacy and motivation. *Computers and Education: Artificial Intelligence*, *4*, 100147. DOI: 10.1016/j.caeai.2023.100147

Zhu, L. (2023, May). Software Engineering as the Linchpin of Responsible AI. In 2023 IEEE/ACM 45th International Conference on Software Engineering (ICSE) (pp. 3-4). IEEE. DOI: 10.1109/ICSE48619.2023.00012

KEY TERMS AND DEFINITIONS

AI Literacy: The understanding of AI system capabilities, limitations, biases, and ethical implications.

AI-Augmented Software Engineering: A development model in which generative AI systems collaborate with developers over the software lifecycle.

Cognitive Offloading: The strategic transfer of mental effort to external systems like AI tools to reduce cognitive load during problem-solving.

Deskilling: The gradual declination of practiced expertise due to reduced interest in cognitively demanding tasks.

Human-in-the-Loop: A framework in which human oversight is integrated into automated workflows to ensure accountability and validation.

Hybrid Cognitive System: A socio-technical system where reasoning and decision-making are distributed between human and AI agents.

Reskilling: The development of new competencies like oversight, analytical reasoning, and governance to sustain expertise in AI-powered systems.

System-Level Thinking: The ability to reason across architectural layers, constraints, and long-term system impacts beyond local code correctness.

Trust Calibration: The ability to appropriately adjust dependence on AI systems based on their reliability, transparency, and contextual fit.

Chapter 8
Integrating AI Literacy, Secure Coding, and Critical Evaluation

Atul Kumar
http://orcid.org/0000-0003-3859-0686
Dnyaan Prasad Global University, India

Gafur Namazov
Termez University of Economics and Service, Termez, Uzbekistan

Ablayeva Nadira
Mamun University, Khiva, Uzbekistan

Shadiev Rizamat
Karshi State University, Uzbekistan

Mirzayev Bobur
Alfraganus University, Uzbekistan

Kurbonbekova Mohichekhra
Department of Scientific and Innovative Developments, Tashkent, Uzbekistan

Aslanova Ozoda
Navoi State University of Mining and Technologies, Uzbekistan

ABSTRACT

Let's start with something honest: most software teams didn't sit down and decide to adopt AI coding tools. The tools just showed up—in IDEs, in search results, in what colleagues started pasting into Slack—and adoption happened organically, often before anyone thought much about the implications. That's not a criticism. It's just how useful tools tend to spread. But now that GitHub Copilot, ChatGPT, and half a dozen competitors are embedded in real development workflows, the question of what to actually do about them—how to teach engineers to use them well, how to keep security from quietly eroding, how to prevent the gradual atrophy of skills that no one noticed they were losing—has become genuinely urgent. This chapter tries to address that question with something more than general advice. What follows is

DOI: 10.4018/979-8-3373-8450-4.ch008

a framework built around three interconnected competencies: understanding how AI code generation tools actually work (what we're calling AI literacy), maintaining rigorous security habits when using them, and developing the judgment to critically evaluate what they produce. None of these stands alone. Together, they describe what it means to use AI tools as a skilled professional rather than a passive recipient of output. The framework is grounded in recent empirical research—and there's quite a bit of it now, which is useful. It's designed for educators building curricula and for organizations trying to upskill engineering teams. The core argument is simple even if the details aren't: AI assistance is only as good as the human judgment wrapped around it.

1. INTRODUCTION

There's a version of this introduction that starts with statistics—GitHub Copilot users, ChatGPT adoption curves, market size projections. That version isn't wrong, but it misses something. The more interesting story isn't how fast these tools spread. It's what happens after.

Here's what the research is actually showing: developers who use AI coding tools often produce code with more security vulnerabilities than developers who don't, and they feel more confident about it (Perry et al., 2023). Students who get access to these tools before building foundational programming skills sometimes never develop those skills (Finnie-Ansley et al., 2022; Becker et al., 2023). And even experienced engineers accept AI suggestions without adequate review far more often than they probably would if you asked them directly whether that was a good idea (Barke et al., 2023; Vaithilingam et al., 2022).

None of this means the tools are bad. It means using them badly has real costs. And the profession hasn't yet done the work of figuring out what "using them well" actually requires.

That's what this chapter is about. Specifically, it's about three things: AI literacy (understanding the tools well enough to use them intelligently), secure coding practices that hold up in AI-augmented workflows, and critical evaluation—the habit of actually looking at what AI generates rather than treating it as ground truth. These aren't three separate topics that happen to share a chapter. They're deeply entangled. You can't evaluate AI output well if you don't understand where it comes from. You can't maintain security practices if you don't know what to look for. The framework we're proposing treats them as a unified whole.

1.1 What AI Tools Actually Change About the Job

The question worth sitting with is: what does AI assistance change about software engineering, specifically? Not in a hand-wavy "everything is different now" sense, but concretely.

The clearest answer is that certain tasks get cheaper—faster, easier, more automated. Boilerplate, common algorithmic patterns, test scaffolding, translations between languages: AI tools handle these with increasing reliability. What doesn't get cheaper, or at least shouldn't, is the judgment work. Deciding whether a generated function actually does what you need. Catching the SQL injection vector buried three levels down. Determining whether a component fits the architecture of the system it's being added to. Recognizing that "correct on common inputs" and "correct" are not the same thing.

The tools are large language models, which means they generate code by predicting statistically likely continuations of whatever input they receive (Xu et al., 2022; Biderman et al., 2023). They're very good at this in ways that can look like understanding but isn't quite. Patterns that appear frequently in their training data—popular libraries, standard algorithms, well-documented APIs—tend to come out right. Novel requirements, unusual edge cases, security-critical operations where common practice is also insecure practice: these are where the statistical prediction machinery starts producing plausible-looking nonsense.

The practical capability of current tools is genuinely broad: function completion from signatures, test generation, cross-language translation, code explanation, refactoring suggestions, even whole-component scaffolding from high-level descriptions (Denny et al., 2023; Nam et al., 2024; Sarsa et al., 2022). The breadth is real. But breadth isn't the same as reliability, and reliability isn't uniform across task types.

1.2 Chapter Roadmap

Section 2 covers the research background—the evolution of the technology, what studies have found about educational and security implications. Section 3 addresses AI literacy in detail. Section 4 takes on secure coding with AI assistance. Section 5 examines critical evaluation methods. Section 6 pulls these together into a practical framework for both academic programs and professional development. Sections 7 and 8 address limitations, future directions, and concrete recommendations.

2. BACKGROUND: WHERE WE ARE AND HOW WE GOT HERE

Code generation tools have existed for decades. Template systems, scaffolding frameworks, macro expanders, IDE code completion—none of this is new. What's new is the fluency. Earlier tools required rigid specifications and produced rigid outputs. What's happened in the last few years, driven primarily by the transformer architecture and massive increases in training data and compute, is that the outputs have become flexible enough to be genuinely useful across a wide range of tasks.

The inflection point most researchers point to is Chen et al. (2021), whose Codex model demonstrated that language models trained specifically on code could solve programming problems with real accuracy. Their HumanEval benchmark gave the field a consistent measurement tool, and subsequent work has shown steady improvement across it and similar evaluations (Li et al., 2023; Roziere et al., 2023). Whether benchmark improvement maps cleanly to real-world utility is a separate question—it often doesn't, at least not one-to-one—but it's a reasonable proxy for progress.

2.1 The Tools Themselves

GitHub Copilot was the tool that brought AI code generation into mainstream practice, mostly because it showed up inside VS Code and other common editors without requiring any particular deliberate adoption decision. Developers started using it because it was there. Studies found that it could meaningfully accelerate certain tasks while also generating insecure or incorrect code at rates that warranted concern (Dakhel et al., 2023; Pearce et al., 2022; Nguyen & Nadi, 2022).

ChatGPT changed the interaction model. In-line completion is useful for finishing what you've started. Conversational AI is useful for working out what you're trying to do—iterating on requirements, debugging conceptual issues, getting explanations (Poldrack et al., 2023). For a lot of developers, the conversational interface turned out to feel more natural for complex problems than the autocomplete metaphor. The two approaches aren't competing; most developers end up using both.

Open-source alternatives—StarCoder, Code Llama, and others—have expanded the ecosystem significantly, giving teams more control over data handling and allowing organizations with strict compliance requirements to run models locally (Li et al., 2023; Roziere et al., 2023). The competitive landscape is now broad enough that there's no single tool that covers all use cases, and organizations are increasingly mixing approaches.

2.2 What the Research Finds About Learning

The educational research on AI code generation is, if we're being honest, somewhat alarming for anyone involved in teaching programming—though the implications are more nuanced than they might first appear.

Finnie-Ansley et al. (2022) established early on that tools like Codex could solve the kinds of problems assigned in introductory programming courses. This isn't surprising in retrospect, but it crystallized a real problem: if the tool can do the assignment, what is the assignment actually for? The answer, presumably, is that wrestling with the assignment is how students build the skills that let them later handle problems the tool can't solve. Remove the wrestling and you might remove the learning.

Becker et al. (2023) pushed this analysis further, examining what specifically gets lost when AI handles the cognitive work that programming exercises are designed to develop. Syntax acquisition, debugging fluency, the ability to decompose complex problems—these emerge from struggle in ways that don't have obvious substitutes. Their work triggered significant discussion about restructuring programming education around higher-order skills rather than trying to ban tools that students will use anyway.

Lau and Guo (2023) surveyed programming instructors to see how they were actually responding. The range was huge—from outright prohibition to enthusiastic integration—with most instructors acknowledging they didn't have a clear framework for either. That's an honest assessment of where things stood, and probably still stands for many programs.

2.3 The Security Problem

The security findings are where things get genuinely troubling, and they deserve more attention than they typically get in discussions of AI tool adoption.

Pearce et al. (2022) ran a systematic analysis of Copilot's security posture across multiple languages and task types. Roughly 40% of generated code contained exploitable security weaknesses. SQL injection flaws, weak cryptographic implementations, inadequate input validation—these showed up with disturbing regularity. The tool was producing code that would fail a basic security review, without any indication that anything was wrong.

Perry et al. (2023) ran the more troubling experiment: they tested whether developers using AI assistance actually wrote more insecure code than those working without it. They did. And—this is the part that keeps security researchers up at night—the developers using AI assistance reported higher confidence in their code's security, despite the objective evidence showing the opposite. The tool was introducing vulnerabilities while simultaneously making developers feel better about the code.

The mechanism is fairly clear once you understand how these models are trained. Public repositories—the dominant training data source—contain enormous amounts of insecure code. Legacy code that predates modern security standards, code written by developers who weren't prioritizing security, code where the vulnerability isn't obvious without specialized knowledge. Models learn the statistical patterns of this code without learning anything about why certain patterns are dangerous. The output looks correct. It may even be functionally correct. The security flaw is invisible to the model because the model has no concept of security—only of patterns (Dakhel et al., 2023).

3. AI LITERACY: WHAT ENGINEERS ACTUALLY NEED TO UNDERSTAND

AI literacy is a term that gets thrown around a lot, usually without much specificity. In the context of software engineering, what it actually needs to mean is: understanding the tools well enough to use them intelligently, recognize their failure modes before those failures become costly, and make informed decisions about when AI assistance is helpful versus when it's actively getting in the way.

This is distinct from just knowing how to open Copilot or type a prompt into ChatGPT. The bar is higher than that. It involves developing what might be called calibrated skepticism—not reflexively distrust AI outputs, but not accept them uncritically either. The developers who use these tools most effectively treat them like a smart but fallible colleague: useful, worth listening to, worth pushing back on (Kasneci et al., 2023).

Figure 1. AI Code Generation Workflow and Security Touchpoints

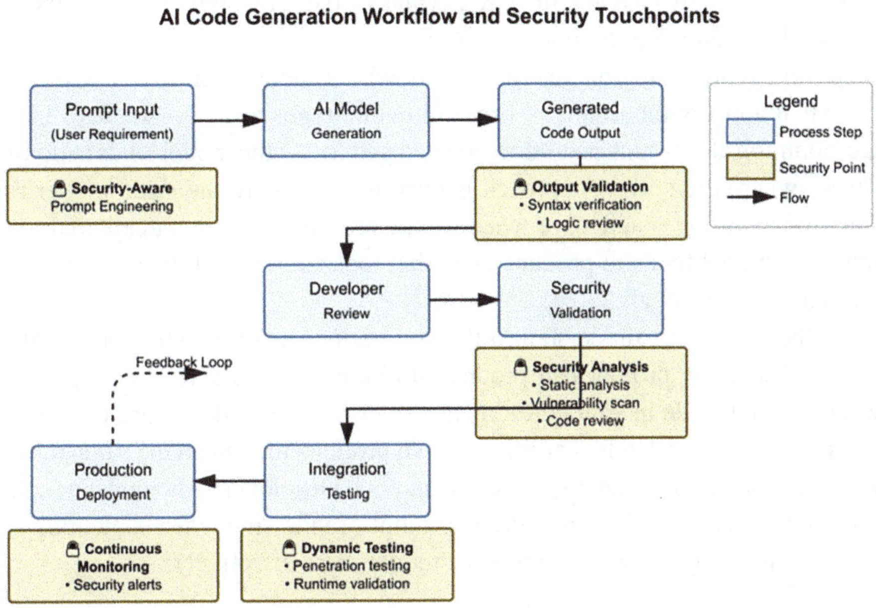

Figure 1 illustrates the complete AI-assisted development workflow from initial prompt input through production deployment, highlighting five critical security validation touchpoints. The diagram demonstrates how security considerations must be integrated throughout the development lifecycle rather than addressed as an afterthought. Feedback loops between stages enable continuous improvement as security issues identified in later stages inform refinements to earlier processes, creating a comprehensive defense-in-depth approach to AI-assisted secure coding.

3.1 How These Models Actually Work

You don't need a PhD in machine learning to use AI coding tools well. But a rough conceptual model of what's happening under the hood turns out to be genuinely useful.

Large language models generate code by statistical prediction. Given some input—your prompt, the surrounding code in your file, whatever context the model has access to—the model predicts what tokens are statistically likely to follow, drawing on patterns learned from its training data (Biderman et al., 2023). This process doesn't involve anything that resembles understanding in the way a developer understands code. The model isn't reasoning about what the code should do and then writing it. It's asking, in effect, "what kind of code typically appears after input like this?" and then producing that.

The implications are concrete. For tasks where the answer is "the same kind of code that appears thousands of times in public repositories"—standard library usage, common algorithms, well-documented patterns—the model tends to do well. For tasks where the correct approach is uncommon, where the right answer runs counter to prevailing practice, or where subtle requirements aren't captured in the prompt, the model tends to produce code that looks correct while being wrong in important ways (Xu et al., 2022).

The other key thing to understand is that suggestions are probabilistic and context-sensitive. The same prompt can produce different outputs across multiple runs. The surrounding code in your editor influences what the model suggests. Phrasing matters in ways that often feel arbitrary—two prompts that mean the same thing to a developer can produce notably different outputs. Developers who understand this can use it deliberately: running multiple prompts, rephrasing when something isn't working, structuring context to guide the model more effectively.

3.2 Prompt Engineering Is a Real Skill

There was a period when "prompt engineering" as a phrase attracted a certain amount of eye-rolling, as though it were a fancy name for figuring out how to ask questions. It's more than that. How you describe a task to an AI coding tool meaningfully affects the quality of what comes back, and the strategies that consistently work better are learnable (White et al., 2023; Denny et al., 2023).

A few things that actually help: providing complete function signatures with descriptive parameter names (the model uses these as strong signals about intent); including docstrings that specify not just what a function does but its constraints, edge cases, and what it should explicitly not do; offering concrete examples of expected inputs and outputs rather than abstract descriptions; and—critically—being explicit about security requirements. Saying "validate and sanitize all input" or "use parameterized queries" in the prompt produces noticeably better security outcomes than leaving it implicit (White et al., 2023).

The bigger mindset shift is treating the interaction as iterative. Research by Vaithilingam et al. (2022) found that developers who treated AI assistance as a back-and-forth process—refining prompts based on what came back, asking follow-up questions, requesting explanations for outputs they didn't understand—consistently got better results than those who expected a single prompt to deliver final-quality code. This parallels good human collaboration in fairly obvious ways.

Zamfirescu-Pereira et al. (2023) documented something useful here: non-expert users consistently struggle with prompt design in ways that more experienced users don't even notice they're doing differently. The skill is real, it's learnable, and it needs to be taught explicitly rather than assumed.

Table 1. Prompt Engineering Strategies and Their Effectiveness

Strategy	What It Involves	Effectiveness	Where It Helps Most
Complete function signatures	Full type annotations, descriptive parameter names, clear return type	High	Function generation, API implementations
Example-driven prompts	Concrete input/output pairs that demonstrate intended behavior	Very High	Algorithm implementations, data transforms
Explicit constraint specification	Stating security, performance, style requirements directly in the prompt	High	Production code, regulated environments
Iterative refinement	Treating the first output as a draft, not a solution	Medium-High	Complex or exploratory problems
Rich context provision	Including imports, adjacent code, relevant dependencies	Very High	Integration work, existing codebases
Negative constraints	Specifying what not to do—deprecated APIs, known bad patterns	Medium	Security-critical code, migration tasks

3.3 Knowing the Failure Modes

Part of using AI tools well is having a realistic map of where they reliably go wrong. This isn't about distrust—it's about knowing where to look harder.

Novel or rare scenarios are the most consistent weak point. Models produce better results for patterns well-represented in their training data. When asked to work with newly released frameworks, implement unusual algorithms, or address domain-specific requirements that didn't appear much in public repositories, the output is less reliable—and often confidently less reliable, which is the dangerous part (Wermelinger, 2023). Code written for cutting-edge or niche contexts should be treated as a rough first draft until carefully reviewed.

Architectural consistency across large codebases is another persistent limitation. Models work within a context window. They don't have a view of the whole system. They can generate a component that is locally correct but inconsistent with patterns elsewhere in the project—different error handling conventions, different abstraction levels, dependencies that conflict with existing choices. The model has no idea, because the model can only see what's in its context.

Security deserves its own flag. This is the limitation with the highest real-world cost, and it's discussed at length in Section 4.

4. SECURE CODING WHEN AI IS WRITING (SOME OF) YOUR CODE

Security is the area where the gap between "AI tool produces correct-looking output" and "AI tool produces safe output" is most consequential—and most consistently underestimated. The research covered in Section 2 should make clear why treating AI-generated code as secure by default is a mistake. This section is about what to do instead.

The approach has to be layered. No single practice is sufficient. Using prompts strategically to reduce obvious vulnerabilities, applying automated analysis to catch known patterns, and building review practices that specifically target the areas where AI-generated code most often fails—these work together, not as alternatives to each other.

4.1 The Vulnerability Patterns That Keep Appearing

It's worth being specific about what Pearce et al. (2022) actually found, because the categories are instructive.

Input validation failures were the most common class of problem—code that processes user input without adequate sanitization, creating vectors for injection attacks. SQL injection showed up in roughly 40% of database-related code in their study. That's not a rounding error; it's a structural issue with how the training data looks. Insecure database interaction patterns are extremely common in public repositories, so the model generates them.

Cryptographic weaknesses were the second major category. Outdated algorithms, fixed initialization vectors, insufficient randomness, improper key management—these appear partly because legacy code is heavily represented in training data and partly because the model has no understanding of why certain cryptographic choices are dangerous. It generates what it's seen. Code that uses MD5 to hash passwords is common in training data, so it can appear in generated code (Dakhel et al., 2023).

Authentication and authorization flaws—hard-coded credentials, inadequate session management, missing access control checks—showed up regularly, as did resource management issues: unclosed file handles, potential memory leaks, error handling that inadvertently exposes internal state. These aren't exotic vulnerability classes. They're the same issues security teams have been fighting for a generation. The AI tools are reproducing them from training data.

4.2 Making Prompts Security-Aware

The easiest intervention is also surprisingly underutilized: ask for security. Explicitly.

Prompts that include direct security constraints—"use parameterized queries exclusively," "validate and sanitize all user input before processing," "implement error handling that doesn't expose internal details"—produce meaningfully better security outcomes than prompts that describe only functional requirements (White et al., 2023). The model responds to explicit guidance. Leaving security implicit is essentially hoping the model will infer it from context, which it often won't.

Adding security-relevant context to prompts also helps. Noting that a function will handle untrusted user input, that the code will run with elevated privileges, that the implementation must meet PCI DSS or similar compliance requirements—this gives the model information it can use to generate more appropriate code. Even a brief description of the threat model tends to improve results.

The important caveat—worth stating clearly—is that better prompts reduce risk, not eliminate it. Every piece of AI-generated code going into production needs verification, regardless of how carefully the prompt was constructed.

Figure 2. Security Validation Framework for AI-Generated Code

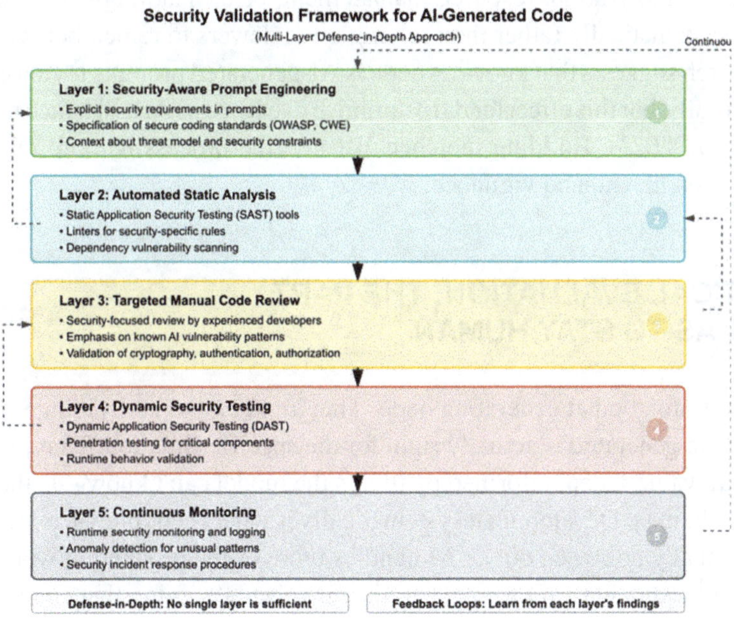

Figure 2 presents a multi-layered security validation framework implementing defense-in-depth principles for Al-generated code. Each layer-from security-aware prompt engineering through continuous monitoring-provides independent verification while feedback loops enable learning across layers. This approach recognizes that no single validation method sufficiently addresses all security risks, necessitating multiple complementary controls that balance thoroughness with practicality without undermining productivity benefits.

4.3 Verification in Practice

Static analysis tools are the first line of automated defense. Semgrep, CodeQL, SonarQube, and language-specific linters can automatically detect many common vulnerability patterns: SQL injection vectors, XSS risks, insecure cryptographic usage, potential authentication bypasses. Integrating these into CI pipelines rather than running them manually means every commit gets checked, not just the ones that happen to get careful review. These tools have real false positive and false negative rates, so they can't substitute for human review—but they catch a substantial portion of obvious problems before they get far.

Code review for AI-generated code benefits from explicit checklists that reflect the known risk areas. Input validation, cryptographic implementations, authentication and authorization, resource management, error handling—these should be checked systematically rather than relying on reviewers to remember what to look for. Research suggests that knowing code is AI-generated prompts reviewers to look more carefully, but this effect tends to diminish over time as AI assistance normalizes (Perry et al., 2023). Building the checklist into the process is more reliable than depending on heightened vigilance.

5. CRITICAL EVALUATION: THE PART THAT HAS TO STAY HUMAN

AI tools are good at generating code. They're not good at deciding whether the code they've generated is actually right for the specific situation. That judgment—contextual, value-laden, informed by things the model can't know—is the part that has to stay human. Developing it systematically is what keeps human expertise from being gradually hollowed out as AI handles more of the production work.

Critical evaluation isn't a single skill. It involves verifying that code does what it's supposed to do (correctness), that it does so in ways that will hold up over time (quality), and that it's appropriate for the specific deployment context it's heading into (fitness for purpose). These dimensions require different knowledge and different approaches.

5.1 Correctness Verification

The core problem with correctness verification for AI-generated code is that the code often looks correct. It handles the common cases. It passes the obvious tests. The failures tend to show up at boundaries, in edge cases, under unusual inputs—exactly the places where casual testing doesn't look (Wermelinger, 2023).

Specification-based testing is the most rigorous approach: define expected behavior precisely, including boundary conditions, error cases, and side effects, and then test against those definitions systematically. This is more work than running a few examples and calling it done—which is exactly why it's valuable. AI-generated solutions that work on typical inputs but fail at edges are a real pattern in the literature.

For reimplementations and refactoring, behavioral comparison offers an additional check: run both the AI-generated version and a reference implementation on the same inputs and compare outputs. This surfaces subtle correctness issues that might not be visible from code inspection alone. It's not a guarantee—identical behavior on a test set doesn't prove correctness across all inputs—but it's a useful additional layer.

5.2 Code Quality Beyond Correctness

A function that works today but that no one can modify six months from now without breaking something is not actually a good function. Code quality assessment has to look past whether the code runs.

Readability and maintainability evaluation asks whether the code follows team conventions, uses clear naming, provides appropriate documentation, and structures logic in ways that a future developer can follow without heroic effort. Research by Nam et al. (2024) found that AI-generated code sometimes exhibits unusual patterns—technically correct implementations that are nonetheless harder than necessary to understand. Part of evaluation is asking whether complexity is justified by requirements or is just an artifact of how the model generates output.

Architectural consistency is particularly important when AI-generated components get integrated into existing systems. The model doesn't know your architecture. It generates code that makes local sense. Whether that code fits the broader design—respects module boundaries, maintains appropriate abstraction levels, follows established patterns—is a judgment call that requires understanding the system the model doesn't have.

5.3 Fitness for Context

The hardest evaluation dimension is also the one most often skipped: whether the code is appropriate for the specific operational environment it will run in, not just whether it works in isolation.

Performance characteristics are context-dependent in ways the model can't account for. A solution that works fine at development-time data volumes may be unusable in production. AI tools generate solutions that are often algorithmically reasonable but not necessarily optimized for actual usage patterns. For performance-sensitive code, profiling and benchmarking against realistic conditions is necessary, not optional.

Operational context considerations include error handling, resource cleanup, logging and monitoring, compatibility with infrastructure constraints, and behavior under failure conditions. AI tools tend to generate code that assumes things go right. Experienced developers know that things often don't, and they build for it. That perspective has to be applied explicitly in evaluation because it won't come from the tool.

6. A FRAMEWORK FOR DEVELOPING THESE COMPETENCIES

The previous three sections have treated AI literacy, secure coding, and critical evaluation as distinct topics. They're not, really. Understanding how models generate code informs how to evaluate their outputs. Security habits shape what to look for in review. Evaluation skills are what make literacy practically valuable. The framework we're proposing treats these as an integrated competency set rather than a list of separate skills.

The central premise is this: effective AI-augmented development isn't primarily about learning specific tools or techniques. Tools change too fast and techniques become obsolete. It's about developing a mental model of how to work with AI systems—when to use them, how to prompt effectively, what to verify and how, when to override or discard suggestions entirely. That mental model can be taught and assessed even as specific tools evolve.

6.1 The Four Competency Domains

The framework organizes competencies into four interconnected domains, each building on the previous.

Foundational Understanding covers what engineers need to know about how AI code generation works: the statistical prediction mechanism, capabilities and limitations of current tools, common vulnerability patterns in generated code, and basic secure coding principles. Proficiency here doesn't require deep technical knowledge of model architectures. It means being able to explain what the tool is doing well enough to predict where it's likely to go wrong.

Interaction Skills covers practical tool use: prompt engineering, iterative refinement, integrating AI assistance into real workflows without disrupting them. Proficiency means consistently eliciting useful outputs and recognizing—quickly, without excessive iteration—when an AI-assisted approach isn't working for a given problem.

Quality Assurance covers the verification and evaluation practices discussed in Sections 4 and 5. Security-focused review, specification-based correctness testing, quality assessment across the relevant dimensions, appropriate use of automated analysis tools. Proficiency means having reliable practices that actually catch the problems AI tools introduce rather than just going through the motions.

Professional Judgment is the most important domain and the hardest to teach explicitly. It covers the meta-level decision-making that integrates the other three: knowing when to trust AI output versus when more scrutiny is warranted, maintaining critical distance without undermining productivity, making sound tradeoff calls. This develops through deliberate practice and reflection, not through instruction alone.

6.2 How to Implement This in Academic Settings

The single most important implementation principle for academic settings is sequence. AI tools should come after foundational skills, not alongside them or instead of them.

The rationale comes directly from the research: Becker et al. (2023) showed that students who get access to AI tools before building foundational competencies often don't develop the deeper understanding that comes from working through hard problems. The tools make the tasks easier in ways that short-circuit the learning the tasks were designed to produce. This isn't an argument for banning the tools—it's an argument for sequencing their introduction.

A practical sequence: begin with traditional programming instruction through the point where students can solve problems independently, debug systematically, and reason about complexity. Then introduce AI tools for specific, constrained tasks with clear evaluation criteria—explicitly teaching students to assess what the tool produces, not just use it. Expand to more complex scenarios as evaluation skills develop. Eventually integrate professional-style workflows where AI assistance and human judgment work together.

Figure 3. Relative Importance of Evaluation Dimensions by Development Context

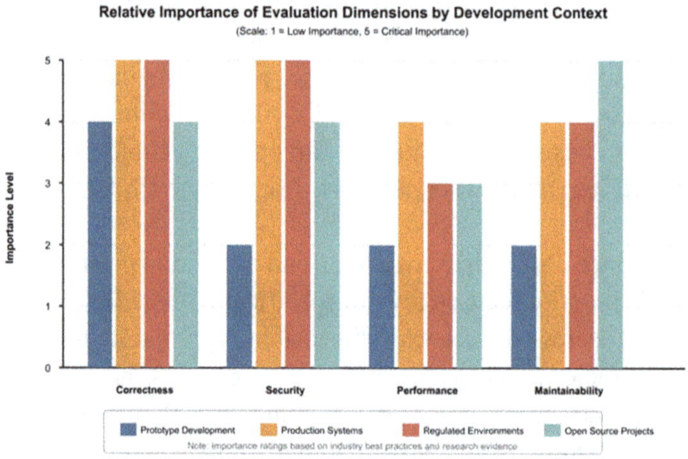

Figure 3: quantifies how evaluation priorities shift across different development contexts: prototype development, production systems, regulated environments, and open source projects. The visualization reveals that while correctness remains consistently critical, security importance varies dramatically from moderate in prototypes to critical in production settings. Maintainability proves essential for opensource projects but less

Critical evaluation needs to be an explicit learning objective from the moment AI tools are introduced. Rubrics, checklists, code review exercises, assignments specifically designed around identifying and correcting AI-generated errors—these make evaluation a skill rather than an afterthought. Students who are told to review AI output carefully but not taught how to do it tend not to do it well.

6.3 Professional Development for Practicing Engineers

Experienced engineers present different challenges than students. They have strong foundational skills—often much stronger than they're given credit for in discussions that focus on what AI can replicate. What they may lack is exposure to how these tools actually work, strategies for integrating them without disrupting established workflows, and frameworks for thinking about the new risks they introduce.

Start with honest skills assessment. Organizations should evaluate where their engineers actually are across the four competency domains and build targeted development programs from those findings, rather than running generic training that assumes everyone starts in the same place. Senior engineers and junior engineers need different things. Specialists need different things than generalists.

The approaches that actually work for building professional competency are experiential. Pair programming where one developer uses AI tools while the other reviews and questions outputs. Code review sessions focused specifically on AI-generated code, using explicit checklists. Challenge exercises built around identifying and improving AI output that's been deliberately flawed. Real project work with mentoring from engineers who have thought carefully about AI-augmented development. Practice with feedback builds the intuition that instruction alone doesn't.

7. CHALLENGES, LIMITATIONS, AND WHAT COMES NEXT

No framework for a rapidly evolving technology can be complete. This one isn't. The goal is to make the limitations explicit rather than leave them to be discovered.

The most fundamental challenge is pace. AI code generation capabilities improve continuously—sometimes incrementally, occasionally with step changes that meaningfully shift what the tools can do. Development programs built around current tools risk obsolescence before they're fully implemented. The framework tries to address this by emphasizing durable principles rather than tool-specific techniques. But maintaining that emphasis requires real discipline, particularly when new capabilities emerge that seem to change the picture.

7.1 Organizational Barriers

Implementation runs into obstacles that have nothing to do with the quality of the framework.

Policy vacuum is a real problem. Many organizations don't have clear policies governing AI tool use, which leaves individual developers uncertain about expectations and best practices. Some organizations prohibit AI tools entirely due to security or IP concerns; others allow unrestricted use without guidance. Neither position serves engineers well. The former wastes genuine productivity benefits; the latter leaves engineers without the framework to avoid the costs.

Resource constraints are genuine, especially for smaller organizations and under-resourced educational programs. Building comprehensive training programs takes time and money. The framework as described here may be aspirational for organizations that can't invest heavily in formal programs—which suggests the need for lighter-weight implementations that capture the most critical elements without requiring full curriculum development.

Cultural resistance comes from both directions. Engineers who view AI tools as threats to professional identity may resist engagement. Engineers who embrace the tools uncritically may resist the slower, more deliberate practices the framework requires. Overcoming both requires leadership that demonstrates why thoughtful adoption produces better outcomes than either extreme—and ideally, concrete evidence from within the organization.

7.2 Assessment Challenges

Assessing whether engineers have actually developed the competencies the framework describes is methodologically difficult. Traditional programming assessment—does the code work?—doesn't capture the meta-skills that matter most here. How do you assess judgment? How do you evaluate someone's ability to identify subtle security vulnerabilities in AI-generated code that they've never seen before?

Performance-based assessment is more promising than knowledge testing. Effective assessment tasks include evaluating and improving AI-generated code with deliberate issues; completing development tasks where AI tool use is optional and analyzing the decisions made; conducting code reviews of mixed human and AI-generated code; and explaining the reasoning behind accepting or rejecting specific suggestions. These reveal whether competencies can be applied, not just recalled.

Longitudinal questions remain largely unanswered. Do competencies developed in training transfer to real development work? Do they persist over time? Do critical evaluation habits erode as AI assistance normalizes? These questions matter for designing programs that produce durable rather than momentary improvement, and the research to answer them is just beginning.

7.3 Where the Technology Is Heading

A few near-term trends seem likely to require framework adaptations.

Multi-modal AI systems that can process diagrams, specifications, and other non-code inputs may change how developers communicate requirements to tools—and what effective prompting looks like. Models with larger context windows or codebase-level access may generate more architecturally consistent code, potentially reducing some of the concerns about local versus global consistency. Models specifically trained for security-critical domains may reduce vulnerability rates, though the track record of security-specialized tools suggests that complete elimination of the problem is a long way off.

The framework should be treated as a living document. Some current recommendations may prove overly cautious or insufficiently rigorous as real-world evidence accumulates. The field would benefit from more longitudinal research on skill development and retention, comparative studies of different training approaches, and serious investigation of how expert developers actually exercise judgment in AI-augmented workflows.

8. CONCLUSION

The argument here is not complicated: AI code generation tools are now a real part of software engineering practice, using them badly has real costs, and the profession hasn't done enough work on what using them well requires.

Three principles have come up repeatedly in the preceding sections. First, AI tools work best as supplements to human expertise rather than substitutes for it. The tools handle pattern-based tasks reliably; the judgment, contextual understanding, and quality assessment that determine whether code actually belongs in a production system have to come from somewhere else. Second, critical evaluation is not a courtesy—it's the core of what keeps AI assistance from being a liability rather than an asset. Without it, AI tools amplify poor decisions as easily as they accelerate good ones. Third, security requires deliberate, active attention throughout AI-assisted development. Assuming the tool got security right is a bet the research literature consistently shows you will lose.

For educational programs, the implication is sequenced integration: build real programming competency first, introduce AI tools in ways that develop rather than bypass evaluation skills, and make critical evaluation an explicit learning objective from day one of AI tool use.

For organizations, the implication is that the soft infrastructure of AI adoption—clear policies, targeted training, security verification processes embedded in workflows, leadership that models thoughtful use—matters as much as the technical capabilities of the tools themselves. Teams that assume their engineers will figure it out on their own are taking on more risk than they probably realize, and the research on false confidence in AI-generated security is not reassuring.

The future of software engineering will be shaped by how well the profession handles this transition. Not by whether AI tools are used—they will be—but by whether engineers develop the competency to use them in ways that produce reliable, secure, maintainable software. That's the work the framework here is designed to support.

REFERENCES

Barke, S., James, M. B., & Polikarpova, N. (2023). Grounded Copilot: How programmers interact with code-generating models. Proceedings of the ACM on Programming Languages, 7(OOPSLA1), 85–111. DOI: 10.1145/3586030

Becker, B. A., Denny, P., Finnie-Ansley, J., Luxton-Reilly, A., Prather, J., & Santos, E. A. (2023). Programming is hard—Or at least it used to be: Educational opportunities and challenges of AI code generation. *Proceedings of the 54th ACM Technical Symposium on Computer Science Education*, 500–506. DOI: 10.1145/3545945.3569759

Biderman, S., Schoelkopf, H., Anthony, Q., Bradley, H., O'Brien, K., Hallahan, E., & Belrose, N. (2023). Pythia: A suite for analyzing large language models across training and scaling. *Proceedings of the 40th International Conference on Machine Learning*, 2397–2430. DOI: 10.48550/arXiv.2304.01373

Chen, M., Tworek, J., Jun, H., Yuan, Q., Pinto, H. P. D. O., Kaplan, J., . . . Zaremba, W. (2021). Evaluating large language models trained on code. arXiv preprint arXiv:2107.03374. /arXiv.2107.03374DOI: 10.48550

Dakhel, A. M., Majdinasab, V., Nikanjam, A., Khomh, F., Desmarais, M. C., & Jiang, Z. M. (2023). GitHub Copilot AI pair programmer: Asset or liability? *Journal of Systems and Software*, *203*, 111734. DOI: 10.1016/j.jss.2023.111734

Denny, P., Kumar, V., & Giacaman, N. (2023). Conversing with Copilot: Exploring prompt engineering for solving CS1 problems using natural language. *Proceedings of the 54th ACM Technical Symposium on Computer Science Education*, 1136–1142. DOI: 10.1145/3545945.3569823

Finnie-Ansley, J., Denny, P., Becker, B. A., Luxton-Reilly, A., & Prather, J. (2022). The robots are coming: Exploring the implications of OpenAI Codex on introductory programming. *Australasian Computing Education Conference*, 10–19. DOI: 10.1145/3511861.3511863

Kasneci, E., Sessler, K., Küchemann, S., Bannert, M., Dementieva, D., Fischer, F., Gasser, U., Groh, G., Günnemann, S., Hüllermeier, E., Krusche, S., Kutyniok, G., Michaeli, T., Nerdel, C., Pfeffer, J., Poquet, O., Sailer, M., Schmidt, A., Seidel, T., & Kasneci, G. (2023). ChatGPT for good? On opportunities and challenges of large language models for education. *Learning and Individual Differences*, *103*, 102274. DOI: 10.1016/j.lindif.2023.102274

Lau, S., & Guo, P. (2023). From 'Ban it till we understand it' to 'Resistance is futile': How university programming instructors plan to adapt as more students use AI code generation and explanation tools such as ChatGPT and GitHub Copilot. *Proceedings of the 2023 ACM Conference on International Computing Education Research*, 106–121. DOI: 10.1145/3568813.3600138

Li, R., Allal, L. B., Zi, Y., Muennighoff, N., Kocetkov, D., Mou, C., . . . von Werra, L. (2023). StarCoder: May the source be with you! arXiv preprint arXiv:2305.06161. /arXiv.2305.06161DOI: 10.48550

Nam, D., Macvean, A., Hellendoorn, V., Vasilescu, B., & Myers, B. (2024). Using an LLM to help with code understanding. *Proceedings of the 46th International Conference on Software Engineering*, 784–796. DOI: 10.1145/3597503.3639187

Nguyen, N., & Nadi, S. (2022). An empirical evaluation of GitHub Copilot's code suggestions. *Proceedings of the 19th International Conference on Mining Software Repositories*, 1–5. DOI: 10.1145/3524842.3528470

Pearce, H., Ahmad, B., Tan, B., Dolan-Gavitt, B., & Karri, R. (2022). Asleep at the keyboard? Assessing the security of GitHub Copilot's code contributions. 2022 IEEE Symposium on Security and Privacy (SP), 754–768. DOI: 10.1109/SP46214.2022.9833571

Perry, N., Srivastava, M., Kumar, D., & Boneh, D. (2023). Do users write more insecure code with AI assistants? *Proceedings of the 2023 ACM SIGSAC Conference on Computer and Communications Security*, 2785–2799. DOI: 10.1145/3576915.3623157

Poldrack, R. A., Lu, T., & Beguš, G. (2023). AI-assisted coding: Experiments with GPT-4. arXiv preprint arXiv:2304.13187. /arXiv.2304.13187DOI: 10.48550

Roziere, B., Gehring, J., Gloeckle, F., Sootla, S., Gat, I., Tan, X. E., . . . Synnaeve, G. (2023). Code Llama: Open foundation models for code. arXiv preprint arXiv:2308.12950. /arXiv.2308.12950DOI: 10.48550

Sarsa, S., Denny, P., Hellas, A., & Leinonen, J. (2022). Automatic generation of programming exercises and code explanations using large language models. *Proceedings of the 2022 ACM Conference on International Computing Education Research*, 27–43. DOI: 10.1145/3501385.3543957

Vaithilingam, P., Zhang, T., & Glassman, E. L. (2022). Expectation vs. experience: Evaluating the usability of code generation tools powered by large language models. Extended Abstracts of the 2022 CHI Conference on Human Factors in Computing Systems, 1–7. DOI: 10.1145/3491101.3519665

Wermelinger, M. (2023). Using GitHub Copilot to solve simple programming problems. *Proceedings of the 54th ACM Technical Symposium on Computer Science Education*, 172–178. DOI: 10.1145/3545945.3569830

White, J., Fu, Q., Hays, S., Sandborn, M., Olea, C., Gilbert, H., . . . Schmidt, D. C. (2023). A prompt pattern catalog to enhance prompt engineering with ChatGPT. arXiv preprint arXiv:2302.11382. /arXiv.2302.11382DOI: 10.48550

Xu, F. F., Alon, U., Neubig, G., & Hellendoorn, V. J. (2022). A systematic evaluation of large language models of code. *Proceedings of the 6th ACM SIGPLAN International Symposium on Machine Programming*, 1–10. DOI: 10.1145/3520312.3534862

Zamfirescu-Pereira, J. D., Wong, R. Y., Hartmann, B., & Yang, Q. (2023). Why Johnny can't prompt: How non-AI experts try (and fail) to design LLM prompts. *Proceedings of the 2023 CHI Conference on Human Factors in Computing Systems*, 1–21. DOI: 10.1145/3544548.3581388

KEY TERMS AND DEFINITIONS

AI Literacy: The capacity to understand AI systems well enough to use them intelligently. For software engineers, this means knowing how code generation works mechanistically, what kinds of tasks the tools handle reliably versus poorly, how to interact with them effectively, and how to evaluate their outputs critically. It's more than knowing the tools exist—it's knowing what they actually are.

ChatGPT: A conversational AI system from OpenAI capable of generating, explaining, and iterating on code through natural language dialogue. The conversational interface makes it useful for working through complex problems and refining requirements, not just completing code. Generated output requires verification—it can appear confident and be wrong.

Code Generation Tools: Software that produces source code from natural language descriptions, partial code contexts, or high-level specifications. Modern tools are built on large language models and can handle a wide range of tasks—from completing function bodies to scaffolding entire components—but require consistent human verification to catch the errors and vulnerabilities they introduce.

Critical Evaluation: Systematic assessment of whether AI-generated code is actually right—functionally, securely, architecturally, and in the specific deployment context. This involves more than running basic tests. It requires examining whether code meets specifications, checking for known vulnerability patterns, assessing maintainability, and exercising the contextual judgment that AI systems lack.

Deskilling: The erosion of professional competencies through underuse. The concern in software engineering is that over-reliance on AI tools prevents engineers—especially early-career ones—from developing the foundational programming abilities, debugging fluency, and problem-solving capacity that come from wrestling with hard problems directly. The risk is real and requires deliberate countermeasures in both education and professional practice.

GitHub Copilot: An AI code completion tool developed by GitHub and OpenAI, integrated directly into common development environments. It provides real-time suggestions based on surrounding code and prompts. Widely studied in the research literature, it is both genuinely useful for accelerating routine tasks and a documented source of security vulnerabilities when outputs are accepted without review.

Human–AI Collaboration: The working relationship between human engineers and AI tools in software development. Effective collaboration means AI handles pattern-based, repetitive tasks while humans provide the judgment, contextual understanding, and quality assurance that current models cannot replicate. Success requires calibrated trust—neither blanket skepticism nor uncritical acceptance.

Prompt Engineering: The practice of crafting inputs to AI systems to elicit better outputs. For code generation this involves providing function signatures, constraints, examples, and explicit security requirements rather than vague descriptions. The difference between a well-crafted prompt and a careless one can be significant in both quality and security of the output.

Reskilling: Building new competencies to work effectively in changed circumstances. In AI-augmented development this means developing prompt engineering skills, learning to evaluate AI outputs systematically, and acquiring the security verification practices that AI assistance requires—while maintaining the foundational engineering knowledge that remains essential.

Secure Coding: Writing software that actively guards against security vulnerabilities rather than hoping they're absent. In AI-augmented development this requires understanding that AI tools reproduce insecure patterns from training data and building verification practices that specifically account for this—input validation, cryptographic correctness, proper authentication, safe error handling.

Software Engineering Education: The preparation of engineers in the principles, practices, and judgment required for professional software development. This now necessarily includes learning to work effectively alongside AI assistance while maintaining the foundational skills and independent judgment that remain essential regardless of what the tools can do.

Vulnerability Detection: Identifying security weaknesses in software before they can be exploited. For AI-generated code this requires both automated tools—static analyzers like Semgrep and CodeQL—and structured human review targeting the specific vulnerability categories that AI tools most commonly introduce: injection flaws, cryptographic issues, authentication gaps, resource management problems.

Chapter 9

Artificial Intelligence and the Transformation of Software Engineering Skills:

Deskilling Risks, Reskilling Imperatives, and Future Workforce Pathway

SP. Arunkumar
http://orcid.org/0000-0002-2726-0529
Nehru Institute of Engineering and Technology, India

G. Ashwin Prabhu
http://orcid.org/0000-0001-5673-647X
St. Joseph's College of Engineering, India

M. Revathy
Coimbatore Institute of Technology, India

Batchu Ramanjaneyulu
CVR College of Engineering, India

Banakara Nagaraj
Ballari Institute of Technology and Management, India

G. V. Maruthi
Global Academy of Technology, India

T. V. Harshan
St. Joseph's College of Engineering, India

S. Hariharan
St. Joseph's College of Engineering, India

DOI: 10.4018/979-8-3373-8450-4.ch009

ABSTRACT

Artificial intelligence is transforming software engineering skills, creating deskilling risks while highlighting urgent reskilling imperatives and evolving workforce pathways. This chapter per the authors examines the adoption of intelligent code generation, automated testing, and AI-assisted development tools, showing how these technologies reshape programming practices, cognitive demands, and professional identities. It explores the tension between productivity gains and the potential loss of foundational competencies, emphasizing adaptive skill frameworks that integrate computational thinking, system-level reasoning, and human–AI collaboration. Organizational and educational responses, including continuous learning, industry–academia partnerships, and competency-based training, are discussed to future-proof the workforce. The chapter synthesizes research and industry trends to outline strategies for resilient, ethically grounded, and innovation-oriented software engineering roles in the age of AI.

1. INTRODUCTION

Software engineering has historically evolved through a sequence of paradigm shifts, each redefining how humans conceptualize, design, and construct software systems. From early handcrafted machine code to structured programming, object-oriented design, and model-driven and agile methodologies, progress has largely been characterized by increasing abstraction and tool support. Each stage reduced certain forms of manual effort while preserving the centrality of human cognition in problem formulation, architectural reasoning, and algorithmic design. The emergence of artificial intelligence (AI)–driven development tools represents a fundamentally different transformation. Rather than merely automating well-specified tasks, contemporary AI systems increasingly participate in cognitive dimensions of software engineering, including code synthesis, architectural suggestion, defect prediction, documentation, and operational decision-making. This shift positions AI not as a conventional productivity aid, but as a structural turning point in how software work is performed and how engineering expertise itself is constituted. The historical arc of software engineering illustrates a persistent drive toward higher-level representations. Structured programming abstracted away unrestrained control flow; object orientation organized systems around reusable entities; frameworks and libraries encapsulated complex behaviors; and DevOps platforms automated large portions of build, test, and deployment pipelines. Yet across these transitions, engineers retained primary responsibility for translating domain problems into formal specifications and executable logic. AI-augmented engineering disrupts this continuity. Large language models trained on massive code corpora can now generate syntactically correct and semantically plausible code, refactor existing systems, and propose solutions based on natural language descriptions (Chen et al., 2021). Comparable AI-driven systems are also being applied in agriculture and IoT-enabled environments, where intelligent agents automate crop health management, vertical farming, and smart traffic control, demonstrating the cross-domain impact of AI (Dhanushya et al., 2025; Gowthaman et al., 2025; Poovithaa et al., 2025). Intelligent DevOps platforms extend this capacity into operations, using machine learning to forecast failures, optimize resources, and recommend interventions. The software lifecycle is thus increasingly mediated by systems that learn from data rather than execute only predefined rules. This development reframes the role of AI from that of a deterministic tool to that of a cognitive collaborator. Unlike compilers, integrated development environments, or traditional automation scripts, AI-driven systems exhibit adaptive and probabilistic behavior. They infer intent, generalize across tasks, and generate novel outputs that were not explicitly programmed. Human–AI interaction research emphasizes that such systems actively shape user decision-making, attention, and skill development, rather than merely accelerating existing workflows (Amershi et al., 2019). In software engineering contexts, this collaboration allows developers to offload not only routine coding but also aspects of design reasoning, testing strategy, and debugging. As a result, engineers increasingly operate as supervisors, curators, and integrators of machine-generated artifacts.

The productivity implications of this shift are substantial. Empirical and industry evidence consistently associates AI-enabled automation with accelerated development cycles, reduced entry barriers, and expanded capacity for rapid prototyping. By compressing the time between ideation and implementation, AI systems promise to democratize software creation and allow organizations to respond more fluidly to evolving requirements. These dynamics align with broader economic observations that intelligent technologies amplify the speed and scale of knowledge work (Brynjolfsson & McAfee, 2014). In software engineering, such amplification manifests in faster feature delivery, automated quality assurance, and continuous operational optimization. However, these gains generate a paradox of productivity. As AI tools abstract increasing layers of technical complexity, they may erode the deep competencies that historically underpinned engineering practice. Over-reliance on generative code systems can reduce opportunities for engineers to engage in algorithmic reasoning, low-level debugging, and architectural trade-off analysis. When systems reliably produce functional solutions, foundational skills risk becoming latent, underdeveloped, or unevenly distributed across the workforce. This phenomenon reflects classic deskilling dynamics observed in other technologically mediated professions, where automation redistributes expertise from practitioners to embedded systems (Brynjolfsson & McAfee, 2014). In the context of software engineering, such deskilling threatens not only individual career trajectories but also the collective innovation capacity of the field, as deep understanding is a prerequisite for building novel infrastructures, ensuring long-term maintainability, and governing complex socio-technical systems. At the same time, AI introduces urgent imperatives for reskilling and workforce transformation. The competencies demanded of software professionals are shifting from primarily syntactic and implementation-level proficiency toward higher-order capabilities: problem framing, system orchestration, critical evaluation of machine outputs, ethical and security reasoning, and the design of human–AI workflows. Effective collaboration with AI systems requires engineers to understand their limitations, biases, and failure modes, and to develop strategies for verification, oversight, and continuous learning. Reskilling in this sense is not limited to acquiring new tools, but involves a reconceptualization of professional identity—from sole author of code to steward of adaptive computational systems.

This chapter is framed around the intertwined dynamics of deskilling, reskilling, and systemic workforce redesign. Deskilling is examined not as an inevitable outcome, but as a risk that emerges when productivity pressures outpace educational and organizational adaptation. Reskilling is treated as a multidimensional process encompassing technical, cognitive, and socio-organizational competencies. Workforce transformation extends beyond individual engineers to include teams, institutions, and governance structures that must evolve to integrate AI responsibly and sustainably. The objectives of this chapter are threefold. First, it seeks to conceptualize AI in software engineering as a structural shift that reconfigures the distribution of cognitive labor between humans and machines. Second, it analyzes the mechanisms through which AI-augmented development may simultaneously enhance productivity and undermine deep expertise. Third, it outlines the foundations for a reskilling-oriented response that emphasizes long-term capability building, ethical oversight, and innovation resilience. Methodologically, the chapter adopts an interdisciplinary orientation, synthesizing insights from software engineering research, human–AI interaction studies, and the economics of technological change. Rather than focusing on specific tools, it emphasizes underlying patterns of work reorganization and skill transformation. By situating contemporary AI systems within the broader historical evolution of software engineering, the chapter aims to provide a conceptual framework for understanding not only what is changing, but why these changes represent a decisive turning point for the profession.

2. AI TECHNOLOGIES RESHAPING THE SOFTWARE ENGINEERING LIFECYCLE

Contemporary artificial intelligence technologies are profoundly reconfiguring the software engineering lifecycle, shifting it from a predominantly human-centered, manual discipline toward an AI-mediated development ecosystem. Machine learning models, large language models (LLMs), and data-driven automation platforms are increasingly embedded across requirements engineering, design, programming, testing, deployment, and maintenance. These systems do not merely support developers; they actively participate in decision-making, artifact generation, and quality control, thereby redefining how software is conceived, built, and evolved. The result is an emerging paradigm in which software engineering becomes a hybrid cognitive process distributed between human professionals and intelligent computational agents (Allamanis et al., 2018).

2.1 Intelligent Requirements Engineering

Requirements engineering has traditionally relied on interviews, workshops, and documentation practices that are often subjective, ambiguous, and time-consuming. AI technologies are now reshaping this phase through natural language processing (NLP) techniques capable of extracting, structuring, and validating requirements from heterogeneous sources such as stakeholder documents, emails, chat logs, and issue trackers. By learning from large corpora of software artifacts, AI systems can identify functional intents, non-functional constraints, and domain-specific terminology, thereby accelerating requirements elicitation and reducing misinterpretation. Automated stakeholder analysis is another emerging capability. Machine learning models can cluster stakeholder inputs, detect conflicting expectations, and highlight latent risks embedded in natural language descriptions. Ambiguity resolution mechanisms, supported by probabilistic language models, can propose alternative interpretations of vague requirements and recommend clarifications, enabling earlier convergence on shared understanding. Moreover, AI-driven tools are increasingly capable of transforming unstructured requirements into structured user stories, acceptance criteria, and traceability matrices. Leveraging generative language models, systems can automatically generate and prioritize user stories based on historical project data, business value signals, and risk profiles, supporting more adaptive and evidence-informed planning processes. Through these capabilities, requirements engineering evolves from manual knowledge capture into an intelligent, continuously learning activity.

2.2 AI-Augmented Design and Architecture

The design and architectural stages are also undergoing significant transformation through AI augmentation. Generative design models can synthesize architectural patterns, propose modular decompositions, and recommend technology stacks aligned with functional goals and anticipated workloads. Trained on large repositories of software systems, these models infer latent design regularities and map high-level requirements to candidate architectures, offering developers a spectrum of viable solutions rather than a single prescriptive blueprint. Predictive system modeling further extends AI's role in design. By analyzing historical performance data, simulation outputs, and architectural metrics, AI systems can forecast scalability limits, reliability risks, and cost-performance trade-offs before implementation begins. Such predictive capabilities enable proactive optimization, allowing architects to experiment with alternative designs and evaluate their long-term implications. Additionally, automated technical debt detection at the design stage is becoming feasible. Machine learning techniques can identify architectural smells, excessive coupling, and violation of design principles in early models, thereby preventing the entrenchment of costly structural weaknesses. In this way, AI shifts architectural practice from reactive refactoring toward anticipatory, data-driven design intelligence.

2.3 Automated Programming and Code Intelligence

Perhaps the most visible impact of AI is occurring in programming and code-related activities. Modern code intelligence systems perform automated code generation, refactoring, and optimization by learning from massive code corpora. Large language models trained on multilingual software repositories can translate natural language prompts into executable code, complete partial implementations, and recommend idiomatic constructs, dramatically lowering the barrier between conceptual design and functional realization. Beyond generation, AI-driven refactoring and optimization tools can detect code smells, propose performance enhancements, and enforce consistency with architectural standards. Self-healing code capabilities are also emerging, in which autonomous debugging agents monitor runtime behavior, localize faults, and suggest or apply corrective patches. Similar resilience strategies have been explored in hardware and embedded systems, where high-performance memory architectures and AI-driven cybersecurity approaches enhance reliability and fault tolerance (Kameswaran et al., 2017; Krithika et al., 2025). These systems leverage learned associations between failure patterns and remediation strategies, reducing mean time to repair and supporting continuous reliability. However, these advances also reshape cognitive practices in software development. Algorithmic thinking and programming fluency increasingly shift from low-level syntax construction toward higher-level problem framing, specification, and critical evaluation of AI outputs. Developers are required to articulate intent, assess generated artifacts, and integrate them coherently into evolving systems. Consequently, programming becomes a collaborative activity between human engineers and machine intelligence, emphasizing oversight, interpretive judgment, and system-level reasoning.

2.4 AI in Testing, Deployment, and Maintenance

AI technologies are equally transformative in testing, deployment, and long-term maintenance. Autonomous test generation systems can derive test cases from specifications, user behavior logs, and inferred program models, enabling broader coverage and earlier defect detection. Machine learning techniques can prioritize test execution, predict fault-prone components, and support continuous quality assurance pipelines that adapt as systems evolve. Within operations, AIOps platforms apply AI to large-scale monitoring, log analysis, and incident management. By correlating metrics across infrastructure and applications, these systems can detect anomalies, forecast failures, and trigger preventive interventions. Predictive maintenance capabilities allow organizations to anticipate performance degradation, capacity bottlenecks, and security threats before they escalate into outages. Recent work on AI-enhanced predictive analytics for wind turbine maintenance demonstrates how intelligent monitoring can improve reliability management and optimize resource allocation in energy-intensive systems (Cloudin et al., 2026). Furthermore, AI-enabled DevSecOps integrates security intelligence into deployment pipelines, automating vulnerability detection, configuration auditing, and compliance verification. As a result, operational activities increasingly transition from reactive troubleshooting to anticipatory governance supported by continuous machine learning feedback loops.

2.5 Implications for Professional Roles

The diffusion of AI across the software lifecycle is dissolving traditional boundaries between professional roles. Developers, testers, architects, and operations engineers increasingly operate within integrated environments where AI systems perform tasks that once defined disciplinary distinctions. Automated test generation, infrastructure-as-code synthesis, and continuous monitoring blur separations between development and operations, reinforcing cross-functional collaboration mediated by intelligent tools. Simultaneously, new professional identities are emerging. AI engineers design, fine-tune, and evaluate models embedded within development pipelines. Prompt engineers and interaction designers specialize in structuring effective human–AI communication for requirements elicitation, code generation, and design exploration. Model integrators orchestrate AI services within complex software ecosystems, ensuring interoperability, reliability, and ethical compliance. Parallel advances in IoT-enabled wearable health monitoring systems illustrate how engineers must integrate AI with sensor networks and emergency response platforms, reinforcing the socio-technical nature of modern engineering roles (Sibiya et al., 2025). These evolving roles underscore a broader shift: software engineering is no longer solely about constructing artifacts, but about managing intelligent socio-technical systems in which learning models are core infrastructural components. Parallel developments in robotics and control systems illustrate this shift, as AI-enabled rover platforms and smart inspection systems require engineers to orchestrate complex socio-technical interactions. Overall, AI technologies are reshaping the software engineering lifecycle into a continuously adaptive, data-driven process. Each phase is increasingly characterized by intelligent automation, predictive analytics, and generative capabilities that extend human cognition. This transformation signals not the obsolescence of software professionals, but the redefinition of expertise toward strategic oversight, interdisciplinary integration, and responsible governance of AI-mediated development environments.

3. DESKILLING RISKS AND THE CHANGING COGNITIVE PROFILE OF SOFTWARE ENGINEERS

The growing integration of artificial intelligence (AI) into software development workflows is reshaping not only productivity and efficiency, but also the cognitive profile of software engineers. Tools such as large language models, automated code generators, and intelligent debugging assistants increasingly mediate how engineers design, implement, and validate software systems. While these technologies offer substantial benefits, they also introduce significant deskilling risks. Deskilling in this context extends beyond the automation of discrete tasks to encompass deeper transformations in how engineers learn, reason, and construct technical knowledge. This section critically examines the evolving nature of deskilling, highlighting technical, cognitive, and organizational consequences associated with increasing reliance on AI-assisted development.

3.1 Conceptualizing Deskilling in the AI Era

Historically, deskilling has been associated with mechanical automation, where machines displaced manual or routine labor and reduced the need for artisanal expertise. In the AI era, however, deskilling increasingly manifests as cognitive offloading—the transfer of reasoning, memory, and problem-solving functions from humans to intelligent systems. Rather than merely executing predefined procedures,

AI tools now participate in abstraction, pattern recognition, and decision support, thereby altering the distribution of cognitive labor between engineers and machines. From a labor economics perspective, AI exemplifies what Autor describes as task reconfiguration rather than wholesale job replacement, wherein certain cognitive functions are automated while others are reweighted or diminished (Autor, 2015). Applied to software engineering, this implies not only the automation of coding tasks, but also a gradual erosion of opportunities to engage deeply with algorithmic construction, low-level reasoning, and system optimization. Complementing this view, Brynjolfsson and Mitchell (2017) emphasize that machine learning systems increasingly perform perception, classification, and prediction, functions that were previously central to professional expertise. As these capabilities become embedded in development environments, engineers may shift from active problem solvers to supervisors of algorithmic outputs.

Cognitive science further frames this transition through the lens of cognitive offloading, where individuals rely on external artifacts to store information or perform mental operations. Risko and Gilbert (2016) argue that while offloading can enhance efficiency, it may also reduce internal cognitive engagement and long-term skill acquisition. In software engineering, persistent reliance on AI-generated code and solutions risks weakening the internalization of programming schemas, architectural reasoning, and debugging heuristics that traditionally underpin professional mastery.

3.2 Technical Deskilling

One of the most visible manifestations of deskilling is the declining emphasis on low-level programming and algorithmic construction skills. AI-driven development tools increasingly generate boilerplate code, data processing pipelines, and even complex functional modules. While this accelerates development cycles, it reduces the frequency with which engineers manually implement core data structures, memory management routines, or algorithmic optimizations. Over time, limited engagement with these foundational tasks may undermine engineers' ability to reason about computational complexity, performance trade-offs, and system constraints (Brynjolfsson & Mitchell, 2017). Reduced exposure to debugging, optimization, and system internals further compounds this risk. AI assistants often propose fixes, refactor code, and identify vulnerabilities with minimal explanation. When engineers accept such recommendations without reconstructing the underlying logic, debugging becomes an act of selection rather than investigation. Autor (2015) notes that when technology absorbs core components of expert work, remaining tasks may become narrower and less cognitively demanding, weakening experiential learning pathways. In software practice, this can translate into limited familiarity with runtime behavior, concurrency issues, or hardware–software interactions—areas where tacit knowledge is critical for system reliability. Moreover, as AI abstracts away complexity, engineers may develop systems without a robust understanding of their internal dependencies.

3.3 Cognitive and Epistemic Risks

Beyond technical skill erosion, AI reliance introduces significant cognitive and epistemic risks. Overreliance on AI recommendations may cultivate automation bias, whereby individuals disproportionately trust algorithmic outputs even when they conflict with contextual evidence or domain knowledge. Brynjolfsson and Mitchell (2017) caution that machine learning systems excel at prediction but lack causal understanding, making uncritical acceptance of their outputs particularly hazardous in complex engineering contexts. When engineers defer to AI-generated solutions, they may disengage from hypothesis testing, alternative exploration, and adversarial reasoning. This dynamic threatens critical evaluation and verification capabilities. Traditional software engineering pedagogy emphasizes reasoning about correctness, edge cases, and failure modes. If AI tools routinely supply "working" solutions, engineers may spend less time validating assumptions or stress-testing systems. Risko and Gilbert (2016) suggest that cognitive offloading can diminish internal monitoring processes, weakening individuals' capacity to detect errors independently. In software engineering, such attenuation undermines epistemic vigilance—the disciplined skepticism required to evaluate system behavior, model limitations, and emergent risks.

Shallow learning and reduced experiential mastery further exacerbate these challenges. Mastery in software engineering historically emerges through iterative cycles of design, failure, debugging, and optimization. AI-mediated workflows compress or bypass these cycles, offering immediate solutions without the accompanying cognitive struggle that consolidates long-term knowledge. Autor (2015) emphasizes that learning opportunities embedded within work tasks are critical for skill formation. When AI removes these opportunities, engineers may acquire tool-specific operational competence but lack transferable mental models, diminishing adaptability in novel or high-stakes scenarios.

3.4 Organizational and Professional Implications

At the organizational level, deskilling risks manifest acutely in junior engineer development. Entry-level roles have traditionally functioned as apprenticeship spaces, where novices build competence through hands-on engagement with foundational tasks. If AI systems now perform these tasks, junior engineers may progress rapidly in surface productivity while lacking deep conceptual grounding. Brynjolfsson and

Mitchell (2017) argue that such shifts can hollow out middle layers of expertise, producing a workforce polarized between a small group of high-level architects and a larger cohort of tool operators. This polarization contributes to the fragility of expertise pipelines. Education-focused studies highlight similar challenges, where conversational AI, smart pedagogies, and intercultural communication frameworks are reshaping how technical expertise is cultivated in higher education environments (Santhini et al., 2025). Comparable challenges are evident in healthcare contexts, where AI-driven systems are being leveraged to ensure equitable care delivery during crises, underscoring the importance of ethical and inclusive design in socio-technical transformations (Ponkarthika et al., 2026). When fewer engineers cultivate low-level or diagnostic skills, organizations become dependent on limited pools of deep expertise, increasing vulnerability to turnover, system failures, and technological disruptions. Autor (2015) highlights that task displacement without corresponding skill regeneration can undermine long-term workforce resilience. Cognitive offloading may insulate engineers from these frictions, narrowing the experiential basis from which novel architectures and paradigms emerge. Risko and Gilbert (2016) note that while offloading enhances immediate performance, it may reduce opportunities for cognitive exploration. Over time, organizations that prioritize AI-mediated efficiency without deliberate skill cultivation may experience diminishing returns in creativity, robustness, and strategic technological leadership. Collectively, these dynamics suggest that deskilling in the AI era is not an inevitable outcome, but a contingent risk shaped by how tools are integrated into education, professional practice, and organizational design. Recognizing deskilling as a cognitive and epistemic transformation rather than mere task automation is essential for developing interventions that preserve deep technical competence, critical reasoning, and sustainable innovation capacity.

4. RESKILLING IMPERATIVES: EMERGING COMPETENCY FRAMEWORKS

The acceleration of artificial intelligence across the software development lifecycle reframes workforce challenges from mere tool adoption to deeper processes of skill reconstitution. As AI-driven systems increasingly participate in requirements analysis, coding, testing, deployment, and maintenance, the core competencies of software engineers are being reorganized around higher-level systems thinking, continuous oversight, and socio-technical responsibility. Traditional programming proficiency, while still necessary, is no longer sufficient as the dominant professional anchor. Instead, sustainable practice in AI-rich environments depends on integrated competency clusters that combine technical fluency with critical reasoning, ethical accountability, and lifelong learning capacity. This section outlines emerging frameworks that characterize reskilling imperatives for contemporary software engineering, emphasizing the shift toward systems-centric roles, new technical literacies, higher-order cognitive capabilities, and institutionalized learning architectures (Shneiderman, 2020).

4.1 From Programming-Centric to Systems-Centric Skill Models

4.1.1 Engineering oversight and AI orchestration

AI-enabled development environments increasingly automate discrete programming tasks, such as code generation, test synthesis, and defect detection. As a result, the engineer's role evolves from direct code authoring to orchestration and oversight of heterogeneous intelligent components. This includes supervising model behavior, validating system outputs, configuring toolchains, and managing dependencies between data pipelines, learning systems, and conventional software modules. Research on machine learning production systems demonstrates that failures rarely stem from isolated algorithms, but from brittle interactions among models, data, and surrounding infrastructure (Sculley et al., 2015). Consequently, reskilling must emphasize architectural reasoning, operational monitoring, and intervention strategies when automated components drift, degrade, or behave unexpectedly.

4.1.2 Socio-technical system design

Beyond technical integration, AI systems increasingly shape organizational processes, decision workflows, and human roles. Engineers are therefore required to design socio-technical systems that align technical performance with human values, institutional constraints, and contextual realities. This involves anticipating how users interpret AI outputs, how authority is redistributed between humans and machines, and how feedback loops reshape behavior. Human-centered AI research stresses that effective systems emerge not from algorithmic optimization alone, but from careful coordination between technical functions and human practices. Emerging work on intelligent campuses reinforces this perspective, showing how socio-technical integration can transform institutional practices and workforce readiness. Reskilling efforts must therefore cultivate competencies in participatory design, stakeholder communication, and interdisciplinary collaboration alongside conventional engineering expertise.

4.2 New Technical Competencies

4.2.1 AI literacy and model interpretability

AI literacy extends beyond familiarity with machine learning APIs or frameworks. It encompasses conceptual understanding of how models learn, what assumptions underlie training processes, and which limitations constrain inference. Engineers must be able to reason about uncertainty, bias, overfitting, and distributional shift, as well as communicate these properties to non-specialist stakeholders. Interpretability techniques—such as feature attribution, error analysis, and behavioral probing—become core professional tools for diagnosing system behavior and ensuring alignment with requirements. Studies of human–AI interaction highlight that engineers who understand model affordances and failure modes are better positioned to design systems that support appropriate human trust and effective collaboration. Hardware-level AI integration also demonstrates the importance of interpretability, as FPGA-based adaptive systems highlight how transparency in algorithmic behavior supports trust and reliability (Shanmugaraja et al., 2023).

4.2.2 Data-centric engineering

As learning systems derive performance primarily from data rather than handcrafted logic, software engineering increasingly becomes a data-centric discipline. Competency in dataset design, curation, governance, and quality assurance is therefore foundational. Engineers must manage data pipelines, detect contamination and leakage, and establish processes for continuous dataset refinement. The technical debt associated with unmanaged data dependencies, unstable feature representations, and opaque training processes has been identified as a dominant risk factor in production AI systems. Reskilling frameworks must thus reposition data engineering, dataset auditing, and pipeline observability as first-order software engineering skills rather than peripheral specializations.

4.2.3 Human-in-the-loop system development

Human-in-the-loop paradigms recognize that AI systems rarely function autonomously in complex real-world environments. Instead, performance and reliability emerge through structured interactions between automated components and human judgment. Engineers must therefore design mechanisms for feedback incorporation, escalation handling, and collaborative decision-making. This includes constructing interfaces that allow users to contest or correct model outputs, building workflows that combine automated recommendations with human review, and establishing monitoring systems that surface meaningful signals to operators. Empirical studies indicate that such designs require specialized competencies at the intersection of software engineering, interaction design, and applied AI.

4.3 Higher-Order Cognitive and Professional Skills

4.3.1 Problem framing and requirements reasoning

As AI systems increasingly shape problem definitions, engineers must develop advanced skills in framing objectives, constraints, and success criteria. Unlike deterministic software, learning-based systems operate probabilistically, making early design decisions about data sources, optimization goals, and evaluation metrics especially consequential. Engineers are thus required to translate ambiguous organizational goals into measurable system behaviors, anticipate unintended consequences, and iteratively refine requirements in response to observed performance. This elevates conceptual modeling, domain analysis, and stakeholder negotiation as central engineering competencies.

4.3.2 Critical validation and algorithmic auditing

The opacity and adaptivity of AI systems necessitate rigorous validation practices that extend beyond conventional testing. Engineers must cultivate habits of critical skepticism, continuously interrogating system outputs, training data assumptions, and operational impacts. Algorithmic auditing—encompassing bias detection, robustness testing, and post-deployment surveillance—becomes an ongoing professional responsibility. The literature on machine learning systems emphasizes that unexamined dependencies and hidden feedback loops can quietly erode system reliability over time. Reskilling initiatives must therefore foreground analytical rigor, evidence-based evaluation, and long-term system stewardship.

4.3.3 Ethical reasoning and accountability engineering

AI-infused systems increasingly mediate access to resources, shape public discourse, and influence consequential decisions. Engineers are thus implicated not only as technical implementers but as moral agents whose design choices carry social and institutional implications. Human-centered AI frameworks stress the need for professionals who can embed values such as transparency, fairness, and human control into system architectures (Shneiderman, 2020). This requires formal training in ethical reasoning, regulatory awareness, and accountability mechanisms, as well as organizational cultures that support responsible dissent and reflective practice.

4.4 Lifelong Learning Architectures

4.4.1 Continuous skill renewal models

Given the rapid evolution of AI techniques and platforms, reskilling cannot be treated as a one-time intervention. Instead, sustainable software engineering depends on continuous learning models that integrate education into everyday professional practice. This includes workplace learning loops, communities of practice, and reflective engineering processes that enable practitioners to update competencies as tools and norms evolve. Research on AI development teams underscores the importance of shared knowledge infrastructures, cross-functional mentoring, and iterative capability building to manage system complexity.

4.4.2 Micro-credentialing and adaptive learning platforms

Emerging professional ecosystems increasingly rely on modular learning pathways that allow engineers to acquire targeted competencies in areas such as data governance, model evaluation, or socio-technical design. Micro-credentials, adaptive learning systems, and experiential training platforms support flexible reskilling aligned with evolving project demands. These architectures shift professional identity from static qualification toward dynamic capability portfolios. Within AI-rich environments, such models enable engineers to remain epistemically agile, supporting the sustained oversight, ethical reflexivity, and technical integration skills demanded by complex intelligent systems (Shneiderman, 2020).

5. EDUCATIONAL TRANSFORMATION AND INDUSTRY-LED RESKILLING STRATEGIES

The rapid advancement of artificial intelligence (AI) and automation necessitates a fundamental rethinking of how education and workforce training are designed, delivered, and evaluated. Traditional models of learning and professional development—often siloed within academic institutions or corporate training departments—are insufficient to prepare learners for the pace and scale of AI-driven change. This chapter examines how software engineering education must evolve to foreground AI fluency, how corporate organizations can build reskilling ecosystems that leverage internal and external learning assets, and how public policy and professional standards must adapt to support ethical, scalable workforce transitions.

5.1 Rethinking Software Engineering Education

Software engineering education is at an inflection point. Curricula that were once focused on language syntax, algorithmic complexity, and standalone systems must now account for AI-enhanced development workflows, human–AI collaboration, and emerging ethical and societal considerations.

AI-integrated curricula: Embedding AI throughout software engineering education moves beyond isolated "AI modules" towards a holistic integration of intelligent systems into core learning outcomes. AI should not be confined to elective courses; rather, concepts such as machine learning pipelines, data ethics, prompt engineering, and model evaluation need to be threaded through foundational courses. AI-integrated curricula prepare learners to reason about both opportunities and limitations of intelligent systems in real-world contexts. For example, incorporating AI case studies into database systems or software testing courses enables students to understand not just how to build systems, but how AI reshapes requirements, validation, and risk.

Studio-based and problem-centered learning models: Conventional lecture–exam teaching formats are increasingly mismatched with the skills needed in AI-augmented engineering environments. Studio-based learning—where learners engage in iterative, collaborative project work—mirrors professional practice more closely than isolated programming assignments. Problem-centered learning challenges students with open-ended tasks that require interdisciplinary thinking, such as designing an ethical recommendation system for healthcare or optimizing an AI-driven energy grid. These approaches build higher-order cognitive skills: strategic planning, adaptive problem solving, and reflective evaluation of AI artifacts. This shift emphasizes learning by doing, with instructors acting as facilitators rather than content deliverers, enabling learners to engage deeply with complex, ambiguous problems typical of AI work.

Assessment reform beyond code output: Educational assessment in software engineering has traditionally focused on correct code execution, performance metrics, or discrete project deliverables. However, AI-related work demands evaluative frameworks that capture design rationale, ethical reasoning, collaboration patterns, and iterative refinement. Assessment reform should incorporate portfolios, peer evaluation, reflective journals, and demonstrations of AI system behavior under varying conditions. These forms of assessment help educators gauge competencies that static code output cannot—such as a learner's ability to identify bias in training data or to articulate the societal implications of an algorithmic decision. Reframing assessment aligns learning incentives with the multidimensional competencies required in an AI-enabled workforce.

5.2 Corporate Reskilling Ecosystems

As technological disruption accelerates, corporations increasingly recognize that hiring for future capabilities is insufficient. Instead, organizations must cultivate internal ecosystems that support continuous learning and strategic redeployment of talent.

Internal AI academies and bootcamps: Establishing internal academies and intensive bootcamp programs enables organizations to rapidly upskill existing talent in AI and data competencies. Such initiatives signal strategic commitment to workforce transformation and help retain institutional knowledge while building new capabilities. Internal bootcamps should be designed with clear alignment to business needs, offering targeted pathways in areas such as data literacy, AI model deployment, and human–AI interaction design. By embedding these programs within an organizational learning infrastructure, corporations can balance standardized learning with role-specific customization, fostering a culture of growth and innovation (Davenport & Ronanki, 2018).

Role-based upskilling pathways: Not all roles require deep technical expertise; instead, progressive upskilling must be tailored to the nuanced demands of different functions. A developer may need advanced understanding of neural architectures, while a product manager may need fluency in AI risk frameworks and model interpretability. Role-based pathways articulate clear competency milestones, mixing micro-credentials, project assignments, and collaborative learning. This approach helps employees visualize their career trajectories in an AI-enhanced organization. By defining the skills needed at each rung of professional progression, corporations can better allocate training resources and build internal talent pipelines.

Mentorship and hybrid human–AI teams: Learning does not occur in isolation. Mentorship—especially in complex domains like AI—amplifies knowledge transfer, contextualizes learning, and models professional judgment. Pairing learners with mentors who have navigated real-world AI projects fosters tacit knowledge that formal training alone cannot convey. Moreover, corporations are experimenting with hybrid human–AI teams, where AI systems act as "teammates" augmenting human creativity and productivity. This dynamic necessitates mentoring that addresses not only technical skills but also how to collaborate with AI: understanding when to trust AI suggestions, how to validate outputs, and how to balance machine efficiency with human values. Such mentoring models strengthen organizational resilience and accelerate competency growth (Davenport & Ronanki, 2018).

5.3 Public Policy and Professional Standards

Education and corporate efforts must be reinforced by public policy and professional standards that ensure equitable access, quality assurance, and ethical grounding in workforce development.

Accreditation reform: Traditional accreditation frameworks for educational programs often lag behind the pace of technological change. Policy efforts should encourage accrediting bodies to incorporate AI-relevant competencies into program standards. This includes data literacy, interdisciplinary problem solving, ethical reasoning, and familiarity with AI systems lifecycle. By updating accreditation criteria, policymakers can incentivize institutions to innovate curricula while maintaining quality and consistency across programs. Alignment between accreditation and industry needs helps ensure that graduates are prepared for the realities of AI-integrated work environments (Manyika et al., 2017).

Workforce transition programs: Governments have a central role in supporting displaced workers and facilitating transitions into growth sectors. Workforce transition programs—such as subsidized training, portable benefits during reskilling, and targeted apprenticeships—reduce barriers to mobility and provide safety nets during career pivots. These programs must be flexible, evidence-based, and responsive to labor market signals. Public–private partnerships can amplify impact by aligning training supply with real demand and by sharing data on emerging skill gaps. Effective transition programs contribute to social stability and ensure that the benefits of technological progress are broadly shared.

Ethical and regulatory literacy integration: As AI systems permeate business and society, ethical and regulatory literacy must be integrated into both education and professional standards. This includes understanding bias, fairness, privacy, accountability, and compliance frameworks. Public policy can catalyze this integration by establishing guidelines for ethical AI education and by incentivizing certification standards that emphasize socio-technical awareness. Workers across sectors—not only engineers—need grounding in ethical and regulatory dimensions to navigate an AI-mediated world responsibly (Manyika et al., 2017).

6. ORGANIZATIONAL AND SOCIO-TECHNICAL TRANSFORMATION

Artificial Intelligence (AI) is radically transforming how software development organizations are structured, how teams collaborate, and how governance and trust are configured in socio-technical systems. Rather than being limited to tooling enhancements, AI's integration touches organizational design, roles and responsibilities, coordination practices, and risk and trust frameworks. This chapter examines these themes across three key dimensions: teams, collaboration models, and governance.

6.1 Redesigning Software Teams

AI integration necessitates revisiting traditional team structures and practices within software development organizations. Agile teams, in particular, are adapting to incorporate AI tools not only as assistants but as active collaborators.

6.1.1 AI-Augmented Agile Teams

Traditional agile teams emphasize human collaboration, iterative delivery, and cross-functional roles. The introduction of AI augments these teams in ways that change both the nature of work and team interactions. AI agents can accelerate routine tasks and provide predictive insights, enabling teams to achieve faster feedback cycles and higher productivity. However, this transformation is not merely technical; it reshapes socio-technical dynamics, as teams must integrate AI as co-working entities rather than passive tools (Tavantzis et al., 2025). Effective AI-augmented agile teams thus blend human creativity with AI-driven automation, requiring adaptive communication and coordination mechanisms that transcend traditional human-only team models. Yet, optimizing these teams means addressing skill gaps, redefining roles, and enabling continuous learning. Organizations must invest in up-skilling team members to work with AI tools and empower them to interpret and guide AI contributions, ensuring that AI complements rather than displaces human agency (Tavantzis et al., 2025).

6.1.2 Shifting Leadership and Coordination Roles

In AI-augmented organizations, leadership functions become more distributed. Rather than centralized command-and-control structures, leadership in AI contexts often involves facilitating human-AI interactions, mediating trust, and coordinating across both human and AI participants. Leaders need to understand AI capabilities and limitations to set goals, evaluate performance, and resolve conflicts that may arise from human-AI decisions (Tavantzis et al., 2025). This shift expands the traditional role of the project manager to include responsibilities such as overseeing ethical AI use, advocating for transparent AI decision practices, and maintaining team coherence when AI agents participate in planning and execution.

6.2 Human–AI Collaboration Models

How humans and AI systems collaborate is central to the socio-technical transformation of software development.

6.2.1 Supervisory Engineering

Supervisory engineering models position humans as overseers and facilitators of AI-driven processes. In this paradigm, AI systems perform complex tasks autonomously, while human engineers provide high-level supervision, ensuring alignment with organizational goals and compliance with quality standards. This model acknowledges the need for continuing human control even as AI systems gain autonomy, emphasizing trustworthy integration through monitoring and justification frameworks (Engin, 2025). Humans thus take on supervisory roles that include validating outputs, interpreting AI recommendations, and intervening when systems behave unpredictably. Supervisory engineering also underscores the importance of explainability, requiring AI systems to offer transparent reasoning so that human overseers can build accurate mental models of AI behavior. Without this transparency, human supervisors may either over-rely on opaque AI decisions or under-trust systems they do not understand, both of which undermine effective collaboration.

6.2.2 Co-Creative Development Paradigms

Beyond supervision, co-creative paradigms place humans and AI systems in collaborative roles where both contribute actively to problem solving and innovation. In co-creative models, AI acts not just as an assistant but as a teammate capable of generating novel ideas, proposing solutions, and responding to human feedback iteratively. This model treats AI as an interactive agent within development workflows, facilitating shared agency in design and coding tasks. Co-creative paradigms challenge traditional boundaries between human labor and automation. They require holistic socio-technical integration that supports mixed-initiative workflows, where tasks shift fluidly between human and AI contributors. Organizations embracing co-creative development must align work practices, incentives, and metrics to reward joint human-AI achievements rather than human effort alone.

6.3 Governance, Accountability, and Trust

Effective governance and accountability frameworks are essential for responsible AI integration in software enterprises. These frameworks uphold trustworthiness and manage risks associated with increasingly autonomous systems.

6.3.1 Validation Pipelines and Audit Frameworks

AI governance in software development must extend beyond technical performance to encompass organizational processes that validate and verify AI outputs. Validation pipelines include automated and human-mediated checks that ensure AI-generated artifacts meet defined quality, safety, and ethical standards. Continuous auditing, both automated and manual, provides traceability and accountability throughout the development lifecycle. These audit frameworks help organizations detect errors, identify bias, and enforce transparency in AI actions. Moreover, governance practices increasingly emphasize auditability—the capacity to reconstruct AI decision paths and justify outcomes. Audit trails support accountability by enabling teams to explain how and why AI influenced specific design decisions, thus reducing ambiguity and building stakeholder trust.

6.3.2 Risk Management in Autonomous Development Systems

Autonomous AI systems introduce new risk vectors into organizational operations. Risk management must adopt socio-technical lenses that consider system behaviors, organizational contexts, and human trust relationships. Trust is not a static property but emerges from repeated successful collaborations where systems behave reliably and transparently (Engin, 2025). Organizations must therefore calibrate trust by balancing AI autonomy with appropriate human oversight and clear escalation paths for exceptions. Risk management strategies include scenario analysis, impact modeling, and safeguards that prevent undesirable behavior. These approaches ensure that organizations retain control over AI outcomes while enabling AI systems to operate at scale and at pace. Embedding risk management practices within organizational governance cultivates resilience and preparedness for unexpected AI behavior.

7. FUTURE WORKFORCE PATHWAYS AND PROFESSIONAL IDENTITY

The accelerating pace of technological change is reshaping not only the tasks that software engineers perform, but also the identities they construct and the careers they pursue. As artificial intelligence (AI), distributed ecosystems, and socio-technical concerns become central to software practice, traditional conceptions of the software engineer—as coder, debugger, and systems integrator—are being challenged. This chapter projects the most salient emerging professional trajectories and examines how professional identity is being reconstituted in response to technological, organizational, and societal pressures.

7.1 Emerging Roles and Career Pathways

7.1.1 AI System Steward

The role of the AI system steward represents a shift from developer-centric technical work toward ongoing governance of AI systems throughout their lifecycle. This emerging professional trajectory reflects recognition that deploying AI in realistic settings requires continuous calibration, transparency, and interpretability. Traditional software maintenance roles focus primarily on code correctness and performance optimization, but AI systems introduce new complexities: data drift, ethical alignment, and context-sensitive outputs. The AI system steward integrates technical expertise with domain understanding and governance perspectives to ensure that AI systems remain reliable and aligned with organizational objectives and societal norms over time. Research on future work emphasizes that as automation and intelligent systems proliferate, human roles will increasingly emphasize supervision, interpretation, and strategic oversight rather than routine coding alone (Davenport & Kirby, 2016). Thus, AI stewards are envisioned as hybrid professionals who bridge the gap between machine autonomy and human accountability. They require skills in machine learning interpretability, system monitoring, and stakeholder communication, reshaping the competencies expected of tomorrow's software workforce.

7.1.2 Algorithmic Auditor

As algorithmic decision-making becomes pervasive, the need for algorithmic auditors emerges as a professional imperative. Unlike traditional testers who verify functionality against specifications, algorithmic auditors interrogate systems for fairness, bias, transparency, and regulatory compliance. This role is informed by rising public and regulatory scrutiny over discriminatory outputs, opaque decision logics, and unforeseen harms arising from automated systems. Algorithmic auditing draws on interdisciplinary knowledge—statistics, ethics, law, and domain expertise—to evaluate systems not just for performance but for societal impact. It represents a departure from purely technical evaluation toward normative assessment. The professional identity of auditors is thus shaped by both engineering rigor and ethical stewardship. Davenport and Kirby (2016) suggest that as algorithmic systems assume critical societal roles, new careers will arise that blend analytical depth with ethical judgment, a pattern well captured in the figure of the algorithmic auditor. This evolution also signals a broader shift in software engineering education and practice, where curricula and organizational roles increasingly must embed ethical reasoning, interpretive frameworks, and sociotechnical awareness as core competencies—rather than optional "soft skills."

7.1.3 Digital Product Ecosystem Architect

The third emerging trajectory is that of the digital product ecosystem architect—a professional responsible for integrating diverse technologies, platforms, and stakeholder needs into coherent and adaptive product ecosystems. Traditional "software architect" roles emphasize technical design patterns, modularity, and scalability within bounded systems. In contrast, digital product ecosystem architects work at the intersection of technology and strategy, orchestrating interconnected components such as cloud services, AI modules, third-party APIs, user communities, and business partners. Ecosystem architects require a holistic perspective that transcends code and embraces networked value creation. The architect's identity becomes less about optimizing internal system structure and more about shaping extensible, resilient systems that evolve with user needs and external innovations. Literature on digital transformation emphasizes the rise of such boundary-spanning roles as organizations seek to embed agility and innovation at scale (Wilson & Daugherty, 2018). These professionals are expected to translate business strategy into modular, interoperable technical designs while managing socio-cultural relationships across organizational boundaries.

7.2 Global Workforce Implications

7.2.1 Redistribution of Technical Labor

The transformation of software careers is tightly coupled with global shifts in technical labor distribution. Advances in cloud computing, collaborative platforms, and automated development tools are lowering barriers to entry and enabling geographically dispersed contributions. Software labor is no longer concentrated in a handful of high-tech hubs; instead, it can be distributed across global talent pools where education, cost structures, and innovation ecosystems vary widely. This redistribution has implications for equity, competition, and workforce mobility. On one hand, accessible tooling and remote collaboration open opportunities for skilled workers in underrepresented regions to participate in high-impact projects. On the other hand, the commoditization of routine technical tasks can intensify global competition, pressuring workers to specialize in high-value, creative, and strategic roles. As Davenport and Kirby (2016) note, automation will displace certain types of work but also amplify the demand for uniquely human capabilities, such as complex problem-solving, ethical judgment, and cross-cultural communication. The identity of the software engineer is thus becoming more global and diversified, encompassing a spectrum from localized technical contributors to globally networked strategists who coordinate across time zones, cultures, and regulatory environments.

7.2.2 Inclusion, Accessibility, and New Entry Pathways

Emerging pathways into software professions emphasize inclusion and accessibility, challenging entrenched educational and credentialing barriers. Bootcamps, micro-credentials, online learning platforms, and competency-based assessments are reshaping how individuals enter and advance within the field. These alternative pathways democratize access, enabling learners from diverse socioeconomic backgrounds to build relevant skills. However, inclusion is not just about access to education; it also entails creating work environments that value diverse perspectives and mitigate bias. As digital systems impact broader populations, the importance of representative engineering teams becomes more salient. A professional identity rooted in inclusivity encourages engineers to attend to not only technical excellence but also the lived experiences of the end-users they serve. Collectively, these trends suggest that the future software workforce will be more heterogeneous, with varied educational backgrounds, fluid career trajectories, and a shared commitment to designing systems that are accessible and equitable.

7.3 Ethical, Social, and Economic Futures

7.3.1 Responsibility in AI-Mediated Engineering

As AI permeates engineering practice, questions of responsibility and accountability intensify. Engineers are increasingly called upon not only to build efficient systems but to anticipate ethical dilemmas, mitigate risks, and respond to unintended consequences. Professional identity, therefore, is expanding beyond technical mastery to encompass ethical reflexivity. Scholarly work on AI futures underscores that responsibility in AI-mediated contexts must be distributed across teams and institutions, embedding ethical lenses into every phase of design and deployment (Wilson & Daugherty, 2018). This transformation challenges the "neutral engineer" archetype, urging professionals to adopt a more proactive, values-oriented stance. The resulting identity is one that integrates moral agency with technical expertise, positioning engineers as stewards of socio-technical integrity.

7.3.2 Long-Term Employability and Professional Sustainability

The rapid evolution of tools and roles raises concerns about long-term employability. Continuous learning, adaptability, and interdisciplinary fluency are becoming essential for sustainable careers. Rather than linear progression within predefined roles, engineers will likely navigate fluid trajectories shaped by emerging technologies, shifting market demands, and evolving organizational forms. Investments in lifelong learning, reflective practice, and portfolio careers help individuals maintain relevance and resilience. Professional sustainability thus hinges on cultivating not only technical depth but also meta-skills—learning how to learn, collaborating across domains, and negotiating ethical and societal trade-offs. In summary, the future of software work will be defined by hybrid roles that blend technical, ethical, and strategic competencies. Professional identity will be reconstructed around stewardship, critical reflection, and global collaboration, reflecting the changing relationship between technology, society, and human agency.

8. CONCLUSION

Artificial intelligence fundamentally reconfigures the knowledge base, skill structures, and socio-technical functions of software engineering, going beyond mere automation of existing tasks and presenting both transformative opportunities and critical challenges for long-term innovation systems. Contemporary research underscores that AI's capacity to enhance productivity, reliability, and adaptability across planning, coding, testing, and maintenance phases represents more than incremental efficiency gains; it signals a paradigm shift toward an AI-augmented engineering ecosystem where human and machine capabilities co-evolve. However, this shift carries inherent risks that, if left unmanaged, can undermine the sustainability of professional practice, erode deep technical competencies, and destabilize innovation ecosystems that rely on robust human expertise. Empirical evidence from the software industry highlights that while there is a notable surge in interest around sustainability competencies—encompassing technical, social, and environmental dimensions—in current practice, professionals frequently lack adequate foundational knowledge to integrate these competencies across development activities, pointing to an emergent gap that threatens the resilience and ethical quality of future engineering outcomes. This gap is closely linked to the broader discussion of AI's impact on the workforce. For example, industry analyses predict that a significant majority of software engineers will need to upskill in response to the proliferation of generative and AI-native tools. These tools, while promising to offload repetitive tasks and free engineers for higher-order problem solving, also risk fostering long-term deskilling if practitioners become overly reliant on automation without maintaining grounding in core engineering principles, systems thinking, and contextual judgment. Upskilling in areas such as prompt engineering, AI system oversight, and hybrid human-AI collaboration becomes not a luxury but a strategic imperative to sustain innovation capacity, preserve quality, and ensure that engineers remain central to the interpretive and ethical dimensions of software design and evolution. Indeed, research focused on responsible software engineering for AI highlights that ethical decision-making, accountability, and interdisciplinary competencies are critical for operationalizing responsible practices within the AI-augmented software life cycle, and that without concerted efforts to integrate ethical frameworks into everyday engineering routines, organizations risk perpetuating practices that prioritize speed and automation at the expense of fairness, transparency, and societal impact (Murali Rani et al., 2025). Instead, proactive strategies in education, organizational practice, and policy are required to shape an AI-augmented engineering future that is resilient, creative, and ethically grounded. In the educational domain, curricula must evolve beyond traditional software engineering competencies to incorporate sustainability literacy, ethical reasoning, and human-AI interaction skills. This includes fostering critical reflection on the limits of automation, equipping learners with the ability to interrogate AI outputs, and cultivating interdisciplinary fluency that bridges technical, ethical, and societal considerations. In practice, organizations must invest in continuous reskilling programs that empower engineers to steward AI tools responsibly, rather than outsourcing key cognitive tasks to algorithms. Upskilling pathways should emphasize not only tool proficiency but also domains such as responsible data practices, socio-technical risk assessment, and collaborative problem solving within AI-enhanced teams. Without such investments, organizations risk creating innovation ecosystems that are fragile, susceptible to systemic biases, and lacking the adaptive capacity to navigate future disruptions. Policymakers also have a crucial role in shaping a sustainable AI-augmented engineering landscape. Regulatory frameworks can incentivize transparency, accountability, and fairness in AI systems, while public investment in workforce development can help mitigate inequities arising from rapid technological change. Standards bodies and professional societies should update codes of practice to reflect the ethical and sustainability implications of AI within software engineering, ensuring that practitioners are held to shared norms that balance innovation with the public good. Moreover, funding agencies can support research that explores long-term impacts of AI augmentation on professional practice, organizational dynamics, and societal outcomes, generating evidence to guide responsible adoption paths.

Finally, future research must delve deeper into the co-evolution of human and AI capabilities in professional work. Key questions remain about how knowledge structures in software engineering will adapt as AI systems become more autonomous, how ethical and sustainability considerations can be embedded into AI-driven workflows, and how organizations can balance the efficiency gains from automation with the cultivation of human creativity and critical judgment. Longitudinal studies that track the effects of AI augmentation on skill development, innovation quality, and labor dynamics will be particularly valuable. In summary, sustainable AI-augmented software engineering requires a holistic orientation that embraces technology's potential while consciously shaping its integration through education, practice, and governance, ensuring that the future workforce is both capable and conscientious in stewarding digital transformation.

REFERENCES

Allamanis, M., Barr, E. T., Devanbu, P., & Sutton, C. (2018). A survey of machine learning for big code and naturalness. *ACM Computing Surveys*, *51*(4), 1–37. DOI: 10.1145/3212695

Amershi, S., Begel, A., Bird, C., DeLine, R., Gall, H., Kamar, E., . . . Zimmermann, T. (2019, May). Software engineering for machine learning: A case study. In 2019 IEEE/ACM 41st International Conference on Software Engineering: Software Engineering in Practice (ICSE-SEIP) (pp. 291-300). IEEE. DOI: 10.1109/ICSE-SEIP.2019.00042

Autor, D. H. (2015). Why are there still so many jobs? The history and future of workplace automation. *The Journal of Economic Perspectives*, *29*(3), 3–30. DOI: 10.1257/jep.29.3.3

Brynjolfsson, E., & McAfee, A. (2014). The second machine age: Work, progress, and prosperity in a time of brilliant technologies. WW Norton & company.

Brynjolfsson, E., & Mitchell, T. (2017). What can machine learning do? Workforce implications. *Science*, *358*(6370), 1530–1534. DOI: 10.1126/science.aap8062 PMID: 29269459

Chen, M., Tworek, J., Jun, H., Yuan, Q., Pinto, H. P. D. O., Kaplan, J., . . . Zaremba, W. (2021). Evaluating large language models trained on code. arXiv preprint arXiv:2107.03374.

Cloudin, S., Priya, R. S., Prabhu, G. A., Ruba, M., Joel, R., & Vanitha, R. (2026). AI-Enhanced Predictive Analytics and Reliability Management for Wind Turbine Maintenance. In AI-Powered Analysis, Modeling, and Monitoring of Wind Energy Systems (pp. 191-218). IGI Global Scientific Publishing.

Davenport, T. H., & Kirby, J. (2016). *Only humans need apply: Winners and losers in the age of smart machines* (Vol. 1). Harper Business.

Davenport, T. H., & Ronanki, R. (2018). Artificial intelligence for the real world. *Harvard Business Review*, *96*(1), 108–116.

Dhanushya, J., Ruba, M., Ponkarthika, M., Soundarya, B., Sakthi Priya, V., Dhanushri, S., & Harikrishnan, S. (2025, April). AI-Powered Multipurpose Agrobot for Precision Farming: Crop Health Management, Fertilizer Recommendation and Yield Prediction. In *2025 International Conference on Recent Advances in Electrical, Electronics, Ubiquitous Communication, and Computational Intelligence (RAEEUCCI)* (pp. 1-6). IEEE.

Engin, Z. (2025). Human-AI Governance (HAIG): A Trust-Utility Approach. arXiv preprint arXiv:2505.01651.

Gowthaman, N., Ruba, M., Aswath, S., Hemavarshni, S. N., Bragadeshwaran, R., & Nithish, S. J. (2025, November). Iot Integrated Solution For Smart Vertical Crop Cultivation. In 2025 IEEE 7th International Conference on Computing, Communication and Automation (ICCCA) (pp. 1-6). IEEE.

Kameswaran, A., Nanthakumar, K., & Ruba, M. (2017). High performance pre-computation based self-controlled precharge-free content-addressable memory. *Journal of Electronics and Communication Systems*, *2*, 1–9.

Krithika, S., Jayachandran, T., Raghapriya, N. R., Ruba, M., Janani, C., & Sathiyavathi, S. (2025, April). An Effective Denial of Service Texture Features from Malware Grayscale Image. In 2025 3rd International Conference on Artificial Intelligence and Machine Learning Applications Theme: Healthcare and Internet of Things (AIMLA) (pp. 1-7). IEEE. DOI: 10.1109/AIMLA63829.2025.11041501

Manyika, J., Remes, J., Mischke, J., & Krishnan, M. (2017). The Productivity Puzzle, A Closer Look at the United States. McKinsey Global Institute, Discussion Paper.

Ponkarthika, M. G., A. P., Ruba, M., Kishore, Y. R., M., K., & G. V., M. (2026). Bridging Health Equity in Times of Crisis: Ensuring Inclusive Care During Emergencies and Disasters. In E. Matsumoto, F. Andres, & R. Agrawal (Eds.), Advancing Equity in Global Healthcare Systems (pp. 27-54). IGI Global Scientific Publishing. DOI: 10.4018/979-8-3373-1330-6.ch002

Poovithaa, M., Ruba, M., Ponkarthika, M., Ragul, N., Ragul, V., & Sangeetha, K. (2025, November). IoT Smart Traffic Control System for Hill Roads with Emergency Vehicle Priority. In 2025 IEEE 7th International Conference on Computing, Communication and Automation (ICCCA) (pp. 1-6). IEEE.

Rani, L. M., Mohammadi, F., Feldt, R., & Svensson, R. B. (2025). An Empirical Study on Decision-Making Aspects in Responsible Software Engineering for AI. arXiv preprint arXiv:2501.15691. DOI: 10.1109/ICSE-SEIP66354.2025.00056

Risko, E. F., & Gilbert, S. J. (2016). Cognitive offloading. *Trends in Cognitive Sciences*, *20*(9), 676–688. DOI: 10.1016/j.tics.2016.07.002 PMID: 27542527

Santhini, C., Ruba, M., Sakthi Priya, V., & Hemalatha, R. (2025). Intercultural communication and assessment practices in the integration of AI with education. In *Generative AI Approaches to Sustainable Development in Higher Education*. IGI Global. DOI: 10.4018/979-8-3693-5623-4.ch010

Sculley, D., Holt, G., Golovin, D., Davydov, E., Phillips, T., Ebner, D., & Dennison, D. (2015). Hidden technical debt in machine learning systems. *Advances in Neural Information Processing Systems*, •••, 28.

Shanmugaraja, T., Ruba, M., Priya, V. S., Venkatesh, T., Supriya, M., & Nallamuthu, M. (2023, September). ECG noise elimination using an FPGA version of a modified error normalized LMS adaptive filter. In AIP Conference Proceedings (Vol. 2764, No. 1, p. 060033). AIP Publishing LLC. DOI: 10.1063/5.0144367

Shneiderman, B. (2020). Human-centered artificial intelligence: Reliable, safe & trustworthy. *International Journal of Human-Computer Interaction*, *36*(6), 495–504. DOI: 10.1080/10447318.2020.1741118

Sibiya, S., Ruba, M., Ponkarthika, M., Vijayasabariswari, M., Sheba, S., Vignesh, S., . . . Sankar, S. S. (2025, October). Integrated Wearable Health Monitoring and Emergency Response System With IOT Sensors, AED and Mobile App for Enhanced Patient Outcomes. In 2025 IEEE 2nd International Conference on Green Industrial Electronics and Sustainable Technologies (GIEST) (pp. 1-6). IEEE.

Tavantzis, T., Lambiase, S., Russo, D., & Feldt, R. (2025). From Challenge to Change: Design Principles for AI Transformations. arXiv preprint arXiv:2512.05533. DOI: 10.2139/ssrn.5912868

Wilson, H. J., & Daugherty, P. R. (2018). Collaborative intelligence: Humans and AI are joining forces. *Harvard Business Review*, *96*(4), 114–123.

Chapter 10
The Future of Software Engineering:
Augmented Engineers, Human Judgment, and Intelligent Automation

Sanjeev Kumar
http://orcid.org/0000-0002-7375-7341
Lovely Professional University, India

Pardeep Kumar
http://orcid.org/0000-0003-0308-7634
Lovely Professional University, India

ABSTRACT

Transforming the future of software engineering and have been dubbed augmented engineers since they have been intersecting intelligent automation, artificial intelligence, and the human-centered design. With this dynamism, day-to-day coding, testing, and deploying applications have become more in line with AI-based solutions, and engineers are left to work on more challenging issues and innovative design and ethical decision-making. When the factors of judgment, contextualization and strategic thinking are paramount, augmented engineers with the help of these intelligent systems may achieve a greater productivity, decrease the number of errors and hasten the software delivery process without losing the control over the process to humans. The transformation is also curling the conventional software engineering, organizational process and team functioning and requires new talents, including AI literacy, human-AI interaction and creative thinking

DOI: 10.4018/979-8-3373-8450-4.ch010

INTRODUCTION TO THE FUTURE OF SOFTWARE ENGINEERING

The sphere of software engineering as a specialization has been evolving in the past several decades. It has also been engaged in systematic designing, creation, testing and maintenance of software systems very conscientiously by use of methodologies, frameworks and the code practices so as to deliver the credible software. However, the increasing pace of technology advancement, diffusion of smart technologies, and sophistication of the software-derived products are redefining the nature of the subject. The term software engineering is no longer used to connote the human ability to write codes in a flowing manner having the capacity of artificial intelligence (AI) and smart automation with the elements of human-focused design (Jain et al., 2021). This new paradigm is also most likely to redeem the roles, the duties and capabilities of software engineers as it has established the present-day term of augmented engineers. The essence of this change is summed up by the fact that manual and repetitive labour force is substituted by the processes of automation development. The traditional software engineering job kept the engineers busy with an enormous portion of their time doing a monotonous task of coding, debugging and testing. The operations are also resource intensive as they are necessary to develop a functional software and are highly prone to be attributed to the human error. The introduction of AI-powered technologies and intelligent automation systems could now undertake most of these activities at a faster, routine, and correct method. One example is the use of AI code generators to produce boilerplate code, and automated testing infrastructures to identify bugs and vulnerabilities in millions of lines of code without necessarily spending the time that would otherwise be spent it in a manual testing infrastructure (Corrigan, 2012). The alteration can help the engineers to focus on the limited activities that only human beings can undertake such as creative problem solving, system architecture design and strategic decisions.

Machine intelligence integrated on a human intelligence, which is referred to the concept of the augmented engineer. Intelligent systems are partners that do not substitute human engineers as they provide knowledge, ideas and support to enhance the human productivity and decision making. Some of the applications of AI to augmented engineers are writing and code optimization, predictive debugging, and anomaly detection, but has the capability to make judgment at those aspects where it is required to be situation specific, use moral cognition, and long-term levels. This kind of close symbiosis of human beings and AI software is changing what software engineering can do, what software engineering can do, and it is possible to develop more complex, reliable, and flexible software systems. The change has also great effects on software engineering learning and career development. The advent of intelligent automation requires engineers to acquire other skills other than the traditional programming (Madni, 2023). AI literacy, data-driven thinking, human-AI collaboration and adaptive problem-solving are some of the new competencies. Alternatively, schools and colleges are also taking the option of interdisciplinary education, which involves the fundamentals of computer science and AI, machine learning, ethics, and systems thinking. It is expected that the future engineers not only know how to write a code and understand the outcomes of AI and how to calculate risks and make a decision with the help of automated systems (Abrahão et al., 2025).

A change in work processes and group life in organizations is a reality. Agile and DevOps processes are being fed with AI-based inputs based on the principle of constant integration, cooperation, and instant iterations. The intelligent project management systems will assist in forecasting the bottlenecks, managing the resources in the most appropriate way, and giving a real time review performance of a team (Northern Kentucky University et al., 2022). This helps the teams in providing a more significant workflow, reduced time-to-marketing and maintaining the software standards on higher levels. In the meantime, companies are recommended to overcome potential dilemmas such as over-reliance on automation, the danger of deskilling, the need to hold AI-based decision-making accountable. The moral and social factor is the other factor that significantly contributes to the future of the profession of software engineering. As the representatives of the software development, engineers would have been required to struggle with the issues of bias in the automated decision making, the transparency of the AI-enhanced code, and the social implications of software, in general. There should also be the application of human judgment that can guarantee that the software systems are not only technical wise efficient but that it is also consistent with ethics and rules other than those of the user. The augmented engineer according to this is a professional and an ethical custodian (Madni, 2020).

The future of software engineering, which is also the last but not the least, is defined by the appearance of hybrid solutions which are developed due to the usage of the benefits of human intelligence and intelligent automation. The AI-driven technologies, combined with the human resource, innovation, and intelligence, can take the software development world to the heights of previously unfeasible innovativeness, stability, and sustainability. Such a hybrid paradigm will assist in enhancing the software delivery in the limited time span, system robustness and enable the engineers to deal with more complex and dynamic issues, autonomous systems and the large-scale enterprise software. The future prognosis of the profession that is software engineering is very likely to indicate that the industry is undergoing a major transformation (Amalfitano et al., 2026). Software engineering has since outgrown being a manual code and traditional approach and now it is taking the form of an ecosystem of co-operation between human experience and intelligent automation. The future of the software development world will be the AI controlled enhanced engineers, whose competencies and experience will have the AI capabilities. There is a cost in education, behavior and ethnics in organization, but the exciting possibilities of having such revolution are some higher, creative and strategic thinking on the part of the engineers in arriving at a decision. The future will enable the software engineering profession to remain in the steep of the curve in the technological advancement and work with additional complexity and social impacts of the present software systems (Hoeschl et al., 2017).

SOFTWARE ENGINEERING PRACTICE

Software engineering practice is a term that is applied to the practices, principles, and actions employed by the developers in the design, development, testing, and maintenance of software systems in an efficient and reliable way. It is based on the application of engineering concepts to software development in order to produce the final product being of high quality, scalable, and easy to maintain. Requirements analysis is one of the practices in software engineering. At this phase, developers interact with the clients or users to know what the software is required to do. Specifications assist in preventing confusion and preventing future errors during development. The other important practice is software design. At this stage, the engineers design the software architecture, such as modules, components, and data flow. An efficient system is simple to construct, to test and to upgrade. Coding standards are also a concern of software engineering practice. In the case of a developer writing code, there are established rules that they follow so as to make sure that the code is clean, readable and consistent. This makes it easy to read and modify the program by other developers. It is a significant procedure that can ensure that the software is operating well and as the user would have anticipated. The process of testing is done in order to identify the errors and the errors are rectified and the software is subsequently launched by the use of various types of testing, which are unit testing, integration testing and system testing. The other practice is the version control which is useful in the management of the changes on the code as time progress. In this case, such tools as Git allow several (two or more) developers to work together without necessarily losing the previous versions of the software. The software should be updated and maintained once it has been published. Bugs are fixed, performance increased and new features are added depending on the feedbacks of the users. Software engineering practices can overall assist developers to develop high-quality, efficient, and reliable software systems.

EXPANDING ENGINEERS IN THE CURRENT SOFTWARE DEVELOPMENT

The advanced technology flux and the state of the art of the software systems have developed a breed of professionals in the software engineering horizon augmented engineers. It is the synergy between the human intelligence and the artificial intelligence (AI) itself because the engineers apply intelligent devices and automation to be more productive, inventive and creative and able to handle their problems better. Unlike the efforts of traditional software engineers, whose work is mostly centered on writing computer code manually, testing and debugging, augmented engineers operate in a hybrid ecosystem, with less complex labor being handled by AI, and more complex work, and human cognition, being open to highly sophisticated thought (Heroux, 2022). The idea of augmented engineers is anchored mostly on the creation of AI sourced development platforms, smart code assistants, and testing frameworks. Such technologies have radically changed the nature of labor of software engineers. As a guide, AI code completion allows searching a large amount of existing code, offering the most efficient solutions, as well as potential bugs and stopping them before they turn into critical issues. Similarly, automated testing will be in a position to perform a full-fledged regression, performance and security testing with minimum human intervention. The potential of these tools is to save on the time of development by eliminating the manual labor and providing less space to make a mistake and these tools can liberate the engineers to devote their time to more creative and strategic software design matters such as architecture design, user experience design, and scalability of a system (Boehm, 2011).

Communication with intelligent systems is one of the enormous values that augmented engineers possess. The alliance is greater than the matter of utilizing the tools, or the chance to comprehend the recommendations, triage, and decision-making created by AI, depending on the perception of the scenario and morals. In an example, an artificial intelligence device can propose a specific algorithm to be applied in the data processing process, but, in a scenario, the augmented engineer can attempt to examine its suitability basing on other considerations, including the performance requirement, security and maintenance (Stevanoviü et al., 2020). The end product of this symbiotic relationship is the quality and efficiency of software development that leads to a work force which is more agile informed, and capable of working on more complex problems. The augmented engineer skills are far superior to the traditional programming skills. They also will not be able to simply master the code; they will have to learn the AI literacy and data analytics and human-AI interaction abilities. The functioning of the AI models in action, the discovery of the potential biases, and the evaluation of the precision of the automated discovery are interesting points to be made in building AI and human judgment as the complementary rather than substitutive ones (Burnett & Myers, 2014). In addition to this, adaptive thinking, problem solving and ethical thinking are also developing into a soft skill, especially since the engineers are now in a position where their robotic decision-making problem can have a significant impact on business or the society. In a simple sense, augmented engineers are not merely technical employees like the con is, but on the other hand, strategic workers who are able to implement technology, ethics, and human gut in their work (Wnuk et al., 2011).

The organization is also affected by augmented engineers. Those companies providing the process of switching to the AI-assisted solutions have increased software releases, the highest grades of precision, and they became flexible to the market changes. These smart project management systems would also assist the team to identify the project bottlenecks, project risk and the optimal use of the resources. Meanwhile, engineers obtain the opportunity to explore deeper into the realm of design thinking, innovation, and solution to certain complex issues. Such transformation is a modification of the traditional dynamics of a team that implies a trade between machine efficiency and human innovation (Hawthorne & Perry, 2005). In order to exploit as much of the potential of augmented engineers as possible, the organizations will need to create the environment, which will assist in maintaining the continual learning, experimentation and error, or inter-functional interaction. Although augmented engineer is found to have such great advantages, there also exist issues surrounding this paradigm. The threat of deskilling the labour force is one of the main issues since the application of AI might lead to loss of the engineering skills (core programming or problem-solving skills). The organizations and education institutes should strive towards coming up with the curricula and training programs that would not only guarantee that the learners know how to use the tools, but the knowledge behind it, critical thinking and ethical decision making (Heaton & Carver, 2015). The other one is the problem of accountability, as AI-oriented systems are used in software development, it will be extremely more difficult to retrieve who will be answerable at the occasion when an error has been made or a miscalculation of outcomes has occurred. Augmented engineers must be ready to respond to such moral and legal questions to ensure that one of the machine aspects is central to the decision-making.

The bigger change in occupation of software engineering in the rise of augmented engineers is also available. It is no longer the technical performance that characterizes the job but rather the human-smarts ability to work in a complex ecosystem of systems and people. Engineers need to push the human-AI so that automation is applied to enhance the innovativeness and, at the same time, not to hamper ethical concerns, contextual knowledge and control (Monasor et al., 2010). Bimodality in this case is the capability of software teams to solve an unseen problem of a totally new complexity such as the real-time artificial intelligence systems and massive distributed systems and the critical infrastructure software. As software systems grow increasingly complex and demand faster delivery, intelligent automation will play an essential role in shaping the future of software development, establishing a new era where humans and machines collaborate to achieve unprecedented efficiency, innovation, and resilience. Future of Software Engineering: Chapters Overview are shown in table 1.,

Table 1. Future of Software Engineering: Chapters Overview; Source: Author Contributions.

Chapter Title	Key Focus / Description
Introduction to the Future of Software Engineering	Overview of how AI, intelligent automation, and human-centered design are reshaping software engineering; rise of augmented engineers.
Emergence of Augmented Engineers in Modern Software Development	Concept of augmented engineers; collaboration between humans and AI; skills and roles for future engineers.
Intelligent Automation: Tools, Techniques, and Applications	Overview of AI, ML, RPA, and predictive analytics in software development; applications in coding, testing, maintenance, and workflow optimization.
Human Judgment and Strategic Decision-Making in Software Engineering	Role of human insight, contextual understanding, and ethical decision-making alongside AI (to be elaborated).
AI-Enhanced Software Development: Opportunities and Challenges	Benefits and limitations of AI integration; efficiency gains, risks of bias, and accountability considerations.
Impact on Software Engineering Education and Skill Development	New educational approaches; AI literacy, adaptive thinking, and interdisciplinary training for engineers.
Transforming Organizational Workflows and Team Dynamics	Integration of AI in DevOps and agile workflows; team collaboration, productivity, and project management improvements.
Ethical Considerations, Bias, and Accountability in Automation	Ethical implications, bias mitigation, and ensuring responsible AI-assisted software development.
Hybrid Approaches: Combining Human Expertise with AI Capabilities	Strategies for blending human judgment with AI precision; best practices for collaboration.
Future Outlook: Innovation, Reliability, and Resilience in Software Development	Long-term implications of AI-human collaboration; driving innovation and sustainable software practices.

HUMAN JUDGMENT AND STRATEGIC DECISION-MAKING IN SOFTWARE ENGINEERING

Although it is true that smart automation and AI-driven software are entering the process of development as participants, human judgment is turning into an even more important contributor toward software engineering. Despite the fact that automation is competitive when dealing with repetitive, rule based and data intensive processes, the human engineer offers insight, creativity and strategic thought processes, which could not have been simulated by machines. Human judgment and potential AI are the key to the contemporary software engineering that enables to make more reasonable decisions, exercise more moral control over the areas, and be more innovative in the solutions to the issues. Software engineering cannot be done in a single step of writing code, it is a complex and cyclic process that should be re-evaluated in terms of architecture, resource utilization, risk management and achievement of organizational goals. Software scaling, software maintainability, software security and software usability are all dependent upon the timing of the software development, which cannot be determined without the human presence of human engineers and their capacity to sense the situation (Tang et al., 2017). To be more precise, an example is when making a decision on microservice or monolithic architecture, one of the factors to take into consideration is the experience of the team, infrastructure, user load estimated and long-term maintenance. Although the forecast and recommendations of the performance can be provided by AI, the human engineers should take these values and the experience, interests of the company, and the ethical considerations into account to identify the most effective solutions (Becker et al., 2017).

These are those spheres, which have to do with ambiguity, moral reasoning and subjective analysis and human judgment is particularly required. Although AI can make the process easier, and offer predictive analytics, it cannot consider situations in a particular manner, social effects, or value-based decision-making. The engineers should consider there are ethical implications, fairness and long-term implications that should be considered in the decision-making process like designing recommendation system or introducing privacy sensitive features in the design of the recommendation system. In the same vein, human only is required in intuitiveness, experience and strategic perspective in the user experience design, innovative systems architecture and new product features (Harris, 2017). Even augmented engineers, who speed up the testing process, simulate options and handle data through the help of AI tools, use judgment to determine how the most effective manner to do things, prioritize features, and an intelligent orientation of the solutions. Organized decision-making mechanisms are normally combined with human judgment and data that is informed by information. The decision matrices, risk assessment schemes and multi-criteria analysis structures allow the engineers to analyze the alternatives methodically and it can take the qualitative input. It is human engineers who analyze the predictive information, optimize the utilization of the resources, and identify risks provided with the assistance of AI-based analytics, calculate the possible bias, and make the decisions which consider the big picture. The results of such a combination of

AI skills and information (quantitative) and human thought (qualitative) are more harmonious, productive, and creative. The human judgment is another human need in a scenario when it is impossible to determine fairness or privacy and even social responsibility of AI. The engineers are the custodians of the reasonable software development, the engineers consider the risks, they comply with ethical laws and they keep the trust of the users (Mendes et al., 2018).

One of the aspects that facilitate the rising level of quality of software engineering domain and its efficiency is the interaction of humans and AI in the sphere of strategic decision-making. Similar to the possibility to test faster, finding patterns, and simulating complex situations and to optimize resources, nevertheless, human decisions should still be taken about architecture, feature or risk priorities, etc. Inappropriate use of AI without critical thinking may also result into deskilling, propagation of bias or even lack of fit between the results of the project and the tasks to be undertaken. The engineers therefore have the role of critically thinking and being discretionary and proactive in how the AI outputs are interpreted in a way that the automated recommendations would align with the project objectives, organizational ideals and ethics (Cunha et al., 2016). Human judgment is the other key factor of trade-offs in the complex software projects. The various development teams are usually limited in the areas of time, cost, technical viability and user demand. In these states of dynamism and uncertainty, one has to rely on adaptive thinking when arriving at decisions and requires experience-based intuition and strategic foresight. Human engineers are able to take into account several sides and see the implications of the future as well as predict the challenges that are not obvious to the automated systems. The ability to cross over and capability of knowledge, such contextualization, is what makes the software projects not only powerful but also scalable, and also open to business intentions, and needs of the user (Li & Li, 2009).

Moral factors and risk evaluation and responsibility are also elements that require human decision-making. The algorithms of AI are also trained using the past that could be biased and its results could not be easily deciphered without the human knowledge. Such outputs will also be evaluated by the engineers and probable ethical or societal consequences and will be tasked to make decisions that will implicate the users and other stakeholders. It is a human control to ensure that the software development practices are accountable, open and in line with the general values of the society, and the organization as a whole. Finally, these days such sides of the software engineering as human judgment and strategic decision-making cannot be separated. On the one hand, the AI and intelligent automation will contribute to the field of productivity, faster and more analytical processing, but it is the human engineer, who introduces the precious insight, innovation, and ethical considerations, in case of some complex and high-stakes decision (Duan et al., 2012). The accuracy of AI can be subjected to the situational intelligence, foresight, and ethical concern of human engineers in order to take the software development to the new level of innovation, excellence, and resilience. The augmented engineering, human-to-intelligent hybrid approach would make sure that the software is more efficient and reliable besides being consistent with the long-term organizational goals and expectations of the society. With the development of the state-of-the-art software systems and further development of AI, human judgment will continue to be the pillar of responsible, innovative and sustainable software engineering.

ARTIFICIAL INTELLIGENCE SOFTWARE DEVELOPMENT: POTENTIAL AND ISSUES

One of the major changes in the development of the software engineering is the improvement of the software engineering as AI and machine learning (ML) technologies are currently implemented in the software development life cycle. AI will enable the software engineers to automate the repetitive processes, make informed decisions, and advance speedy software development, which will eventually increase productivity, code quality, as well as reliability of the system. Nevertheless, some difficulties concerning this integration also exist which are associated with the problems of ethics, prejudice, responsibility, and workforce readjustment that must be addressed in the right way to reveal the full potential of the AI-enhanced development (Deshmukh et al., 2023). The opportunities open to AI so far as software development is considered are enormous and include the code generation, testing, debugging, optimizing, and project management. The code assistants based on AI offer snippets of code, identify potential failures, and optimize algorithms, which enable an engineer to find more solutions to problems, develop a better architecture, and provide new features at an additional level. AI is also useful in saving time and human error during the development process since it is automated and expands and shortens the development cycles and creates a high-quality software product. These advantages can be also added with intelligent testing which automatically passes unit testing, regression testing and performance testing and detects possible flaws and deviations. This has made the software applications more powerful and safe by forming small patterns in the massive codebases which may not have been detected by human engineers (Khaliq et al., 2022).

The AI is also used in maintenance and support of software. Predictive analytics enables engineers to plan the breakdown of the system and aggressively assign resources and in addition resolve performance concerns in advance. The monitoring tools are coded to monitor the behavior of their systems within the time frame that notifies and warns engineers in case there is a possibility of a bottleneck or a threat occurring, before it becomes a serious problem. The AI-based debugging systems are able to recognize the root causes of the error and suggest the potential solution to minimize the downtimes and increase the reliability of the system. On the same note, AI project management software can forecast the delivery schedule, make the staff work automated, and forecast the risks, which may facilitate making critical strategic decisions. Such integration will allow the software teams become more concentrated and assured with their work and they can commit their energy in innovation and problem solving instead of the daily routine activities of operations. Although these strengths are present, AI-enhanced software development has a number of disadvantages. The biases and unintended consequences are one of the largest problems (Meziane & Vadera, 2010). The previous data is used to carry out training of AI algorithms and it can be the current bias or biased data. These biases are spread to the software outputs unless these biases are mitigated and therefore affect fairness, security or user trust. By being skeptical about the recommendation, ensuring that the outputs are delivered, and the choice made by the artificial intelligence is a just decision in a sensible ethical context is the responsibility of the engineers to ensure that the correspondence of AI with the organization is ethical and achieves its objective. The other weakness is accountability. The more the AI system is used to create the product, the less one understands who should take responsibility in case of mistakes, vulnerability, or unintended consequences. In the situation when AI is doing a major share of the job, human control and strict rules of governance are required to make sure that engineers will be responsible in terms of quality of the software (Nascimento et al., 2020).

Another factor of importance is workforce adaptation. AI is being taken up more routine and analytical work and the engineers turn deskilled in the crucial fields of core programming or problem solving. In reaction to this, it is needed to bring the continuous learning and upskilling which ought to be based on the AI literacy, data analysis, the collaboration between the human beings and the AI, and the ethical decision-making. The engineers are expected to not only be taught how to employ the AI tools positively, but also how to employ their result, how to identify their negative aspects and how to think critically during automated processes. The organizations are to develop an organizational culture that would not be over-reliant on AI and neglect the human know-how and be ready to utilize it so as to be creative and come up with solutions to the strategic problems (Khan et al., 2023).

It is also difficult to incorporate with the old systems and old software. AI tools may need a lot of computing and infrastructures to be integrated with machines, which may not be provided to the current environment. The deployment of AI requires the guarantee of safety and efficiency by keeping information of high quality, compatibility of the systems and the cyber-safety of the systems. Cost and intricacy of implementing AI may also be a constraint to a smaller organization or team, and it is worth mentioning the degree to which they will recuperate and how much will expand upon doing so. Social and ethical factors are also the necessity to treat them in an adequate way. When the AI software is being developed, the questionable issues include the problem of transparency, fairness, and social impact. The engineers will guarantee that the automated decisions will not have a negative impact on the users without their intentions, spread discrimination, and infringe their privacy (Ellahham et al., 2020). Explainability, accountability, and bias mitigation are some of the responsible AI practices, which would ensure trust and legitimacy of software systems. Human control will be the very heart of such issues because it is proposed to balance AI activities and ethical decisions, strategic orientation, and vision.

TRANSFORMING ORGANIZATIONAL WORKFLOWS AND TEAM DYNAMICS

The rapid adoption of AI, intelligent automation and augmented engineering is literally changing the way processes are performed and relationships in the organization in the field of software development. The intensely teamwork-based, fast and AI-enhanced practices are substituting the traditional processes, relying on linear processes, manual coordination, and silos of expertise. The primary driver of this change is the need to productivity, accelerate the delivery of the software, reduce mistakes, dynamically respond to the changes in the market and technology. Integration of smart tools into the software engineering team is not only changing the manner in which things are done; it is also changing the roles and responsibilities as well as the interaction of the team members in the team (Marion & Fixson, 2021). In modern processes where AI is used to augment operations, most routine operations such as coding, testing, debugging, and deployment is automated. This will allow human engineers to focus on the activity that requires creativity, critical thinking and situational knowledge and enhance the quality of work the team performs. The intelligence systems may be employed so as to streamline the development cycle and generally to increase efficiency within organization, by assigning the repetitive or time-consuming tasks to the intelligent systems. The automation of project management may be regarded as other methods of streamlining the processes since it provides the opportunity to monitor the progress of the work in real-time, identify the potential bottlenecks, anticipate risks, and suggest the most successful resources allocation. These tools allow the teams to anticipate the challenges and reduce the delays in terms of time and guarantee high standards of quality, even in the big projects (Irayani et al., 2025).

The group dynamics are also affected by AI penetration into the organizational processes. The human-AI interaction should be based on the change of mindset where the human-AI interaction, trust, and monitoring should be the priorities of the collaboration. The engineers will be required to be oriented on how to abide by AI-driven recommendations, test automated products, and make decisions based on the project objectives and ethics. This human-AI collaboration distorts the essence of the traditional power dynamics and decision making since machines, which make decisions using data, and people-centered decision making have responsibilities and power. The teams, which are sufficiently adaptable to such a hybrid environment, will be able to reap the rewards of speed and accuracy of AI with creative and strategic thinking and ethical sensitivity of human engineers, and creativeness and inventiveness will enhance. Agile and DevOps approaches are particularly introduced to adapt to the AI-enhanced workflow. These approaches put emphasis on the iterative development, continuous integration, teamwork and looped feedback. Agile teams may apply intelligent automation to conduct the tests automatically, release updates with a simple gesture and monitor the functioning of the system in real time (Neves, 2024). The data can be made to formulate the decisions based on the information they can obtain using AI-based dashboards about the performance metrics, the tasks performed, and the potential risks. This integration not only assists in accelerating the provision of software but enhances the adaptation, the responsiveness of the teams so that organizations are in a position to deal with the dynamism of the markets (Neves, 2024).

The reorganization of working processes and work teams also provokes the need of new skills and professional behaviors. The engineers are expected to be proficient in dealing with intelligent systems and how to process information that was created by AI and how to think critically in automated processes. The communication, coordination, and knowledge-sharing skills assist the teams to emerge out of the difficulties of human-AI collaboration that happen rather complexly. The other factor of leadership variations that managers and team heads need to find a balance between the effectiveness of technology and human touch, morality and team spirit. The firms must invest in capacity building sessions, group and team building workshops and platforms to build onto such skills and culture of learning and learning constantly.

Along with the advantages, AI-enhanced workflow raises concerns that must be addressed by the organizations. With too much automation, there can be reduced interaction, the lack of critical thinking, and the potential deskilling of a group member. It is also possible that engineers are stressed or distressed when AI systems offer the recommendations that contradict their judgment, and they will be obliged to be able to resolve the conflicts and make decisions. In addition, there are certain ethical, legal, and organizational implications of AI implementation within a team that should be considered, in particular, when the choices made by machines impact users, clients, or stakeholders. It is of utmost importance that the process of preserving trust at the team and corporate level is quite dependent on being responsible and applying the concept of visibility to the AI-augmented processes. There is also the Alteration of the nature of collaboration among various cross-functional teams through the use of AI. Teams have become human engineers, project managers, AI systems and sometimes agents with AI that convey and operate without human interventions. Effective team dynamics require that there is a good understanding between human role and responsibility and AI role and responsibility, and scope of the decision. Trust is a key fact about such partnerships as engineers must feel that the outcomes of AI can be relied on yet they must have the right to act according to their authority and responsibility and do the required actions. The more successful companies in building trust and communication and mutual understanding on AI-enhanced teams, there are higher chances of achieving high performance, more productivity, and more innovations. AI and intelligent automation are transforming work processes of organizations and work dynamics of teams in the software engineering sector. Repetitive processes, prediction, and resource optimization AI can assist the team to work more efficiently, deliver software faster, and perform high-value work. At the same time, human engineers will remain the focus of data interpretation and be creative, judgmental, ethically, and strategically aligned. This mixed model changes the model of collaboration, team designs, and leadership operations that concentrate on human-AI synergy as an origin of innovation and resiliency. Those that are capable of navigating such a change will not just grow productivity and quality of the software but they will also create dynamic, collaborative and visionary teams that are capable of emerging in an ever more complex technological environment.

FUTURE PERSPECTIVES: NOVICE, RELIABILITY AND ROBUSTNESS IN SOFTWARE-DEVELOPMENT

The convergence of intelligent automation, artificial intelligence, and human-oriented design is quickly becoming a characteristic of the future of software development wherein the areas of innovation, reliability, and as well as resilience become central issues. As business and society become more complex, more interrelated and dependent on software systems, organizations must undertake measures to ensure that they do not only accelerate their rate of development, but also offer system resilience, protection, and adaptability. The emergence of augmented engineers' individuals who will be employed in a leading role of using intelligent tools, is the reason why the tilt toward automation and human judgment will define the future of software engineering and influence the development of technological understanding and organization culture. The human creativity and AI capabilities are becoming the basis of the promotion of innovation in software development. The AI is able to generate solutions fast, process extensive data, to simulate outcomes and suggest optimization and as a consequence expand the range of options engineers can consider. Human engineers, in their turn, contribute the strategic knowledge, moral reasoning as well as contextual knowledge necessary to select, refine and put such solutions to the right practice. It is also the combined effort that enables the organizations to experiment with new architecture, develop new applications, and add new complex features in a faster duration than ever. This means that software engineers are now able to focus on problem-solving, system design, and user-experience which are the main product characteristics in competitive markets by automating more routine tasks. The AI-enabled natural language processing also results in maximizing the iterative and exploratory development, which allows numerous options to be tested within a short period, feedback, which may be provided in real time, and solutions to be dynamically processed, based on the data of users and systems.

One of the core issues is the question of reliability since the systems become autonomous, distributed and necessary in the sale of business. Moreover, intelligent automation is useful in improving reliability, decreasing human error, and strenuous testing, as well as keeping a keen watch on how the system performs alongside predicting imminent failure ahead of time. The predictive analytics and AI-based monitoring solutions can be used to lower the downtime and enhance the stability of systems as the engineers can discover the patterns and anomalies that may indicate the possible problem and take preventive measures. Despite all these possibilities the human control is obligatory to interpret the outcomes of automated systems and make the decision in ambiguous situations, and also ensure that the policies are made based on the strategic goals and ethical principles. The augmented engineers also have the mandate of seeing to it that the balance is achieved between efficiency and reliability which are realized through automation and the one that is human guided so that systems become robust, scaled and reliable during their lifetime. Software development Resilience Software development refers to the ability of software development systems and organizations to endure change, recover post-disturbance, and continue on diverse conditions. The combination of the AI-enhanced procedures, the workflow flexibility, and the human consideration establishment also contributes to the development of the resilience capacity in the form of a quick response to the alterations of the requirements, unexpected malfunctions, or any external risks. The AI can also be employed by the software teams to recreate the stress situations, test the vulnerability of their system, and implement measures to correct the situation, and the human engineers ensure that the responses would be in alignment with the organizational priorities and ethical issues. Other resilient development practices comprise the creation of modular and maintainable architectures and DevOps, continuous integration and continuous deployment patterns so as to allow quick iteration and recovery. This will reduce the probability of systemic failures and ensure the fact that its programs can be created to accommodate the new challenges without compromising the performance and user experience.

The moral and responsible features of AI and intelligent automation implementation also reveal the importance of these in the future of software development. The engineers would be needed to ensure that the software would be transparent, fair, and safe with more autonomy in the systems. Prejudice, unintended consequences and responsibility are also issues of concern and engineers should exhibit discretion and develop governance systems that can be employed whenever making a decision with assistance of AI. This technical competence and moral discernment and ability to think in situations will become a trait of a quality software development team, in which innovation does not come at the cost of social trust and corporate integrity. The other notable observation in the future perspective is the constant fluctuation of the working force and the organizational culture. It will be necessary that the software engineers embrace the concept of continuous learning and adapt to new technologies, instruments, and paradigms that are introduced in the AI-enhanced environment at an almost lighting speed. The companies should develop the cultures of collaboration, innovativeness, and knowledge sharing, in which human capabilities and intelligent technologies will interact to enable the organizations to become effective and creative. The leadership will have to be capable of managing human-AI hybrid teams, whereas productivity, innovation, and moral control should be balanced to achieve strategic goals. Companies who are able to unite human and machine strengths effectively will be capable of maintaining a competitive edge, generate high quality software at a rapid pace manner and dynamically react to market and technology shocks. In conclusion, innovation, reliability, and resilience are elements of software creation made possible as a result of human and intelligent interaction. AI and robots help companies to become more efficient, offer predictive intelligence, and enable them to iterate, although human engineers retain situational awareness, ethical practice, and direction. The key to this vision will be the concept of augmented engineers since this will assist in reducing the gap between automated and human-judged software to develop a novel, powerful, and versatile software. Companies that implement this hybrid model, invest in lifelong learning, and develop collaborative and human-AI workflows will be highly likely to achieve success in an environment that is highly dynamic in terms of technology. That the future of software engineering is not only the code that runs faster or algorithms smarter but making resilient systems, which innovate in a responsible manner and offer consistency of results as well as adapt to change. The combination of human intelligence and AI-driven tools may lead to the productive, innovative, and strategically influential development of the software in a completely new manner, and it has to be ensured that the sphere of study does not fall behind the requirements of the ever more sophisticated and dynamic world.

CHALLENGES AND ETHICAL CONSIDERATIONS IN THE FUTURE OF SOFTWARE ENGINEERING

Software engineering has a great future that is full of opportunities, yet it involves a number of challenges and ethical issues are also to be considered. With the current high rate of development in technology, the software engineers should make sure that the systems they develop are safe, reliable and useful to the society. The data privacy and security are one of the major issues. The contemporary software systems amass and store enormous user data. It is highly relevant to prevent the hacking and abuse of this information. The engineers have to come up with systems that retain personal data safely and are sensitive to privacy of users. The other problem is a fast rate of changing technology. Such new technologies as artificial intelligence, cloud computing, automation are evolving rapidly. To keep up with the latest trends and develop efficient solutions, software engineers have to keep acquiring new tools, languages, and frameworks. There is also growing complexity of the system. Software systems comprising global platforms, smart infrastructure, and others, have millions of lines of code and different teams. Such complex systems are hard to manage and maintain and can cause an error unless taken care of. Morally, the software engineers should reflect on how the technology affects the society. As an example, the artificial intelligence can be biased when trained on unequal data. Engineers should take care of the fairness, transparency, and anti-discrimination of software systems to individuals or groups. One more ethical issue is automation and displacement. With software and AI coming in and automating most activities, certain jobs can be downsized or eliminated. Organizations and engineers ought to consider responsible innovation, which aids the society and generates new opportunities. The future of software engineering is bright, but engineers should cope with technical issues and act in accordance with good ethical standards to create technology that will be helpful to mankind

CONCLUSION

The future of software engineering is coming to be determined by the coincidence of human insight and intelligent automatic implementation. Augmented engineers, which are the ones who will work with the AI-based technologies, is a change in the paradigm in the sphere, which will make it possible to develop more efficient, more accurate, and creative software-writing. Although automation is useful in repetitive, data saturated and computational learning, the human engineers can be creative, strategic, morally judgmental and contextually sensitive whereby the technology can be generalized to the organizational and societal requirements. This ambivalent practice changes education, the working processes, the processes in groups, and competence demands. The engineers will be obliged to gain AI literacy, adaptable thought, and moral reasoning and organizations must embrace collaborative, agile, and knowledge-based environment. IAA will be more productive, quality, and resilient but have issues, such as biases, responsibility, and adaptation in employees. In order to overcome these barriers, life-long education and responsible government and a reasonable approach to introducing AI into the decision-making can be seen as assistants. Finally, the complementary capability of human beings and machines is the future of software engineering. The precision, speed and computation of AI together with the creativity, intelligence and moral resolution of human engineers will provide the sector with new degrees of creativity, stability and reliability. The flexibility of this software development, its accountability and the ability to manage the complex technological issues of the following few decades will be provided by the adoption of this paradigm.

REFERENCES

Abrahão, S., Grundy, J., Pezzè, M., Storey, M.-A., & Tamburri, D. A. (2025). Software Engineering by and for Humans in an AI Era. *ACM Transactions on Software Engineering and Methodology*, *34*(5), 1–46. DOI: 10.1145/3715111

Amalfitano, D., Metzger, A., Autili, M., Fulcini, T., Hey, T., Keim, J., Pelliccione, P., Scotti, V., Koziolek, A., Mirandola, R., & Vogelsang, A. (2026). A Research Roadmap for Augmenting Software Engineering Processes and Software Products with Generative AI. *ACM Transactions on Software Engineering and Methodology*, *3788879*, 3788879. Advance online publication. DOI: 10.1145/3788879

Becker, C., Walker, D., & McCord, C. (2017). Intertemporal Choice: Decision Making and Time in Software Engineering. *2017 IEEE/ACM 10th International Workshop on Cooperative and Human Aspects of Software Engineering (CHASE)*, 23–29. DOI: 10.1109/CHASE.2017.6

Boehm, B. (2011). Some Future Software Engineering Opportunities and Challenges. In Nanz, S. (Ed.), *The Future of Software Engineering* (pp. 1–32). Springer Berlin Heidelberg., DOI: 10.1007/978-3-642-15187-3_1

Burnett, M. M., & Myers, B. A. (2014). Future of end-user software engineering: Beyond the silos. *Future of Software Engineering Proceedings*, 201–211. DOI: 10.1145/2593882.2593896

Corrigan, J. M. (2012). Augmented intelligence—The new AI — Unleashing human capabilities in knowledge work. *2012 34th International Conference on Software Engineering (ICSE)*, 1285–1288. DOI: 10.1109/ICSE.2012.6227098

Cunha, J. A. O. G., Moura, H. P., & Vasconcellos, F. J. S. (2016). Decision-making in Software Project Management: A Systematic Literature Review. *Procedia Computer Science*, *100*, 947–954. DOI: 10.1016/j.procs.2016.09.255

Deshmukh, A., Patil, D. S., Shyam Mohan, J. S., Balamurugan, G., & Tyagi, A. K. (2023). Transforming Next Generation-Based Artificial Intelligence for Software Development: Current Status, Issues, Challenges, and Future Opportunities. In Ortiz-Rodriguez, F., Tiwari, S., Hernández-González, L. M., & Tiburcio, A. (Eds.), (pp. 30–66). Advances in Logistics, Operations, and Management Science. IGI Global., DOI: 10.4018/978-1-6684-8088-5.ch003

Duan, Y., Ong, V. K., Xu, M., & Mathews, B. (2012). Supporting decision making process with "ideal" software agents – What do business executives want? *Expert Systems with Applications*, *39*(5), 5534–5547. DOI: 10.1016/j.eswa.2011.11.065

Ellahham, S., Ellahham, N., & Simsekler, M. C. E. (2020). Application of Artificial Intelligence in the Health Care Safety Context: Opportunities and Challenges. *American Journal of Medical Quality*, *35*(4), 341–348. DOI: 10.1177/1062860619878515 PMID: 31581790

Harris, D. (2017). *Decision Making in Aviation* (D. Harris & W.-C. Li, Eds.; 1st ed.). Routledge. DOI: 10.4324/9781315095080

Hawthorne, M. J., & Perry, D. E. (2005). Software engineering education in the era of outsourcing, distributed development, and open source software: Challenges and opportunities. *Proceedings of the 27th International Conference on Software Engineering - ICSE '05*, 643. DOI: 10.1145/1062455.1062581

Heaton, D., & Carver, J. C. (2015). Claims about the use of software engineering practices in science: A systematic literature review. *Information and Software Technology*, *67*, 207–219. DOI: 10.1016/j.infsof.2015.07.011

Heroux, M. A. (2022). Research Software Science: Expanding the Impact of Research Software Engineering. *Computing in Science & Engineering*, *24*(6), 22–27. DOI: 10.1109/MCSE.2023.3260475

Hoeschl, M. B., Bueno, T. C. D., & Hoeschl, H. C. (2017). Fourth Industrial Revolution and the future of Engineering: Could Robots Replace Human Jobs? How Ethical Recommendations can Help Engineers Rule on Artificial Intelligence. *2017 7th World Engineering Education Forum (WEEF)*, 21–26. DOI: 10.1109/WEEF.2017.8466973

Irayani, I., Melvani, F. N., Azrin, A., & Mikial, M. (2025). Behavioral Theory and Organizational Culture: The Interplay of Transformational Leadership, Team Dynamics, and Motivation in Driving Change at Tridinanti University of Palembang. *The Eastasouth Management and Business*, *3*(02), 220–229. DOI: 10.58812/esmb.v3i02.375

Jain, H., Padmanabhan, B., Pavlou, P. A., & Raghu, T. S. (2021). Editorial for the Special Section on Humans, Algorithms, and Augmented Intelligence: The Future of Work, Organizations, and Society. *Information Systems Research*, *32*(3), 675–687. DOI: 10.1287/isre.2021.1046

Khaliq, Z., Farooq, S. U., & Khan, D. A. (2022). *Artificial Intelligence in Software Testing: Impact, Problems, Challenges and Prospect* (Version 1). arXiv. DOI: 10.48550/ARXIV.2201.05371

Khan, B., Fatima, H., Qureshi, A., Kumar, S., Hanan, A., Hussain, J., & Abdullah, S. (2023). Drawbacks of Artificial Intelligence and Their Potential Solutions in the Healthcare Sector. *Biomedical Materials & Devices, 1*(2), 731–738. DOI: 10.1007/s44174-023-00063-2 PMID: 36785697

Li, S., & Li, J. Z. (2009). Hybridising human judgment, AHP, simulation and a fuzzy expert system for strategy formulation under uncertainty. *Expert Systems with Applications, 36*(3), 5557–5564. DOI: 10.1016/j.eswa.2008.06.095

Madni, A. M. (2020). Exploiting Augmented Intelligence in Systems Engineering and Engineered Systems. *Insight - International Council on Systems Engineering, 23*(1), 31–36. DOI: 10.1002/inst.12282

Madni, A. M. (2023). Augmented Intelligence: A Human Productivity and Performance Amplifier in Systems Engineering and Engineered Human–Machine Systems. In Verma, D. (Ed.), *Systems Engineering for the Digital Age* (1st ed., pp. 375–391). Wiley., DOI: 10.1002/9781394203314.ch17

Marion, T. J., & Fixson, S. K. (2021). The Transformation of the Innovation Process: How Digital Tools are Changing Work, Collaboration, and Organizations in New Product Development*. *Journal of Product Innovation Management, 38*(1), 192–215. DOI: 10.1111/jpim.12547

Mendes, E., Rodriguez, P., Freitas, V., Baker, S., & Atoui, M. A. (2018). Towards improving decision making and estimating the value of decisions in value-based software engineering: The VALUE framework. *Software Quality Journal, 26*(2), 607–656. DOI: 10.1007/s11219-017-9360-z

Meziane, F., & Vadera, S. (2010). Artificial Intelligence in Software Engineering: Current Developments and Future Prospects. In Meziane, F., & Vadera, S. (Eds.), (pp. 278–299). Advances in Computational Intelligence and Robotics. IGI Global., DOI: 10.4018/978-1-60566-758-4.ch014

Monasor, M. J., Vizcaino, A., Piattini, M., & Caballero, I. (2010). Preparing Students and Engineers for Global Software Development: A Systematic Review. *2010 5th IEEE International Conference on Global Software Engineering*, 177–186. DOI: 10.1109/ICGSE.2010.28

Nascimento, E., Nguyen-Duc, A., Sundbø, I., & Conte, T. (2020). *Software engineering for artificial intelligence and machine learning software: A systematic literature review* (Version 1). arXiv. DOI: 10.48550/ARXIV.2011.03751

Neves, R. (2024). Collaboration and Team Dynamics. In R. Neves, *The Engineering Leadership Playbook* (pp. 113–179). Apress. DOI: 10.1007/979-8-8688-0140-2_3

Northern Kentucky University. Paul, S., Yuan, L., Iowa State University, Jain, H., The University of Tennessee at Chattanooga, Sporher, J., ISSIP.org, Lifshitz-Assaf, H., & Warwick University. (2022). Intelligence Augmentation: Human Factors in AI and Future of Work. *AIS Transactions on Human-Computer Interaction*, 426–445. DOI: 10.17705/1thci.00174

Stevanoviü, J., Atanasijeviü, S., Atanasijeviü, T., & Zahar, M. (2020). Expanding the level of engineer knowledge for software modeling within corporate education by active and collaborative learning. *2020 IEEE Global Engineering Education Conference (EDUCON)*, 1807–1814. DOI: 10.1109/EDUCON45650.2020.9125250

Tang, A., Razavian, M., Paech, B., & Hesse, T.-M. (2017). Human Aspects in Software Architecture Decision Making: A Literature Review. *2017 IEEE International Conference on Software Architecture (ICSA)*, 107–116. DOI: 10.1109/ICSA.2017.15

Wnuk, K., Regnell, B., & Berenbach, B. (2011). Scaling Up Requirements Engineering – Exploring the Challenges of Increasing Size and Complexity in Market-Driven Software Development. In Berry, D., & Franch, X. (Eds.), *Requirements Engineering: Foundation for Software Quality* (Vol. 6606, pp. 54–59). Springer Berlin Heidelberg., DOI: 10.1007/978-3-642-19858-8_6

Chapter 11
The Reskilling Imperative
Redefining Software Engineering Skills in the Age of AI-Generated Code

Nikhil Kumar Goyal
http://orcid.org/0009-0007-4532-8033
Poornima University, Jaipur, India

Aman Kumar
http://orcid.org/0009-0005-1872-2129
Poornima University, Jaipur, India

Yash Agarwal
http://orcid.org/0009-0001-9184-5249
Poornima University, Jaipur, India

Prince Kumar Choudhary
http://orcid.org/0009-0000-3306-8026
Poornima University, Jaipur, India

ABSTRACT

The fact of artificial intelligence gaining ground along with its instant progress with artificial intelligence as a particular example of the given phenomenon fundamentally changes the situation in software engineering. This chapter discusses the rising reskilling demand with developers leaving behind conventional coding jobs and moving into more agile, artificially intelligent jobs. It discusses the influence that tools that are run on large language models have had on the development processes, particularly how they are now prioritizing problem-solving, system design, and code validation rather than manual code writing. The discussion indicates the changes in

DOI: 10.4018/979-8-3373-8450-4.ch011

the skills requirements such as instant engineering, critical thinking and the sense of ethics, as well as the essential value of the basic knowledge of programming. Besides, the chapter examines the implication in education, workforce development as well as organizational training where the continuity of learning and curriculum modification are paramount.

1. INTRODUCTION

1.1 The Rise of AI in Software Development

The use of AI in software development has brought a new revolution of designing, developing, and maintaining applications. Both the creation of code and the proposal of improvements are becoming increasingly possible with AI-powered tools and can even be automated to perform standard tests and even debugging itself. The improvement in machine learning and natural language processing is a key factor contributing to this change, having allowed human-like code to be generated by systems based on context and developer intent.

The implementation of AI-driven coding tools has transformed the conventional development protocols. Manual operations that previously took place on a large scale are now done with ease with the help of AI. GitHub Copilot and ChatGPT are some of the tools being used by developers to speed up their code, minimize bugs and improve their productivity. These tools do not only create the code snippets but they offer explanations and advice as well; hence, it has become one of the rich resources of a contemporary software engineering (Kausik & Kausik, 2024).

The development of AI in software development is as well conditioned by the growing sophistication of systems and the need to develop quickly. Organizations face increasing pressure to deliver high-quality software more rapidly., and AI is a solution to this consideration, as it can automate most of the processes, streamline the creation process. Consequently, AI is becoming a part of the software development cycle.

This increased use of AI emphasizes the necessity of developers to evolve into new tools and approaches. To work successfully with AI systems is becoming a very important skill that makes the start of another era of software engineering (Kumari et al., 2026).

1.2 Changing Nature of Software Engineering Roles

The usage of AI-generated code changes the positions and the functions of software engineers radically. Conventionally, the tasks of code writing, code testing, and code maintenance were mainly the role of developers. But as AI replaces most of the common coding work, the emphasis is on more advanced work, including problem-solving, system design, and decision-making.

The expectations put on developers are increasingly that they be facilitators of AI processes and not just coders. This entails steering AI tools, verifying their results and quality and security assurance of the code generated. The job is becoming increasingly technical and strategic in that the software engineer position is a multifaceted occupation (Gadekar, 2024).

This transition also brings changes when it comes to the distribution of work in terms of different levels of experience. Such skilled workers as developers on the entry-level might have lower chances of participating in simple coding duties, whereas more experienced specialists need to acquire new skills connected with the implementation of AI functions and control. The conventional career ladder in software engineering is hence being re-furnished.

Roles change and thus cooperation becomes relevant. To build and sustain AI-enabled systems, developers will have to collaborate with data scientists, AI specialists, and other stakeholders. This multidisciplinary aspect can be explained by the ability of software engineering in the era of AI to change (Senapathi et al., 2018).

1.3 Need for Reskilling in the AI Era

The high pace of AI technology adoption in the software development domain has led to the immediate necessity of reskilling among the professionals. The older programming skills are not enough anymore to accommodate the requirement of the new-fangled development surroundings. The developers will have to learn new skills that would allow them to successfully cope with AI tools and respond to the changes in workflow (Kumari & Goyal, 2026).

The concept of reskilling entails not only the acquisition of technical skills, but also learning cognitive and behavioral skills. As an example, the skill of communicating with AI systems on a timely basis has become an essential one, and this is what has come to be named as prompt engineering. Likewise, problem-solving, adaptability, and critical thinking are necessary in dealing with AI-assisted development due to its complex nature.

Organizations are realizing the value of reskilling and are allocating funds to train programs in order to empower their employees. Nowadays learning is not an option but a necessity because technological change is so rapid that any professional has to refresh his/her knowledge and skills on a regular basis. Critical to AI, educational institutions are changing the curriculum to include issues that are related to AI and equip students with the vocation trends of the future (Akter et al., 2021).

Reskilling is not exclusive to individual professionals but also the whole ecosystem. Industry leaders, governments, and academic institutions should cooperate and develop structures that can facilitate a lifelong learning process and labor change. This team-work is necessary to make the work force relevant in the AI-driven world.

1.4 Scope and Objectives of the Chapter

The purpose of this chapter is to identify and discuss the revolutionary nature of the idea of AI-generated code on software engineering and the necessity to reskill. It gives in-depth discussion on how AI technologies are transforming development practices, roles and skills. The chapter aims at providing a comprehensive picture of the changing landscape by looking at the technical and human aspects of the same.

The chapter scope will also cover the discussion of new tools and technologies, evolution in software engineering roles, and skills expected in order to navigate in an AI-driven world. It addresses the dilemmas and dangers of AI adoption as well like excessive dependence on the automation process and the possible degradation of skills. These challenges are important to comprehend in order to come up with effective reskilling strategies.

Besides that, the chapter also highlights the significance of education and organizational support in the process of bringing to the fore AI-enhanced development. It emphasizes how training programs, changes of curriculum and industry efforts help professionals to be prepared to the future. The chapter will seek to offer action steps by incorporating theoretical knowledge with practical implications.

On the whole, this chapter aims at contributing to the further discussion of the future of software engineering. It aims at educating policymakers, educators and practitioners on the significance of reskilling and introduces a model of how to go through the transformations caused by AI-generated code.

1.5 Key Concepts and Terminology

The transformation of software engineering in the age of artificial intelligence has introduced several new concepts that are often used interchangeably in academic and industry discussions. To ensure conceptual clarity, this chapter defines the key terms used throughout the analysis.

AI-generated code refers to source code that is automatically produced by artificial intelligence systems, typically large language models trained on extensive datasets of programming languages and software repositories. These models can interpret natural language prompts or partial code inputs and generate syntactically valid programming outputs.

AI-assisted development refers to development workflows in which artificial intelligence tools support programmers by providing suggestions for code completion, debugging assistance, documentation generation, and test case recommendations. In this model, AI functions as a productivity-enhancing tool that complements human developers rather than replacing them.

Augmented engineers are software developers who collaborate with AI systems as part of their everyday workflow. Instead of writing every line of code manually, augmented engineers supervise AI outputs, refine prompts, validate generated solutions, and integrate them into broader system architectures.

Intelligent automation describes the broader integration of artificial intelligence technologies into software engineering processes in order to automate tasks such as code generation, testing, documentation, and deployment.

Human judgment remains a critical element in AI-assisted development environments. While AI systems can generate code and recommendations, developers must evaluate correctness, ensure architectural coherence, assess security risks, and make strategic design decisions.

By clarifying these concepts, the chapter establishes a conceptual foundation for analyzing how artificial intelligence reshapes the roles, skills, and professional identities of software engineers.

Figure 1. Conceptual Framework of Reskilling in AI-Driven Software Engineering

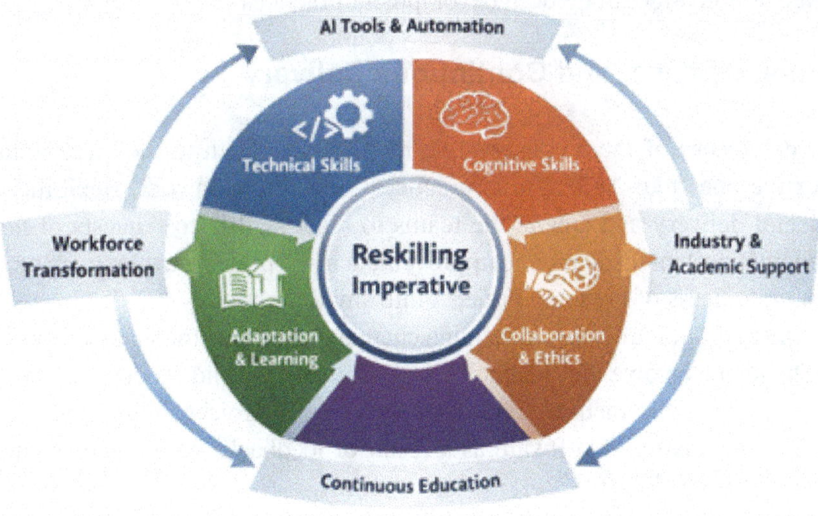

2. EVOLUTION OF SOFTWARE ENGINEERING

2.1 Traditional Software Development Practices

The origins of software engineering lie in documented and managed development practices, which focused on planning, describing, and developing by stages. The initial models like waterfall adhered to a linear approach and thus each stage namely; requirements, design, implementation, testing and maintenance had to be completed before proceeding to the next. This would have been clear and controlled but with inflexibility to meet emerging demands (Alenezi & Akour, 2025).

The old development methods were highly manual based and highly human-intensive. The developers used to write the code snippets, debugging the bugs and making sure that the system worked well by conducting thorough testing. It was both technically complex and time and labor-consuming especially when dealing with large and complicated systems.

Documentation has been a key part of the traditional software engineering, with all the aspects of the system being clear and traceable. Although this enhanced accountability and maintainability, it brought in some rigidness and therefore changes were hard to fit within the development lifecycle. Consequently, projects were usually delayed and overrun (Sharma et al., 2026).

In spite of these shortcomings, the traditional practices formed the basis of the present software engineering. Some of the fundamental principles that they put in place between them include modularity, quality of the code, and systematic testing, which are still in effect in modern development practices.

2.2 Agile, DevOps, and Continuous Delivery

The drawbacks of more conservative models gave birth to the more iterative and flexible ones like Agile. Agile practices focus on teamwork, flexibility and incremental delivery and enable the teams to react swiftly to requests of needs. Agile allows constant feedback and improvement in the project development process through the process of breaking projects into small iterations.

The practices of Agile became a huge change towards customer based development. The teams involve the stakeholders in ensuring the end product can be used by the end user. This method minimizes chances of project failure and general increase in the quality of software as a result of feedbacks being incorporated at each phase (Smith, 2024).

DevOps goes even further to expand the concepts of Agile by incorporating both development and operations. It encourages coordination among software construction and deployment teams with the aim of allowing more dependable and quicker issues. The development pipeline mechanisms like continuous integration and continuous deployment (CI/CD) are automated to eliminate manual work and enhance efficiency.

Constant delivery is becoming a norm in contemporary software engineering, which enables companies to publish new releases regularly and keep pace with the market competition. These methodologies have changed the dynamics of development workflow, making it dynamic and efficient and responsive to change (Ferrari et al., 2021).

2.3 Emergence of AI-Assisted Development

The development of software engineering has entered a new stage due to the development of AI-assisted development. The field of artificial intelligence is becoming popular in assisting different phases of the software development life cycle, Code production and testing, as well as debugging and optimization. Such transition signifies movement towards automation and smart support during development process (Farooqi et al., 2026).

The AI-based code development tools use machine learning algorithms to examine patterns of code, discover errors, and propose their solutions. GitHub Copilot and ChatGPT are programs that can help developers to write code snippets, to automate their routine tasks, and to become more productive. These aids are virtual assistants, as they offer support and guidance as they appear in real-time.

The introduction of AI-assisted development has minimized the time taken to code and test by a wide margin. The developers can be able to concentrate on high-level activities like system design and problem-solving, and AI addresses routine tasks. This not only increases the efficiency, but also increases the quality of software as it reduces the number of human mistakes (Hymel, 2024).

Nonetheless, the introduction of AI into the development processes is met by new challenges, too. The developers should know how these tools can be used well and how to authenticate their output. The dependency on AI means a change of mindset whereby collaboration between humans and machines is incorporated instead of the full automation.

2.4 Transition to AI-Generated Code

The shift towards the use of AI in the development process to the creation of AI codes is a significant milestone in the development of software engineering. The AIG code presupposes using sophisticated models to write working code automatically in response to natural language input or high-level specifications. The feature can revolutionize the process of developing and supporting software.

The AI-based code systems are capable of developing whole functions or applications at a bare minimum human interaction based on the requirements made by users. This saves on manual coding activities and aggressively minimizes the development process. This is leading to a situation where software engineering is being made more accessible and thus people with some little experience with programming are able to develop an application (Nettur et al., 2025).

The transition is also transforming the role of developers, and taking them to roles of reviewers of codes and integrators. It is the role of engineers to guarantee that AI-produced code is of quality and secure, as well as performance. Such a change will demand new capabilities, such as how to assess and filter AI outputs.

Figure 2. Evolution of Software Engineering Toward AI-Generated Development

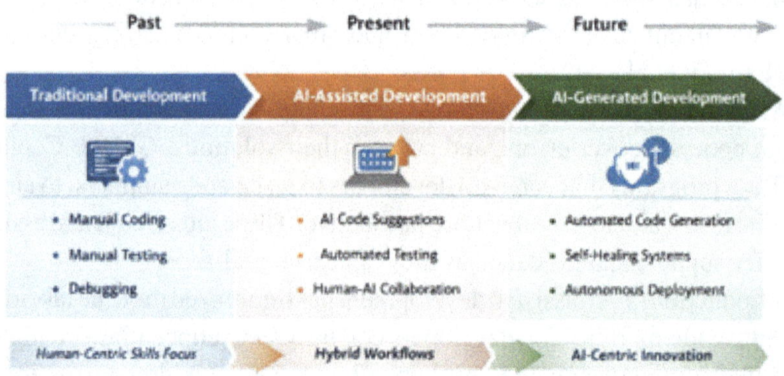

To a certain degree, AI-generated code has the potential to provide substantial benefits, but other aspects of it, such as reliability, security, and considerations of morals and ethics, are also problematic. It has been a serious issue to make sure that the code generated is correct and safe. Since the technology is still developing, it will be necessary to balance the automation and human control to ensure the effectiveness and trust in the software development. While these methodological changes improved flexibility and collaboration in software engineering, the emergence of artificial intelligence introduces an even more significant transformation. The following section therefore examines the technologies that enable AI-generated code and their role in modern development practices. (Goyal et al., 2026).Top of Form

3. AI-GENERATED CODE: CONCEPTS AND TECHNOLOGIES

3.1 Definition and Overview of AI-Generated Code

AI-generated code is when artificial intelligence systems are used to generate a source code automatically as prompted, prompted, or understanding. These systems utilise complex machine learning models to act on executing instructions in natural language and convert them to executable programming statements. This is a major departure in the traditional codes where code was written explicitly and in a structural form by developers.

The idea of the AI-generated code lies in the fact that AI models learn through enormous amounts of the already existing code and patterns of coding existing in large volumes of information. Through the analysis of their datasets, the AI systems are able to determine the relationship among the inputs and outputs allowing them to produce code that is in line with the requirements of the users. This potential has revolutionised the development process in that it has become more efficient and accessible (Nabeel, 2024).

The code provided by AI is not confined to simple assignments but to more complicated functions, such as code generation of the application, code generation of APIs, and code generation of a testing process. Such flexibility gives developers the opportunity to work at a higher design level and concentrate on the problem-solving aspect, leaving the implementation specifics to the AI. Due to this, coding work is taking a new shape as it is no longer a manual work, but rather a more cooperative task between a human being and a machine.

AI-generated code is not flawless even with all its positives. The human coordination is necessary, which is proven by the problems of misrepresentation, deficit of contextual knowledge, and their possible security threat. Code developers have to ensure that code generated is of high quality and that it is understandable to the project needs (Marar, 2024).

3.2 Role of Large Language Models (LLMs)

The large language models (LLM) have been considered as the facilitator or focal point of AI-generated code in that they bring the intelligence that is needed to receive and generate programming language outputs. The models are trained with large amounts of data consisting of both code repositories, documentation, and natural language text, and are able to comprehend both programming syntax and human instructions.

The goal of LLMs is on the one hand capable of completing a broad variety of tasks, such as code generation, completion, translation, and explanation. They are also able to create code snippets, based on the user prompts, matching the desired functionality. This capability to connect natural language and programming languages allows LLCMs to become a powerful tool of developers (Goyal et al., 2026).

The capability of ET to generalise across programming languages and frameworks is what makes the LLMs effective. These models enable developers to operate with various technologies without the explicit knowledge of any technology. This increases the level of productivity and allows prototyping and experimenting quickly.

Nevertheless, reliability and bias are also an issue concerning the use of LLMs. The quality of code generated is determined by the training data and the condition offered in prompts. Output validation and care in developers is thus critical to prevent inaccuracy and lack of security. The strengths and limitations of LLMs are the key aspects of using these systems in software development (Siahaan et al., 2023).

3.3 Tools and Platforms (GitHub Copilot, ChatGPT, etc.)

A variety of tools and platforms enabling the integration of AI capabilities into the environment of development make the practical implementation of AI-generated code possible. Tools like GitHub Copilot and ChatGPT have been widely adopted and they come with features like autocompletion, generation and real time support. The tools will improve the productivity of developers and simplify the work process.

Examples include GitHub Copilot that can be directly integrated with code editors and generates suggestions based on code context as the developer composes the code. It is capable of creating complete functions, proposing improvements and even making documentation. ChatGPT, in the same approach, allows developers to communicate with AI in a natural language, where developers can create code, debug problems, and learn about complex problems (Albaroudi et al., 2025).

Such tools have saved a lot of time on the process of coding and debugging, leaving developers to attend higher level tasks. Explanations and examples also help in the learning and the development of the skills in individuals involved, thus, they prove useful to both new and professional individuals.

Nevertheless, the use of these tools should be thought over. One has to make sure that code generated to take is correct, secure, and meets project requirements. Processes and skills also require modification as the application of AI tools to development processes requires an elasticity to be an essential principle in the contemporary software engineering environment (Dandotiya et al., 2026).

3.4 Capabilities and Limitations

The AI-created code has a wide range of features that contribute to the software development process. These are quick code generation, automated testing and debugging support in real time. AI systems have the ability of processing dense code volumes and defining patterns, which can be utilised to generate effective and efficient solutions. This enhances productivity to a high level and also saves on time to develop.

The other skill that may be of great benefit is the capacity to help in learning and transfer of knowledge. Explanations, recommendations on best-practise, and assisting developers with the unfamiliar technologies can be supported by AI tools. This renders them useful in terms of education as well as professional development to bridge any gap in knowledge and learn faster (Aslam, 2024).

In spite of such benefits, AI-generated code has a number of drawbacks. The possibility of errors and miscalculation especially in the complicated or contextual situations is one of the biggest challenges. AI systems can produce code (which seems to work) but has hidden bugs or inefficiency. This requires intensive testing and validation by programmers.

There are also security and ethical concerns that are also a challenge. Stolen code can contain bugs or alternatives to best practises, which further risk a security breach. Moreover, the problem of intellectual property and data security should be properly handled. To resolve these limitations, it is necessary to find a middle ground between the assets of AI and the human factor that would ensure the responsible and reliable development of the software (Khan et al., 2023).

3.5 Practical Challenges of AI-Generated Code

Although AI-generated code can significantly improve development productivity, practitioners frequently encounter practical challenges when integrating these tools into real software engineering environments. One commonly reported issue is the generation of hallucinated APIs or non-existent libraries. Large language models sometimes produce code that appears syntactically correct but references functions or modules that do not exist in the relevant framework.

Security vulnerabilities also represent a major concern. AI-generated code may include insecure authentication mechanisms, weak encryption practices, or insufficient input validation. Because such vulnerabilities may not always be immediately visible, developers must carefully review generated code to ensure system security.

Another challenge relates to architectural consistency. AI tools typically generate solutions for localized programming tasks but often lack awareness of the broader system architecture. As a result, generated code may conflict with established design patterns or system structures.

Licensing and intellectual property concerns also arise when AI models trained on public code repositories generate outputs that resemble existing copyrighted software. Organizations must therefore establish policies regarding the acceptable use of AI-generated code.

Finally, development teams often experience a rework burden after initial productivity gains. While AI tools may accelerate early coding stages, developers may later spend additional time correcting structural issues, integrating generated components into existing systems, and adapting them to architectural requirements. These practical challenges highlight the importance of maintaining strong human oversight and rigorous validation processes within AI-assisted development workflows.

3.6 Human–AI Collaboration in Software Development

Modern software engineering increasingly involves collaborative interactions between developers and artificial intelligence systems. Rather than functioning as fully autonomous tools, AI-based coding assistants operate as collaborative partners that support programmers during various stages of the development lifecycle.

In typical AI-assisted development environments, developers provide prompts or partial code structures while AI systems generate suggestions that can be accepted, modified, or rejected. This interactive process creates a form of human–AI co-production in which both actors contribute to the final software artifact.

Human–AI collaboration also transforms how developers access technical knowledge. Instead of relying solely on personal expertise or documentation, developers can leverage knowledge embedded within machine learning models trained on large repositories of code.

However, effective collaboration with AI systems requires new competencies. Developers must understand how to formulate precise prompts, evaluate machine-generated outputs critically, and recognize potential biases or inaccuracies in generated solutions.

These collaborative practices demonstrate that the future of software engineering lies not in replacing human developers but in creating hybrid development environments in which human expertise and artificial intelligence complement one another.

4. IMPACT ON SOFTWARE ENGINEERING ROLES

4.1 Changing Responsibilities of Developers

The emergence of the AI-generated code is also dramatically changing the role of software developers. Conventionally, the developers used to work mostly on code writing, debugging and maintenance of systems. Now, the task of developing a computer programme is, however, being pushed into a more strategic and managerial role due to the automation of a significant part of these routine activities occurring through AI. The developers have now been anticipated to direct AI tools, interpret their results and also have to check that the output codes meet the project demands.

Such a change demands developers to pay further attention to learning the problem areas and converting business requirements into technical services. Instead of wasting hours of manual labour on coding, they have to outline clear requirements and give accurate instructions to artificial intelligence systems. This shall entail a further involvement with system architecture and design whereby the general structure of the application is healthy and scalable (Kumari et al., 2026).

The other task of significant importance is the validation of AI-generated code and its refinement. The developers should also check outputs to confirm correctness, performance, and safety, and in this case refer to the possible problems that might be missed by AI tools. This demands good analytical ability and thorough knowledge of programming principles because even though one does not need technical expertise when using AI, it is impossible to do without it.

Generally, the evolving role of developers is an indication of the move towards undertaking execution centred jobs that become oversight oriented and decision making. The focus of this evolution is the significance of flexibility and life-long learning in the current software engineering environment (Kaur et al., 2020).

4.2 Shift from Coding to Problem-Solving

The fact that the emphasis is left on the problem-solving rather than on coding is one of the most remarkable effects of AI-generated code. As much as coding is a crucial skill, it is no longer the major activity of developers. Rather, it focuses on knowledge about the intricate issues, systems creation, and using AI-tools to execute them effectively (Haefner et al., 2023).

This change puts emphasis on critical thinking and analytical skills. The developers should have the capacity to scale the more complex requirements into simple manageable units and know the most appropriate way in which they can engage AI tools to get the desired results. This includes weighing alternative options, trade-offs and making rational decisions.

Problem-solving is also applicable to the unexpected challenges and the system reliability. It is the duty of developers to be able to foresee the possible problems and come up with resilient and adaptable solutions. This involves profound knowledge of not only the problem sphere but also of the technical environment on which solutions are used (Kumari et al., 2026).

The shift towards problem-solving, instead of coding, is a fundamental shift in the skills one would need to perform software engineering. It highlights the importance of developers that should build higher order of thinking and leave the monotonous operations and get into more elaborate and dynamic positions.

4.3 Rise of AI-Augmented Engineers

The application of AI into software development has created a new type of professional who is called an AI-augmented engineer. These users use AI to increase their productivity and abilities and merge human skills with artificial intelligence. This mixed methodology helps the developers to do more within few hours without compromising the quality (Kusal et al., 2023).

The essence of AI-augmented engineers is that they are able to communicate with AI systems. They know how to create prompts, how to interpret outputs and refine results to achieve a particular requirement. This is the skill set that is commonly known as prompt engineering that is gaining significance in the AI-driven environment of development.

Besides the technical competencies, AI-enhanced engineers are to be equipped with good cooperation and communication skills. They will frequently collaborate in a team comprising data scientists, specialists in AI, and experts in the field. That needs the capacity to convey sophisticated concepts and organise activity in the capacity of various fields of expertise (Sheikh et al., 2026).

The emergence of AI-enhanced engineers shows the changing trend in the practises of software engineering. It emphasises the significance of applying AI to day-to-day work processes and keeping up with new technology. With the further development of AI, this position is most likely to take the place of the industry standard.

4.4 Impact on Entry-Level and Senior Roles

The entry of AI-generated code has varied implications on the entry-level and senior software engineering. In the case of entry-level developers, it could lessen chances to have a practical experience in creating code as the simple code processes are being automated. This may cause a disruption in the conventional learning pathways and might have to adopt new methods of learning skills.

Nevertheless, AI tools could also be useful learning materials in novices. These tools will make the learning process faster because they can give live feedback, explanations, and examples that allow new developers to develop more efficiently. The issue is how to make sure that the use of AI does not interfere with the acquisition of basic programming skills (Kazi et al., 2023).

In case of senior developers, the effect is narrowed down to the addition of responsibilities and leadership. During the process of integration of AI, teams, and quality and security of software systems, experienced professionals are expected to lead the process. They are also very important in overseeing multidomestic projects and handling problems that cannot be done simply by AI tools.

The fluctuation of job descriptions of entry and senior levels is a reason to change the approach to career development as adaptive. Companies and schools should reconsider the training and mentoring strategies and equip their employees with the skills and knowledge required by the changing needs of software engineering sector (Jim et al., 2024).

4.5 Industry Examples of AI-Assisted Development

The adoption of AI-assisted coding tools is already visible across a wide range of software development organizations. Companies using tools such as GitHub Copilot have reported improvements in developer productivity, particularly for repetitive programming tasks such as writing boilerplate code and generating documentation.

In large software organizations, AI tools are also used to support debugging and code review processes. Automated suggestions help developers identify potential errors, optimize algorithms, and recommend alternative implementations, thereby improving development efficiency.

Start-up environments provide another illustration of AI-assisted development. Small development teams frequently use generative AI tools to rapidly prototype applications and experiment with new features. By combining natural language prompts with automated code generation, developers can iterate more quickly and test multiple design ideas with minimal manual coding.

These industry examples demonstrate that AI-generated code is already influencing everyday software engineering practices. At the same time, they highlight the continuing importance of human oversight, as developers must review and refine AI-generated solutions before deploying them in production environments.

5. SKILLS TRANSFORMATION IN THE AI ERA

5.1 Core Technical Skills Revisited

The introduction of AI-generated code does not deprive the presence of basic technical skills; it simply changes their significance and use. Basic knowledge in programming, including knowledge on data structures, algorithms, and software design principles, is still needed to assess and improve the outputs of AI. Still, developers need to have a good understanding of the functionality of systems to make sure that created code is efficient, maintainable and it meets project requirements (Liu et al., 2022).

Moreover, the knowledge of the programming languages remains a critical factor. Although the AI tools may compile the code in other languages, the developers have to be aware of syntax, semantics, and best practises to ensure that the code fits, and that the performance is desired. This is in order to guarantee that dependence on AI does not undermine the quality of any code, nor does it cause inefficiencies.

The other thing that should be learned is software development tools and environments. The developers will need to be conversant with version control systems and integrated development environments (IDEs). These tools are at the centre of codebase management and collaborative development, despite the use of artificial intelligence for assistance (Pachouly et al., 2022).

Finally, basic technical skills are the building blocks meant to be used by the development of new competencies. Instead of being made obsolete, these skills are being modified to assist in the development process in a more supervisory and analytical way.

5.2 Prompt Engineering and AI Interaction Skills

Prompt engineering becomes one of the essential skills in the era of AI-generated code. It is a practise that includes the formulation of effective and accurate instructions on how AI systems will generate accurate and relevant results. The quality of the input provided is highly crucial in the effectiveness of the generated AI-generated code hence a skill that is necessary in the developers.

Developers should be trained to code prompts to give context, limitations, and expected results. This will need to understand how AI models perceive language and come up with responses. With prompts being refined, developers are able to make the generated code more accurate and useful and require only limited modifications (Yang et al., 2022).

The work with AI systems is based on the iterative refinements as well. The developers tend to have to discuss the work with the AI tools, giving feedback and modifying inputs in order to obtain the best outcomes. This is an interactive process that is time consuming and involves trial and error.

The evolution of prompt engineering talents is a change in the communication of developers with technology. It modifies coding as a purely technical action turned into a collaborative process between a human and AI with a focus on communication and clarity.

5.3 System Design and Architecture Thinking

In an environment where AI automates routine coding tasks, system design and architecture thinking are becoming more and more crucial. The developers should be concerned with creation of scalable, reliable and efficient systems that are capable of fulfilling the complex requirements. This is meaning to know how the different components are interacting and to be able to ensure that the overall architecture facilitates performance, security and maintainability (Yadav et al., 2024).

System design involves a whole view approach taking into account the aspects like data flow, integration and scalability. It is the expectation of the future needs that developers shall have to consider and come up with systems that will be able to support the needs as they arise. It is a progressive strategy that is necessary towards the construction of sound applications in dynamism settings.

The AI tools may be utilised to create codes, and it does not eliminate strategic decision-making in system design. The developers have to consider trade-offs, choose the right technologies, and make sure that the choices made in architecture would correspond to the business goals. This involves the profound knowledge of technical and organisational contexts (Lacerda et al., 2020).

The focusing on the system design is indicative of a larger move by software engineering to thinking at a higher level. Developers are supposed to go beyond the details of implementation and started developing solutions that provide value in the long term.

5.4 Code Review, Debugging, and Validation Skills

Review, debug and validation of code is becoming more significant in an AI-driven development environment. Although AI tools can be used to produce a code more fast, they are not always accurate and can lead to errors or inefficient solutions. The developers are thus required to make sure that there is quality, security, and performance in the code generated (Iorliam & Ingio, 2024).

The skills of code review are related to the critical analysis of AI-generated output to find possible problems. These involve the detection of logical errors, inefficiency and compliance to best practises. The developers should also make sure that the code is compatible with the existing systems and it does not create vulnerabilities.

The skill of debugging will also keep becoming important because AI-generated code might harbour hidden bugs, which need significant investigation. The developers should be in a position to be able to trace errors and the root causes of the same as well as be able to put proper solutions. This process normally entails keen knowledge of the system behind it and the behaviour.

Validation does not only cover technical correctness but also requires compliance with requirements and standards. A developer needs to make sure that the code is developed with the purpose and in line with the needs of the user. Through the development of these skills, specialists will be able to handle the issues that are related to the AI-generated code that will be useful, and the practises of software development can be maintained at high standards.

5.5 Security and Quality Assurance in AI-Generated Code

As AI-generated code becomes increasingly integrated into development workflows, the importance of quality assurance and security review grows significantly. Developers must ensure that machine-generated outputs satisfy reliability, security, and maintainability requirements.

One important concern involves hidden dependencies introduced by generated code. AI tools may recommend external libraries or software packages that introduce compatibility issues or security vulnerabilities. Developers must therefore carefully examine dependencies before integrating generated code into production systems.

Prompt fragility represents another challenge. Small variations in prompts or surrounding context may produce significantly different outputs from AI systems, making reproducibility difficult in collaborative development environments.

Model drift also presents risks. As AI models evolve and are updated by platform providers, the behavior of generated code may change over time. Development teams must therefore maintain strong testing and validation practices to ensure long-term system stability.

These considerations demonstrate that AI-assisted development does not eliminate the need for rigorous software engineering practices. Instead, it reinforces the importance of testing, verification, and security analysis within modern development environments.

6. HUMAN SKILLS AND COGNITIVE ABILITIES

6.1 Critical Thinking and Analytical Skills

Critical thinking and analytical skills have been recognised as more essential than ever to the job of a software engineer in the era of AI-generated code. Although AI applications are able to write code, make suggestions, they lack real knowledge and awareness of context. Programmers will therefore have to analyse AI generated work, test their accuracy and see whether it responds to the desired goals. This involves the skills to challenge assumptions, spot inconsistencies and make an informed decision.

The developers can have analytical skills that will aid them to deconstruct complicated problems into small manageable parts. The awareness of the logic behind the proposed solution as well as the important consideration that the method used is correct should never be overlooked by the developers even when AI is used to help facilitate solutions. This includes the interpretation of requirements, analysis of constraints and projection of the most successful strategies to be undertaken (Siam et al., 2024).

Such abilities are also very important in the risk assessment and error detection. The developers have to foresee the possible problems, including the bottlenecks in the performance (or security weaknesses) and deal with them in advance. Any AI-based tools might fail to consider such concerns, and human monitoring is required to ensure quality and reliability.

Finally, critical thinking and analytical skills allow developers to go beyond the AI dependency and is actively involved in defining solutions. All these skills will be the basis of successful decision making in more automated development setting.

6.2 Creativity and Innovation

The two human qualities that make developers stand out concurrently in an AI-oriented world are creativity and innovation. At the same time, though AI is excellent in the recognition and reproduction of patterns, it cannot think creatively or come up with original ideas. The developers need to use their creativity to develop distinctive solutions, experiment and challenge the limits of what technology can do.

Software engineering is an area of innovation whereby one will not only be coming up with new products but also optimising processes and systems that are already in place. The developers will need to find challenges to optimise and come up with results that are more efficient and user-friendly. This demands both technical expertise as well as creative ideas (Vasiliniuc & Groza, 2023).

It is true that the implementation of AI within the processes of development can positively affect the level of creativity, as it will lessen the load of mechanicalized procedures. As coding tasks are monotonous and attended to by artificial intelligence, developers have increased time to work conceptually and innovatively. The change will help them explore new concepts and come up with more complex solutions.

Development of creativity and innovation needs an environment that promotes exploration and on-going learning. The developers need to be encouraged to investigate new technologies and methods within organisations and see how much damage they can do with their creative capacity in the AI era.

6.3 Ethical Reasoning and Responsible AI Use

When developers employ AI in the development of software, there are critical ethical issues that they need to consider. Ethical reasoning entails being knowledgeable of the consequences of AI generated codes and making sure that they are utilised responsibly. These will involve the concerns on AI systems of bias, fairness, transparency, and accountability.

The developers should understand what risks can AI-created code hold such as security issues and data abuse. Code compliance that ensures it complies with ethical and legal standards is a crucial role especially in applications that affect the privacy and well-being of users. This needs an excellent grasp of ethical standards and regulatory standards.

Other aspects of responsible AI usage encompass transparency in the use of AI tools and decision-making. The outputs of AI systems that are generated by developers should be explicable and justified in such a way that they would be coherent and credible. This is especially so in a situation where the outcomes of a decision are of great importance.

Ethical reasoning will have a more significant role as AI is plotted further into software development. The developers have to weigh between the advantages of automation and the need to safeguard the users and preserve trust. This emphasises the role of applying ethics both to education and to practise.

6.4 Collaboration and Communication Skills

The ability to communicate and collaborate are relevant software engineering skills, especially in case of AI-driven development. The developers tend to operate in cross-functional teams comprising the data scientists, AI experts, designers, and business partners. There should be proper communication to make sure that every team member is aware of project objectives, and he/she is productive.

The communication with the machines is also affected by the use of AI tools as developers need to speak to the machines clearly. The art of making good prompts and decoding AI text includes some sort of correspondence that combines technical and language abilities. This brings into focus the need to have clear and accurate communication when one wants to attain certain desired results.

Teamwork is not limited to the team interactions but also to interactions with larger communities, through open-source communities and professional networks. Exchanging information and best practises assists the developers to keep abreast with current times and enhance their expertise. It is a teamwork strategy that is vital in dealing with the fast changing technology (Pandey et al., 2024).

Effective communication and teamwork are valuable skills that help to make decisions, accomplish projects and effective group dynamics. These abilities will be crucial in the success of the AIs era as software engineering is increasingly more complex and ubiquitous.Bottom of Form

7. RESKILLING AND UPSKILLING STRATEGIES

7.1 Continuous Learning and Lifelong Education

In the rapidly evolving landscape of AI-driven software development, continuous learning has become an essential requirement rather than an optional pursuit. The pace at which technologies such as AI-generated code, machine learning frameworks, and development tools are advancing demands that software engineers consistently update their knowledge and skills. Lifelong education ensures that professionals remain relevant and capable of adapting to new paradigms, particularly as traditional coding practices are being reshaped by automation and intelligent systems.

Continuous learning involves engaging with a variety of resources, including online courses, technical documentation, research publications, and hands-on projects. Developers must actively seek opportunities to expand their understanding of emerging technologies and integrate them into their workflows. This proactive approach to learning not only enhances technical proficiency but also fosters adaptability, enabling individuals to navigate complex and dynamic environments effectively.

Moreover, lifelong education extends beyond technical skills to include cognitive and behavioral competencies. Skills such as critical thinking, problem-solving, and adaptability are essential for working effectively with AI tools. As the nature of software engineering evolves, developers must be prepared to learn, unlearn, and relearn concepts to stay aligned with industry demands.

The emphasis on continuous learning also highlights the need for a growth mindset, where individuals view challenges as opportunities for development. By embracing lifelong education, software engineers can position themselves to thrive in an AI-driven ecosystem and contribute meaningfully to innovation and progress.

7.2 Role of Online Platforms and Certifications

Online learning platforms and professional certifications have emerged as key enablers of reskilling and upskilling in the AI era. These platforms provide accessible and flexible learning opportunities, allowing developers to acquire new skills at their own pace. Courses covering topics such as artificial intelligence, machine learning, cloud computing, and prompt engineering are widely available, catering to diverse learning needs and skill levels.

Certifications offered by industry leaders and educational institutions serve as formal recognition of acquired skills and knowledge. They provide a structured pathway for learning and help professionals demonstrate their expertise to employers. In a competitive job market, certifications can enhance credibility and open up new career opportunities, particularly in specialized domains related to AI and software development (Baqar & Khanda, 2024).

Online platforms also facilitate interactive learning through hands-on projects, coding exercises, and real-world case studies. These practical experiences are essential for understanding how theoretical concepts can be applied in real-world scenarios. Additionally, many platforms incorporate AI-driven learning tools that personalize content and provide feedback, further enhancing the learning experience.

The accessibility of online learning has democratized education, enabling individuals from diverse backgrounds to acquire advanced skills. However, learners must carefully select credible platforms and relevant courses to ensure that their efforts align with industry requirements. By leveraging online platforms and certifications, developers can effectively navigate the reskilling journey.

7.3 Organizational Training Programs

Organizations play a crucial role in facilitating reskilling and upskilling by providing structured training programs for their employees. As businesses increasingly adopt AI-driven development tools, they must invest in workforce development to ensure that employees can effectively utilize these technologies. Organizational training programs help bridge skill gaps and align employee capabilities with strategic objectives.

These programs often include workshops, training sessions, mentorship initiatives, and collaborative learning opportunities. By creating an environment that supports continuous learning, organizations can foster a culture of innovation and adaptability. Employees are encouraged to experiment with new tools, share knowledge, and develop skills that enhance their performance and productivity.

In addition to technical training, organizations must also focus on developing soft skills such as communication, teamwork, and ethical decision-making. These skills are essential for navigating the complexities of AI-driven development and collaborating effectively in interdisciplinary teams. Comprehensive training programs that address both technical and human skills are therefore critical for success.

Furthermore, organizations benefit from investing in employee development by improving retention, enhancing productivity, and maintaining a competitive edge.

A well-trained workforce is better equipped to leverage AI technologies and drive innovation, contributing to overall organizational growth and success.

7.4 Self-Learning and Peer Learning Models

Self-learning and peer learning models have become increasingly important in the context of reskilling, offering flexible and collaborative approaches to skill development. Self-learning empowers individuals to take control of their learning journey, allowing them to explore topics of interest and develop skills at their own pace. This approach is particularly valuable in the fast-changing field of software engineering, where new tools and technologies emerge frequently.

Peer learning complements self-learning by fostering collaboration and knowledge sharing among individuals. Developers can learn from each other's experiences, exchange ideas, and solve problems collectively. This collaborative approach enhances understanding and promotes the development of practical skills, as individuals are exposed to diverse perspectives and approaches (Deming et al., 2021).

Communities such as developer forums, open-source platforms, and professional networks play a significant role in facilitating peer learning. These platforms provide opportunities for interaction, discussion, and collaboration, enabling developers to stay updated on industry trends and best practices. Participation in such communities also helps build professional networks and enhances career growth.

The combination of self-learning and peer learning creates a dynamic and supportive learning environment. By leveraging these models, developers can continuously improve their skills, adapt to new challenges, and remain competitive in the AI-driven software engineering landscape.

7.5 Future Trajectories of AI-Assisted Software Engineering

The transformation of software engineering through AI-generated code can be better understood by distinguishing between current realities, near-term developments, and longer-term possibilities.

Current Reality. Today, AI coding assistants primarily function as productivity tools that help developers complete routine programming tasks such as writing boilerplate code, generating documentation, and suggesting test cases. Human developers remain responsible for architectural design, debugging complex problems, and ensuring system reliability.

Near-Term Developments. In the coming years, AI tools are likely to become more deeply integrated into development pipelines, supporting automated testing, code review, and infrastructure configuration. Development teams may increasingly adopt hybrid workflows in which human engineers collaborate with AI systems throughout the software development lifecycle.

Long-Term Possibilities. Over a longer time horizon, artificial intelligence may reshape the organization of software engineering work itself. Developers may transition toward roles centered on system architecture, governance of AI-generated artifacts, and high-level problem solving.

Distinguishing these time horizons helps clarify how current technological developments may evolve into broader transformations of software engineering practice.

CONCLUSION

The quick rate of AI-generated code being integrated into the software development industry has radically altered the profession of software engineers, defining the character of their work and the abilities one needs to achieve success. This chapter has pointed out the changes of more strategic, analytical and supervisory roles of traditional coding centric jobs where developers and AI systems work together to design, validate and optimize solutions. The development of AI-assisted, and AI-generated development has not decreased the relevance of technical skills but has rather intensified the demand of more advanced thinking, the ability to design systems, as well as the understanding of fundamental principles of programming.

Simultaneously, the increased use of AI machinery has triggered an urgent necessity to undergo constant reskilling/upskilling. New skills like prompt engineering, critical assessment of AI output, ethical decision-making, and enhancement of human-focused skills like creativity, teamwork, and communication have to be learned by developers. The chapter has highlighted the relevance of lifelong learning with the help of online platform, organizational training programs and collaborative learning environment by making professionals relevant in a fast changing technologically advanced world.

In summary, the future of software engineering is in the art of human-AI cooperation, whereby the synergies of the two are exploited to make breakthroughs and deliver outputs. Although AI is able to robotize a number of ordinary actions and make them more efficient, the role of human judgment, creativity, and ethical responsibility cannot be ignored. Through reskilling as an ongoing process and providing adaptive learning ecosystems, individuals and organizations will be able to overcome the challenges of AI-driven development and develop a resilient and future-oriented workforce in software engineering successfully.

REFERENCES

Akter, S., McCarthy, G., Sajib, S., Michael, K., Dwivedi, Y. K., D'Ambra, J., & Shen, K. N. (2021). Algorithmic Bias in Data-Driven Innovation in the Age of AI. *International Journal of Information Management*, *60*, 102387. DOI: 10.1016/j.ijinfomgt.2021.102387

Albaroudi, E., Mansouri, T., Hatamleh, M., Elbehairy, M., & Alameer, A. (2025). Generative AI and the Future of Software Engineering in Saudi Arabia: Governance, Innovation, and Workforce Transformation. *International Journal of Theoretical and Applied Computational Intelligence.*, *2025*, 84–105.

Alenezi, M., & Akour, M. (2025). AI-Driven Innovations in Software Engineering: A Review of Current Practices and Future Directions. *Applied Sciences (Basel, Switzerland)*, *15*(3), 1344. Advance online publication. DOI: 10.3390/app15031344

Aslam, M. (2024). *A User Centric Approach to Explainable Artificial Intelligence in Industry*. Loughborough University.

Baqar, M., & Khanda, R. (2024). The Future of Software Testing: AI-Powered Test Case Generation and Validation, 1424, arXiv preprint arXiv.05808.

Dandotiya, M., Goyal, N. K., Yadav, P., Sankhla, K., & Kumari, M. (2026). GENALYTICS: A Deep Dive Into Real-Time Insights via Generative AI. In Elbaghazaoui, B., Amnai, M., & Gherabi, N. (Eds.), *Generative AI-Powered Data Architectures: From Governance to Autonomous Analytics* (pp. 105–134). IGI Global Scientific Publishing., DOI: 10.4018/979-8-3373-5616-7.ch005

Deming, C., Khair, M. A., Mallipeddi, S. R., & Varghese, A. (2021). Software Testing in the Era of AI: Leveraging Machine Learning and Automation for Efficient Quality Assurance. *Asian Journal of Applied Science and Engineering.*, *10*(1), 66–76. DOI: 10.18034/ajase.v10i1.88

Farooqi, A., Das, D., Tripathi, M., Dutta, R., Goyal, N. K., & Sheikh, M. F. (2026). Navigating Ethical Frontiers in AI-Driven Geriatric Care. In Stolakis, K., & Efthymiou, I. (Eds.), *AI for Geriatric Care in an Aging Society: Ethical, Clinical, and Policy Challenges* (pp. 243–266). IGI Global Scientific Publishing., DOI: 10.4018/979-8-3373-5462-0.ch009

Ferrari, A., Zhao, L., & Alhoshan, W. (2021). NLP for Requirements Engineering: Tasks, Techniques, Tools, and Technologies, 2021 IEEE/ACM 43rd International Conference on Software Engineering: Companion Proceedings (ICSE-Companion), IEEE.

Gadekar, S. (2024). How AI-Powered Tools Like GitHub Copilot Are Transforming Software Development, https://dev.to/gadekar_sachin/-how-ai-powered-tools-like-github-copilot-are-transforming-software-development-1h23, 24 February 2025.

Goyal, N. K., Goyal, N. K., Kumar, S., Dutta, R., Kothari, V., & Sinha, S. K. (2026). Empowering Elderly Care Through Artificial Intelligence. In Stolakis, K., & Efthymiou, I. (Eds.), *AI for Geriatric Care in an Aging Society: Ethical, Clinical, and Policy Challenges* (pp. 1–28). IGI Global Scientific Publishing., DOI: 10.4018/979-8-3373-5462-0.ch001

Goyal, N. K., Gulati, K., Avasthi, A., Kapoor, S. K., Keswani, B., & Gupta, S. (2026). Securing the Imagination: Security and Privacy Challenges in Generative AI Systems. In Elbaghazaoui, B., Amnai, M., & Gherabi, N. (Eds.), *Generative AI-Powered Data Architectures: From Governance to Autonomous Analytics* (pp. 239–266). IGI Global Scientific Publishing., DOI: 10.4018/979-8-3373-5616-7.ch010

Haefner, N., Parida, V., Gassmann, O., & Wincent, J. (2023). Implementing and Scaling Artificial Intelligence: A Review, Framework, and Research Agenda. *Technological Forecasting and Social Change*, *197*, 122878. DOI: 10.1016/j.techfore.2023.122878

Hymel, C. The AI-Native Software Development Lifecycle: A Theoretical and Practical New Methodology, 2024, arXiv preprint arXiv.03416.

Iorliam, A., & Ingio, J. A. (2024). A Comparative Analysis of Generative Artificial Intelligence Tools for Natural Language Processing. *Journal of Computing Theories and Applications.*, *1*(3), 311–325. DOI: 10.62411/jcta.9447

Jim, J. R., Talukder, M. A. R., Malakar, P., Kabir, M. M., Nur, K., & Mridha, M. F. (2024). Recent Advancements and Challenges of NLP-Based Sentiment Analysis: A State-of-the-Art Review. *Natural Language Processing Journal.*, *6*, 100059. DOI: 10.1016/j.nlp.2024.100059

Kaur, K., Singh, P., & Kaur, P. A Review of Artificial Intelligence Techniques for Requirement Engineering, Computational Methods Data Engineering: *Proceedings of ICMDE*, 2020, Singapore, Springer, 259–278.

Kazi, S., Khoja, S., & Daud, A. (2023). A Survey of Deep Learning Techniques for Machine Reading Comprehension. *Artificial Intelligence Review*, *56*(S2, no. S2), 2509–2569. DOI: 10.1007/s10462-023-10583-4

Khan, W., Daud, A., Khan, K., Muhammad, S., & Haq, R. (2023). Exploring the Frontiers of Deep Learning and Natural Language Processing: A Comprehensive Overview of Key Challenges and Emerging Trends. *Natural Language Processing Journal.*, *4*, 100026. DOI: 10.1016/j.nlp.2023.100026

Kumari, M., & Goyal, N. K. (2026). Artificial Intelligence in the Cryptocurrency Ecosystem: Crime Mechanisms, Detection Strategies, and Legal Perspectives. In Lin, L. (Ed.), *Innovations in Cryptocrime and Financial Fraud* (pp. 245–282). IGI Global Scientific Publishing., DOI: 10.4018/979-8-3373-0675-9.ch007

Kumari, M., Khan, S. T., Gulati, K., Sharma, P., Goyal, N. K., & Sheikh, M. F. (2026). Innovative Procedural Content Generation (PCG) Using Generative AI: A New Paradigm in Game Design. In Sousa, J., & Tavares, R. (Eds.), *Reshaping the Video Game Landscape With AI and GenAI* (pp. 205–232). IGI Global Scientific Publishing., DOI: 10.4018/979-8-3373-4637-3.ch007

Kumari, M., Kumawat, R., Dutta, R., Khan, S. T., Goyal, N. K., & Sheikh, M. F. (2026). Wireless Communication and IoT Integration in Smart Clothing. In Saxena, P., Singh, M., Singh, S., & Rashid, M. (Eds.), *Next-Generation Electronic Textiles and Conductive Materials for Smart Wearables* (pp. 195–232). IGI Global Scientific Publishing., DOI: 10.4018/979-8-3373-4287-0.ch008

Kumari, M., Kumawat, R., Tripathi, M., Suganthi, K., Goyal, N. K., & Sheikh, M. F. (2026). Blockchain for Transparency and Traceability in Supply Chains. In Khan, M., Mehmood, T., & Rao, M. (Eds.), *Maximizing Operational Efficiency at the Intersection of Supply Chain Management and Marketing* (pp. 35–64). IGI Global Scientific Publishing., DOI: 10.4018/979-8-3373-3109-6.ch002

Kusal, S., Patil, S., Choudrie, J., Kotecha, K., Vora, D., & Pappas, I. (2023). A Systematic Review of Applications of Natural Language Processing and Future Challenges With Special Emphasis in Text-Based Emotion Detection. *Artificial Intelligence Review*, *56*(12), 15129–15215. DOI: 10.1007/s10462-023-10509-0

Lacerda, G., Petrillo, F., Pimenta, M., & Guéhéneuc, Y. G. (2020). Code Smells and Refactoring: A Tertiary Systematic Review of Challenges and Observations. *Journal of Systems and Software*, *167*, 110610. DOI: 10.1016/j.jss.2020.110610

Liu, K., Reddivari, S., & Reddivari, K. (2022). Artificial Intelligence in Software Requirements Engineering: State-of-the-Art, 2022 IEEE 23rd International Conference on Information Reuse and Integration for Data Science (IRI), IEEE.

Marar H. W. (2024). Advancements in Software Engineering Using AI, Computer Software Media Applications. 6, no. 1.

Nettur, S. B., Karpurapu, S., Nettur, U., Gajja, L. S., Myneni, S., & Dusi, A. The Role of GitHub Copilot on Software Development: A Perspective on Productivity, Security, Best Practices and Future Directions, 2025, arXiv preprint arXiv.13199.

Pachouly, J., Ahirrao, S., Kotecha, K., Selvachandran, G., & Abraham, A. (2022). A Systematic Literature Review on Software Defect Prediction Using Artificial Intelligence: Datasets, Data Validation Methods, Approaches, and Tools. *Engineering Applications of Artificial Intelligence*, *111*, 104773. DOI: 10.1016/j.engappai.2022.104773

Pandey, R., Singh, P., Wei, R., & Shankar, S. (2024). Transforming Software Development: Evaluating the Efficiency and Challenges of GitHub Copilot in Real-World Projects, arXiv preprint arXiv.17910.

Rashid, A. B., & Kausik, M. D. A. K. (2024). AI Revolutionizing Industries Worldwide: A Comprehensive Overview of Its Diverse Applications. *Hybrid Advances.*, *7*, 100277. DOI: 10.1016/j.hybadv.2024.100277

Senapathi, M., Buchan, J., & Osman, H. DevOps Capabilities, Practices, and Challenges: Insights From a Case Study, *Proceedings of the 22nd International Conference on Evaluation and Assessment in Software Engineering*, 2018, New York, NY, United States, Association for Computing Machinery. DOI: 10.1145/3210459.3210465

Sharma, P., Kumawat, R., Jain, G., Keswani, G., Goyal, N. K., & Sheikh, M. F. (2026). Machine Learning-Based Intrusion Detection Systems for Healthcare Internet of Things (HIoT). In Shieh, C., Goel, P., Horng, M., & Pandey, H. (Eds.), *Resilient Healthcare Internet of Things Systems: Architectures, Security, and Trust* (pp. 185–214). IGI Global Scientific Publishing., DOI: 10.4018/979-8-3373-7610-3.ch007

Sheikh, M. F. A., Kapoor, S. K., Goyal, N. K., & Tuba, E. rao, A. (2026). Enhancing Healthcare Security with Fog Computing and Blockchain Technology. In: Nayak, R., Mittal, N., Khunteta, A., Kumar, M. (eds) Recent Advancements in Artificial Intelligence. ICRAAI 2025. Lecture Notes in Networks and Systems, vol 1468. Springer, Singapore. DOI: 10.1007/978-981-96-7760-3_38

Siahaan, D., Raharjana, I. K., & Fatichah, C. (2023). User Story Extraction From Natural Language for Requirements Elicitation: Identify Software-Related Information From Online News. *Information and Software Technology*, *158*, 107195. DOI: 10.1016/j.infsof.2023.107195

Siam, M. K., Gu, H., Cheng, J. Q., & Programming With, A. I. Evaluating ChatGPT, Gemini, AlphaCode, and GitHub Copilot for Programmers, 2024, arXiv preprint arXiv.09224.

Smith, H. K. (2024). *Leveraging AI for Proactive Software Quality Assurance: Predictive Analytics.* Machine Learning, and Agile Test Automation.

Vasiliniuc, M.-S., & Groza, A. (2023). Case study: Using AI-Assisted Code Generation in Mobile Teams, 2023 IEEE 19th International Conference on Intelligent Computer Communication and Processing (ICCP), IEEE.

Yadav, A., Usman, M., Sati, A., & Jain, S. (2024). Revolutionizing Software Development: Enhancing Quality and Performance Through Code Refactoring, *Proceedings of the 2024 Sixteenth International Conference on Contemporary Computing*, DOI: 10.1145/3675888.3676139

Yang, Y., Xia, X., Lo, D., & Grundy, J. (2022). A Survey on Deep Learning for Software Engineering. *ACM Computing Surveys*, *54*(10s, no. 10s), 1–73. DOI: 10.1145/3505243

Zahaib Nabeel, M. (2024). AI-Enhanced Project Management Systems for Optimizing Resource Allocation and Risk Mitigation. *Asian Journal of Multidisciplinary Research and Review.*, *5*(5), 53–91. DOI: 10.55662/AJMRR.2024.5502

Chapter 12
Leading AI Transition:
Deskilling, Reskilling, and Frameworks for Engineering Managers

Nikhil Akkiraju
http://orcid.org/0009-0008-0846-8894
PayPal, USA

ABSTRACT

AI coding tools are now firmly embedded in engineering teams toolkits. What is still up for debate is what this means for how engineers grow and whether the productivity gains come with a cost. This chapter draws on experience leading larger teams through the shift to AI, and it looks closely at one tension that kept showing up along the way: the AI tools accelerating output today may be quietly eroding the foundational skills teams will need when things go wrong. A framework is offered for thinking about which skills to protect, which to build through AI collaboration, and which to hand off entirely. It covers hiring, career development, team dynamics, and the harder question of what makes an engineer valuable when AI can generate the code. This chapter does not seek to reassess the merits of AI adoption but instead aims to support engineering managers in navigating the transition while preserving long-term capability alongside near-term productivity gains.

DOI: 10.4018/979-8-3373-8450-4.ch012

INTRODUCTION: THE AI DISRUPTION IN SOFTWARE ENGINEERING

The Velocity of Change (2021-2025)

The focus when AI adoption began around 2021 was on management issues related to CI/CD pipelines and code review turnaround. By early 2023, the conversation had shifted entirely, and the question engineering managers were focused on was no longer about deployment frequency. Instead, it became this: Are engineers learning to code, or learning to prompt?

The change happened faster than most people expected. Before 2021, AI in development was focused on relatively small areas: autocomplete, syntax highlighting, and basic linting. The launch of GitHub Copilot in June 2021 marked a real turning point. For the first time, engineers could describe what they wanted and get working code in return. ChatGPT followed in late 2022, opening up debugging, explanation, and even architectural thinking through conversation.

By 2023, AI tools were part of daily workflows across many teams. By 2024, entire functions, test suites, and API integrations were being generated through prompts. Now, in 2026, AI agents are capable of increasingly autonomous coding in constrained domains.

The productivity gains are real. Tasks that once took hours now take minutes. The more important question is whether the way engineers approach problem-solving (their habits, their depth of understanding, and their ability to work through difficult problems independently) is keeping pace with the increase in output.

The Manager's Dilemma

Engineering management has traditionally operated on a fundamental principle: hire capable people and facilitate their growth through direct experience. Engineers develop expertise by engaging with complex problems, navigating documentation, and debugging systems they have not yet mastered. This process is deliberate, often challenging, but it cultivates the judgment that distinguishes competent practitioners from exceptional ones.

AI is fundamentally altering the environment in which that growth has historically occurred. The central question is no longer simply how quickly teams can deliver, but whether the experiences that build genuine capability remain embedded in the work itself.

A junior engineer today can leverage AI to implement features, integrate services, and produce functional code without deeply understanding connection pooling behavior, the practical implications of timeout configurations, or how to diagnose network failures independently. The software functions as intended, but the learning that traditionally accompanied its construction is often more superficial than in previous eras.

Senior engineers encounter a more nuanced version of this transformation. Knowledge of concurrency, distributed systems behavior, and asynchronous execution (competencies that once required years to internalize) can now be retrieved instantly. This expertise remains critical when evaluating AI-generated solutions. However, the discipline of maintaining and deepening that knowledge can erode when answers are perpetually available on demand.

Engineering managers find themselves navigating two responsibilities that do not always align: maximizing team output in the present while developing engineers for careers spanning decades. Whether these objectives can remain compatible in an AI-augmented environment is an open question, and the answer carries significant implications for hiring practices, performance evaluation, and approaches to long-term professional development.

Why This Matters Now

The deskilling-reskilling dynamic is already here. It is happening in teams now, and the decisions engineering managers take today about the skills to develop, automate, and let go will shape organizational capabilities for the next decade. AI capabilities are advancing faster than the frameworks for managing their impact on teams. Market pressure is forcing adoption faster, and the competitive advantage of AI-assisted development is real, which creates pressure to move fast without thinking carefully about what gets lost. The effects of deskilling are slow to surface. An engineer relying heavily on AI can produce results faster and appear productive until they encounter something AI cannot solve, and by then the gap may already be substantial. This makes this transition different from previous technology shifts. Desktop to web, monolithic to distributed, on-premises to cloud - those required new skills while keeping existing ones. There are no established playbooks yet, but this one potentially removes the need for certain skills entirely.

AI Adoption as an Organizational, Not Individual, Decision

Much of the public discourse around AI-assisted development treats adoption as a personal choice. Engineers decide whether to use AI tools, how often, and for what kinds of tasks. In practice, AI adoption is mostly an organizational decision. Tooling, performance expectations, delivery timelines, and unspoken norms do more to shape usage than individual preference. Even when explicit policies are absent, teams quickly infer what is rewarded by observing which behaviors lead to recognition, promotion, and continued trust.

When organizations emphasize velocity, feature throughput, and rapid iteration without simultaneously articulating expectations around validation and understanding, AI use naturally expands to fill that gap. Engineers respond rationally to the incentives in front of them. If AI-generated solutions pass tests, clear code review, and meet delivery deadlines, there is little immediate reason to slow down and interrogate the output more deeply. Over time, this creates a local equilibrium where reliance on AI is normalized and questioning it feels inefficient or even obstructive.

This matters because it shifts responsibility from individual engineers to management systems. Deskilling in this context isn't about negligence or lack of curiosity. It's what happens when you optimize environments for speed while tools get more capable. Organizations that treat AI reliance as a personal failing risk misdiagnosing the problem and implementing counterproductive interventions, such as discouraging tool use without addressing the incentives that made it attractive in the first place.

Recognizing AI adoption as an organizational phenomenon also clarifies why its effects are uneven across teams. Groups with strong architectural leadership, robust review practices, and explicit learning expectations tend to integrate AI in ways that augment existing strengths. Teams lacking these structures may experience rapid output gains alongside a gradual erosion of shared understanding. The difference lies less in individual discipline than in how responsibility, learning, and judgment are distributed across the organization.

BACKGROUND

This chapter starts by defining what deskilling and reskilling means in an AI context, then works through observations from managing engineering teams through the transition. A three-category skill framework is introduced (commoditized, augmentable, and human-unique skills) followed by strategies for reskilling without sacrificing productivity. A few case studies will be explored on what worked and what has not. The chapter closes with predictions for where AI is heading and recommendations for managers at any stage of the adoption curve.

DEFINING THE DESKILLING-RESKILLING PARADOX

What Is Deskilling?

Sociologist Harry Braverman documented something similar in manufacturing decades ago. Labor and Monopoly Capital (Braverman,1974) traced how industrial automation encoded crafts people's knowledge into machines, leaving workers as operators rather than practitioners. The knowledge did not disappear; it just moved somewhere the worker could no longer access or build on. Something analogous is happening in software engineering now.

Deskilling in this context refers to AI handling tasks that previously required engineers to develop and maintain capabilities. A few repeated patterns to highlight:

- Junior engineers often turn to AI tools before they've had a chance to build their own mental model of how to diagnose problems. The immediate issue gets fixed, but they miss the chance to develop the pattern recognition that helps experienced engineers quickly zero in on what's likely going wrong.
- Mid-level engineers can start drifting away from algorithmic thinking once AI consistently produces optimized solutions. It's not that they fully mastered time complexity and then chose to stop using it - more often, they simply haven't needed to engage with it, and over time the habit fades.
- Senior engineers tend not to focus on language internals and platform details that AI now handles. The depth they once had begins to thin.
- Engineers across all levels focus on AI instant summaries rather than reading documentation carefully. Building comprehensive mental models of systems gets replaced by surface familiarity that is enough for the immediate task but not for the edge cases.

AI-assisted engineers still ship working code and pass code reviews. The gap only becomes visible when AI fails or produces incorrect code, and the engineer does not have enough context or foundations to recognize it.

What Is Reskilling?

Reskilling means developing capabilities suited to AI work - new competencies and not necessarily just focusing on updates to existing ones. On actual teams this looks like engineers learning how to drive and check the tools, not just keep up with the latest framework.

Prompt engineering is a skill that did not exist in software engineering before. It involves understanding how language models interpret instructions, providing the right context, iterating when results fall short, and knowing when changing the approach entirely will work better than refining the prompt. AI validation goes beyond traditional code review cycles. It requires recognizing common AI error patterns, understanding which problem categories AI handles reliably versus which it consistently gets wrong, and maintaining enough judgment to catch what AI misses.

Tool chain orchestration means identifying which AI tools excel at specific tasks and connecting them into workflows that make sense for the team. Meta-problem solving involves breaking complex problems into pieces AI can address effectively while holding overall architecture and sequencing decisions as a human responsibility. These are not nice to have add-ons. They decide whether AI makes the team faster or hide gaps for a while.

Beyond these technical skills, architectural thinking grows in importance as AI handles more implementation detail. Cross-domain synthesis is an area AI struggles with, hence judgment about when to use AI and when not to is increasingly a professional competency.

The Paradox: Both Simultaneously

Deskilling and reskilling are happening at the same time to the same people. Traditional frameworks assume one happens before the other. That assumption does not hold here. A mid-level engineer's output on routine tasks has tripled. They scaffold features quickly, generate tests, and implement standard patterns, but at the same time their ability to debug without AI has gotten worse. They have developed a tendency to accept AI suggestions they do not understand fully because the output looks correct, deriving more productivity in the short term but becoming less capable independently. Both things are true simultaneously, and traditional management frameworks do not have a clean answer for that.

It's important to recognize not all skills are affected equally. Some are being commoditized and can be delegated to AI. Others are augmented by AI, stronger in combination but still requiring human capability to work well. Others remain genuinely human and need more investment now, not less. Engineering managers need to distinguish between these and make deliberate choices about where to invest, where to automate, and where to hold the line even when it looks less effective in the short term.

MAIN FOCUS OF THE CHAPTER

Observations from Engineering Teams (2021-2025)

Impact on Junior Engineers (0-2 Years Experience)

Junior engineer onboarding is much faster with AI. Engineers who previously needed several months before contributing meaningfully now ship code to production within weeks. The cost of not knowing something feels lower, thereby increasing the confidence to engage with unfamiliar technologies. AI fills the gap immediately without the friction of asking a colleague a question that might seem basic. The fundamental gap between shipping code and understanding it is increasing, as AI can often describe what their code does, but the engineers cannot always explain why it works that way, what the edge cases are, or what they would do differently if the approach failed.

Consider Arun, a junior engineer who implements a mobile API integration following Copilot's suggestions without consulting the API documentation. It passes testing. In production under load it fails - the generated code made incorrect assumptions about rate limiting that the documentation would have surfaced. In the post-incident review, Arun says: "I'm not sure - Copilot just suggested this pattern." The integration was feasible and the code looked correct. But certain issues around how the backend behaves were not visible because the underlying model was never understood. The current setup (reaching for AI before reaching for documentation) made that gap almost inevitable.

The deeper issue with Arun's situation is not that he used Copilot. It is that nothing in the workflow required him to understand what Copilot generated before it shipped. The code passed tests. It cleared review. It looked correct to everyone who touched it. The rate-limiting failure was not in the code's surface behavior; it was in an assumption baked into the generated pattern that nobody had reason to question because nobody had read the documentation that would have surfaced it.

This is the part that does not show up in velocity metrics. Arun's feature was delivered on time. His throughput was solid. From a sprint perspective, he had a good quarter. The problem only became visible under production load, weeks later, in a post-incident review where the honest answer was "I don't know why it was written this way."

The fix is not to ban AI. It is to make documentation review a non-negotiable step before any external API integration, regardless of how confident the generated code looks. A short checklist works: read the authentication docs, check the rate limit behavior, confirm the error response contract. Takes twenty minutes. Catches the class of failures that AI tools consistently miss because they generalize from patterns rather than reading the specific contract in front of them. Arun now does this on every integration. The habit took one bad incident to form. The goal is to build it before the incident, not after. That means twenty minutes reading documents now beats hours debugging in production later and an engineer who knows why rate limit matters over one who just prompts past the problem.

Arun's pattern is not isolated. GitHub (2022) found that developers using Copilot reported 55% faster task completion. What the study did not measure is comprehension depth or ability to maintain AI-generated code over time. That gap is what Arun hit in production.

Prather et al. (2023) documented similar patterns across computing education, where students using generative AI completed assignments faster but struggled with fundamental concept mastery.

Impact on Mid-Level Engineers (3-7 Years Experience)

Mid-level engineers get the clearest productivity lift from AI, and the tradeoffs are subtler and slower to surface. Productivity gains of 3-5x on routine tasks are common. The time freed up should go toward architecture, mentorship, and harder problems. Whether it does depend on the individual and on what the team's incentives reward. The pattern worth watching is the growing gap between output and comprehension.

Consider Dave, a mid-level engineer who uses AI to optimize a data processing pipeline and achieves a 40% performance improvement - real, measurable, good work. In code review he cannot fully explain the async patterns AI generated. He did not need to understand them to get the result. Deeper review surfaces a race condition he could not have caught independently because he did not fully work through the code he submitted. The optimization was real. The understanding was not there to sustain it when things went wrong.

Vaithilingam et al. (2022) documented this exact problem in their study of GitHub Copilot users. Participants completed tasks faster but struggled to explain their solutions when the tool was removed. Output and understanding can diverge significantly. Dave's case confirms it.

The current setup for many mid-level engineers is producing results without the comprehension to maintain or debug them reliably. That is not a problem until the next outage, when three engineers stare at logs and nobody remembers how the pieces fit together anymore. Metrics looked great. The shared system knowledge quietly faded.

Impact on Senior Engineers (8-12 Years Experience)

Senior engineers show the widest range of responses to AI tools, and the stakes of getting the balance wrong are highest for this group. The engineers who integrate AI well are almost always the ones who already think architecturally. They use AI to move faster on implementation details while holding system design themselves. They validate AI suggestions quickly because they have enough depth to recognize when something is off. For these engineers, AI is genuinely additive - it makes them faster without creating dependency.

The harder case is the engineer who resists. Consider a senior engineer with fifteen years of strong delivery who views AI assistance as unnecessary given their existing speed. As teammates accelerate, this engineer becomes a relative bottleneck, not because their absolute output drops, but because the gap widens. After eventually trying AI tools seriously, productivity increases substantially. But something else changes: the ongoing investment in platform updates, language features, and API changes that had been a professional habit for years quietly stops. "AI handles that now." Six months later, a technical interview at another company requires coding without AI access. Skills that were sharp for over a decade have atrophied in months. The offer does not come through.

The problem is not about whether to use AI. The problem is that maintaining foundational knowledge while also leveraging AI cannot be dropped without cost. More AI adoption does not necessarily help if the underlying depth is not being maintained alongside it. It might be counterproductive.

The identity question underneath all of this does not get enough attention. An engineer who spent years mastering concurrent programming may feel genuinely devalued when AI generates correct concurrency code more reliably than they can recall the edge cases. What makes a senior engineer valuable when AI can produce the code they spent years learning to write? That is not rhetorical. It affects morale and retention in ways that do not show up in productivity metrics until someone leaves.

A different senior engineer on the same team took almost the opposite path. Instead of resisting AI, he adopted it aggressively but kept a personal rule that any pattern he accepted had to be something he could implement by hand a week later. That rule forced him to keep reading language release notes, platform changelogs, and RFCs even when AI could have filled the gaps. It also changed how he mentored others. When a junior brought an AI-generated solution to a design review, he would ask them to whiteboard the core idea without the code. If they could not do it yet, he treated that as a growth opportunity rather than a failure. Over time, the team started to see him less as the person who always had the answer and more as the person who could tell when an AI-generated answer was safe to trust. His value shifted, but it did not disappear. This kind of adaptation is harder to measure than lines of code or closed tickets, yet it is exactly what keeps senior engineers relevant when tools can now do large parts of what used to define seniority.

Impact on Staff and Principal Engineers (12+ Years Experience)

Staff+ engineers face a different problem. Their value never came from code volume. It came from judgment, architectural vision, and the ability to influence technical decisions across teams. AI does not directly threaten that. But it changes what influence looks like.

A Staff engineer used to build credibility through depth. "I have debugged this class of problem five times. Here is what breaks and why." That still matters, but it is not enough anymore. Now they also need to teach critical evaluation. "Here is what AI gets wrong in distributed systems. Here is how you validate its suggestions before you trust them." The mentorship shifts. It used to be "let me show you how to implement this." Now it is "let me show you how to think about whether this AI-generated approach is sound."

Organizations that keep evaluating Staff+ engineers primarily on technical output are missing the point. Judgment development and team capability building matter more in an AI-augmented environment. If you reward the Staff engineer who ships the most code instead of the one who makes the team better at spotting bad AI suggestions, you are optimizing for the wrong thing.

Team Dynamics

The most noticeable change in how teams work shows up when an engineer gets stuck. A decade ago, a junior developer might walk over to a senior and say, "Can I show you something weird?" They would step through the logs and the debugger together while the senior narrated their thinking. The bug might take thirty minutes to fix, but the junior would leave with a reusable mental model for the next problem.

Today, that same junior pastes the error and a code snippet into Claude, Copilot, or ChatGPT. The answer appears in seconds, with a patch and an explanation, and nobody had to be interrupted. Throughput improves, but the informal apprenticeship (watching how a more experienced engineer reasons about the system) quietly disappears. Over time, the team ships more fixes but shares fewer ways of thinking.

Code review has shifted in a similar way. With AI handling much of the boilerplate and syntax, reviewers spend more time on architecture, boundaries, and edge cases, which is usually an improvement. The risk is that when both author and reviewer leaned on AI for the implementation, review can devolve into asking whether the output looks reasonable, not whether it is correct. Subtle correctness or performance issues slip through unless someone still has enough independent understanding to mentally execute the code and challenge what the AI produced.

Documentation decays even more quietly. When AI can explain the codebase on demand, writing and maintaining design docs feels less urgent. But those explanations only reflect what is in the code today, not why it ended up that way, what failed in the past, or which constraints shaped key decisions. If that context is never written down and the people who remember it leave, it is gone. Teams that rely on AI as their de facto source of institutional memory often do not notice the foundation eroding until they start re-learning lessons they once already paid for.

Tech Leads sit between architecture and implementation, and AI is changing what that role requires. Reviewing AI-generated code is different from reviewing human-written code. Consistency becomes harder when five engineers are using different prompting strategies, different tools, and producing solutions that all work but follow incompatible patterns.

Maintaining coding standards across a team where everyone leans on AI requires explicit conversations about what AI should and should not handle. It requires agreed-upon validation steps before code hits review. It requires enough technical depth to catch when AI has subtly violated an architectural decision the team made months ago. The Tech Lead who tries to enforce consistency purely through code review, without addressing how the team uses AI upstream, will spend all their time rewriting AI output instead of guiding system design.

The role is shifting. It used to be "write the hardest code." Now it is "decide what the team builds in-house versus what gets delegated to AI, then make sure those boundaries hold.

The Disappearance of Friction and Its Consequences for Learning

Friction has traditionally played a central role in how engineers learn. Difficulty navigating a codebase, uncertainty about system behavior, and the effort required to debug unfamiliar failures all create moments where learning is unavoidable. AI tools dramatically reduce this friction by providing immediate answers, plausible explanations, and ready-to-apply fixes. While this improves efficiency, it also removes many of the cues that historically signaled the need for deeper engagement.

Reduced friction changes what engineers learn and how they evaluate their own competence. When progress is smooth and obstacles are resolved quickly, it is easy to conclude that understanding is sufficient. No struggle does not mean mastery. Most of the time it just means the learning opportunity never happened. This dynamic is particularly subtle because AI explanations often reinforce confidence by offering coherent narratives that feel indistinguishable from genuine comprehension.

From a managerial perspective, reduced friction complicates skill assessment. A manager looking at a dashboard sees "unblocked quickly" and "high throughput" and has no easy way to tell whether that came from real depth or pasting better prompts. The usual signals of growth how quickly an engineer can unblock themselves, how independently they deliver features become less reliable when AI mediates much of the problem-solving process. An engineer may appear highly autonomous while remaining dependent on tools in ways that only surface under atypical conditions, such as outages, novel requirements, or partial system failures.

The long-term risk is not that engineers stop learning. It is that they get really good at working with specific tools without building skills that transfer. When the tool changes or the problem does not fit what AI handles well, the learning does not carry over.

Hiring and Onboarding

Technical interviews assume something that is no longer reliably true: that candidates built real coding skill through hands-on practice and can demonstrate it under controlled conditions. When someone has learned to code with AI in the loop, what appears to be fluency may be skillful prompting. That distinction matters because it shapes how the engineer will behave when they encounter a genuinely difficult problem.

Live coding interviews have become uncomfortable in both directions. If AI is not allowed, candidates are asked to work in a way that does not match how they build software. If AI is allowed, the exercise no longer reveals much about their depth of understanding. In either case, the signal is noisy.

Technical interviews need to move closer to how engineers really work. System design interviews remain relatively effective, because AI still struggles with context-heavy, integrative reasoning, and strong candidates can still distinguish themselves here. Debugging exercises are also promising for example, giving candidates AI-generated code with a few subtle defects and asking them to identify and fix the issues. This approach shows whether they read code critically, recognize edge cases, and understand the failure modes common in AI-produced code. Likewise, asking candidates to critique an AI-proposed architecture often reveals more about their judgment and independence than asking them to design one from scratch.

There is also a question worth standardizing across interviews: when would you use AI for this problem, and when would you avoid it? How candidates respond exposes their engineering judgment in ways that most implementation tasks no longer do.

Onboarding is shifting along similar lines. New engineers now expect AI access from the start, because that is how they learned to code. Traditional onboarding patterns that relied on struggling through a codebase to build deep understanding are fading, replaced by asking AI to explain unfamiliar code. This can yield faster early productivity but may produce shallower long-term comprehension. Whether that tradeoff is acceptable depends on the role and on the complexity of the system, and it is something organizations should decide explicitly rather than drifting toward whatever gets new hires productive the fastest.

THE SKILL ASSESSMENT FRAMEWORK

Managing the deskilling-reskilling tension requires a way to distinguish which skills to protect, which to reshape through AI collaboration, and which to largely hand off. Three categories are useful for framing this shift.

Category 1: Commoditized Skills

These are skills AI now performs reliably enough that continued heavy investment offers diminishing returns: syntax memorization, boilerplate generation, basic CRUD flows, standard library lookups, simple bug fixes where the error message points directly to the problem, format conversions, and routine documentation comments. The management response is to stop treating these as core development or evaluation criteria. Whether a junior engineer has memorized UIKit lifecycle callbacks or Android's Activity stack matters far less than it once did; AI will supply the correct signatures more consistently than most people can recall under pressure. What matters is whether the engineer understands why a particular lifecycle hook is appropriate, or when to choose a Fragment versus a composable. Baseline competence still has value when AI is unavailable or inappropriate, but these skills should no longer anchor development plans or performance reviews.

Category 2: Augmentable Skills

These are skills where human-AI collaboration is stronger than either alone. The underlying capabilities remain important, but the engineer's role shifts from direct execution to validation, correction, and refinement. This includes algorithm design and optimization, debugging complex issues, API integration, testing strategy, refactoring, and performance work. The task moves from "write an algorithm" to "evaluate and improve the algorithm AI proposed." A productive code review question becomes: What did AI suggest, why is it right or wrong, how would you improve it, and what alternatives did you consider? This develops critical evaluation, comparative reasoning, and design judgment - the skills that retain value even as AI becomes more capable.

Category 3: Human-Unique Skills

These are capabilities where humans retain clear, durable advantages: system architecture and high-level design, problem framing and scope definition, cross-functional communication, ethical judgment, domain and business understanding, mentorship, strategic technical planning, and trade-off analysis grounded in organizational reality. As AI absorbs more implementation detail, the most valuable engineers are not the fastest coders but the ones asking the right questions, choosing the right problems, and designing systems that fit constraints. System architecture illustrates this clearly: AI can propose patterns, but it cannot meaningfully weigh team capabilities, existing technical debt, regulatory requirements, or strategic priorities. That synthesis (deciding what should be built and how it should fit into the organization) remains a human responsibility.

Table 1. Skill categories and managerial responses

Skill Category	What good looks like	Warning Signs	Management response
Commoditized	AI handles boilerplate, syntax, routine look ups. Engineer focuses attention on harder problems	Engineer cannot explain generated code at all. Skips documentation entirely for any external API	Require documentation review before integration. Add "explain this" step to review
Augmentable	Engineer catches AI review in error. Modifies suggestions before submitting. Can explain why changes were made.	Accepts AI output without modification consistently. Cannot identify where AI code could fail	Introduce validation annotations, shift review focus to "where could this break"
Augmentable	Test coverage reflects understanding of edge cases, not just happy path	Tests generated by AI accepted without reviewing what they cover	Require engineer to write atleast one edge case test manually per feature
Human-unique	Can articulate tradeoffs made in design. Pushes back on scope when requirements are unclear	Defers all design decisions to AI suggestions or to senior engineers without engaging	Assigned scope design decisions. Debrief the reasoning in one-on-ones
Human-unique	Communicate clearly across team boundaries. Translates technical constraints for non-technical stakeholders	Relies on AI-generated summaries for cross-team communication without personalizing them	Involve in cross-functional meetings. Coach on stakeholder communication

The Framework as a Moving Target

The boundaries between these targets are not fixed. Skills classified as human-unique today may become augmentable as AI systems improve. Some augmentable skills will eventually commoditize. System architecture, currently a clear human advantage, may shift as AI models get better at understanding organizational context and constraint trade-offs.

The framework's value is not in permanent categorization. It is in forcing regular reassessment. Engineering Managers should revisit these distinctions quarterly. Which skills have AI systems begun handling reliably? Which human capabilities remain genuinely differentiated? The goal is not to predict where boundaries will settle. It is to avoid anchoring on outdated assumptions about what engineers must master versus what they can safely delegate.

Using the Framework to Assess Teams

Managers can assess teams at the level of individual engineers rather than in the abstract. For each person, the key questions are: Is over-reliance on AI confined to commoditized work, or is it also creeping into augmentable and human-unique tasks? Has genuine collaboration skill developed, or is the engineer either avoiding AI altogether or accepting its outputs without real scrutiny? And is there visible, sustained investment in human-unique capabilities, or has easy access to AI made it simpler to sidestep the harder developmental work?

A lightweight assessment matrix per engineer can surface these patterns early enough to act on them. Teams with clear patterns act faster. Others drift toward tool dependency without noticing until hiring lags or incidents expose the gaps. Early signals let managers course-correct before velocity masks deeper problems. The aim is not to constrain AI use, but to ensure that people are building capabilities that retain value as AI systems advance, rather than concentrating growth only in areas that are useful so long as AI remains at its current level.

Why Traditional Engineering Excellence Metrics Break Down

Many of the metrics organizations use to assess engineering excellence were developed in environments where implementation effort closely tracked understanding. Code quality, delivery speed, and defect rates functioned as rough proxies for competence because producing reliable software generally required internalizing how systems behaved. AI weakens this connection. You can ship high-quality code without understanding it.

In AI-augmented workflows, you get high quality artifacts without equivalent internal understanding. Generated code may follow best practices, handle common edge cases, and pass automated tests even when the engineer integrating it lacks a deep mental model of the system. As a result, metrics that focus on artifact quality alone increasingly fail to distinguish between engineers who can reason independently and those who rely heavily on tools.

This breakdown has implications for promotion, compensation, and talent retention. You start rewarding the people who ship the most, not the people you most want in the room when things go wrong. The incentives drift. The capability follows. Both happen slowly until they do not. Engineers who invest time in maintaining foundational skills may appear slower in environments optimized for throughput, while those who rely more heavily on AI may outperform in the short term. Over time, this can invert incentives, rewarding behaviors that maximize immediate output at the expense of long-term capability.

Recalibrating excellence metrics requires acknowledging that AI has shifted where value is created. Judgment, validation, and architectural coherence become more important as implementation becomes cheaper. Organizations that keep rewarding volume and speed without changing how they evaluate people will underinvest in the skills they need when things break.

RECOMMENDATIONS FOR ENGINEERING MANAGERS

Managing the deskilling–reskilling paradox requires deliberate intervention rather than passive adaptation. AI adoption alone does not determine long-term engineering capability; managerial choices about training, incentives, evaluation, and culture shape whether AI becomes an amplifier of expertise or a substitute for it. The following five strategies synthesize practical actions engineering managers can take to preserve foundational skills, cultivate effective AI collaboration, and sustain organizational resilience while benefiting from AI-driven productivity gains.

Strategy 1: Preserve Foundational Skills Through Deliberate Practice

The most direct risk of widespread AI use is the quiet erosion of foundational engineering skills that only surface during system failure, incident response, or novel problem solving. To counter this, managers should create structured opportunities for engineers to practice without AI assistance. The intent is not to recreate everyday work, but to keep the independent reasoning muscle from fading.

Practical approaches include setting aside regular “fundamentals” time blocks in which engineers debug unfamiliar code, reason through system behavior, or solve constrained problems with AI tools explicitly disabled. Occasional AI-free pair programming and post-incident reviews that require manual reconstruction of failure modes serve a similar purpose. Resistance is common, as these activities feel slower and less immediately productive. However, teams that sustain such practices typically show improved debugging depth, stronger code review quality, and greater confidence in challenging AI-generated outputs. Framed as skill preservation instead of resisting automation, this becomes an investment in robustness, not nostalgia.

Handling Organizational Pushback

Managers proposing fundamentals training often face resistance from leadership focused on velocity metrics. The conversation shifts when you frame it in risk terms instead of skill development. "We ship fast now, but what happens during the next major outage if no one can debug without AI?" That question lands differently than "we should preserve skills."

Referencing recent incidents where AI reliance delayed resolution makes the case concrete. Some managers pilot fundamentals blocks with a single team, measure impact on debugging speed or code review quality, then present results to leadership as "insurance against fragility" rather than "slowing down to preserve skills." The data usually wins the argument that short-term productivity metrics miss.

Strategy 2: Make AI Collaboration an Explicit, Teachable Skill

Most engineers adopt AI tools informally and let habits form through trial and error. This approach produces uneven outcomes and often reinforces dependency rather than judgment. Managers should instead treat AI collaboration as a professional competency that can be taught, evaluated, and improved over time.

Effective AI collaboration encompasses both prompt construction and output validation. Engineers must learn how to supply sufficient context, constrain AI behavior to match organizational standards, iterate when results fall short, and recognize when changing approaches is preferable to refining a prompt. Denny et al. (2023) demonstrated that prompt engineering quality directly affects solution correctness and code comprehension in AI-assisted development. Equally important is the ability to critically evaluate AI-generated code: identifying common failure patterns, understanding where models are unreliable, and validating correctness, security, and performance independently.

A practical mechanism is an AI collaboration rubric integrated into code review. Barke et al. (2023) found that effective programmers using code-generating models employ iterative refinement strategies and maintain critical distance from AI suggestions. The rubric approach formalizes these behaviors. Reviewers can routinely ask: What did the AI suggest? Why is this solution appropriate or not? Where was the output modified, and why? What alternatives were considered? Over time, these questions normalize AI use while reinforcing accountability for judgment rather than prompt fluency alone.

Common AI Failure Modes Engineers Should Recognize

AI tools fail in predictable ways. Engineers who recognize these patterns validate outputs more effectively. Four categories show up repeatedly.

Hallucinated Dependencies

AI suggests importing libraries or packages that do not exist, or references API methods that were deprecated years ago or never shipped. This happens because models train on a mix of documentation, GitHub repositories, and forum discussions where proposed features and actual releases blur together. An engineer who does not verify imports against current package repositories will ship code that breaks at build time.

Outdated or insecure patterns

AI often generates code that follows older idioms or includes patterns flagged by modern static analysis tools. String concatenation for SQL queries instead of parameterized statements. Authentication flows that skip token validation. The code works in a narrow test case but introduces vulnerabilities that only surface during security review or in production.

Incorrect async behavior

Concurrency is where AI-generated code most often looks correct but behaves wrong under load. Race conditions, improper error handling in promise chains, missing await keywords. All these passes initial testing but fail when request volume increases or network latency spikes. Engineers need to mentally trace execution paths, not just check that the code runs locally.

Wrong performance characteristics

AI frequently generates algorithms that work but scale poorly. A nested loop that performs acceptably on ten items becomes a bottleneck at ten thousand. An engineer who accepts the solution without considering time complexity or reviewing how the data structures interact will ship code that degrades unpredictably.

Teaching engineers to recognize these categories turns AI validation from "does this look okay?" into "which failure mode am I checking for?" It makes review concrete instead of vague.

Validation Thresholds and Techniques

Organizations should establish explicit thresholds for when AI-generated code requires deeper validation. High-risk categories trigger mandatory manual review with AI explicitly disabled during the validation pass. Authentication, payment processing, data deletion, anything touching user privacy. For lower-risk work, a lighter checklist suffices. Verify imports exist, check error handling covers expected failure modes, confirm the solution does not introduce new dependencies without justification.

Some teams maintain a running log of "AI mistakes we caught in review" and use it to train newer engineers on what to watch for. This turns validation from individual discipline into shared team knowledge that improves as the team encounters more failure modes.

Strategy 3: Recenter Development on Meta-Skills and Engineering Judgment

As AI absorbs more implementation detail, the skills that differentiate strong engineers shift toward meta-capabilities that endure across technologies. Systems thinking, problem framing, decomposition of complex challenges, cross-domain synthesis, and trade-off analysis grounded in organizational context become increasingly central. AI does not displace these skills. It either amplifies them if they are present or exposes the gap when they are not.

Managers can reinforce this shift by refocusing development conversations and evaluations. In one-on-one meetings and performance reviews, emphasis should move from volume of output to the reasoning behind decisions: why a solution was chosen, which alternatives were rejected, how the design fits within broader architecture, and what risks were accepted or mitigated. This signals that judgment, not just speed, defines growth when AI is part of the work.

Strategy 4: Redesign Career Ladders and Performance Expectations with AI-Augmented Work

Traditional career progression models place disproportionate weight on coding output and domain-specific implementation expertise. While these remain relevant, their relative importance must shift toward evaluation, validation, and architectural responsibility.

For junior engineers, expectations should emphasize understanding and validating code regardless of authorship, including the ability to explain AI-generated solutions and debug them independently. Mid-level engineers should demonstrate critical evaluation of AI suggestions, disciplined problem decomposition, and coherent integration of AI-assisted work into existing systems. Senior engineers should be assessed primarily on architectural judgment, strategic decision-making, and mentorship. At staff and principal levels, shaping organizational AI strategy, governance, and long-term technical direction becomes central.

Performance evaluation systems must reinforce these priorities. If organizations continue to reward raw throughput while claiming that judgment and architecture matter more, engineers will follow incentives rather than guidance. Clear alignment between evaluation criteria and stated values is essential to sustaining capability as AI adoption accelerates.

Strategy 5: Redesign Hiring, Onboarding and Accountability Practices

Hiring and onboarding practices must adapt to an environment where apparent coding fluency may reflect effective prompting rather than deep understanding. Interviews that prohibit AI no longer reflect real working conditions, while interviews that allow unrestricted AI use often fail to surface independent reasoning.

More reliable signals come from tasks that require candidates to actually think about AI-generated code. Debugging exercises using AI-produced code with subtle defects reveal whether candidates can read code skeptically and recognize failure modes. Architecture critiques of AI-proposed designs test judgment, trade-off awareness, and contextual reasoning. Asking candidates when to use AI and when not to often reveals more about their judgment than how fast they code.

Onboarding should similarly balance early productivity with long-term comprehension. While AI can accelerate initial contribution, organizations should decide explicitly where deep understanding is non-negotiable and ensure that critical system knowledge is actively developed rather than outsourced to tools. Throughout this process, accountability must remain unambiguous: engineers own the systems they ship, regardless of who or what generated the first draft. Engineers need to feel safe saying "I don't understand this yet" while also knowing they own what ships. That combination keeps AI as an amplifier for good work, not a shield for bad calls.

Putting the Strategies into a Quarter

Most managers do not have time to launch a full transformation program. A more realistic path is to pick a single quarter and wire three changes into work that is already happening. First, choose one recurring meeting and make AI use explicit there. For example, start each incident review by asking whether AI was involved in the original change and, if so, how it was validated. This alone surfaces patterns that were previously invisible. Second, pick one onboarding cohort and pilot a different balance between AI-assisted work and fundamentals. Give them access to tools but also schedule a few "no AI" sessions where they have to find answers the old way and then compare the two experiences. Third, identify one promotion packet or performance review cycle and deliberately weight judgment and architecture more heavily than raw output, then watch how that changes the conversation. None of these changes require new headcount or tooling. They simply bring AI out of the background and into explicit discussion, which is where better decisions get made.

Table 2. Quarterly implementation roadmap

Timeline	Action	Outcome Measured
Week 1-2	Conduct skill assessment for Table 1 for each engineer	Identify engineers over-reliant on AI for augmentable/human-unique tasks
Week 3-6	Pilot fundamental blocks with 2-3 engineers (2hrs/ week, AI disabled)	Track debugging depth improvement in code review comments
Week 7-10	Integrate AI on collaboration rubric into team code review process	Measure quality of "What did AI suggest?" responses
Week 11-13	Update one promotion packet criteria to explicitly weight judgment over output	Document shift in performance review conversations and criteria discussed

ETHICAL CONSIDERATIONS

The strategies outlined above are not value neutral. Decisions about how AI is adopted, how skills are preserved, and how accountability is assigned carry ethical implications for individuals, teams, and organizations. This section highlights the most salient ethical considerations engineering managers must confront during AI-driven transformation.

Job Displacement

Managers owe their teams honesty about how the market is shifting. It is very likely that some junior roles will shrink as AI takes over more entry-level implementation work, and the "start with straightforward tickets and grow from there" path that many of us followed will not look the same for the next generation. Being honest does not mean being fatalistic. It means saying out loud that certain tasks and roles may contract, helping people build skills that travel well as AI improves, supporting those who need to move into different kinds of roles, and pushing for adoption plans that weigh human impact alongside throughput and cost.

Equity

AI does not land on a level playing field. Teams with more budget can buy better tools. Engineers with strong foundations get more lift from AI, while those who are already struggling can fall further behind. People in well-connected networks hear about effective practices sooner. Organizations that invest in deliberate reskilling give their engineers advantages that others may never see. From a distance, it is easy to treat this as a neutral technology shift. Up close, you start to see that access, training, and psychological safety determine who benefits.

As a manager, you have some room to push back on that gradient: making sure the whole team has access to core tools, offering structured training instead of assuming people will "catch up" on their own time, and building spaces where it is acceptable to admit confusion and ask basic questions. Democratizing access and learning is not a nice-to-have in this context; it is part of keeping the team cohesive rather than quietly creating a two-tier organization.

The Shadow AI Problem

A less visible equity issue emerges around tooling that exists outside official channels. Engineers who hit friction with approved AI tools often turn to personal ChatGPT accounts, browser extensions, or other unapproved services to maintain productivity. This creates risk the organization cannot see. Proprietary code leaving the network. Inconsistent quality across the team. Engineers building skills around tools the company does not support or may eventually block.

From a management perspective, the answer is not to crack down harder. It is to close the gap between what the organization provides and what engineers need to get work done. If approved tools are too slow, too locked down, or missing critical capabilities, engineers will route around them. The solution involves faster procurement for legitimate tools, clearer policies on what is acceptable, and enough transparency that engineers feel safe asking "can I use this?" instead of quietly adopting it and hoping nobody notices.

Organizations that treat unsanctioned tool use as a compliance failure rather than a signal of unmet need often make the problem worse.

Responsibility and Accountability

Finally, someone owns the code. If AI-generated code causes an outage or a security incident, that responsibility cannot be handed back to the tool. Engineers own the systems they ship, regardless of who or what wrote the first draft. That needs to be said clearly and backed up with practice.

In concrete terms, this means setting expectations that AI outputs are starting points, not answers; designing review practices that treat AI-generated code with appropriate skepticism; and creating enough psychological safety that people feel able to say "I do not fully understand this suggestion yet" without fear. The combination of clear accountability and real safety is what keeps AI as an amplifier for good engineering rather than a shield for bad calls.

Long-Term Organizational Resilience in an AI Environment

The cumulative effects of AI-assisted development extend beyond individual careers and team dynamics to influence organizational resilience. Resilience in software systems has historically depended on a distributed base of understanding: multiple engineers with overlapping knowledge who could diagnose issues, reason about failures, and adapt systems under pressure. As AI absorbs more implementation and reasoning tasks, this distribution can narrow without obvious warning signs.

Organizations may find that critical knowledge becomes increasingly concentrated in a small number of individuals or externalized into tools whose limitations are poorly understood. When incidents occur, recovery depends not only on access to AI assistance, but on the presence of engineers who can interpret outputs, challenge assumptions, and navigate situations where models fail. If that capacity has eroded broadly, the organization becomes more brittle despite appearing productive.

This risk is amplified by the speed of AI advancement. As tools improve, it becomes tempting to defer investment in human capability under the assumption that future models will handle remaining gaps. This logic misses something basic: building organizational capability takes years. Adopting new tools takes weeks. Once foundational expertise is lost, rebuilding it is far more costly than maintaining it incrementally.

From a strategic perspective, resilience requires treating human capability as a complement to AI, not a temporary bridge. Organizations that succeed over the long term will be those that integrate AI deliberately while preserving the conditions under which engineers continue to develop judgment, intuition, and independent reasoning. The goal is not to slow progress, but to ensure that acceleration does not come at the cost of fragility.

Limitations

This chapter reflects a particular slice of the industry: larger product organizations with established platforms, high deployment frequency, and strong pressure to deliver. Smaller teams, research groups, or organizations with heavy regulatory constraints will experience some of these dynamics differently. In addition, most of the examples here come from full stack engineering rather than embedded or safety-critical systems, where AI adoption is slower and guardrails are tighter. The patterns described should be read as signals, not universal laws. They are meant to help managers ask better questions about their own environment, then adapt the frameworks and strategies to fit the constraints they face.

The regulatory and legal landscape around AI-generated code is evolving. Questions of code ownership, liability for AI-introduced bugs, and compliance with data privacy regulations (GDPR, CCPA) remain unsettled in many jurisdictions. These considerations fall outside this chapter's scope of managerial practice. Engineering leaders should monitor developments in partnership with their legal and compliance teams.

Similarly, economic impacts at the market level merit separate analysis by economists and workforce researchers. Shifts in offshore development models, changes in salary structures for different experience levels, the viability of coding bootcamps as a talent pipeline. These are real questions, but they are not questions an individual engineering manager can answer or control.

For safety-critical systems (medical devices, automotive, aerospace, financial infrastructure), AI adoption follows different risk calculus. Regulatory requirements, formal verification needs, and liability exposure mean AI-assisted development in these domains requires specialized treatment beyond this chapter's scope. Managers in safety-critical contexts should treat the frameworks here as starting points requiring significant adaptation to their stricter validation requirements.

This chapter focuses on what individual managers can control: their team's capability development and organizational resilience within their sphere of influence.

CONCLUSION

Engineering managers occupy a central position in navigating an AI-driven transition for which established playbooks do not yet exist. The future configuration of engineering capability will be shaped by present decisions about which skills to cultivate, which to automate, and which to preserve despite short-term efficiency arguments.

This role entails safeguarding foundational skills that support robustness under failure, embracing AI fluency as a non-optional competency, fostering meta-skills and critical thinking that current AI systems cannot replicate reliably, and supporting engineers through adaptation.

Although AI's precise trajectory remains uncertain, several expectations are reasonable. Engineers combining strong fundamentals with AI collaboration outperform peers with only one dimension. Teams integrating AI thoughtfully while maintaining human capabilities prove more resilient than those embracing or resisting it wholesale. Meta-skills such as systems thinking, problem decomposition, and communication will increase in importance as AI mediates more implementation, with adaptability outweighing specific technical proficiency.

Increased AI adoption risks eroding engineering depth, making velocity-focused optimization potentially counterproductive. A phased approach incorporating AI incrementally while protecting sound judgment habits offers greater durability than abrupt overhauls.

One thing that does not get said enough in discussions about AI and engineering is that the managers navigating this transition did not sign up for it on a clear timeline. The shift from AI as a niche tool to AI as a default workflow happened in roughly three years. That is faster than most organizations update their hiring criteria, their career ladders, or their onboarding programs. The gap between how fast the tools moved and how fast the organizational systems responded is where most of the problems described in this chapter live.

This is not a failure of foresight. It is a structural problem. The organizations that managed previous technology shifts, desktop to web, monolithic to distributed, on premises to cloud, had more time. The skills being automated now are closer to core engineering identity than any previous shift. Writing code is not a peripheral skill that got absorbed into a framework. It is what many engineers were hired to do and what they spent years getting good at. Asking them to redefine what they are valuable for, on a compressed timeline, while also delivering against quarterly goals, is a significant ask.

The managers who navigate this well are not the ones with the clearest framework. They are the ones who take the human dimension seriously alongside the technical one. They make space for engineers to say "I am not sure where I fit in this new environment" without that being treated as a performance problem. They invest in capability deliberately, even when the short-term incentives push toward throughput. And they are honest with their teams about what is changing, what is uncertain, and what the organization is still figuring out. That honesty is not a soft skill. In a transition this fast, it is a precondition for keeping good engineers from walking out the door.

This transition also represents software engineering's largest productivity inflection point in decades. Successfully adapting engineers become substantially more capable, enabling teams to accomplish previously infeasible work. Those best positioned combine foundational grounding, AI fluency, meta-skill strength, and learning agility. Success will belong not to the most aggressive adopters or firmest resisters, but to those integrating AI deliberately while preserving engineers core strengths: curiosity, critical judgment, and capacity for novel problem-solving.

AI DISCLOSURE STATEMENT

Grammarly and Claude were used solely for grammar, spelling, and readability improvements. No AI tools were used to create, generate, or contribute to the scholarly content of this chapter.

REFERENCES

Barke, S., James, M. B., & Polikarpova, N. (2023). Grounded Copilot: How programmers interact with code-generating models. Proceedings of the ACM on Programming Languages, 7(OOPSLA1), 85-111. DOI: 10.1145/3586030

Braverman, H. (1974). *Labor and monopoly capital: The degradation of work in the twentieth century*. Monthly Review Press. DOI: 10.14452/MR-026-03-1974-07_1

Denny, P., Kumar, V., & Giacaman, N. (2023). Conversing with Copilot: Exploring prompt engineering for solving CS1 problems using natural language. In *Proceedings of the 54th ACM Technical Symposium on Computer Science Education* V. 1 (pp. 1136-1142). Association for Computing Machinery. DOI: 10.1145/3545945.3569823

GitHub. (2022, September 7). Research: Quantifying GitHub Copilot's impact on developer productivity and happiness. *GitHub Blog*. https://github.blog/2022-09-07-research-quantifying-github-copilots-impact-on-developer-productivity-and-happiness

Prather, J., Denny, P., Leinonen, J., Becker, B. A., Albluwi, I., Craig, M., Keuning, H., Kiesler, N., Kohn, T., Luxton-Reilly, A., MacNeil, S., Petersen, A., Pettit, R., Reeves, B. N., & Savelka, J. (2023). The robots are here: Navigating the generative AI revolution in computing education. Proceedings of the 55th ACM Technical Symposium on Computer Science Education V. 1 (SIGCSE 2024). ACM.DOI: 10.1145/3623762.3633499

Vaithilingam, P., Zhang, T., & Glassman, E. L. (2022). Expectation vs. experience: Evaluating the usability of code generation tools powered by large language models. In *CHI Conference on Human Factors in Computing Systems Extended Abstracts* (pp. 1–7). Association for Computing Machinery. DOI: 10.1145/3491101.3519665

ADDITIONAL READING

Davenport, T. H., & Mittal, N. (2023). *All in on AI: How smart companies win big with artificial intelligence*. Harvard Business Review Press.

Ford, M. (2021). *Rule of the robots: How artificial intelligence will transform everything*. Basic Books.

Karpathy, A. (2017, November 11). Software 2.0. *Medium*. https://karpathy.medium.com/software-2-0-a64152b37c35

Molick, E. (2024). *Co-intelligence: Living and working with AI*. Portfolio/Penguin.

Sculley, D., Holt, G., Golovin, D., Davydov, E., Phillips, T., Ebner, D., & Young, M. (2015). Hidden technical debt in machine learning systems. In *Advances in Neural Information Processing Systems* (Vol. 28).

KEY TERMS AND DEFINITIONS

AI-Assisted Development: A software engineering workflow in which AI tools such as GitHub Copilot or ChatGPT are used to generate, explain, debug, or optimize code, accelerating development while changing the nature of the skills engineers apply.

AI Output Validation: The critical evaluation of AI-generated code to determine correctness, security, and appropriateness before integration into a codebase, requiring independent engineering judgment.

Augmentable Skills: Engineering capabilities that are enhanced through human-AI collaboration, where human judgment and AI generation together produce better results than either could independently.

Commoditized Skills: Technical capabilities that AI performs reliably enough that continued investment in developing them delivers diminishing returns relative to other areas of growth.

Deskilling: The gradual erosion of technical skills as automation absorbs tasks that previously required human expertise, reducing the depth of understanding needed to perform a given role.

Deskilling-Reskilling Paradox: The simultaneous occurrence of skill erosion in foundational technical areas and skill development in AI collaboration competencies within the same engineering workforce.

Human-Unique Skills: Engineering capabilities where humans maintain clear advantages over current AI, including system architecture, ethical judgment, cross-domain synthesis, and organizational context understanding.

Meta-Skills: Transferable capabilities that apply across technologies and problems, including systems thinking, problem decomposition, cross-domain synthesis, and strategic judgment.

Prompt Engineering: The practice of crafting inputs to AI language models to produce accurate, useful, and contextually appropriate outputs; a hybrid technical and communication skill specific to AI-augmented work.

Reskilling: Developing new capabilities to adapt to changed technological conditions, particularly skills that complement or manage new automation rather than competing with it directly.

Compilation of References

Abrahão, S., Grundy, J., Pezzè, M., Storey, M.-A., & Tamburri, D. A. (2025). Software Engineering by and for Humans in an AI Era. *ACM Transactions on Software Engineering and Methodology*, *34*(5), 1–46. DOI: 10.1145/3715111

Ahmad, A., Waseem, M., Liang, P., Fahmideh, M., Aktar, M. S., & Mikkonen, T. (2023, June). Towards human-bot collaborative software architecting with chatgpt. In *Proceedings of the 27th international conference on evaluation and assessment in software engineering* (pp. 279-285). DOI: 10.1145/3593434.3593468

Akter, S., McCarthy, G., Sajib, S., Michael, K., Dwivedi, Y. K., D'Ambra, J., & Shen, K. N. (2021). Algorithmic Bias in Data-Driven Innovation in the Age of AI. *International Journal of Information Management*, *60*, 102387. DOI: 10.1016/j.ijinfomgt.2021.102387

Alanazi, M., Soh, B., Samra, H., & Li, A. (2025). The Influence of Artificial Intelligence Tools on Learning Outcomes in Computer Programming: A Systematic Review and Meta-Analysis. *Computers*, *14*(5), 185. DOI: 10.3390/computers14050185

Albaroudi, E., Mansouri, T., Hatamleh, M., Elbehairy, M., & Alameer, A. (2025). Generative AI and the Future of Software Engineering in Saudi Arabia: Governance, Innovation, and Workforce Transformation. *International Journal of Theoretical and Applied Computational Intelligence.*, *2025*, 84–105.

Alenezi, M., & Akour, M. (2025). AI-Driven Innovations in Software Engineering: A Review of Current Practices and Future Directions. *Applied Sciences (Basel, Switzerland)*, *15*(3), 1344. Advance online publication. DOI: 10.3390/app15031344

Allamanis, M., Barr, E. T., Devanbu, P., & Sutton, C. (2018). A survey of machine learning for big code and naturalness. *ACM Computing Surveys*, *51*(4), 1–37. DOI: 10.1145/3212695

Almer, J. (2022). Deskilling as an effect of AI: A group of students' attitudes towards AI and their worries about deskilling.

Amalfitano, D., Metzger, A., Autili, M., Fulcini, T., Hey, T., Keim, J., Pelliccione, P., Scotti, V., Koziolek, A., Mirandola, R., & Vogelsang, A. (2026). A Research Roadmap for Augmenting Software Engineering Processes and Software Products with Generative AI. *ACM Transactions on Software Engineering and Methodology, 3788879*, 3788879. Advance online publication. DOI: 10.1145/3788879

Amershi, S., Begel, A., Bird, C., DeLine, R., Gall, H., Kamar, E., Nagappan, N., Nushi, B., & Zimmermann, T. (2019). Software engineering for machine learning: A case study. *Proceedings of the 41st International Conference on Software Engineering: Software Engineering in Practice (ICSE-SEIP)*, 291–300. DOI: 10.1109/ICSE-SEIP.2019.00042

Arboh, F., Zhu, X., Atingabili, S., Yeboah, E., & Drokow, E. K. (2025). From fear to empowerment: The impact of employees AI awareness on workplace well-being–a new insight from the JD–R model. *Journal of Health Organization and Management*. Advance online publication. DOI: 10.1108/JHOM-06-2024-0229 PMID: 39875341

Asiedu, E., & Tenakwah, E. S. (2025). Future-proofing your workforce: Upskilling and reskilling as HR's top priorities. *Strategic HR Review, 24*(4), 169–173. Advance online publication. DOI: 10.1108/SHR-01-2025-0008

Aslam, M. (2024). *A User Centric Approach to Explainable Artificial Intelligence in Industry*. Loughborough University.

Aspra, N. O., & Chong, C. H. (2025, May). Developing an AI-Driven NC Programming Assistant: A Productive Failure Approach in CNC Education. In *2025 Systems and Information Engineering Design Symposium (SIEDS)* (pp. 438-443). IEEE. DOI: 10.1109/SIEDS65500.2025.11021219

Asrifan, A., Said, U. M. R., Jakob, J. C., & Wanci, R. (2025). AI literacy: foundations, importance, and broader implications. In *Transforming vocational education and training using AI* (pp. 17–48). IGI Global Scientific Publishing.

Asvestopoulou, E. (2024). AI revolution: Trust and the perceived threat to job security (Master's thesis). http://hdl.handle.net/10071/33859

Autor, D. H. (2015). Why are there still so many jobs? The history and future of workplace automation. *The Journal of Economic Perspectives, 29*(3), 3–30. DOI: 10.1257/jep.29.3.3

Avila-Chauvet, L., Mejía, D., & Acosta Quiroz, C. (2023). CHATGPT as a support tool for online behavioral task programming. *SSRN*. Obtenido de https://ssrn.com/abstract=4329020

Ayyagari, R., Grover, V., & Purvis, R. (2011). Technostress: Technological antecedents and implications. *Management Information Systems Quarterly, 35*(4), 831–858. DOI: 10.2307/41409963

Bainbridge, L. (1983). Ironies of automation. *Automatica, 19*(6), 775–779. DOI: 10.1016/0005-1098(83)90046-8

Baqar, M., & Khanda, R. (2024). The Future of Software Testing: AI-Powered Test Case Generation and Validation, 1424, arXiv preprint arXiv.05808.

Barke, S., James, M., & Polikarpova, N. (2023). Grounded copilot: How programmers interact with code-generating models. *Proceedings of the ACM on Programming Languages, 7*(OOPSLA1), 85-111. DOI: 10.1145/3586030

Battisti, M., Del Gatto, M., & Parmeter, C. (2022). Skill Biased Technical Change and Labor Market. Available at *SSRN* 3977544. DOI: 10.1016/j.jedc.2022.104428

Becker, B. A., Craig, M., Denny, P., Keuning, H., Kiesler, N., Leinonen, J., ... & Quille, K. (2023). Generative ai in introductory programming. Computer Science Curricula, 438-439.

Becker, C., Walker, D., & McCord, C. (2017). Intertemporal Choice: Decision Making and Time in Software Engineering. *2017 IEEE/ACM 10th International Workshop on Cooperative and Human Aspects of Software Engineering (CHASE)*, 23–29. DOI: 10.1109/CHASE.2017.6

Becker, B. A., Denny, P., Finnie-Ansley, J., Luxton-Reilly, A., Prather, J., & Santos, E. A. (2023). Programming is hard—or at least it used to be. *Proceedings of the 54th ACM Technical Symposium on Computer Science Education*, 500–506. DOI: 10.1145/3545945.3569759

Bender, E. M., Gebru, T., McMillan-Major, A., & Shmitchell, S. (2021). On the dangers of stochastic parrots: Can language models be too big? *Proceedings of the 2021 ACM Conference on Fairness, Accountability, and Transparency*, 610–623. DOI: 10.1145/3442188.3445922

Benraouane, S. A. (2024). AI management system certification according to the ISO/ IEC 42001 standard. In *Productivity Press eBooks*. DOI: 10.4324/9781003463979

Berretta, S., Tausch, A., Ontrup, G., Gilles, B., Peifer, C., & Kluge, A. (2023). Defining human-AI teaming the human-centered way: A scoping review and network analysis. *Frontiers in Artificial Intelligence, 6*, 1250725. Advance online publication. DOI: 10.3389/frai.2023.1250725 PMID: 37841234

Bhalla, J. S., & Jodhka, M. K. (2025). Leveraging large language models in the software development lifecycle: Opportunities and challenges. *International Journal of Advanced Computer Science and Applications, 16*(11). Advance online publication. DOI: 10.14569/IJACSA.2025.0161105

Biderman, S., Schoelkopf, H., Anthony, Q., Bradley, H., O'Brien, K., Hallahan, E., & Belrose, N. (2023). Pythia: A suite for analyzing large language models across training and scaling. *Proceedings of the 40th International Conference on Machine Learning*, 2397–2430. DOI: 10.48550/arXiv.2304.01373

Bird, C., Menzies, T., & Zimmermann, T. (Eds.). (2015). *The art and science of analyzing software data*. Elsevier.

Bjerg, J. (2024). *The Early-Career Professional's Guide to Generative AI*. Apress. DOI: 10.1007/979-8-8688-0456-4

Bodea, C. N., Paparic, M., Mogos, R. I., & Dascalu, M. I. (2024). Artificial intelligence adoption in the workplace and its impact on the upskilling and reskilling strategies. *Amfiteatru Economic, 26*(65), 126–144. DOI: 10.24818/EA/2024/65/126

Boehm, B. (2011). Some Future Software Engineering Opportunities and Challenges. In Nanz, S. (Ed.), *The Future of Software Engineering* (pp. 1–32). Springer Berlin Heidelberg., DOI: 10.1007/978-3-642-15187-3_1

Braverman, H. (1998). Labor and monopoly capital: The degradation of work in the twentieth century. nyu Press.

Braverman, H. (1974). *Labor and monopoly capital*. Monthly Review Press. DOI: 10.14452/MR-026-03-1974-07_1

Brod, C. (1984). Technostress. Addison-Wesley. https://cir.nii.ac.jp/crid/1970023484968949634

Brown, T. B., Mann, B., Ryder, N., Subbiah, M., Kaplan, J., Dhariwal, P., Neelakantan, A., Shyam, P., Sastry, G., Askell, A., Agarwal, S., Herbert-Voss, A., Krueger, G., Henighan, T., Child, R., Ramesh, A., Ziegler, D. M., Wu, J., Winter, C., & Amodei, D. (2020). Language models are few-shot learners. *Advances in Neural Information Processing Systems, 33*, 1877–1901. DOI: 10.48550/arXiv.2005.14165

Brynjolfsson, E., & McAfee, A. (2014). The second machine age: Work, progress, and prosperity in a time of brilliant technologies. WW Norton & company.

Brynjolfsson, E., & Mitchell, T. (2017). What can machine learning do? Workforce implications. *Science, 358*(6370), 1530–1534. DOI: 10.1126/science.aap8062 PMID: 29269459

Bughin, J. R. (2024). Corporate Ai Play and Skill-Biased Ai Change. Available at *SSRN* 4852540. DOI: 10.2139/ssrn.4852540

Burnett, M. M., & Myers, B. A. (2014). Future of end-user software engineering: Beyond the silos. *Future of Software Engineering Proceedings*, 201–211. DOI: 10.1145/2593882.2593896

Buschmann, F., Henney, K., & Schmidt, D. C. (2007). *Pattern-oriented software architecture: A pattern language for distributed computing* (Vol. 4). John Wiley & Sons.

Cavestro, W. (2024). Automation, new technology and work content. In *The Transformation of Work?* (pp. 219–234). Routledge. DOI: 10.4324/9781003502913-11

Chaker, B., & Damak, C. (2024). Navigating tomorrow: Strategies for effective workforce reskilling. In *Reskilling the Workforce for Technological Advancement* (pp. 62–81). IGI Global Scientific Publishing., DOI: 10.4018/979-8-3693-0612-3.ch004

Chattopadhyay, S., Nelson, N., Au, A., Morales, N., Sanchez, C., Pandita, R., & Sarma, A. (2022). Cognitive biases in software development. *Communications of the ACM*, *65*(4), 115–122. DOI: 10.1145/3517217

Chen, M., Tworek, J., Jun, H., Yuan, Q., Pinto, H. P. D. O., Kaplan, J., . . . Zaremba, W. (2021). Evaluating large language models trained on code. arXiv preprint arXiv:2107.03374.

Cheng, Z., & Jin, X. (2024). The Impact of Job Anxiety Caused by Artificial Intelligence Substitution on Organizational Members' Turnover Intention: The Mediating Role of Job Insecurity and the Moderating Effect of Job Uncertainty. : , 38(3), 67-103.https://www.dbpia.co.kr/Journal/articleDetail?nodeId=NODE12011895

Cheng, R., Wang, R., Zimmermann, T., & Ford, D. (2024). "It would work for me too": How online communities shape software developers' trust in AI-powered code generation tools. *ACM Transactions on Interactive Intelligent Systems*, *14*(2), 1–39. DOI: 10.1145/3651990

Cloudin, S., Priya, R. S., Prabhu, G. A., Ruba, M., Joel, R., & Vanitha, R. (2026). AI-Enhanced Predictive Analytics and Reliability Management for Wind Turbine Maintenance. In AI-Powered Analysis, Modeling, and Monitoring of Wind Energy Systems (pp. 191-218). IGI Global Scientific Publishing.

Corrigan, J. M. (2012). Augmented intelligence—The new AI — Unleashing human capabilities in knowledge work. *2012 34th International Conference on Software Engineering (ICSE)*, 1285–1288. DOI: 10.1109/ICSE.2012.6227098

Crowston, K., & Bolici, F. (2025). Deskilling and upskilling with AI Systems. *nformation Research an International Electronic Journal, 30*(iConf), 1009-1023. DOI: 10.47989/ir30iConf47143

Cruz, L., Fernandes, J. P., Kirkeby, M. H., Martínez-Fernández, S., Sallou, J., Anwar, H., Barba Roque, E., Bogner, J., Castaño, J., Castor, F., Chasmawala, A., Cunha, S., Feitosa, D., González, A., Jedlitschka, A., Lago, P., Muccini, H., Oprescu, A., Rani, P., & Yamshchikov, I. P. (2025). Greening ai-enabled systems with software engineering: A research agenda for environmentally sustainable ai practices. *Software Engineering Notes*, *50*(3), 14–23. DOI: 10.1145/3743095.3743099

Cunha, J. A. O. G., Moura, H. P., & Vasconcellos, F. J. S. (2016). Decision-making in Software Project Management: A Systematic Literature Review. *Procedia Computer Science, 100*, 947–954. DOI: 10.1016/j.procs.2016.09.255

Daigle, K. (2024). *Survey: The AI wave continues to grow on software development teams*. Obtenido de https://github.blog/author/kdaigle/

Dandotiya, M., Goyal, N. K., Yadav, P., Sankhla, K., & Kumari, M. (2026). GENALYTICS: A Deep Dive Into Real-Time Insights via Generative AI. In Elbaghazaoui, B., Amnai, M., & Gherabi, N. (Eds.), *Generative AI-Powered Data Architectures: From Governance to Autonomous Analytics* (pp. 105–134). IGI Global Scientific Publishing., DOI: 10.4018/979-8-3373-5616-7.ch005

Daun, M., & Brings, J. (2023, June). How ChatGPT will change software engineering education. In *Proceedings of the 2023 Conference on Innovation and Technology in Computer Science Education* V. 1 (pp. 110-116). DOI: 10.1145/3587102.3588815

Davenport, T. H., & Kirby, J. (2016). *Only humans need apply: Winners and losers in the age of smart machines* (Vol. 1). Harper Business.

Davenport, T. H., & Ronanki, R. (2018). Artificial intelligence for the real world. *Harvard Business Review*, *96*(1), 108–116.

De Witte, H. (2005). Job insecurity: Review of the international literature on definitions, prevalence, antecedents and consequences. *SA Journal of Industrial Psychology*, *31*(4), 1–6. https://hdl.handle.net/10520/EJC89073. DOI: 10.4102/sajip.v31i4.200

Demerouti, E., & Bakker, A. B. (2022). Job demands-resources theory in times of crises: New propositions. *Organizational Psychology Review*, *13*(3), 209–236. DOI: 10.1177/20413866221135022

Deming, C., Khair, M. A., Mallipeddi, S. R., & Varghese, A. (2021). Software Testing in the Era of AI: Leveraging Machine Learning and Automation for Efficient Quality Assurance. *Asian Journal of Applied Science and Engineering.*, *10*(1), 66–76. DOI: 10.18034/ajase.v10i1.88

Denny, P., Kumar, V., & Giacaman, N. (2023). Conversing with Copilot: Exploring prompt engineering for solving CS1 problems using natural language. *Proceedings of the 54th ACM Technical Symposium on Computer Science Education*, 1136–1142. DOI: 10.1145/3545945.3569823

Denny, P., Prather, J., Becker, B. A., Finnie-Ansley, J., Hellas, A., Leinonen, J., Luxton-Reilly, A., Reeves, B. N., Santos, E. A., & Sarsa, S. (2024). Computing education in the era of generative AI. *Communications of the ACM*, *67*(2), 56–67. DOI: 10.1145/3624720

Deshmukh, A., Patil, D. S., Shyam Mohan, J. S., Balamurugan, G., & Tyagi, A. K. (2023). Transforming Next Generation-Based Artificial Intelligence for Software Development: Current Status, Issues, Challenges, and Future Opportunities. In Ortiz-Rodriguez, F., Tiwari, S., Hernández-González, L. M., & Tiburcio, A. (Eds.), (pp. 30–66). Advances in Logistics, Operations, and Management Science. IGI Global., DOI: 10.4018/978-1-6684-8088-5.ch003

Dhanushya, J., Ruba, M., Ponkarthika, M., Soundarya, B., Sakthi Priya, V., Dhanushri, S., & Harikrishnan, S. (2025, April). AI-Powered Multipurpose Agrobot for Precision Farming: Crop Health Management, Fertilizer Recommendation and Yield Prediction. In *2025 International Conference on Recent Advances in Electrical, Electronics, Ubiquitous Communication, and Computational Intelligence (RAEEUCCI)* (pp. 1-6). IEEE.

Diaz Alfaro, G., Fiore, S. M., & Oden, K. (2024, September). Externalized and Extended Cognition: Cognitive Offloading for Human-Machine Teaming. [). Sage CA: Los Angeles, CA: SAGE Publications.]. *Proceedings of the Human Factors and Ergonomics Society Annual Meeting*, *68*(1), 290–293. DOI: 10.1177/10711813241275506

Duan, Y., Ong, V. K., Xu, M., & Mathews, B. (2012). Supporting decision making process with "ideal" software agents – What do business executives want? *Expert Systems with Applications*, *39*(5), 5534–5547. DOI: 10.1016/j.eswa.2011.11.065

Dwivedi, Y. K., Hughes, D. L., Ismagilova, E., Aarts, G., Coombs, C., Crick, T., Duan, Y., Dwivedi, R., Edwards, J., Eirug, A., Galanos, V., Ilavarasan, P. V., Janssen, M., Jones, P., Kar, A. K., Kizgin, H., Kronemann, B., Lal, B., Lucini, B., & Williams, M. D. (2021). Artificial intelligence (AI): Multidisciplinary perspectives on emerging challenges, opportunities, and agenda for research, practice and policy. *International Journal of Information Management*, *57*, 101994. DOI: 10.1016/j.ijinfomgt.2019.08.002

Ellahham, S., Ellahham, N., & Simsekler, M. C. E. (2020). Application of Artificial Intelligence in the Health Care Safety Context: Opportunities and Challenges. *American Journal of Medical Quality*, *35*(4), 341–348. DOI: 10.1177/1062860619878515 PMID: 31581790

Endsley, M. R. (2017). From here to autonomy: Lessons learned from human–automation research. *Human Factors*, *59*(1), 5–27. DOI: 10.1177/0018720816681350 PMID: 28146676

Engin, Z. (2025). Human-AI Governance (HAIG): A Trust-Utility Approach. arXiv preprint arXiv:2505.01651.

Ersanlı, C. Y., Çelik, F., Barjesteh, H., Duran, V., & Manoochehrzadeh, M. (2025). A review of global reskilling and upskilling initiatives in the age of AI. *AI and Ethics*, *5*(6), 1–10. DOI: 10.1007/s43681-025-00767-9

EU High-Level Expert Group on AI. (2020). *Ethics guidelines for trustworthy AI.* European Commission.

Evans, R. M. (2022). Perceived benefits of upskilling and reskilling by persons who are among the employed, underemployed, and unemployed.https://digitalcommons.acu.edu/etd/482

Fakhoury, S., Naik, A., Sakkas, G., Chakraborty, S., & Lahiri, S. K. (2024). LLM-based test-driven interactive code generation: User study and empirical evaluation. *IEEE Transactions on Software Engineering*, *50*(9), 2254–2268. DOI: 10.1109/TSE.2024.3428972

Faraj, S., Pachidi, S., & Sayegh, K. (2018). Applied extensively 2020–2024). Working and organizing in the age of the learning algorithm. *Information and Organization*, *28*(1), 62–70. DOI: 10.1016/j.infoandorg.2018.02.005

Farhan, A. (2023). The impact of artificial intelligence on human workers. *Journal of Communication Education*, *17*(2), 93–104. DOI: 10.58217/joce-ip.v17i2.350

Farooqi, A., Das, D., Tripathi, M., Dutta, R., Goyal, N. K., & Sheikh, M. F. (2026). Navigating Ethical Frontiers in AI-Driven Geriatric Care. In Stolakis, K., & Efthymiou, I. (Eds.), *AI for Geriatric Care in an Aging Society: Ethical, Clinical, and Policy Challenges* (pp. 243–266). IGI Global Scientific Publishing., DOI: 10.4018/979-8-3373-5462-0.ch009

Felemban, H., Sohail, M., & Ruikar, K. (2024). Exploring the readiness of organisations to adopt artificial intelligence. *Buildings (Basel, Switzerland)*, *14*(8), 2460. DOI: 10.3390/buildings14082460

Ferdman, A. (2025). AI deskilling is a structural problem. *AI & Society*, •••, 1–13. DOI: 10.1007/s00146-025-02686-z

Ferrari, A., Zhao, L., & Alhoshan, W. (2021). NLP for Requirements Engineering: Tasks, Techniques, Tools, and Technologies, 2021 IEEE/ACM 43rd International Conference on Software Engineering: Companion Proceedings (ICSE-Companion), IEEE.

Finnie-Ansley, J., Denny, P., Becker, B. A., Luxton-Reilly, A., & Prather, J. (2022). The robots are coming: Exploring the implications of OpenAI Codex on introductory programming. *Australasian Computing Education Conference*, 10–19. DOI: 10.1145/3511861.3511863

Fitts, P. M. (1951). *Human engineering for an effective air-navigation and traffic-control system*. National Research Council.

Foerster, J. N., Assael, Y. M., de Freitas, N., & Whiteson, S. (2018). Counterfactual multi-agent policy gradients. In *Proceedings of the Thirty-Second AAAI Conference on Artificial Intelligence* (pp. 2974– 2982).

Ford, D., Zimmermann, T., Bird, C., & Nagappan, N. (2017). Characterizing software engineering work with personas based on knowledge worker actions. *Proceedings of the 2017 ACM/IEEE International Symposium on Empirical Software Engineering and Measurement (ESEM)*, 394–403. DOI: 10.1109/ESEM.2017.54

Fui-Hoon Nah, F., Zheng, R., Cai, J., Siau, K., & Chen, L. (2023). Generative AI and ChatGPT: Applications, challenges, and AI-human collaboration. Journal of information technology case and application research, 25(3), 277-304.

Gadekar, S. (2024). How AI-Powered Tools Like GitHub Copilot Are Transforming Software Development, https://dev.to/gadekar_sachin/-how-ai-powered-tools-like-github-copilot-are-transforming-software-development-1h23, 24 February 2025.

Galanakis, M. D., & Tsitouri, E. (2022). Positive psychology in the working environment. Job demands-resources theory, work engagement and burnout: A systematic literature review. *Frontiers in Psychology*, *13*, 1022102. DOI: 10.3389/fpsyg.2022.1022102 PMID: 36204770

Gardella, N., Pettit, R., & Riggs, S. L. (2024). Performance, workload, emotion, and self-efficacy of novice programmers using AI code generation. In *Proceedings of the 2024 Innovation and Technology in Computer Science Education* V. 1 (pp. 290–296). ACM. DOI: 10.1145/3649217.3653615

Gausen, A., Mitra, B., & Lindley, S. (2024, June). A framework for exploring the consequences of AI-mediated enterprise knowledge access and identifying risks to workers. In *Proceedings of the 2024 ACM conference on fairness, accountability, and transparency* (pp. 207-220). DOI: 10.1145/3630106.3658900

Gemlau, K. B., Hasseln, H. V., & Ernst, R. (2022, October). Industry-track: System-level logical execution time for automotive software development. In *2022 International Conference on Embedded Software (EMSOFT)* (pp. 21-23). IEEE. DOI: 10.1109/EMSOFT55006.2022.00017

George, A. S. (2024). Artificial intelligence and the future of work: Job shifting not job loss. *Partners Universal Innovative Research Publication*, *2*(2), 17–37. DOI: 10.5281/zenodo.10936490

Gerlich, M. (2025). AI tools in society: Impacts on cognitive offloading and the future of critical thinking. *Societies (Basel, Switzerland)*, *15*(1), 6. Advance online publication. DOI: 10.3390/soc15010006

GitHub. (2022, September 7). Research: Quantifying GitHub Copilot's impact on developer productivity and happiness. *GitHub Blog*. https://github.blog/2022-09-07-research-quantifying-github-copilots-impact-on-developer-productivity-and-happiness

Giuntella, O., König, J., & Stella, L. (2023). Artificial intelligence and workers' well-being (No. 16485). IZA Discussion Papers. https://hdl.handle.net/10419/282612

Goel, A., Dede, C., Garn, M., & Ou, C. (2024). AI-ALOE: AI for reskilling, upskilling, and workforce development. *AI Magazine*, *45*(1), 77–82. DOI: 10.1002/aaai.12157

Gowthaman, N., Ruba, M., Aswath, S., Hemavarshni, S. N., Bragadeshwaran, R., & Nithish, S. J. (2025, November). Iot Integrated Solution For Smart Vertical Crop Cultivation. In 2025 IEEE 7th International Conference on Computing, Communication and Automation (ICCCA) (pp. 1-6). IEEE.

Grimmelikhuijsen, S. (2023). Explaining why the computer says no: Algorithmic transparency affects the perceived trustworthiness of automated decision-making. *Public Administration Review*, *83*(2), 241–262. DOI: 10.1111/puar.13483

Gruenewald, H., & Mueller, M. (2025). Challenges and Opportunities in Reskilling and Upskilling. In *Reskilling and Upskilling in a Globalized Economy. Future of Business and Finance*. Springer., DOI: 10.1007/978-3-658-48384-5_7

Hackman, J. R., & Oldham, G. R. (1976). Motivation through the design of work: Test of a theory. *Organizational Behavior and Human Performance*, *16*(2), 250–279. DOI: 10.1016/0030-5073(76)90016-7

Haefner, N., Parida, V., Gassmann, O., & Wincent, J. (2023). Implementing and Scaling Artificial Intelligence: A Review, Framework, and Research Agenda. *Technological Forecasting and Social Change*, *197*, 122878. DOI: 10.1016/j.techfore.2023.122878

Hajam, A. A., & John, A. S. (2024). Reskilling and Upskilling Strategies in the Era of Automation: A Human-Centered Approach to Workforce Development. *International Journal of Multidisciplinary Research Transactions*, *6*(10). Advance online publication. DOI: 10.5281/zenodo.13912971

Hancock, P. A., Billings, D. R., Schaefer, K. E., Chen, J. Y. C., de Visser, E. J., & Parasuraman, R. (2011). A meta-analysis of factors affecting trust in human–robot interaction. *Human Factors*, *53*(5), 517–527. DOI: 10.1177/0018720811417254 PMID: 22046724

Harris, D. (2017). *Decision Making in Aviation* (D. Harris & W.-C. Li, Eds.; 1st ed.). Routledge. DOI: 10.4324/9781315095080

Hasan, M., Haque, M. A., Nishat, S. S., & Hossain, M. M. (2024). Upskilling and reskilling in a rapidly changing job market: Strategies for organizations to maintain workforce agility and adaptability. *European Journal of Business and Management Research*, *9*(6), 118–126. DOI: 10.24018/ejbmr.2024.9.6.2502

Hawthorne, M. J., & Perry, D. E. (2005). Software engineering education in the era of outsourcing, distributed development, and open source software: Challenges and opportunities. *Proceedings of the 27th International Conference on Software Engineering - ICSE '05*, 643. DOI: 10.1145/1062455.1062581

Heaton, D., & Carver, J. C. (2015). Claims about the use of software engineering practices in science: A systematic literature review. *Information and Software Technology*, *67*, 207–219. DOI: 10.1016/j.infsof.2015.07.011

Heroux, M. A. (2022). Research Software Science: Expanding the Impact of Research Software Engineering. *Computing in Science & Engineering*, *24*(6), 22–27. DOI: 10.1109/MCSE.2023.3260475

Hicks, C. M., Lee, C. S., & Foster-Marks, K. (2024). The new developer: AI skill threat, identity change & developer thriving in the transition to AI-assisted software development.

Hobot, Z. (2024). *Navigating the Artificial Intelligence Revolution: Trust*. Fear, and Job Security in the Modern Workplace.

Hoeschl, M. B., Bueno, T. C. D., & Hoeschl, H. C. (2017). Fourth Industrial Revolution and the future of Engineering: Could Robots Replace Human Jobs? How Ethical Recommendations can Help Engineers Rule on Artificial Intelligence. *2017 7th World Engineering Education Forum (WEEF)*, 21–26. DOI: 10.1109/WEEF.2017.8466973

Humlum, A., & Plato, P. (2025). *Reskilling and Resilience (No. w34095)*. National Bureau of Economic Research., DOI: 10.3386/w34095

Huseynova, F. (2024). Addressing Deskilling as a Result of Human-AI Augmentation in the Workplace.

Hutter, C., & Weber, E. (2023). Labour market effects of wage inequality and skill-biased technical change. *Applied Economics*, *55*(27), 3063–3084. DOI: 10.1080/00036846.2022.2108751

Hu, Y., Xu, Y., & Wu, B. (2025). A dual-pathway model of teacher-AI collaboration based on the job demands-resources theory. *Education and Information Technologies*, *30*(11), 15125–15146. DOI: 10.1007/s10639-025-13421-y

Hymel, C. The AI-Native Software Development Lifecycle: A Theoretical and Practical New Methodology, 2024, arXiv preprint arXiv.03416.

Idrisov, B., & Schlippe, T. (2024). Program code generation with generative AIs. *Algorithms*, *17*(2), 62. DOI: 10.3390/a17020062

Imai, S. (2022). Is GitHub Copilot a substitute for human pair-programming? An empirical study. In Proceedings of the ACM/IEEE 44th International Conference on Software Engineering: Companion Proceedings (pp. 319–321). ACM. DOI: 10.1109/ICSE-Companion55297.2022.9793778

Iorliam, A., & Ingio, J. A. (2024). A Comparative Analysis of Generative Artificial Intelligence Tools for Natural Language Processing. *Journal of Computing Theories and Applications.*, *1*(3), 311–325. DOI: 10.62411/jcta.9447

Irayani, I., Melvani, F. N., Azrin, A., & Mikial, M. (2025). Behavioral Theory and Organizational Culture: The Interplay of Transformational Leadership, Team Dynamics, and Motivation in Driving Change at Tridinanti University of Palembang. *The Eastasouth Management and Business*, *3*(02), 220–229. DOI: 10.58812/esmb.v3i02.375

Isaacs, W. (1999). Dialogue: The art of thinking together. Crown Business. Dietterich, T. G. (2000). Ensemble methods in machine learning. In Kittler, J., & Roli, F. (Eds.), *Multiple Classifier Systems* (pp. 1–15). Springer.

Jabłoński, M. (2025). Changes of Employees' Skill Requirements Caused by Technological Progress. In Moussa, M., & McMurray, A. (Eds.), *The Palgrave Handbook of Breakthrough Technologies in Contemporary Organisations.*, DOI: 10.1007/978-981-96-2516-1_17

Jain, H., Padmanabhan, B., Pavlou, P. A., & Raghu, T. S. (2021). Editorial for the Special Section on Humans, Algorithms, and Augmented Intelligence: The Future of Work, Organizations, and Society. *Information Systems Research*, *32*(3), 675–687. DOI: 10.1287/isre.2021.1046

Jaiswal, A., Arun, J., & Varma, A. (2022). Rebooting employees: Upskilling for artificial intelligence in multinational corporations. *International Journal of Human Resource Management*, *33*(6), 1179–1208. DOI: 10.1080/09585192.2021.1891114

Jamal, A. F., El Nemar, S., & Sakka, G. (2025). The relationship between job redesigning, reskilling and upskilling on organizational agility. *EuroMed Journal of Business*, *20*(2), 474–492. DOI: 10.1108/EMJB-10-2023-0279

Jim, J. R., Talukder, M. A. R., Malakar, P., Kabir, M. M., Nur, K., & Mridha, M. F. (2024). Recent Advancements and Challenges of NLP-Based Sentiment Analysis: A State-of-the-Art Review. *Natural Language Processing Journal.*, *6*, 100059. DOI: 10.1016/j.nlp.2024.100059

Johnson, A., Dey, S., Nguyen, H., Groth, M., Joyce, S., Tan, L., Glozier, N., & Harvey, S. B. (2020). A review and agenda for examining how technology-driven changes at work will impact workplace mental health and employee well-being. *Australian Journal of Management*, *45*(3), 402–424. DOI: 10.1177/0312896220922292

Kahr, P. K., Rooks, G., Willemsen, M. C., & Snijders, C. C. (2024). Understanding trust and reliance development in ai advice: Assessing model accuracy, model explanations, and experiences from previous interactions. *ACM Transactions on Interactive Intelligent Systems*, *14*(4), 1–30. DOI: 10.1145/3686164

Kameswaran, A., Nanthakumar, K., & Ruba, M. (2017). High performance pre-computation based self-controlled precharge-free content-addressable memory. *Journal of Electronics and Communication Systems*, *2*, 1–9.

Karekezi, P., Moore, G., & Luo, J. (2025). Human-centered AI design: Developers' perspectives. *Journal of Engineering Design*, ●●●, 1–16. DOI: 10.1080/09544828.2025.2518907

Karim, M. M., Khan, S., Van, D. H., Liu, X., Wang, C., & Qu, Q. (2025). Transforming data annotation with AI agents: A review of architectures, reasoning, applications, and impact. *Future Internet*, *17*(8), 353. Advance online publication. DOI: 10.3390/fi17080353

Kasneci, E., Seßler, K., Küchemann, S., Bannert, M., Dementieva, D., Fischer, F., Gasser, U., Groh, G., Günnemann, S., Hüllermeier, E., Krusche, S., Kutyniok, G., Michaeli, T., Nerdel, C., Pfeffer, J., Poquet, O., Sailer, M., Schmidt, A., Seidel, T., & Kasneci, G. (2023). ChatGPT for good? On opportunities and challenges of large language models for education. *Learning and Individual Differences*, *103*, 102274. Advance online publication. DOI: 10.1016/j.lindif.2023.102274

Kaur, K., Singh, P., & Kaur, P. A Review of Artificial Intelligence Techniques for Requirement Engineering, Computational Methods Data Engineering: *Proceedings of ICMDE*, 2020, Singapore, Springer, 259–278.

Kazemitabaar, M., Ye, R., Wang, X., Henley, A. Z., Denny, P., Craig, M., & Grossman, T. (2024). CodeAid: Evaluating a classroom deployment of an LLM-based programming assistant that balances student and educator needs. In Proceedings of the 2024 CHI Conference on Human Factors in Computing Systems (CHI '24, Article 650, 20 pages). ACM. DOI: 10.1145/3613904.3642773

Kazemitabaar, M., Chow, J., Ma, C. K. T., Ericson, B. J., Weintrop, D., & Grossman, T. (2023). Studying the effect of AI code generators on supporting novice learners in introductory programming. In *Proceedings of the 2023 CHI Conference on Human Factors in Computing Systems* (pp. 1–23). ACM. https://doi.org/DOI: 10.1145/3544548.3580919

Kazi, S., Khoja, S., & Daud, A. (2023). A Survey of Deep Learning Techniques for Machine Reading Comprehension. *Artificial Intelligence Review*, *56*(S2, no. S2), 2509–2569. DOI: 10.1007/s10462-023-10583-4

Keyes, C. L. M. (2002). The mental health continuum: From languishing to flourishing in life. *Journal of Health and Social Behavior*, *43*(2), 207–222. DOI: 10.2307/3090197 PMID: 12096700

Khaliq, Z., Farooq, S. U., & Khan, D. A. (2022). *Artificial Intelligence in Software Testing: Impact, Problems, Challenges and Prospect* (Version 1). arXiv. DOI: 10.48550/ARXIV.2201.05371

Khan, B., Fatima, H., Qureshi, A., Kumar, S., Hanan, A., Hussain, J., & Abdullah, S. (2023). Drawbacks of Artificial Intelligence and Their Potential Solutions in the Healthcare Sector. *Biomedical Materials & Devices, 1*(2), 731–738. DOI: 10.1007/s44174-023-00063-2 PMID: 36785697

Khan, W., Daud, A., Khan, K., Muhammad, S., & Haq, R. (2023). Exploring the Frontiers of Deep Learning and Natural Language Processing: A Comprehensive Overview of Key Challenges and Emerging Trends. *Natural Language Processing Journal., 4*, 100026. DOI: 10.1016/j.nlp.2023.100026

Khurana, A., Subramonyam, H., & Chilana, P. K. (2024). Why and when llm-based assistants can go wrong: Investigating the effectiveness of prompt-based interactions for software help-seeking. *arXiv.org*. Obtenido de /arxiv.2402.08030DOI: 10.1145/3640543.3645200

Kim, M., Zimmermann, T., & Nagappan, N. (2014). An empirical study of refactoring challenges and benefits at Microsoft. *IEEE Transactions on Software Engineering, 40*(7), 633–649. DOI: 10.1109/TSE.2014.2318734

Kinowska, H., & Sienkiewicz, Ł. J. (2023). Influence of algorithmic management practices on workplace well-being–evidence from European organisations. *Information Technology & People, 36*(8), 21–42. DOI: 10.1108/ITP-02-2022-0079

Klingbeil, A., Grützner, C., & Schreck, P. (2024). Trust and reliance on AI—An experimental study on the extent and costs of overreliance on AI. *Computers in Human Behavior, 160*, 108352. DOI: 10.1016/j.chb.2024.108352

Koripalli, M. (2025). Copilot Impact Studies: Measuring Productivity, Trust, and Skill Evolution in Enterprise Developer Teams. *International Journal of Computational and Experimental Science and Engineering, 11*(4). Advance online publication. DOI: 10.22399/ijcesen.4217

Krithika, S., Jayachandran, T., Raghapriya, N. R., Ruba, M., Janani, C., & Sathiyavathi, S. (2025, April). An Effective Denial of Service Texture Features from Malware Grayscale Image. In 2025 3rd International Conference on Artificial Intelligence and Machine Learning Applications Theme: Healthcare and Internet of Things (AIMLA) (pp. 1-7). IEEE. DOI: 10.1109/AIMLA63829.2025.11041501

Krolikowski, K. A., Bi, M., Baggott, C. M., Khorzad, R., Holl, J. L., & Kruser, J. M. (2022). Design thinking to improve healthcare delivery in the intensive care unit: Promise, pitfalls, and lessons learned. *Journal of Critical Care*, *69*, 153999. DOI: 10.1016/j.jcrc.2022.153999 PMID: 35104692

Kuhail, M. A., Mathew, S. S., Khalil, A., Khalil, A., & Shah, S. J. (2023). "Will I be replaced?" Assessing ChatGPT's effect on software development and programmer perceptions of AI tools. *arXiv.org*. Obtenido de DOI: 10.2139/ssrn.4571482

Kumar, A., Khare, V., Sharma, D., Kumar, S., Saini, V., Yadav, A., Jain, S., Rana, A., Verma, P., Meena, V., & Edubilli, A. (2025). Intuition to evidence: Measuring AI's true impact on developer productivity (arXiv:2509.19708). arXiv. https://arxiv.org/abs/2509.19708

Kumari, M., & Goyal, N. K. (2026). Artificial Intelligence in the Cryptocurrency Ecosystem: Crime Mechanisms, Detection Strategies, and Legal Perspectives. In Lin, L. (Ed.), *Innovations in Cryptocrime and Financial Fraud* (pp. 245–282). IGI Global Scientific Publishing., DOI: 10.4018/979-8-3373-0675-9.ch007

Kumari, M., Khan, S. T., Gulati, K., Sharma, P., Goyal, N. K., & Sheikh, M. F. (2026). Innovative Procedural Content Generation (PCG) Using Generative AI: A New Paradigm in Game Design. In Sousa, J., & Tavares, R. (Eds.), *Reshaping the Video Game Landscape With AI and GenAI* (pp. 205–232). IGI Global Scientific Publishing., DOI: 10.4018/979-8-3373-4637-3.ch007

Kumari, M., Kumawat, R., Dutta, R., Khan, S. T., Goyal, N. K., & Sheikh, M. F. (2026). Wireless Communication and IoT Integration in Smart Clothing. In Saxena, P., Singh, M., Singh, S., & Rashid, M. (Eds.), *Next-Generation Electronic Textiles and Conductive Materials for Smart Wearables* (pp. 195–232). IGI Global Scientific Publishing., DOI: 10.4018/979-8-3373-4287-0.ch008

Kumari, M., Kumawat, R., Tripathi, M., Suganthi, K., Goyal, N. K., & Sheikh, M. F. (2026). Blockchain for Transparency and Traceability in Supply Chains. In Khan, M., Mehmood, T., & Rao, M. (Eds.), *Maximizing Operational Efficiency at the Intersection of Supply Chain Management and Marketing* (pp. 35–64). IGI Global Scientific Publishing., DOI: 10.4018/979-8-3373-3109-6.ch002

Kusal, S., Patil, S., Choudrie, J., Kotecha, K., Vora, D., & Pappas, I. (2023). A Systematic Review of Applications of Natural Language Processing and Future Challenges With Special Emphasis in Text-Based Emotion Detection. *Artificial Intelligence Review*, *56*(12), 15129–15215. DOI: 10.1007/s10462-023-10509-0

Lacerda, G., Petrillo, F., Pimenta, M., & Guéhéneuc, Y. G. (2020). Code Smells and Refactoring: A Tertiary Systematic Review of Challenges and Observations. *Journal of Systems and Software*, *167*, 110610. DOI: 10.1016/j.jss.2020.110610

Lau, S., & Guo, P. (2023). From 'Ban it till we understand it' to 'Resistance is futile': How university programming instructors plan to adapt as more students use AI code generation and explanation tools such as ChatGPT and GitHub Copilot. *Proceedings of the 2023 ACM Conference on International Computing Education Research*, 106–121. DOI: 10.1145/3568813.3600138

Le, H. (2026). Design and Development Effective Learning AI Education: Navigating Deskilling in the Age of Intelligent Automation. In The Intersection of AI and Student Development in Learning (pp. 307-338). IGI Global Scientific Publishing. DOI: DOI: 10.4018/979-8-3373-2927-7.ch010

Le, H. (2025). The Deskilling of Software Development and the Impact of AI Chatbots on Programmers' Skills and Roles. In *Generative AI in Software Engineering* (pp. 397–426). IGI Global Scientific Publishing. DOI: 10.4018/979-8-3373-0370-3.ch013

Leon, R. D. (2023). Employees' reskilling and upskilling for industry 5.0: Selecting the best professional development programmes. *Technology in Society*, *75*, 102393. DOI: 10.1016/j.techsoc.2023.102393

Leveson, N. G. (2012). *Engineering a safer world: Systems thinking applied to safety*. MIT Press., DOI: 10.7551/mitpress/8179.001.0001

Liang, H., & Xue, Y. (2009). Avoidance of information technology threats: A theoretical perspective. *Management Information Systems Quarterly*, *33*(1), 71–90. DOI: 10.2307/20650279

Liang, J. T., Yang, C., & Myers, B. A. (2024). A large-scale survey on the usability of AI programming assistants: Successes and challenges. In *Proceedings of the 46th IEEE/ACM International Conference on Software Engineering* (pp. 616–628). ACM. DOI: 10.1145/3597503.3608128

Li, P. L., Ko, A. J., & Begel, A. (2019). What distinguishes great software engineers? *Empirical Software Engineering*, *25*(1), 322–352. DOI: 10.1007/s10664-019-09773-y

Li, S., & Li, J. Z. (2009). Hybridising human judgment, AHP, simulation and a fuzzy expert system for strategy formulation under uncertainty. *Expert Systems with Applications*, *36*(3), 5557–5564. DOI: 10.1016/j.eswa.2008.06.095

Liu, K., Reddivari, S., & Reddivari, K. (2022). Artificial Intelligence in Software Requirements Engineering: State-of-the-Art, 2022 IEEE 23rd International Conference on Information Reuse and Integration for Data Science (IRI), IEEE.

Liu, N.-C., Wang, Y.-C., & Lin, Y.-T. (2024). Employees' Adaptation to Technology Uncertainty in the Digital Era: An Exploration Through the Lens of Job Demands–Resources Theory. *IEEE Transactions on Engineering Management*, *71*, 7286–7297. DOI: 10.1109/TEM.2023.3264293

Macnamara, B. N., Berber, I., Çavuşoğlu, M. C., Krupinski, E. A., Nallapareddy, N., Nelson, N. E., Smith, P. J., Wilson-Delfosse, A. L., & Ray, S. (2024). Does using artificial intelligence assistance accelerate skill decay and hinder skill development without performers' awareness? *Cognitive Research: Principles and Implications*, *9*(1), 46. Advance online publication. DOI: 10.1186/s41235-024-00572-8 PMID: 38992285

Madni, A. M. (2020). Exploiting Augmented Intelligence in Systems Engineering and Engineered Systems. *Insight - International Council on Systems Engineering*, *23*(1), 31–36. DOI: 10.1002/inst.12282

Madni, A. M. (2023). Augmented Intelligence: A Human Productivity and Performance Amplifier in Systems Engineering and Engineered Human–Machine Systems. In Verma, D. (Ed.), *Systems Engineering for the Digital Age* (1st ed., pp. 375–391). Wiley., DOI: 10.1002/9781394203314.ch17

Malik, S. A. (2023). Unlocking Organizational Potential: Harnessing AI literacy for Dynamic Capabilities through sensing, seizing and reconfiguring initiatives in IT firms.

Manyika, J., Remes, J., Mischke, J., & Krishnan, M. (2017). The Productivity Puzzle, A Closer Look at the United States. McKinsey Global Institute, Discussion Paper.

Marar H. W. (2024). Advancements in Software Engineering Using AI, Computer Software Media Applications. 6, no. 1.

Margulieux, L. E., Prather, J., Reeves, B. N., Becker, B. A., Cetin Uzun, G., Loksa, D., Leinonen, J., & Denny, P. (2024). Self-regulation, self-efficacy, and fear of failure interactions with how novices use LLMs to solve programming problems. In *Proceedings of the 2024 Innovation and Technology in Computer Science Education* V. 1 (pp. 276–282). ACM. DOI: 10.1145/3649217.3653621

Marion, T. J., & Fixson, S. K. (2021). The Transformation of the Innovation Process: How Digital Tools are Changing Work, Collaboration, and Organizations in New Product Development*. *Journal of Product Innovation Management*, *38*(1), 192–215. DOI: 10.1111/jpim.12547

Maslach, C., & Jackson, S. E. (1981). The measurement of experienced burnout. *Journal of Organizational Behavior*, *2*(2), 99–113. DOI: 10.1002/job.4030020205

Mbelekani, N. Y., & Bengler, K. (2023, November). Unequally Yoked [Skilled]: Transformative Views on Human-Automation Skilfulness. In *2023 International Conference on Electrical, Computer and Energy Technologies (ICECET)* (pp. 1-8). IEEE. DOI: 10.1109/ICECET58911.2023.10389238

McGuinness, S., Pouliakas, K., & Redmond, P. (2023). Skills-displacing technological change and its impact on jobs: Challenging technological alarmism? *Economics of Innovation and New Technology*, *32*(3), 370–392. DOI: 10.1080/10438599.2021.1919517

McIntosh, T. R., Susnjak, T., Liu, T., Watters, P., Xu, D., Liu, D., & Halgamuge, M. N. (2025). From Google Gemini to OpenAI Q* (Q-Star): A survey on reshaping the generative artificial intelligence (AI) research landscape. *Technologies*, *13*(2), 51. Advance online publication. DOI: 10.3390/technologies13020051

McKinsey & Company. (2021). How Companies are Reskilling to Address Skill Gaps. https://www.mckinsey.com/business-functions/organization/our-insights/how-companies-are-reskilling-to-address-skill-g

Mendes, E., Rodriguez, P., Freitas, V., Baker, S., & Atoui, M. A. (2018). Towards improving decision making and estimating the value of decisions in value-based software engineering: The VALUE framework. *Software Quality Journal*, *26*(2), 607–656. DOI: 10.1007/s11219-017-9360-z

Menon, S., & Suresh, M. A. (2020). Organizational agility assessment for higher education institution. *Journal of Research on the Lepidoptera*, *51*(1), 561–573. DOI: 10.36872/LEPI/V51I1/301050

Meziane, F., & Vadera, S. (2010). Artificial Intelligence in Software Engineering: Current Developments and Future Prospects. In Meziane, F., & Vadera, S. (Eds.), (pp. 278–299). Advances in Computational Intelligence and Robotics. IGI Global., DOI: 10.4018/978-1-60566-758-4.ch014

Michels, L.-M., Petkova, A., Richter, M., Farley, A., Graziotin, D., & Wagner, S. (2024). Overwhelmed software developers: An interpretative phenomenological analysis. *IEEE Software*, *41*(4), 51–59. Advance online publication. DOI: 10.1109/MS.2024.3374821

Mieczkowski, H. N. (2022). *AI-Mediated communication: Examining agency, ownership, expertise, and roles of AI systems*. Stanford University.

Miranda, J. P. P., Cruz, M. A. D., Fernandez, A. B., Balahadia, F. F., Aviles, J. S., Caro, C. A., ... & Gaña, E. P. (2025). Erosion of Critical Academic Skills Due to AI Dependency Among Tertiary Students.

Mitra, A., Seetharaman, A., & Maddulety, K. (2024, December). Adoption of Artificial Intelligence Enabling Value Creation in Business. In 2024 4th International Conference on Robotics, Automation and Artificial Intelligence (RAAI) (pp. 213-220). IEEE. DOI: 10.1109/RAAI64504.2024.10949520

Mitsugi, N., Ijuin, K., Oshiyama, C., Hara, E., & Nishimura, T. (2025). An AI-mediated framework for recursive learning: Transforming individual experiences into organizational knowledge and autonomous engagement in elderly care. *Frontiers in Digital Health*, *7*, 1529072. DOI: 10.3389/fdgth.2025.1529072 PMID: 40678716

Monasor, M. J., Vizcaino, A., Piattini, M., & Caballero, I. (2010). Preparing Students and Engineers for Global Software Development: A Systematic Review. *2010 5th IEEE International Conference on Global Software Engineering*, 177–186. DOI: 10.1109/ICGSE.2010.28

Moradi Dakhel, A., Majdinasab, V., Nikanjam, A., Khomh, F., Desmarais, M. C., & Jiang, Z. M. (2023). GitHub Copilot AI pair programmer: Asset or liability? *Journal of Systems and Software*, *203*, 111734. Advance online publication. DOI: 10.1016/j.jss.2023.111734

Morandini, S., Fraboni, F., De Angelis, M., Puzzo, G., Giusino, D., & Pietrantoni, L. (2023). The impact of artificial intelligence on workers' skills: Upskilling and reskilling in organisations. *Informing Science*, *26*, 39–68. DOI: 10.28945/5078

Mulgund, P., Singh, R., Gillenson, M., Li, Y., & Oliver, C. (2025, May). "Not My First Choice": Why Software Testing Struggles to Attract Early-Career Professionals. In Proceedings of the 2025 Computers and People Research Conference (pp. 1-8).

Nam, D., Macvean, A., Hellendoorn, V., Vasilescu, B., & Myers, B. (2024). Using an LLM to help with code understanding. *Proceedings of the 46th International Conference on Software Engineering*, 784–796. DOI: 10.1145/3597503.3639187

Nascimento, E., Nguyen-Duc, A., Sundbø, I., & Conte, T. (2020). *Software engineering for artificial intelligence and machine learning software: A systematic literature review* (Version 1). arXiv. DOI: 10.48550/ARXIV.2011.03751

Nettur, S. B., Karpurapu, S., Nettur, U., Gajja, L. S., Myneni, S., & Dusi, A. The Role of GitHub Copilot on Software Development: A Perspective on Productivity, Security, Best Practices and Future Directions, 2025, arXiv preprint arXiv.13199.

Neves, R. (2024). Collaboration and Team Dynamics. In R. Neves, *The Engineering Leadership Playbook* (pp. 113–179). Apress. DOI: 10.1007/979-8-8688-0140-2_3

Nguyen, S., Babe, H. M., Zi, Y., Guha, A., Anderson, C. J., & Feldman, M. Q. (2024). How beginning programmers and Code LLMs (mis)read each other. In Proceedings of the 2024 CHI Conference on Human Factors in Computing Systems (CHI '24, Article 650, 20 pages). ACM. DOI: 10.1145/3613904.3642706

Nguyen, N., & Nadi, S. (2022). An empirical evaluation of GitHub Copilot's code suggestions. *Proceedings of the 19th International Conference on Mining Software Repositories*, 1–5. DOI: 10.1145/3524842.3528470

Nikolic, S., Daniel, S., Haque, R., Belkina, M., Hassan, G. M., Grundy, S., Lyden, S., Neal, P., & Sandison, C. (2023). ChatGPT versus engineering education assessment: A multidisciplinary and multi-institutional benchmarking and analysis of this generative artificial intelligence tool to investigate assessment integrity. *European Journal of Engineering Education*, *48*(4), 559–614. DOI: 10.1080/03043797.2023.2213169

NIST. (2023). *AI Risk Management Framework (AI RMF 1.0)*. National Institute of Standards and Technology. https://www.nist.gov/itl/ai-risk-management-framework

Northern Kentucky University. Paul, S., Yuan, L., Iowa State University, Jain, H., The University of Tennessee at Chattanooga, Sporher, J., ISSIP.org, Lifshitz-Assaf, H., & Warwick University. (2022). Intelligence Augmentation: Human Factors in AI and Future of Work. *AIS Transactions on Human-Computer Interaction*, 426–445. DOI: 10.17705/1thci.00174

Nwaomah, A. E. (2025). Utilization of Artificial Intelligence (AI) and Fear of Job Loss in the Banking Industry: Perspectives of Bank Employees. Pan-African Journal of Education and Social Sciences, 6(1), 88-103.https://www.ajol.info/index.php/pajes/article/view/296667

O'Brien, G. (2025). Threats to scientific software from over-reliance on AI code assistants. *Nature Computational Science*, *5*(9), 701–703. DOI: 10.1038/s43588-025-00845-2 PMID: 40715786

OECD. (2019). OECD skills outlook 2019: Thriving in a digital world. OECD Publishing. https://www.oecd.org/en/publications/2019/05/oecd-skills-outlook-2019_c8896fe0.html

Ojiyi, G., Oji, I., Aikabeli, B. O., Oji, I. N., & Ayegbusi, W. E. (2023). Job Security in the Artificial Intelligence and Automation Era. no. December.https://repositorio.iscte-iul.pt/handle/10071/33859

Orrell, B. (2025). De-Skilling the Knowledge Economy.https://cosm.aei.org/wp-content/uploads/2025/06/De-Skilling-the-Knowledge-Economy-1.pdf

Ozkaya, I. (2023). The next frontier in software development: AI-augmented software development processes. *IEEE Software, 40*(4), 4–9. DOI: 10.1109/MS.2023.3278056

Pachouly, J., Ahirrao, S., Kotecha, K., Selvachandran, G., & Abraham, A. (2022). A Systematic Literature Review on Software Defect Prediction Using Artificial Intelligence: Datasets, Data Validation Methods, Approaches, and Tools. *Engineering Applications of Artificial Intelligence, 111*, 104773. DOI: 10.1016/j.engappai.2022.104773

Pandey, R., Singh, P., Wei, R., & Shankar, S. (2024). Transforming Software Development: Evaluating the Efficiency and Challenges of GitHub Copilot in Real-World Projects, arXiv preprint arXiv.17910.

Pangavhane, S., Raktate, G., Pariane, P., Shelar, K., Wakchaure, R., & Kale, J. N. (2024, December). AI-augmented software development: Boosting efficiency and quality. In *2024 International Conference on Decision Aid Sciences and Applications (DASA)* (pp. 1-5). IEEE. DOI: 10.1109/DASA63652.2024.10836523

Parasuraman, R., Sheridan, T. B., & Wickens, C. D. (2000). A model for types and levels of human interaction with automation. *IEEE Transactions on Systems, Man, and Cybernetics. Part A, Systems and Humans, 30*(3), 286–297. DOI: 10.1109/3468.844354 PMID: 11760769

Pearce, H., Ahmad, B., Tan, B., Dolan-Gavitt, B., & Karri, R. (2022). Asleep at the keyboard? Assessing the security of GitHub Copilot's code contributions. 2022 IEEE Symposium on Security and Privacy (SP), 754–768. DOI: 10.1109/SP46214.2022.9833571

Peiró, J. M. (2025). Applied Psychology and Careers in the 21st Century. Challenges and Opportunities. *Australian Journal of Career Development, 34*(2), 114–123. DOI: 10.1177/10384162251350691

Peoples, K. (2021). *How to write a phenomenological dissertation: A step-by-step guide* (Vol. 56). SAGE.

Perry, N., Srivastava, M., Kumar, D., & Boneh, D. (2023). Do users write more insecure code with AI assistants? In *Proceedings of the 2023 ACM SIGSAC Conference on Computer and Communications Security* (pp. 2785–2799). ACM. DOI: 10.1145/3576915.3623157

Petrovska, O., Clift, L., Moller, F., & Pearsall, R. (2024, January). Incorporating generative AI into software development education. In *Proceedings of the 8th Conference on Computing Education Practice* (pp. 37-40). DOI: 10.1145/3633053.3633057

Pham, P., Nguyen, V., & Nguyen, T. (2022, October). A review of ai-augmented end-to-end test automation tools. In *Proceedings of the 37th IEEE/ACM International Conference on Automated Software Engineering* (pp. 1-4). DOI: 10.1145/3551349.3563240

Ponkarthika, M. G., A. P., Ruba, M., Kishore, Y. R., M., K., & G. V., M. (2026). Bridging Health Equity in Times of Crisis: Ensuring Inclusive Care During Emergencies and Disasters. In E. Matsumoto, F. Andres, & R. Agrawal (Eds.), Advancing Equity in Global Healthcare Systems (pp. 27-54). IGI Global Scientific Publishing. DOI: 10.4018/979-8-3373-1330-6.ch002

Poovithaa, M., Ruba, M., Ponkarthika, M., Ragul, N., Ragul, V., & Sangeetha, K. (2025, November). IoT Smart Traffic Control System for Hill Roads with Emergency Vehicle Priority. In 2025 IEEE 7th International Conference on Computing, Communication and Automation (ICCCA) (pp. 1-6). IEEE.

Pradhan, I. P., & Saxena, P. (2023). Reskilling workforce for the Artificial Intelligence age: Challenges and the way forward. In The adoption and effect of artificial intelligence on human resources management, Part B (pp. 181-197). Emerald Publishing Limited.

Prather, J., Denny, P., Leinonen, J., Becker, B. A., Albluwi, I., Craig, M., Keuning, H., Kiesler, N., Kohn, T., Luxton-Reilly, A., MacNeil, S., Petersen, A., Pettit, R., Reeves, B. N., & Savelka, J. (2023). The robots are here: Navigating the generative AI revolution in computing education. In *Proceedings of the 2023 Working Group Reports on Innovation and Technology in Computer Science Education* (pp. 108–159). ACM. DOI: 10.1145/3623762.3633499

Putri, K. M. H., & Werdini, Y. E. (2025). Artificial Intelligence Adoption, Job Insecurity, and Psychological Resilience: Challenges for Employee Adaptation in Future Work Environments. *International Journal of Issue Science*, *1*(5). Advance online publication. DOI: 10.71364/ijiss.v1i5.12

Rahwan, I., Cebrian, M., Obradovich, N., Bongard, J., Bonnefon, J.-F., Breazeal, C., Crandall, J. W., Christakis, N. A., Couzin, I. D., Jackson, M. O., Jennings, N. R., Kamar, E., Kloumann, I. M., Larochelle, H., Lazer, D., McElreath, R., Mislove, A., Parkes, D. C., Pentland, A. S., & Wellman, M. (2020). Machine behaviour. *Nature*, *568*(7753), 477–486. DOI: 10.1038/s41586-019-1138-y PMID: 31019318

Raisch, S., & Krakowski, S. (2021). Artificial intelligence and management: The automation–augmentation paradox. *Academy of Management Review*, *46*(1), 192–210. DOI: 10.5465/amr.2018.0072

Ramos, T., Dean, A., & McGregor, D. (2025). AI-Augmented Software Engineering: Revolutionizing or Challenging Software Quality and Testing? *Journal of Software (Malden, MA)*, *37*(2), e2741. DOI: 10.1002/smr.2741

Rani, L. M., Mohammadi, F., Feldt, R., & Svensson, R. B. (2025). An Empirical Study on Decision-Making Aspects in Responsible Software Engineering for AI. arXiv preprint arXiv:2501.15691. DOI: 10.1109/ICSE-SEIP66354.2025.00056

Ranjan, B., Sivanesan, I., & Bernie, S. B. (2026). Artificial intelligence and anxiety: The human price of adapting to a smarter workplace. Inspire Intelligence, 1(1), 52-67.https://inspirequill.org/index.php/inspireAI/article/view/12

Rashid, A. B., & Kausik, M. D. A. K. (2024). AI Revolutionizing Industries Worldwide: A Comprehensive Overview of Its Diverse Applications. *Hybrid Advances.*, *7*, 100277. DOI: 10.1016/j.hybadv.2024.100277

Rhoades, L., & Eisenberger, R. (2002). Perceived organizational support: A review of the literature. *The Journal of Applied Psychology*, *87*(4), 698–714. https://psycnet.apa.org/buy/2002-15406-008. DOI: 10.1037/0021-9010.87.4.698 PMID: 12184574

Riazi, M., Rezvani, R., & Ghanbar, H. (2023). Trustworthiness in L2 writing research: A review and analysis of qualitative articles in the Journal of Second Language Writing. *Research Methods in Applied Linguistics*, *2*(3), 100065. Advance online publication. DOI: 10.1016/j.rmal.2023.100065

Rinta-Kahila, T., Penttinen, E., Salovaara, A., Soliman, W., & Ruissalo, J. (2023). The vicious circles of skill erosion: A case study of cognitive automation. *Journal of the Association for Information Systems*, *24*(5), 1378–1412. DOI: 10.17705/1jais.00829

Risko, E. F., & Gilbert, S. J. (2016). Cognitive offloading. *Trends in Cognitive Sciences*, *20*(9), 676–688. DOI: 10.1016/j.tics.2016.07.002 PMID: 27542527

Samuels, A., & Pelser, A.-M. (2025). Transitioning from Industry 4.0 to 5.0: Sustainable supply chain management and talent management insights. *SA Journal of Human Resource Management*, *23*(0), a2874. Advance online publication. DOI: 10.4102/sajhrm.v23i0.2874

Santhini, C., Ruba, M., Sakthi Priya, V., & Hemalatha, R. (2025). Intercultural communication and assessment practices in the integration of AI with education. In *Generative AI Approaches to Sustainable Development in Higher Education*. IGI Global. DOI: 10.4018/979-8-3693-5623-4.ch010

Sarma, A. D. N. (2025). FusionFlow: A Software Development Approach in the Era of Design Thinking and AI. In Innovative Design Thinking Approaches in Software Engineering (pp. 53-84). IGI Global Scientific Publishing. DOI: 10.4018/979-8-3693-9531-8.ch003

Sarsa, S., Denny, P., Hellas, A., & Leinonen, J. (2022). Automatic generation of programming exercises and code explanations using large language models. *Proceedings of the 2022 ACM Conference on International Computing Education Research*, 27–43. DOI: 10.1145/3501385.3543957

Sauvola, J., Tarkoma, S., Klemettinen, M., Riekki, J., & Doermann, D. (2024). Future of software development with generative AI. *Automated Software Engineering*, *31*(1), 26. DOI: 10.1007/s10515-024-00426-z

Schaetz, N., Gagrčin, E., Toth, R., & Emmer, M. (2025). Algorithm dependency in platformized news use. new media & society, 27(3), 1360-1377.

Schieferdecker, I. K. (2025, August). Navigating the growing field of research on AI for software testing–the taxonomy for AI-augmented software testing and an ontology-driven literature survey. In International Conference on Formal Methods for Industrial Critical Systems (pp. 3-20). Cham: Springer Nature Switzerland.

Sculley, D., Holt, G., Golovin, D., Davydov, E., Phillips, T., Ebner, D., Chaudhary, V., Young, M., Crespo, J., & Dennison, D. (2015). Hidden technical debt in machine learning systems. *Advances in Neural Information Processing Systems*, *28*, 2503–2511.

Senapathi, M., Buchan, J., & Osman, H. DevOps Capabilities, Practices, and Challenges: Insights From a Case Study, *Proceedings of the 22nd International Conference on Evaluation and Assessment in Software Engineering*, 2018, New York, NY, United States, Association for Computing Machinery. DOI: 10.1145/3210459.3210465

Sengul, G., Neykova, R., & Destefanis, G. (2024). Software engineering education in the era of conversational AI: Current trends and future directions. *Frontiers in Artificial Intelligence*, *7*, 1436350. Advance online publication. DOI: 10.3389/frai.2024.1436350 PMID: 39268193

Sergeyuk, A., Golubev, Y., Bryksin, T., & Ahmed, I. (2025). Using AI-based coding assistants in practice: State of affairs, perceptions, and ways forward. *Information and Software Technology*, *178*, 107610. DOI: 10.1016/j.infsof.2024.107610

Sergeyuk, A., Zakharov, I., Koshchenko, E., & Izadi, M. (2026). Human-AI experience in integrated development environments: A systematic literature review. *Empirical Software Engineering*, *31*(3), 55. DOI: 10.1007/s10664-025-10793-0

Shah, A., Rexin, T., Tomson, E., Porter, L., Griswold, W. G., & Soosai Raj, A. G. (2025). Evolution of programmers' trust in generative AI programming assistants (arXiv:2509.13253). arXiv. https://arxiv.org/abs/2509.13253 DOI: 10.1145/3769994.3770029

Shanmugaraja, T., Ruba, M., Priya, V. S., Venkatesh, T., Supriya, M., & Nallamuthu, M. (2023, September). ECG noise elimination using an FPGA version of a modified error normalized LMS adaptive filter. In AIP Conference Proceedings (Vol. 2764, No. 1, p. 060033). AIP Publishing LLC. DOI: 10.1063/5.0144367

Sharma, K., Davidson, B. G. J., George, J. P., & Muttungal, P. V. (2025, October). Breeding distrust during artificial intelligence (AI) era: how technological advancements, job insecurity and job stress fuel organizational cynicism? In Evidence-based HRM: a Global Forum for Empirical Scholarship (Vol. 13, No. 4, pp. 763-779). Emerald Publishing Limited. DOI: 10.1108/EBHRM-05-2024-0159

Sharma, P., Kumawat, R., Jain, G., Keswani, G., Goyal, N. K., & Sheikh, M. F. (2026). Machine Learning-Based Intrusion Detection Systems for Healthcare Internet of Things (HIoT). In Shieh, C., Goel, P., Horng, M., & Pandey, H. (Eds.), *Resilient Healthcare Internet of Things Systems: Architectures, Security, and Trust* (pp. 185–214). IGI Global Scientific Publishing., DOI: 10.4018/979-8-3373-7610-3.ch007

Sharma, R. (2024). Governance and Oversight of AI Systems. In *AI and the Boardroom: Insights into Governance, Strategy, and the Responsible Adoption of AI* (pp. 353–370). Apress. DOI: 10.1007/979-8-8688-0796-1_28

Sheikh, M. F. A., Kapoor, S. K., Goyal, N. K., & Tuba, E. rao, A. (2026). Enhancing Healthcare Security with Fog Computing and Blockchain Technology. In: Nayak, R., Mittal, N., Khunteta, A., Kumar, M. (eds) Recent Advancements in Artificial Intelligence. ICRAAI 2025. Lecture Notes in Networks and Systems, vol 1468. Springer, Singapore. DOI: 10.1007/978-981-96-7760-3_38

Shneiderman, B. (2020). Human-centered artificial intelligence: Reliable, safe & trustworthy. *International Journal of Human-Computer Interaction*, *36*(6), 495–504. DOI: 10.1080/10447318.2020.1741118

Siahaan, D., Raharjana, I. K., & Fatichah, C. (2023). User Story Extraction From Natural Language for Requirements Elicitation: Identify Software-Related Information From Online News. *Information and Software Technology*, *158*, 107195. DOI: 10.1016/j.infsof.2023.107195

Siam, M. K., Gu, H., Cheng, J. Q., & Programming With, A. I. Evaluating ChatGPT, Gemini, AlphaCode, and GitHub Copilot for Programmers, 2024, arXiv preprint arXiv.09224.

Sibiya, S., Ruba, M., Ponkarthika, M., Vijayasabariswari, M., Sheba, S., Vignesh, S., . . . Sankar, S. S. (2025, October). Integrated Wearable Health Monitoring and Emergency Response System With IOT Sensors, AED and Mobile App for Enhanced Patient Outcomes. In 2025 IEEE 2nd International Conference on Green Industrial Electronics and Sustainable Technologies (GIEST) (pp. 1-6). IEEE.

Simon, H. A. (1956). Rational choice and the structure of the environment. *Psychological Review*, *63*(2), 129–138. DOI: 10.1037/h0042769 PMID: 13310708

Smith, H. K. (2024). *Leveraging AI for Proactive Software Quality Assurance: Predictive Analytics*. Machine Learning, and Agile Test Automation.

Song, F., Agarwal, A., & Wen, W. (2024). The Impact of Generative AI on Collaborative Open-Source Software Development: Evidence from GitHub Copilot. SSRN *Electronic Journal*. https://doi.org//arXiv.2410.02091DOI: 10.48550

Spinellis, D. (2024). Pair programming with generative AI. *IEEE Software*, *41*(3), 16–18. DOI: 10.1109/MS.2024.3363848

Stevanoviü, J., Atanasijeviü, S., Atanasijeviü, T., & Zahar, M. (2020). Expanding the level of engineer knowledge for software modeling within corporate education by active and collaborative learning. *2020 IEEE Global Engineering Education Conference (EDUCON)*, 1807–1814. DOI: 10.1109/EDUCON45650.2020.9125250

Sun, Y., & Xu, C. (2025). Hybrid cognitive authority and algorithmic subjectivity: Rethinking knowledge management in AI-driven communication. *Journal of Knowledge Management*, •••, 1–26. DOI: 10.1108/JKM-02-2025-0252

Sverke, M., Hellgren, J., & Näswall, K. (2002). No security: A meta-analysis and review of job insecurity and its consequences. *Journal of Occupational Health Psychology*, *7*(3), 242–264. https://psycnet.apa.org/buy/2002-01632-005. DOI: 10.1037/1076-8998.7.3.242 PMID: 12148956

Tang, A., Razavian, M., Paech, B., & Hesse, T.-M. (2017). Human Aspects in Software Architecture Decision Making: A Literature Review. *2017 IEEE International Conference on Software Architecture (ICSA)*, 107–116. DOI: 10.1109/ICSA.2017.15

Tang, N., Chen, M., Ning, Z., Bansal, A., Huang, Y., & McMillan, C. (2024). Developer behaviors in validating and repairing LLM-generated code using IDE and eye tracking. In *Proceedings of the IEEE Symposium on Visual Languages and Human-Centric Computing* (pp. 40–46). IEEE. DOI: 10.1109/VL/HCC60511.2024.00015

Tankelevitch, L., Kewenig, V., Simkute, A., Scott, A. E., Sarkar, A., Sellen, A., & Rintel, S. (2024). The metacognitive demands and opportunities of generative AI. In Proceedings of the 2024 CHI Conference on Human Factors in Computing Systems (Article 680). ACM. DOI: 10.1145/3613904.3642902

Tan, L. (2024). Designing an AI Career Mentor for Early Career Researchers. *CERN ideaSquare Journal of Experimental Innovation*, *8*(3), 42–51.

Tarafdar, M., Cooper, C. L., & Stich, J. (2019). The technostress trifecta. *Information Systems Journal*, *43*(3), 683–712. DOI: 10.1111/isj.12169

Tavantzis, T., Lambiase, S., Russo, D., & Feldt, R. (2025). From Challenge to Change: Design Principles for AI Transformations. arXiv preprint arXiv:2512.05533. DOI: 10.2139/ssrn.5912868

Taylor, A., Green, A., & Hassan, S. (2021). Priorities for up-skilling and re-skilling: what role can and should universities play?.

The Economic Times. 2025;https://economictimes.indiatimes.com/news/new-updates/reskilling-wont-help-200000-tech-jobs-gone-30000-more-lay-offs-likley-in-next-two-months-says-report/articleshow/124989112.cms?from=mdr

The Hindu. 2026; https://www.thehindu.com/business/human-ai-will-define-the-future-of-work-by-2027-nasscom-indeed/article70505399.ece

The times of India, 2025; https://timesofindia.indiatimes.com/education/careers/news/silent-layoffs-on-the-rise-in-indian-tech-sector-subtle-signs-employees-should-watch-out-for/articleshow/124498098.cms

Treude, C., & Gerosa, M. A. (2025, April). How developers interact with AI: A taxonomy of human-AI collaboration in software engineering. In 2025 IEEE/ACM Second International Conference on AI Foundation Models and Software Engineering (Forge) (pp. 236-240). IEEE. DOI: 10.1109/Forge66646.2025.00033

Turvey, K., & Pachler, N. (2025). A topological exploration of convergence/divergence of human-mediated and algorithmically mediated pedagogy. *British Journal of Educational Technology*, bjet.70007. DOI: 10.1111/bjet.70007

Uren, V., & Edwards, J. S. (2023). Technology readiness and the organizational journey towards AI adoption: An empirical study. *International Journal of Information Management*, *68*, 102588. DOI: 10.1016/j.ijinfomgt.2022.102588

Vaithilingam, P., Zhang, T., & Glassman, E. L. (2022). Expectation vs. experience: Evaluating the usability of code generation tools powered by large language models. In *CHI Conference on Human Factors in Computing Systems Extended Abstracts* (pp. 1–7). ACM. DOI: 10.1145/3491101.3519665

Valový, M., & Buchalcevova, A. (2023, October). The psychological effects of AI-assisted programming on students and professionals. In *2023 IEEE International Conference on Software Maintenance and Evolution (ICSME)* (pp. 385-390). IEEE. DOI: 10.1109/ICSME58846.2023.00050

van Voorst, R. (2024). Challenges and limitations of human oversight in ethical artificial intelligence implementation in health care: Balancing digital literacy and professional strain. *Mayo Clinic Proceedings. Digital Health*, *2*(4), 559–563. DOI: 10.1016/j.mcpdig.2024.08.004 PMID: 40206522

Vasiliniuc, M.-S., & Groza, A. (2023). Case study: Using AI-Assisted Code Generation in Mobile Teams, 2023 IEEE 19th International Conference on Intelligent Computer Communication and Processing (ICCP), IEEE.

Vaswani, A., Shazeer, N., Parmar, N., Uszkoreit, J., Jones, L., Gomez, A. N., Kaiser, Ł., & Polosukhin, I. (2017). Attention is all you need. In Advances in Neural Information Processing Systems, 30 (pp. 5998– 6008). https://papers.nips.cc/paper/2017/file/3f5ee243547dee91fbd053c1c4a8 45aa-Paper.pdf

Vaswani, A., Shazeer, N., Parmar, N., Uszkoreit, J., Jones, L., Gomez, A. N., & Polosukhin, I. (2017). Attention is all you need. *Advances in Neural Information Processing Systems*, *30*, 6000–6010.

Wadhwa, S. N., Bhardwaj, G., Srivastava, A. P., & Malik, R. (2025). AI-driven job insecurity and work performance: Unveiling the mediating role of psychological well-being. *International Journal of Information Technology : an Official Journal ofBharati Vidyapeeth's Institute of Computer Applications and Management*, *17*(7), 1–12. DOI: 10.1007/s41870-025-02602-0

Wahn, B., Schmitz, L., Gerster, F. N., & Weiss, M. (2023). Offloading under cognitive load: Humans are willing to offload parts of an attentionally demanding task to an algorithm. *PLoS One*, *18*(5), e0286102. DOI: 10.1371/journal.pone.0286102 PMID: 37205658

Wanner, J., Herm, L. V., Heinrich, K., & Janiesch, C. (2022). The effect of transparency and trust on intelligent system acceptance: Evidence from a user-based study. *Electronic Markets*, *32*(4), 2079–2102. DOI: 10.1007/s12525-022-00593-5

Weis, P. P., & Wiese, E. (2022). Know your cognitive environment! Mental models as crucial determinant of offloading preferences. *Human Factors*, *64*(3), 499–513. DOI: 10.1177/0018720820956861 PMID: 32955351

Wermelinger, M. (2023). Using GitHub Copilot to solve simple programming problems. *Proceedings of the 54th ACM Technical Symposium on Computer Science Education*, 172–178. DOI: 10.1145/3545945.3569830

Wickens, C. D., Hollands, J. G., Banbury, S., & Parasuraman, R. (2013). *Engineering psychology and human performance* (4th ed.). Pearson.

Wilson, H. J., & Daugherty, P. R. (2018). Collaborative intelligence: Humans and AI are joining forces. *Harvard Business Review*, *96*(4), 114–123.

Wnuk, K., Regnell, B., & Berenbach, B. (2011). Scaling Up Requirements Engineering – Exploring the Challenges of Increasing Size and Complexity in Market-Driven Software Development. In Berry, D., & Franch, X. (Eds.), *Requirements Engineering: Foundation for Software Quality* (Vol. 6606, pp. 54–59). Springer Berlin Heidelberg., DOI: 10.1007/978-3-642-19858-8_6

Wooldridge, M., & Jennings, N. R. (1995). Intelligent agents: Theory and practice. *The Knowledge Engineering Review*, *10*(2), 115–152. DOI: 10.1017/S0269888900008122

World Economic Forum. (2023). The Future of Jobs Report 2023. https://www.weforum.org/publications/the-future-of-jobs-report-2023/

Wu, Q., He, P., & Zhou, P. (2025). Skill-biased Productivity Effects of AI Adoption: Evidence from a Financial Shared Service Center Reform. DOI: 10.2139/ssrn.5759446

Xu, J., & He, C. (2024, December). Understanding AI Tools Adoption in Academic Work: Case from Chinese Early-Career Researchers. In International Conference on Asian Digital Libraries (pp. 181-193). Singapore: Springer Nature Singapore.

Xu, F. F., Alon, U., Neubig, G., & Hellendoorn, V. J. (2022). A systematic evaluation of large language models of code. *Proceedings of the 6th ACM SIGPLAN International Symposium on Machine Programming*, 1–10. DOI: 10.1145/3520312.3534862

Yabaku, M., Pombo, N., & Ouhbi, S. (2024, September). Exploring the potential use of generative ai in software engineering education. In 2024 IEEE 18th International Conference on Application of Information and Communication Technologies (AICT) (pp. 1-7). IEEE. DOI: 10.1109/AICT61888.2024.10740416

Yadav, A., Usman, M., Sati, A., & Jain, S. (2024). Revolutionizing Software Development: Enhancing Quality and Performance Through Code Refactoring, *Proceedings of the 2024 Sixteenth International Conference on Contemporary Computing*, DOI: 10.1145/3675888.3676139

Yang, Y., Xia, X., Lo, D., & Grundy, J. (2022). A Survey on Deep Learning for Software Engineering. *ACM Computing Surveys, 54*(10s, no. 10s), 1–73. DOI: 10.1145/3505243

Yan, W., Nakajima, T., & Sawada, R. (2024). Benefits and challenges of collaboration between students and conversational generative artificial intelligence in programming learning: An empirical case study. *Education Sciences, 14*(4), 433. DOI: 10.3390/educsci14040433

Yilmaz, R., & Yilmaz, F. G. K. (2023). The effect of generative artificial intelligence (AI)-based tool use on students' computational thinking skills, programming self-efficacy and motivation. *Computers and Education: Artificial Intelligence, 4*, 100147. DOI: 10.1016/j.caeai.2023.100147

Zahaib Nabeel, M. (2024). AI-Enhanced Project Management Systems for Optimizing Resource Allocation and Risk Mitigation. *Asian Journal of Multidisciplinary Research and Review., 5*(5), 53–91. DOI: 10.55662/AJMRR.2024.5502

Zamfirescu-Pereira, J. D., Wong, R. Y., Hartmann, B., & Yang, Q. (2023). Why Johnny can't prompt: How non-AI experts try (and fail) to design LLM prompts. *Proceedings of the 2023 CHI Conference on Human Factors in Computing Systems*, 1–21. DOI: 10.1145/3544548.3581388

Zheng, J., Zhang, J. Z., Kamal, M. M., Liang, X., & Alzeiby, E. A. (2025). Unpacking human-AI interaction: Exploring unintended consequences on employee Well-being in entrepreneurial firms through an in-depth analysis. *Journal of Business Research, 196*, 115406. DOI: 10.1016/j.jbusres.2025.115406

Zheng, J., & Zhang, T. (2025). Association between AI awareness and emotional exhaustion: The serial mediation of job insecurity and work interference with family. *Behavioral Sciences (Basel, Switzerland), 15*(4), 401. DOI: 10.3390/bs15040401 PMID: 40282023

Zhou, X., Liang, P., Zhang, B., Li, Z., Ahmad, A., Shahin, M., & Waseem, M. (2024). Exploring the problems, their causes and solutions of AI pair programming: A study on GitHub and Stack Overflow. *Journal of Systems and Software, 219*, 112204. Advance online publication. DOI: 10.1016/j.jss.2024.112204

Zhu, L. (2023, May). Software Engineering as the Linchpin of Responsible AI. In 2023 IEEE/ACM 45th International Conference on Software Engineering (ICSE) (pp. 3-4). IEEE. DOI: 10.1109/ICSE48619.2023.00012

Ziegler, A., Kalliamvakou, E., Li, X. A., Rice, A., Rifkin, D., Simister, S., Sittampalam, G., & Aftandilian, E. (2024). Measuring GitHub Copilot's impact on productivity. *Communications of the ACM*, *67*(3), 54–63. DOI: 10.1145/3633453

Zuboff, S. (1988). *In the age of the smart machine: The future of work and power*. Basic Books.

About the Contributors

Hanh Le is a dedicated researcher, Full Stack Software Developer, and manager of a software development team. She holds a Ph.D. in Information Technology and a master's degree in computer science. Her research interests include artificial intelligence (AI), software development, data analytics, data science, and cloud computing. Dr. Le's work focuses on leveraging AI and data-driven technologies to enhance decision-making and optimize software systems across industries such as healthcare, law enforcement, and retail. With expertise in both front-end and back-end development, she designs object-oriented, database-driven applications and values interdisciplinary collaboration to drive innovation and discovery.

***

Nikhil Akkiraju is a Senior Engineering Manager at PayPal, where he leads engineering for Buy Now Pay Later serving millions of users and processing over $40 billion in annual transactions. With 16 years of experience in software development, platform architecture, and engineering leadership, he has managed teams ranging from 10 to 60+ engineers across FinTech, retail, and IoT industries. He has led organizations through major technology transitions including platform modernization, multi-country expansion, and the integration of AI-assisted development tools. He holds an MS in Applied Computer Science from Northwest Missouri State University.

Jasdeep Singh Bhalla is a senior software engineer specializing in cloud platforms, security, and large-scale distributed systems. His work focuses on cloud governance, secure-by-design infrastructure, and policy-driven automation across complex production environments. With extensive experience designing and enforcing security controls in multi-account cloud architectures, he brings a practitioner's perspective to the challenges of AI-augmented software development.

His research interests include human–AI collaboration, skill transformation in software engineering, and the governance of generative AI systems.

Arunima Dutta (Member, IEEE) received the B.E. degree in Electrical Engineering from Jorhat Engineering College, Assam, India, in 2012, and the M.Tech. Degree in Power and Energy systems from the National Institute of Technology Meghalaya, Meghalaya, India, in 2016. She received the doctoral degree from IIT Guwahati in the year 2022. She is currently working as Assistant Professor in the Dept. of Electrical Engineering, NIT Meghalaya. Her research interests include power system operation, model predictive based voltage control and energy management, modeling of electric vehicles and power electronics appliances to be utilized in modern distribution systems.

Deepak Gupta is a distinguished academician with over 20 years of teaching experience and expertise in Computer Science and Engineering. He holds a Ph.D. in Computer Engineering and has an extensive research portfolio, including many international journal papers, multiple conference proceedings, and several books. His research interests span machine learning, artificial intelligence, and data mining. Currently, Dr. Gupta serves as an Associate Professor and Head of Department of CSE (Emerging Branches) at ITM Gwalior, MP, India. He has also contributed significantly to the field through patents and copyrights and actively engages as a reviewer, conference chair and editor.

Vishal Jain currently serves as a Professor and Dean of Accreditation, Statutory Compliances & Institutional Development at the School of Engineering & Technology, Vivekananda Institute of Professional Studies - Technical Campus, New Delhi. His previous roles include Professor at Sharda University, Greater Noida, and Associate Professor at Bharati Vidyapeeth's Institute of Computer Applications and Management (BVICAM), New Delhi. Dr. Jain has actively participated in various academic governance bodies, including the Faculty Board, Board of Planning and Management, Executive Council, Academic Council, Curriculum Development and Review Committee, and Academic Audit across multiple higher education institutions. He collaborates with Kuala Lumpur University of Science and Technology (KLUST), Malaysia, Lincoln University College, Malaysia and the Research Institute of IoT Cybersecurity at National Kaohsiung University of Science and Technology in Taiwan for research initiatives. He has supervised three Ph.D. candidates, with two additional scholars currently pursuing their degrees under his guidance.

Nasiba Jumaniyazova is a faculty member in the Department of Psychology at Mamun University, Khiva, Uzbekistan. She is engaged in teaching and academic activities related to psychological science, human behavior, and educational psychology. Her academic interests include cognitive and developmental psychology, student mental well-being, and the application of psychological principles in educational settings. She is committed to fostering students' analytical thinking, emotional intelligence, and academic growth through learner-centered instruction. Nasiba Jumaniyazova actively contributes to academic and institutional initiatives aimed at strengthening psychology education and promoting research-informed teaching practices in higher education.

Arpan Shaileshbhai Korat is a software engineer and independent researcher based in Jersey City, New Jersey, United States. His work focuses on applied artificial intelligence, multi-agent systems, large language models, and AI-assisted software engineering workflows. He has published research on collaborative AI architectures, natural language interfaces, and intelligent system orchestration, with an emphasis on practical deployment and human–AI collaboration. Arpan has served as a peer reviewer for international journals and conferences, including IEEE, PLOS One, and AI-focused publication venues. In addition to his research activities, he brings industry experience from large-scale enterprise environments, where he has worked on designing and evaluating AI-driven systems for real-world applications. His current interests include deskilling and reskilling dynamics in software engineering, prompt engineering, and the responsible integration of AI tools into development processes.

Sanjeev Kumar Is a Professor in Lovely Professional University Punjab India. He received Undergraduate in Hotel Management from Osmania University, Postgraduate in Tourism Management from Madurai Kamaraj University. He completed Doctor of Philosophy in Hospitality Management in 2019 from Amity University Jaipur India. His research areas lies in food Service Industry, his research focuses on Alcoholic beverages, Event management and Sustainable Management Practices, Metaverse, AI Machine Learning and Artificial Intelligence. He published more than 80 research papers, articles and chapters in Scopus Indexed, UGC Approved and peer reviewed Journals and books. Dr. Sanjeev Kumar participated and acted as resource person in various National and International conferences, seminars, session chair, research workshops and industry talks and his work has been widely cited. Dr. Sanjeev also edited more than 20 books with various International Publishers such as IGI Global, Cambridge Scholars, Emerald, CABI, Bentham Science, Taylor & Francis. Dr Sanjeev is an active researcher and has published numerous research articles in prestigious National and International journals and books.

Rampelli Manojkumar received his Ph.D. in Power Engineering from the Indian Institute of Technology Guwahati in 2023. He obtained his Master of Technology in Power and Energy Systems from the National Institute of Technology Karnataka, Surathkal, India, in 2015. He is currently an Assistant Professor in the Department of Electrical and Electronics Engineering at BVRIT Hyderabad College of Engineering for Women. He is currently the Editorial Board Member of Scientific Reports, Early Career Editor for the International Journal of Ambient Energy and the Guest Editor for PLOS ONE. He has been a speaker at the IEEE Smart Grid webinar series and has contributed to multiple funded research projects on smart transformer-based microgrid systems and distributed generation management. He has published 10 Q1 journal papers, including articles in IEEE Transactions on Power Systems, IEEE Transactions on Industrial Informatics, and Sustainable Cities and Society. His research expertise spans energy management, hybrid AC/DC distribution systems, energy storage, and power electronics applications in modern distribution systems. Additionally, he is an active reviewer for around 30 SCI journals, including IEEE Transactions on Industrial Informatics, IEEE Systems Journal, Journal of Energy Storage, Applied Energy, etc. He has also been actively involved in faculty training programs focused on teaching and learning enhancement, including instructional design, formative assessment, and teaching analytics, thereby strengthening his interdisciplinary expertise in education and technology integration.

Akankshya Panda is a Ph.D. scholar at KIIT Deemed to be University with over three years of combined experience in industry and academia. Her research interests focus on Human Resource Management (HRM) and Organizational Behaviour (OB), with a special emphasis on mental well-being in the workplace. She is passionate about understanding employee psychology, stress management, and creating healthier, more supportive organizational environments. Through her academic and practical exposure, she aims to contribute to research and practices that enhance employee well-being and promote sustainable work cultures.

T. Aditya Sai Srinivas is an accomplished academician currently serving as an Associate Professor in the Department of Computer Science and Engineering at Ravindra College of Engineering for Women, Kurnool. He holds a Ph.D. in Internet of Things (IoT) from the prestigious VIT University, Vellore, where he specialized in cutting-edge IoT frameworks and intelligent systems. With a strong research orientation, he has published over 50 research papers in reputed international journals. His academic contributions extend beyond research, having authored multiple textbooks in computer science and engineering. Dr. Srinivas is actively involved in mentoring students and guiding innovative projects in emerging technologies like ML, IoT, and FL. He is also a regular contributor to academic conferences and technical symposiums. His work reflects a commitment to both scholarly excellence and practical application in the evolving tech landscape.

Ipseeta Satpathy, Senior Professor at KSOM, KIIT Deemed to be University, has over 25 years of experience in teaching, research, and administration. An alumna of Jawaharlal Nehru University (JNU), New Delhi, she has authored five textbooks and edited Economic Growth in India. She has published over 300 research papers, including more than 190 in Scopus-indexed journals. She was a visiting professor at Lynchburg College, USA, and has presented at several international conferences. Under her guidance, 28 scholars have earned Ph.D. degrees. She received the Oxford Journal Distinguished Research Professor Award (2014) and the Times Power Women Award (2023), and has been invited as a resource person by universities in the USA and UK.

Mayank Singh is currently working as Professor and Head CSE (AIML) department at JSS University Noida, UP, India. Prior to this he worked as Dean (Research) at G. L. Bajaj Institute of Technology and Management, Greater Noida, India and Director at Consilio Research Lab, Tallinn, Estonia. He also worked as Postdoctoral Fellow at Univeristy of KwaZulu-Natal Durban, South Africa, and Professor & Head, Department of Computer Science and Engineering at Krishna Engineering College, Ghaziabad from January 2013 to September 2017. He has 21+ years of extensive experience in IT industry, Academics and Research in India and abroad. Dr. Singh has published around 100+ research papers in peer reviewed Transaction, Journals and Conferences of National and International repute and has supervised 14 M. Tech and 9 PhD students. He is currently also serving as a Life Member of Computer Society of India (CSI), Life Member of Indian Science Congress Association (ISCA), Senior Member of IEEE, Senior Member of ACM, Senior Member of IACSIT, and Member of Indian Society for Technical Education (ISTE). He is also serving for IEEE Committees as a TPC Member and designated Reviewer for various IEEE Conferences. He has organized several international conferences with reputed publishers like IEEE, Springer, Taylor and Francis, IOP etc. Dr. Singh is currently serving as Review Member, Research Grants Council (RGC), Hong Kong (Research Council) since 2016. He is also serving as Reviewer for IET Software, IEEE Communications, IEEE TENCON, IEEE Sensors, The Journal of Engineering, IET Wireless Sensor Networks, and Program Committee Member of innumerable IEEE & Springer International Journals and Conferences Worldwide.

Vipin Tyagi is a distinguished academician, researcher and author, currently serving as Dean (Academics and Research) at Jaypee University of Engineering and Technology in Guna, Madhya Pradesh. With a rich background in Computer

Science, his expertise spans across Image Processing, Cyber Forensics and Speech Recognition. Prof. Tyagi has a prolific publication record, contributing significantly to his fields of interest. His scholarly work includes numerous journal articles, conference papers, and books. Some of his notable publications are in the areas of image forgery detection, image denoising and content-based image retrieval. He has authored and edited several books and papers in the field of Computer Science, such as "Digital Image Forgery Detection: Techniques, Challenges and Applications", "Predictive Computing and Information Security" and "Content-Based Image Retrieval: Ideas, Influences, and Current Trends" published by Springer Singapore. His book "Understanding Digital Image Processing" using MATLAB, published by Taylor and Francis is highlighted by Mathworks. His scholarly work has earned him a respectable h-index and numerous citations in the academic community

Neha Yadav, Assistant Professor, Department of Computer Science and Engineering (AIML), JSS University, Noida, India. ORCID Id: 0000-0002-7793-2063. Ms. Neha Yadav, Ph.D. (Submitted), is currently serving as an Assistant Professor in the Department of Computer Science and Engineering (AIML) at JSS University, Noida, India. She is pursuing her PhD and has earned an M.Tech in Computer Science and Engineering from Jaypee Institute of Information Technology (JIIT), Noida, as well as a B.Tech. in Computer Science from Bundelkhand University, India. She is in the final stage of her doctoral studies (PhD thesis submitted) at JIIT. Noida. She has over 15 publications in reputed journals and conferences. She serves as a reviewer for various reputable journals, including Informatica and IEEE Access.

Index

A

C

D

E

G

H

I

J

M

O

P

Q

R

S

T

V

W

www.ingramcontent.com/pod-product-compliance
Lightning Source LLC
LaVergne TN
LVHW080907300926
849162LV00003B/586